An Introduction to Land Law

Second Edition

Simon Gardner

·HART·
PUBLISHING

OXFORD AND PORTLAND, OREGON
2009

Published in North America (US and Canada) by
Hart Publishing
c/o International Specialized Book Services
920 NE 58th Avenue, Suite 300
Portland, OR 97213-3786
USA
Tel: +1-503-287-3093 or toll-free: +1-800-944-6190
Fax: +1-503-280-8832
Email: orders@isbs.com
Website: www.isbs.com

Hart Publishing, 16C Worcester Place, OX1 2JW
Telephone: +44 (0)1865 517530 Fax: +44 (0)1865 510710
E-mail: mail@hartpub.co.uk
Website: http://www.hartpub.co.uk

British Library Cataloguing in Publication Data
Data Available

ISBN-13: 978-1-84113-980-7

Typeset by Forewords, Oxford
Printed and bound in Great Britain by
TJ International Ltd, Padstow, Cornwall

Preface

The rules of land law are numerous, complex, and in some cases substantively baffling. The story that together they tell does not jump out from the page. Students who quickly see what is going on in other areas of law often find themselves beaten by land law. This is a worry. Land law is not, after all, some arcane optional extra: it is the set of rules governing, literally, the foundation of terrestrial life. We ought to be able to get a grip on it.

This book aims to help. It tries to offer students a perspective on the subject; and also to provide an example of how it is possible to develop such a perspective for oneself. For the account given here cannot conceivably be the only way of viewing the material. The most valuable thing it can do is give those reading it the confidence, spur and apparatus to do something similar—but better!—for themselves.

By way of content, this book covers most of the main rules of land law as that subject is captured by most university syllabuses. Given its aim, however, it does not set out to be exactly a textbook on the subject. In the effort to present a vision of what the rules are doing, it sometimes focuses on some details more than others. And throughout, it necessarily contains a large element of opinion. It ought, therefore, to be used alongside—most certainly—the primary sources themselves, and probably also some other secondary sources. There are many textbooks available, of various sizes and (like this book) with different strengths and weaknesses. There are also other books with aspirations not dissimilar to this one, each with its own set of viewpoints and insights. And there are some valuable books of essays, particularly perhaps the biennial volumes of *Modern Studies in Property Law*, presenting the excellent papers delivered to the conferences organised by the Centre for Property Law at the University of Reading. Use this book for ideas, support and reassurance that the material not only should but can add up to something—then see what you can do with it for yourself.

This second edition, two years after the first, was needed above all so as to take account of new decisions of the House of Lords in the areas of proprietary estoppel and family property, *Cobbe v Yeoman's Row Management Ltd*, *Thorner v Majors* and *Stack v Dowden*. The relevant parts of the book have been fully rewritten. Other changes in the law, and developments in the literature, have been incorporated too.

Simon Gardner
1 April 2009

Contents

Table of Cases

Australia

Table of Legislation

United States of America

International

PART 1
The Basic Ideas

This book aims to give an account of that part of English law known as 'land law'.

This label is, however, misleading. It suggests that the topic is the whole set of English law's rules relevant to land. This in turn could mean various things. At its widest, it could mean the set of all the rules applicable to someone using land. Since legal rules are propositions about human behaviour, and nearly all human behaviour takes place on land, 'land law' in this sense would comprise almost the entire law, excluding only the special rules applicable to activities on water or in the air. Less widely, it could mean, within that set, the subset of all the rules making some particular reference to the land dimension. So while the first meaning would take in the rules about pollution generally, the second meaning would include only those rules focusing specifically (though perhaps inter alia) on pollution of the soil. And while the first meaning would include the whole law of contract, the second would take in only those contract rules aimed specifically at arrangements involving land, such as room rental agreements.

One certainly could address such subjects, though the enterprise would be a huge one, because land is in these senses an aspect of so many rules. Even the less wide of the two meanings would, for example, take in areas as distant from one another as agricultural law, planning law, domestic violence, and the crime of burglary.

In practice, the label 'land law' is more often used much more narrowly: as referring, out of all the rules involving land, only—or at any rate principally—to the rules that establish 'rights in rem' in land.[1] And that will be the focus of this book.

The book is divided into three parts. The first, comprising Chapters 1 to 3, concentrates on the basic ideas: the nature of rights in rem, and how they behave. Part 2, comprising Chapters 4 to 8, looks at the ways in which rights in rem can be acquired. Finally, Part 3, comprising Chapters 9 to 15, reviews a number of different sorts of rights in rem.

---

[1] This is not to say that other foci are unworthy of attention. For a reminder of how important the *lack* of rights to land may be, see D Cowan and J Fionda, 'Homeslessness' in S Bright and J Dewar (eds), *Land Law—Themes and Perspectives* (Oxford, 1998) ch 10.

Rights in Rem

1.1 The Idea of a Right in Rem

1.1.1 'Rights in Personam' and 'Rights in Rem'

Say I own a house, but then something occurs which, under the law's rules, means that you now have a right to live in it. The 'something' might be that I make a contract with you to this effect; or that I give you a share in the ownership; or that I marry you; or various other significant happenings. Say then that I sell the house to John. There are two possibilities.

One is that your right cannot affect John. That is, it is effective only against me, and if you want to enforce it you will have to look to me, not to John. It follows, now I have passed the house to John, that you will not be able to insist on living there: as it is said, to maintain your right 'in specie'. Only a right effective against John could allow that. Because your remedy can only be against me, it will have to take the form of a money payment, from me, compensating you for *not* now being able to live in the house. Rights which behave in this way are called 'rights in personam'. Among the rules dealing in rights of this kind are those comprising the ordinary law of contract. Contract has a feature called 'privity', whereby a contract between *A* and *B* cannot bind *C*.[1] That is another way of describing the fact that rights arising under the law of contract alone are in personam.

The other possibility is that your right can affect—bind—John. If your right is of this kind, and the conditions for John being affected are indeed satisfied, your remedy is no longer against me alone: you can enforce the right against John. Just because your right is effective against John does not

---

[1] Distinguish this meaning of privity from another, whereby a contract between *A* and *B* cannot *confer a right* on *C*. This too was a feature of the law of contract, but the relevant rules have been substantially amended by the Contracts (Rights of Third Parties) Act 1999. On privity generally, see eg M Chen-Wishart, *Contract Law* (2nd edn, Oxford, 2008) ch 16.

necessarily mean that you will be able to maintain it in specie, ie insist on living in the house: your remedy might still take the form of money compensation for not being able to live in it, though this time against John rather than me. However, effectiveness against John is certainly a precondition for your being able to claim in specie protection, and commonly this will indeed be forthcoming. If the law treats your right as having the potential to affect John in this way, your right is called a 'right in rem'.[2]

Your right to live in the house might be of either kind. To know which, we need further information. For example, if you simply rent the house from me, your right will be a 'lease', and in rem; but if your right is to live in it with me, as my lodger, it will be a 'licence', and in personam. There are various other possibilities, some of each type. We shall review many, though not all, of them in the course of this book.

1.1.2 'The Potential to Affect John'

The previous section spoke of a right in rem as one 'having the potential to affect John', and noted that John will in fact be affected by it only if certain conditions are satisfied.

In principle, the law could say that rights in rem *will* affect John, full stop. In practice, contemporary English land law takes a more complex position, whereby John will commonly be affected only if certain circumstances are present. The rules on this point have varied over the years, but currently are for the most part stated in the Land Registration Act 2002. We shall look at these in detail in Chapter 2, but, for example, the position may be that John will be affected by your right in rem only if, before John bought my land, your right had been registered at the Government's Land Registry. (A right in personam cannot be registered at the Registry, and even if somehow it were, it would still not bind John. Registration, and certain equivalent phenomena,[3] constitute the circumstances under which rights capable of binding John will actually do so. So they apply only to rights in rem. A right in personam is by definition not capable of binding John, so will not do so, no matter what.)

The idea of a right in rem is sometimes conveyed in the Latin expression *nemo dat quod non habet*, ie no one can give what he[4] does not have. Say I

---

[2] K Gray, 'Property in Thin Air' [1991] *CLJ* 252 at 293, and in other writings, castigates as circular the proposition that a property right—alias a right in rem (§ 1.1.3)—is one having the potential to affect John in this way. This criticism is questionable. The proposition is simply that 'in rem' is a synonym for 'can affect John'. To discover whether a given type of right *is* of this nature, one consults the rules. To decide whether it *ought* to be, one reflects on its standing in terms of the considerations explored in § 1.2.2.

[3] That is, the cases in which the law regards a right in rem as an 'overriding interest': § 2.1.1.

[4] Here, and (unless the context indicates otherwise) throughout this book, masculine pronouns are intended to refer to both sexes.

purport to sell John a house, but in fact it belongs not to me but to you. John does not become owner of the house, because I did not own it previously, so did not have it to give. Equally if I do own the house but have leased it to you for five years, thereby giving you a right in rem over it for that period. If I purport to sell the house to John, what I have to give is the ownership minus your leased interest, so the picture is painted of him acquiring the ownership minus your interest. Which, in both cases, explains why John must respect your interest: he never acquired (because I never gave him, because I never had) the ability to do otherwise.[5] Whereas if your right is only in personam—as where you are my lodger—your claim is against me personally, so all the rights in the house remain mine to give, and I can successfully transfer them to John. If John chooses to evict you, all you can do is sue me for breaking my contract with you.

But this picture does not fit with the fact that English land law's rights in rem affect someone like John *only if certain conditions, such as registration, are met*. I may own a house subject to a lease in your favour, but if that lease is not registered, John may not be affected by it: I will thus have given him the house unencumbered, despite not owning such an unencumbered house myself. So the actual law regarding the behaviour of rights in rem is not in fact fully described by the *nemo dat* image. How should we think about this discrepancy?

A quick answer might be that *nemo dat* is only a metaphor, and its imprecision therefore unimportant. That is not good enough, however. The idea underlying *nemo dat* is that when something 'belongs' to a person, as the house in the above examples belongs wholly or in part (to the extent of the lease) to you, that person's entitlement to it is absolute, impregnable. This idea has a powerful appeal.[6] The fact that the actual law departs from it, in the manner under discussion, therefore requires explanation and justification.

The key is that, for all its appeal seen from your perspective, the pure *nemo dat* idea creates dangers for others such as John. Dealing with me, he may believe that I have the house to sell, and that there are no derogations from this, for example a lease in your favour; and he may proceed on the basis of this belief, most especially by paying me for the house's whole value. If this belief turns out to be ill-founded, John will suffer. He may well have a claim against me for his money, or the relevant fraction of it, but this is distinctly second best to not encountering the problem at all. Of course, John's mistake

---

[5] Likewise if, rather than selling the house to John, I go bankrupt and the house is to be taken and sold to help pay my creditors. If the house is not mine but yours, this cannot happen. If it is mine but you have a lease over it, it can and will happen, but when the house is offered for sale, the offer must be subject to your lease.

[6] It is an aspect of the paradigm conception of property, or ownership. For further discussion of the latter (the reasons why it has a powerful appeal, and the reasons why we may nonetheless not espouse it), see § 1.3.

may be entirely his own fault. But equally it may not be: he may have taken all the care in the world, or—more interestingly—all the care that we should wish him to. For the market in an asset to operate most effectively, so that the asset can move to the person able to extract the greatest profit from it, we need to minimise the 'transaction costs', ie the costs involved in procuring this movement. The more care we expect of John, or that is in effect demanded by our rules about when a right in rem will bind him, the higher will be his transaction costs, frustrating these boons.

From this point of view, then, it makes sense for the law to make John bound by a right in rem only when it ought to be easily discoverable. Hence the rule whereby John will in many cases by bound by your right only if the latter has been registered: registration makes for easy discoverability.[7] The literal idea of *nemo dat quod non habet* is sacrificed to the extent required by such countervailing considerations. But that idea's essential appeal remains, so the rules embodying the departures from it require the most careful design. Those currently in force will be examined and evaluated in Chapter 2.

1.1.3 Two Difficulties with the Terminology

Two difficulties with the terminology, 'in rem' and 'in personam', need exploration.

First, one often encounters other terminology, dividing the universe of rights into 'real', or 'proprietary', or 'property' rights on the one hand and 'personal' rights on the other. Unless it seems that the writer intends otherwise, it should be assumed that 'personal' is a synonym for 'in personam', and that 'real', 'proprietary' and 'property' are synonyms for 'in rem' ... as are 'a right in (or relating to, or affecting) the land', 'an interest in (or relating to, or affecting) the land', or even 'an interest' without more.

These other labels may be preferred because 'in rem' and 'in personam' were originally used in the law of ancient Rome, whose rules gave them specific meanings; and the writer wishes to make clear that the meanings of the corresponding concepts in modern English law are not necessarily quite the same. Those who, like the present writer, use the Roman terms are however usually clear that they do so simply for convenience, with no intention to treat the terms as having the Roman or any other particular meaning. The Roman terms are generally used in this book because, unlike their synonyms, they are not ordinary English words. Their very strangeness,

---

[7] An older rule provided that certain rights bound John only if he was not a 'bona fide purchaser for value without notice' of them. The key element in this, the idea of 'notice', in theory referred to the possibility of discovery by a 'reasonable purchaser'. As such, it was apparently sympathetic to the value under discussion. But the concept of a 'reasonable purchaser' was itself interpreted in various ways, including some quite demanding on John: leaving the concept not so sympathetic after all.

by arresting the mind, helps to flag up the fact that the concepts in question are crucial, and involve technical rules.

Second, a writer will sometimes draw the line between rights in rem and in personam in a different place from that sketched in § 1.1.2, insisting that a right counts as 'in rem' only if it affects John *without further ado*—ie without need of registration or whatever—and that all other rights are thus in personam, including those that have the potential to affect John, but will do so only if certain conditions are met.

This issue arises because there are in fact three classes of right—(i) those that will affect John without further ado; (ii) those that will affect John, but only if certain conditions are met; and (iii) those that cannot affect John—but only two labels (whether Roman or English). A solution would be to adopt a third label, and some take this path, though the third label often chosen—and used for category (ii)—is 'sui generis', meaning 'in a class of their own', which is hardly illuminating. But say we restrict ourselves to only two labels, as is more usual, and treat rights in category (i) as certainly in rem, and those in category (iii) as certainly in personam. We need to group those in category (ii) with one of the other categories. Which? Either answer could be defended, but in practice it is more useful to distinguish category (ii) from (iii) than from (i). The rules creating the boundary between categories (ii) and (iii), ie determining whether a right is capable of binding John at all, are rather firm and long-lived;[8] whereas the rules creating the boundary between (i) and (ii)—ie the precise details about when a given right, capable of binding John, will actually do so—are relatively superficial and ephemeral. Hence the decision in this book (and in most lawyers' parlance) to group categories (i) and (ii) together as rights in rem, treating category (iii) rights alone as in personam.

In short, this book uses the term 'right in rem' to mean a right that is capable of affecting John, and will do so under the conditions prescribed by the law's prevailing rules on the matter, whether these make it affect him without further ado or (as in the current state of English registered land law) only under certain conditions.

1.1.4 Rights in Rem as Effective Against 'Disponees'

So far we have seen that a right in rem over my land is one that can affect John, to whom I sell that land. We need to be a little more precise about the kind of person that can be affected.

To put it abstractly, a right in rem over a piece of land is a right (to use the land in some way, and) effective not merely vis-à-vis the person against whom

---

[8] This is the '*numerus clausus*' effect, and there are reasons for it, discussed in § 1.2.2.

the right arose in the first place, but also, potentially, vis-à-vis people subsequently acquiring rights in the land in question.

People of this kind are called 'disponees'. Disponees include someone who becomes owner of the land in my place, such as John: as owner hitherto, I give John all my rights. They also include those to whom I give only some of my rights, while remaining owner myself. So if I give you a right in rem to live in my house, and then merely rent my house out to Kate, Kate is a disponee. If the conditions for your right affecting Kate are met, therefore, she will be affected by your right.

In this example, your right's 'effect' on Kate is likely to be immediate and obvious. She will probably want to occupy the house herself, or to allow someone else to do so, and your right to do so will frustrate this desire.

Sometimes, however, the effect will be less immediate or obvious, but nonetheless there. Say I give you a right—in rem—to get from your land to a certain road by crossing my land that lies between the two: a 'right of way'. Then I mortgage my land to a bank, to secure my overdraft. As a disponee of the land, the bank will (assuming the relevant conditions for this are met) be affected by your right. But in at any rate the first instance, there will be no practical impact on the bank: your crossing my land is quite compatible with the bank's having its security right. The picture changes, however, if I default on my repayments and the bank repossesses my land so as to sell it and recoup the outstanding debt. Being bound by your right to cross the land, the bank will be able to offer the land for sale only subject to your right, and that will mean fetching a lower price than would otherwise be attainable (since a buyer will be to that extent deprived of the land's use: he will not, for example, be able to build across your route).

Equally, if I mortgage the land to the bank first, then give you your right of way. A mortgage is a right in rem, so assuming the necessary conditions are fulfilled, you—as a disponee—will be affected by it. But at any rate at first, there will be no practical impact on you. The impact will appear if the bank repossesses and sells. Being 'affected' by the mortgage means that you cannot insist on your right of way so as to cut down the bank's rights. So the bank can offer the land for sale free from your right to cross it, and thus attract a higher price.

Sometimes again, the nature of the two rights will be such that even a delayed impact of this kind cannot occur. Say I give you the right to cross my land following route X, then give Liam the right to cross it following route Y, and that the two routes do not cross one another. Assuming the necessary conditions are met, Liam, as a disponee, will be affected by your right, but given the topography it is hard to see how this could ever matter. So when we say that a right in rem is one that is potentially 'effective' against a later disponee of the land in question, we mean that it takes priority—precedence—over the later disponee's interest; but whether this makes a concrete difference will depend on the two rights' specifications, and the ways in which they are in practice used.

This book refers to a person who acquires a right in land—such as Kate, the bank, Liam, and indeed you in these examples—as a 'disponee'. The word 'disponee' has only recently come to be used to describe a person of this kind. Until 2002,[9] the usual term was 'purchaser'. But that term was misleading in suggesting (at any rate to lay ears) someone who *bought* the *ownership* of the land. Neither of these limitations reflected the actual rule, which has always been as described in this section. The word 'disponee' avoids giving such an impression, correctly capturing someone to whom I give any kind of right in my land (like Kate, the bank, Liam and you), and whether for payment or gratuitously. This book will use the word 'disponee', but given the recentness of the change, the word 'purchaser' will still be found in many sources.

1.2 The Kinds of Rights in Rem

So far we have talked about rights in rem in the abstract, though some concrete examples of them—ownership, leases, rights of way, mortgages—have cropped up. Now we shall develop a firmer understanding of the kinds of rights in rem that the law recognises.

1.2.1 The *Numerus Clausus*

Notice the key assumption in this: that the law recognises only rights of certain kinds—ie with certain contents—as able to exist in rem. This contrasts with the position regarding the in personam rights that can be generated by making a contract, which can be given almost[10] any content. So I can effectively contract with you (in personam) for you to occupy my house on a temporary basis in more or less any manner we choose. But if you are to have the relevant right in rem, a lease, we must conform our arrangement to the law's template for the latter. As we shall see in § 11.2.1, this requires the arrangement to give you the right to 'exclusive possession' of the land (so, not sharing with me); for a defined period (so, not simply for as long as you

---

[9] The change occurred in the language used by the Land Registration Act 2002.

[10] The sole exceptions are where the right would give a claim to something that is against the law (eg the supply of illegal drugs), or otherwise contrary to public policy (eg an unacceptable restriction on trade).

like); and, supposedly but perhaps not correctly, in return for some sort of payment.

There are only a certain number of such templates, and they are not exhaustive of all possible rights. So it is not a matter simply of finding the correct label for the right we wish to create. Many rights will not fit any of the templates, and so cannot exist in rem at all. For example, if we try to create a right allowing you exclusive possession of my land, in return for rent, *for an undefined period*, but nonetheless having the potential to bind a disponee of my land, we shall fail, for there is no such right in rem. We shall succeed only in creating a right in personam, which cannot bind a disponee.

So a right can be in rem only if it positively matches the demands of one of the limited number of defined templates, and otherwise can be in personam only. To put it another way, rights in rem, as defined by their respective templates, form a finite subset of all possible rights, the remainder being capable of existing in personam only. The idea that rights in rem are limited to this finite subset is known as the '*numerus clausus*' (closed number) principle.

The *numerus clausus* principle operates at two levels. Hitherto, this section has focused on only one: that concerning individuals who might wish to create rights in rem of their own devising, but who (the principle dictates) cannot.[11] The other concerns the design of the law. When we say that, to be in rem, a right must conform to one of the recognised templates, we do not necessarily say that the law should be shy of enlarging the class of templates. But in fact, the *numerus clausus* principle seems to operate at this level too. The class of rights in rem is small (there are problems about how to count them, but one could certainly defend an assertion that the number of rights in rem recognised by English land law barely reaches double figures); over the last couple of centuries the law has arguably gained four new rights in rem[12] but lost certain others;[13] and the principle may even have received statutory statement, instructing the courts not to develop new rights in rem on their own.[14]

---

[11] The principle is stated in this form in certain decisions, most famously *Keppell v Bailey* (1834) 2 My & K 517, 535–6 (Ch).

[12] The restrictive covenant (Ch 10); the right of pre-emption and the 'mere equity' (Land Registration Act 2002 ss 115, 116(b)); and the 'home right' dealt with in the Family Law Act 1996 s 30 (though the conditions under which the latter will bind a disponee—s 31(10)—are unique to it, and somewhat restrictive).

[13] Until 1925, it was possible to divide up the ownership of land, using a variety of more limited estates which were themselves rights in rem: eg a life estate and an entail. By the Law of Property Act 1925 s 1(1), such interests can no longer exist in their own right (§ 1.3.4). They can however still take effect as beneficial interests under trusts. The latter are traditionally conceived as rights in rem, but § 14.8.2 concludes that the combined effect of a number of contemporary rules is substantially to deprive them too of their effect in rem.

[14] Law of Property Act 1925 s 4(1). 'May', because although this appears to be the provision's literal meaning, many refuse to accept it, finding it a little too strong a reading of the principle. See further § 15.3.3.

1.2.2 Why the *Numerus Clausus*?

Why does the law operate this *numerus clausus* principle? Essentially, to ensure that rights can operate in rem where, but only where, this does more good than harm.

Rights in rem always do harm. Say I own a plot of land, and am negotiating to sell it to John. John will want to know whether, on buying it, he will be bound by any pre-existing rights relating to it. Any such rights will make the land less valuable to him than the same piece of land without such rights, and so diminish the amount of wealth that can be extracted by the sale. Indeed, the mere possibility of such rights—inherent in the fact that rights in rem exist at all—will have this effect, for the need to discover whether the land is affected by such rights will increase John's transaction costs.

One might therefore think it right to prohibit all rights in rem other than ownership (ie to have a *numerus clausus* consisting only of that one right). Then John could buy the land with the freedom to exploit it as he might wish, and could do so without needing even to worry about the matter. But this would be to overlook the arguments in favour of allowing rights to operate in rem. Rights in rem have positive value in two ways. If I, the owner of the land, wish to give you such a right, allowing the right to exist vindicates my wish, so enhancing my liberty. (So too allowing the generation of wealth: the possibility of creating such a right in return for payment gives me another way of extracting value from my land.) And the fact that your right is in rem gives you the opportunity to enforce it against John (not merely against me, as where it is in personam) ... and so, in turn, the possibility of maintaining it in specie, rather than seeing it become merely a compensation right, after the transfer to him. Say the right represents your entitlement to your home: the possibility of maintaining it in specie is likely to be of the greatest importance to you.

The *numerus clausus* principle represents the law's effort to reconcile these sets of opposing considerations: allowing rights to operate in rem where the arguments for their doing so outweigh those against, but forbidding them otherwise. But how does the law perform the calculation? Given how basic the *numerus clausus* is, one would expect the answer to be rather obvious. In fact, commentators have struggled to identify it.[15]

It may be that the task cannot be performed in a formulaic way: that any decision to regard a particular kind of right as in rem or in personam must rest upon contestable value judgments. So one would ask directly whether the

---

[15] See especially B Rudden, 'Economic Theory v Property Law: The *Numerus Clausus* Problem' in J Eekelaar and J Bell (eds), *Oxford Essays in Jurisprudence, Third Series* (Oxford, 1987) ch 11; T Merrill and H Smith, 'Optimal Standardization in the Law of Property: The *Numerus Clausus* Principle' (2000) 110 *Yale Law Journal* 1; H Hansmann and R Kraakman, 'Property, Contract and Verification: The *Numerus Clausus* Problem and the Divisibility of Rights' (2002) 31 *Journal of Legal Studies* S373.

market damage entailed by allowing the right to operate in rem is a price worth paying, perhaps in social terms, for the facility of allowing it to subsist in specie, as an adjunct to the land, against the land's successive owners. Coming at the matter in this way, one would see the *numerus clausus* as containing those rights in respect of which the answer to that question is 'yes'. For example, we might well regard a right to use the land as one's home—given the social importance of homes—as trumping the opposing market arguments in this way, and so as meriting in rem status.

In each chapter dealing with a particular right in rem later in the book, we shall think in this way about the case for accepting it as such.

1.2.3 The Rights

The chapters in Part 3 of this book consider a number of the rights in rem that can exist over land in English law, ie are members of the *numerus clausus*, namely:[16]

— Easements (Chapter 9): rights that one piece of land be used in a certain way, for the benefit of another piece of land. An example is a right of way, ie a right allowing the owner of one piece of land to access it by crossing another.
— Restrictive covenants (Chapter 10): a further class of rights that one piece of land be used in a certain way, for the benefit of another piece of land: for instance, a right that you have, as owner of your house, requiring me not to build in my garden, lest this interrupts your view. Restrictive covenants and easements evidently have similarities: their relationship is considered in § 10.6.
— Leases (Chapter 11): rights allowing one person (or a group) to have exclusive possession of land belonging to another, for a defined period. If you rent a house, or shop, or field from me for 10 years, you will probably do so by way of a lease.
— Mortgages (Chapter 12): rights securing obligations, principally debts. If I owe you money, and grant you a mortgage over my land, you thereby acquire the right to recoup the outstanding debt by seizing my land and selling it.

---

[16] Others are profits (rights allowing one person to enter and take certain things—eg coal, timber, game—from land owned by another); rentcharges (rights allowing someone to own land in return for periodical payments to someone else, but since the Rentcharges Act 1977 usable only in rather exiguous circumstances); rights of entry (rights connected with leases and rentcharges, allowing the land to be taken from its tenant or owner respectively if the required rent is not paid); estate contracts (rights arising where the parties intend to create, or purport to have created, some other right, but have not yet done so: see § 5.2); options and rights of pre-emption (rights to demand a right under certain circumstances); 'mere equities' (rights to rescind a transaction, if it is vitiated by eg misrepresentation); and 'home rights' (occupation rights arising by virtue of a family relationship).

— Rights under trusts (Chapters 13 and 14): rights entitling their owners ('beneficiaries') to the benefit of land nominally held by others ('trustees'), who themselves are not allowed to derive benefit from it. This distinguishes trust rights from the other rights in rem, for in the case of the latter the owner of the land clearly retains all the remaining rights in it. Since the beneficiaries thus collectively enjoy the ownership of the land, trusts can be used to divide the ownership between two or more people. This is perhaps their principal importance.

— Licences coupled with an interest (§ 15.4): rights allowing someone to enter the land of another so as to gain access to some asset that he owns and that is located there. But § 15.4.3 queries whether this class of right exists as a distinct species, or whether it is better understood as a type of easement.

Additionally, Chapter 15 deals with licences in general, which are the rights in personam that may exist in respect of land thanks to its owner's consent. (Others again may exist without the owner's consent, but this book does not extend so far.) Given what was said about the *numerus clausus* principle in § 1.2.1, it will be appreciated that such rights—unlike the specific rights in rem—can have any content their parties wish. It is, however, always possible that licences with a particular type of content will, on account of evolving social perceptions of that content, come to be seen as sufficiently valuable to merit recognition as in rem (ie be added to the *numerus clausus*), notwithstanding the harm that this would entail. In § 15.3.3, we shall see how the courts have experimented with giving in rem status to a certain class of licence in this way, though without producing an enduring change in the law to that effect.

This list of rights in rem to be detailed in later chapters does not include the grandest of all such rights, namely the freehold ownership. It tends to be taken for granted: not unreasonably, since it is so familiar a concept. But some discussion will be useful.

1.3 Ownership

1.3.1 Ownership in English Land Law

It is sometimes said that English law does not recognise the idea of ownership of land.

Certainly, the largest interest in land recognised by English law is officially known, not as 'ownership', but as the 'fee simple absolute in possession'. But if we inquire what this interest amounts to—what is its substance, what it gives its holder—the answer is, quite undoubtedly, ownership of the land.[17]

As we shall see in § 1.3.3, 'ownership' is a rather imprecise term: it does not give very exact information about the content of the interest, ie what the 'owner' can and cannot do. The term 'fee simple absolute in possession' gives greater precision, though only in two particulars. It connotes that the interest in question (whatever its precise content) is enjoyed *immediately* and *indefinitely*. Such an interest contrasts with lesser interests, such as leases and most beneficial rights under trusts, which in terms of their day-to-day content are also candidates for the label 'ownership',[18] but which either begin in the future, or last only for a certain time, or both. The possibility of creating time-limited ownership in this way involves fragmenting the full (immediate and indefinite) ownership interest. This is a valuable possibility, but it also entails problems. We shall look at the law's experience with it in § 1.3.4.

1.3.2 Ownership as a Right in Rem

Unlike at least some of the other members of the *numerus clausus*, ownership could hardly not be in rem: its effectiveness in rem is part and parcel of the very idea of ownership. Say you 'own' a house, but I purport to sell it to John. (Perhaps having squatted in it for a while, and as a result seeming to be its owner.) In stipulating that you 'own' the house, we have already suggested that I have no right to sell it: were it otherwise, it would be harder to call you the house's 'owner'. And if I have no right to sell the house, it follows (*nemo dat quod non habet*) that John cannot acquire it. In stipulating that you 'own' the house, we have therefore also already suggested that John should not be able to acquire it, without your consent.

We can thus continue to say that, as with all rights in rem, your right has the potential to affect John as a disponee of the land. But in this instance, where the right amounts to ownership and as such negatives all rights in the disponee, the 'effect' is so extensive that it seems absurd to call John a disponee at all. This latter observation shows the difference in degree between ownership and the other rights in rem. If I own the house, but you have some other kind of right in rem over it (say, a right of way across its garden), I can indeed make John owner in my place, and accordingly we have no worries about terming him a disponee, going on to say that your right can affect him as such. The relative appropriateness of the word

---

[17] On this and associated issues, see further J Harris, 'Ownership of Land in English Law' in N MacCormick and P Birks (eds), *The Legal Mind—Essays for Tony Honoré* (Oxford, 1986) ch 9.

[18] For leases as a species of ownership, see § 11.1.1; for trust rights, see § 14.1.

'disponee' in the two cases is not the key point, however. The essential idea is the same in both.

1.3.3 The Content of Ownership

The paradigm idea of ownership supposes that an owner has all the rights in the asset concerned, and can lose these rights by, but only by, his consent. In other words, an owner has the legal power to use the asset, to exclude others from it,[19] and to transfer it. It is unlikely, however, that any legal system does or would operate this idea in an unqualified way.[20] Certainly English law does not.

Take even an uncomplicated asset like a pencil. There are few ways in which I may not use my pencil, but there are some: my ownership does not entitle me to commit a crime with it, say by stabbing someone. I can give, sell or bequeath the pencil to someone else largely as I wish, but there are general restrictions on my power to alienate property when approaching bankruptcy, so as to protect my creditors, and on my power to neglect my family and dependants on my death. And while I will generally have the law on my side in objecting to others' behaviour tending to deprive me of the pencil, like all my assets it can be seized to pay my debts (in the organised manner known as bankruptcy), and for certain law enforcement and security reasons, and potentially by government expropriation (probably subject to the payment of compensation); and if someone does take it from me or damages or destroys it, there are certain restrictions (especially time limits) on my legal power to complain.

So while the law's construction of the ownership of a pencil does not diverge hugely from the paradigm idea, even in this simple case it certainly does not follow that idea fully. When the asset is land, the picture is essentially similar, but with different emphases. My right to recover my land from those who seek to steal it is in general better protected, for example, but there is a significantly higher chance of its being expropriated, under the standing

---

[19] For the significance of the ability to exclude others, see K Gray, 'Property in Thin Air' [1991] *CLJ* 252.

[20] Civil law jurisdictions operate a concept called 'dominium', which is represented as being of this kind. But of course it is not: such jurisdictions recognise the sorts of qualifications about to be discussed in the text. Differences between the civil law and English law approaches are thus in practical terms ones of degree (though they may rest on rather widely divergent conceptual foundations). (See further G Samuel, 'The Many Dimensions of Property' in J McLean (ed), *Property and the Constitution* (Oxford, 1999) ch 3.) The differences are perhaps most marked as regards the fragmentation of ownership, a matter discussed in § 1.3.4. English law's experiments with this have certainly been more adventurous than the civil law's ... but as we shall see, English law, having experimented, has now become more cautious, giving unitary ownership greater emphasis.

arrangements for compulsory purchase.[21] It is also much more likely that other people will have rights demanding that the land shall, or shall not, be used in particular ways, such as the right entitling them to cross it (an easement), or to share the occupation of it with me (a licence), or the right that I shall not build on it (a restrictive covenant). It is wholly usual for you and others to have such rights in my land; yet we continue to think of me as owning it.

So English law, and the English language, seems to have no difficulty seeing someone as owner despite their not wholly fitting the paradigm mould. But how far can this be taken? Say I lose certain of the rights that I would otherwise have as owner of the pencil or the land, whether by my consent or otherwise. At what point should I cease to be called 'owner'? Neither the law nor the language has a firm answer to this. But it is noticeable how resilient the idea of ownership is: how great an erosion is tolerated before the term is seen as under pressure, let alone to be abandoned. For example, I can 'own' a piece of land despite its being mortgaged. I normally retain my basic abilities to use the land and transfer it. But my ability to exclude others is heavily impaired: until I have paid off my mortgage loan, I run the risk of having my rights in it sold out from under me. Yet we still think of me as the land's owner.

In thinking about the extent to which 'ownership' may be qualified, in this and other ways, we are concerned not only with the elasticity of the word, but also with what the idea of ownership stands for in moral and political discourse.[22]

Conceived in the terms of the paradigm—as the legal power to use the asset in question, to exclude others from it, and to transfer it—ownership promotes the liberal desideratum of maximising human autonomy, in the particular context of people's dealings with things.[23] Such a maximising of

---

[21] For discussion of some of the respects in which English law currently plays up and plays down the idea of unqualified ownership of land, and why, see K Gray and S Gray, 'The Rhetoric of Realty' in J Getzler (ed), *Rationalizing Property, Equity and Trusts—Essays in Honour of Edward Burn* (London, 2003) ch 10.

[22] The relevant literature is voluminous, and often very distinguished, so that selection is more than usually invidious. But, focusing only on modern work, one might assemble the following as a useful bookshelf: B Ackerman, *Takings—Private Property and the Power of Eminent Domain* (Cambridge MA, 1985); J Waldron, *The Right to Private Property* (Oxford, 1988); J Harris, *Property and Justice* (Oxford, 1996); J Penner, *The Idea of Property in Law* (Oxford, 1997); J Singer, *Entitlement: The Paradoxes of Property* (New Haven, 2000); L Underkuffler, *The Idea of Property: Its Meaning and Power* (Oxford, 2003); T Endicott et al (eds), *Properties of Law—Essays in Honour of Jim Harris* (Oxford, 2006) pt II.

[23] 'Things' is itself interesting. Of tangible things, only some can be owned (land being one of these, and of course pencils), while others (such as natural air) cannot (see further K Gray, 'Property in Thin Air' [1991] *CLJ* 252). The restriction to the former is an important reflection of the fact, about to be explained, that ownership and its liberal driver are by no means omnipotent. On the other hand, 'things' also include—ie rights in the nature of ownership can be had in respect of—certain intangibles, ie conceptual constructs, such as copyright. This extension reflects the potency that the liberal project does possess.

autonomy is a desideratum either for its own libertarian sake, or for the beneficial economic consequences to which it should conduce. But the conception of ownership to which it points is the subject of objections from rival philosophies,[24] emphasising in particular the claims of utility[25] and of community,[26] and indeed from within liberalism itself, for to grant one person unqualified rights regarding a thing may clearly have damaging effects on another's freedom.[27] So there is no surprise at all in the fact that unqualified ownership is not encountered in practice. But it is interesting and significant that, while assimilating the inevitable qualifications, we continue using the word 'ownership' so long as we can. That I remain 'owner' of a thing, despite quite a lot of reasons to think and say otherwise, bespeaks our attraction to the liberal ideal even while we agree the correctness of compromising it.

The observation that 'ownership' is constructed from the interplay of sometimes countervailing considerations has to be distinguished, however, from the argument that 'unqualified ownership' is in fact an impossible *conception*: that certain restrictions—for example, those calculated to protect the environment—are intrinsic to the very idea of ownership.[28] To make such an argument, one might say that the apparently private institution of property is actually the predicate of a more fundamental desideratum which, given the nature of human existence, cannot help but be public, social, communal: in respect of this facet of people's dealings, the institution represents the way of ordering human affairs that is most beneficent to the underlying social given. It follows that the private institution

---

[24] Some however view ownership otherwise than as a liberal idea in the first place, so that certain limitations on the owner's autonomy are intrinsic to it. See eg M Raff, 'Towards an Ecologically Sustainable Property Concept' in E Cooke (ed), *Modern Studies in Property Law, Volume 3* (Oxford, 2005) ch 4.

[25] Provisions for compulsory purchase will normally rest on this basis, for example. See also S Grattan, 'Proprietarian Conceptions of Statutory Access Rights' in E Cooke (ed), *Modern Studies in Property Law, Volume 2* (Oxford, 2003) ch 18.

[26] As when a 'right to roam' arises over my property under the Countryside and Rights of Way Act 2000. Community—or some differently named non-anthropocentric cousin to it—could also limit my rights so as to protect the wider environment: see eg C Rodgers, 'Reforming Property Rights for Nature Conservation' in P Jackson and D Wilde, *Property Law: Current Issues and Debates* (Aldershot, 1999) ch 3.

[27] This is plain as regards my use of my pencil to stab you, which of course is—for this reason—not permitted. The same issue also troubles the phenomenon of a trust. Trusts are explained further in § 1.3.4 and Chs 13–14. But say I have an asset, and seek to arrange—a trust being the principal vehicle for doing so—that you shall have it *but only with certain strings attached* (eg once you marry). I am claiming to transfer the asset very much on my individual terms, rather than in the off-the-peg form of a simple gift. Liberalism argues that I should be able to do so, as a facet of my ownership ... but also recoils at the thought that, as a result, the rights you acquire in the asset will be correspondingly further from full ownership. See S Gardner, *An Introduction to the Law of Trusts* (2nd edn, Oxford, 2003) 46–49.

[28] For an argument configured in this way see eg S Coyle and K Morrow, *The Philosophical Foundations of Environmental Law: Property, Rights and Nature* (Oxford, 2004).

cannot be sustained when insistence on it would not further but corrode this given.[29]

One's view on this has consequences for the question whether a rule affirming a restriction upon ownership needs to provide compensation for those at whom it is aimed. If the rule merely tracks restrictions intrinsic to the idea of ownership, the answer should be 'no'; otherwise, it should be 'yes'. This question is begged by the terms of the US Constitution[30] and the European Convention on Human Rights,[31] and the relevant caselaw gives no stable answer to it.[32] This experience tends to suggest that even if the argument is in principle apt, it does not in practice yield the *necessarily correct* concrete conclusions it promises. We may do better to think of the nature and extent of the qualifications on ownership in an avowedly messier way, as the political (rather than moral) resolution of the conflicting impacts of essentially competing arguments.[33]

1.3.4 The Fragmentation of Ownership

The previous section considered the idea that I may remain 'owner' while my rights actually fall short of the paradigm. Of course, the more my rights are limited in the ways described, the more difficult it becomes to view me as owner. This difficulty is important not only linguistically, but also substantively. The limitations in question, for example, might make it impossible for me to extract full value from the land, or to sell it on terms enabling a buyer to do so. We might well see this as problematic, as diminishing liberty and damaging the market. If we decide to accept it nonetheless, it should be

---

[29] For a map of the ideas in play here, and an exploration of their implications, see M Robertson, 'Liberal, Democratic, and Socialist Approaches to the Public Dimensions of Private Property' in J McLean (ed), *Property and the Constitution* (Oxford, 1999) ch 12.

[30] Fifth Amendment, whereby '... nor shall private property be taken for public use, without just compensation', leaving the question: 'But what is private property?'

[31] First Protocol, Art 1, whereby 'No one shall be deprived of his possessions except in the public interest ...' and then only proportionately, ie normally in return for compensation; but 'the preceding provisions shall not ... impair the right of a State to enforce such laws as it deems necessary to control the use of property in accordance with the general interest ...', leaving the question whether any given restriction is (or can be) a 'deprivation' or a 'control'.

[32] In the context of the US Constitution, the issue is addressed, but settled largely by assertion: see especially *Lucas v South Carolina Coastal Council* (1992) 505 US 1003 (US Supreme Court). (See further J Singer and J Beerman, 'The Social Origins of Property' (1993) 6 *Canadian Journal of Law & Jurisprudence* 217.) In the context of the ECHR, the caselaw appears essentially oblivious of the issue: see especially *Sporrong and Lönnroth v Sweden* (1982) 5 EHRR 35 (ECtHR) and *Holy Monasteries v Greece* (1995) 20 EHRR 1 (ECtHR). (See further T Allen, 'The Human Rights Act (UK) and Property Law' in J McLean (ed), *Property and the Constitution* (Oxford, 1999) ch 7, 148–52.)

[33] See further G Alexander, 'Constitutionalising Property: Two Experiences, Two Dilemmas' in McLean, *ibid* ch 5; but compare A van der Walt, 'Property Theory and the Transformation of Property Law' in E Cooke (ed), *Modern Studies in Property Law, Volume 3* (Oxford, 2005) ch 17.

because we believe that the negative effects of the relevant limitation are outweighed by countervailing advantages.

It is easy to understand how this might be the case as regards limitations imposed on me from outside, such as the prohibition on using my asset to injure others, and the compulsory purchase and environmental protection regimes. It has also to be the case as regards limitations that I myself create, by conferring rights on others. As we saw in § 1.2.2, the point of the *numerus clausus* principle is to ensure that such limitations do more good than harm. In this discussion, we have noted the resilience of the idea of ownership: the fact that, despite the attenuation of my interest in such ways, it generally remains reasonable to regard me as owner. This resilience is no accident. It is the product of a strong moral and political presumption in favour of ownership, so that its attenuation not only demands justification, but is relatively unlikely to be justified.

Given this, it comes as a surprise to discover that English law has experimented with the idea of explicitly dividing the ownership of an asset, especially land, between a number of different people—so that while taken together their interests certainly add up to ownership, individually they are more limited[34]—and no surprise to learn that, as we shall see, it has to a significant extent abandoned the experiment. There have been three principal ventures of this kind, involving estates, trusts, and leases.

The first of these ventures is (or was: as explained below, it has now been discontinued) the most direct. It involves dividing the fee simple absolute in possession—as we have seen, the law's fullest rendition of ownership—into a collection of fragments. The fee simple absolute in possession, and the different fragments into which it can be divided, are known as estates.

The fragments might be sequential, when they are called by such names as the 'life estate' and the 'fee simple absolute in remainder'. For example, I, having the fee simple absolute in possession, might divide it into a life estate for you, giving you an interest for the duration of your life, and a fee simple absolute in remainder for John. On your death, John becomes as much owner as I originally was (his fee simple absolute in remainder became a fee simple absolute in possession). But until then, you do not have a full owner's rights, and nor does John. His interest is in effect ownership-in-waiting: it does not allow him to do anything with the land during your life. And although your interest certainly allows you to do things with the land (eg live on it), the need to think of John coming after you means that you cannot treat it

---

[34] Though the elasticity of the concept of ownership is such that some fragments, while clearly distanced from the paradigm, may still qualify as ownership, though only within their own time frame. For leases, see § 11.1.1; for trust rights, see § 14.1. The important thing here, however, is not the label, but the fact that fragmentation undoubtedly leaves the set of rights held by any one person considerably smaller than (*ceteris paribus*) it would otherwise be.

straightforwardly as your own (eg cut down its trees, extract its minerals, and keep all the proceeds for yourself).

Alternatively, the fragments might be concurrent, as where I make you and John co-owners of the land: ie I give you and him the fee simple absolute in possession to share between you (as opposed to physically dividing the land in two, and giving you each that estate over your own piece).[35] Here again, obviously, neither of you alone is the owner of the land.

The second experiment with fragmenting ownership, which continues to form part of the law, involves the land being held on a trust. We shall look at trusts more fully in Chapters 13 and 14. But broadly speaking, a trust is 'a situation in which property is vested in someone (a trustee), who is under legally recognised obligations, at least some of which are of a proprietary kind [ie in rem], to handle it in a certain way, and to the exclusion of any personal interest'.[36] The obligations can be configured in many ways, but one of these is to benefit two or more people in a manner analogous to one of the forms of fragmentary ownership just discussed.

So say I own some land. I may make myself trustee of it, or the law may impose a trust of it upon me. Then, although I technically continue to have the fee simple absolute in possession in the land, I have no rights as a result, for—as noted—the obligations I owe as trustee must be so great as to exclude all personal interest on my part.[37] The obligations may take various forms, but one could be to use the land for the benefit of you for your life, and thereafter John; or you and John concurrently: ie to let you and (whether later or simultaneously) John live on the land, or receive the income it generates. Here we see the fragmentation of ownership again. Although I have the fee simple absolute in possession, my lack of rights means that I myself certainly cannot be called the owner of the land. The rights which my obligations give you and John add up to something like ownership; but they are split between the two of you.[38]

It may be useful for the law to allow the ownership of land to be divided in the ways permitted in these two experiments: for example, so as to provide for successive generations of a family to have interests in their ancestral estate, or for a couple to co-own their house. But there is a disadvantage too:

---

[35] Or indeed, I might use both sequential and concurrent fragments simultaneously, as where I give you and John together an estate in the land for the life of the first of you to die, and give Kate and Liam jointly the fee simple absolute in remainder.

[36] S Gardner, *An Introduction to the Law of Trusts* (2nd edn, Oxford, 2003) 2.

[37] Though it is possible for me to be trustee for a group of people that includes myself, in which case I shall have rights in the latter capacity.

[38] Although the example in the text involves fragmented ownership, trusts are not always configured in this way. Sometimes, indeed, while the trustee continues to have no rights, nobody else does either. For example, I may hold the land on trust so as to house a religious community. Then, ownership simply disappears. But this raises the same kind of difficulty as fragmentation, namely the prima facie destruction of the land's marketability; to which the law has responded in the same way, by the device of overreaching.

on the face of it, the land's exploitability and hence marketability is damaged. Since, in our examples, the ownership rights are divided between your and John's interests, someone wanting to exploit the land fully, and therefore to acquire it with full ownership (the right to do everything an owner could do with the land, and straight away), would seem to need to buy from both of you. This might be reasonably straightforward, but could easily be more difficult: as where you are amenable to sale but John is not (a possibility which obviously grows as I divide the ownership of the land among larger numbers of people), or indeed—for this is a possible version of the sequential arrangement—where John has not yet been born.

The law has developed a solution to this problem. In the case of a trust, I, as trustee, have the power to sell the full ownership of the land, simultaneously 'overreaching' the rights under it, ie converting them into rights in the money I receive in exchange for the land. The idea of overreaching is considered in more detail in § 14.5, but the key point is that it allows ownership to be fragmented as described, *but re-assembled for the purposes of a sale*. This device operates only where a trust is used, however. There is no equivalent to it where the ownership is divided into fragmentary estates ... except that the latter possibility was abolished in the last century, meaning that all such ventures are now channelled through the trust route, to which overreaching does apply.[39]

The third way in which the law allows the ownership of land to be fragmented is by creating a lease. Say I own a house, and lease it to you for 10 years. The exact nature of a lease is explained in Chapter 11, but in essence you thereby acquire, for the 10 years, the right to occupy the house and to exclude all others, including me; and you can normally transfer this right to someone else. You usually have to pay me rent, and you may have certain other obligations (especially regarding the house's upkeep) as well, but it is fair to view you as the house's owner for the 10 years, while I of course will once again be its unqualified owner thereafter. (In the meantime, I, retaining the freehold in the land, may be referred to as its 'owner', but this is apt only in the sense that I continue to have the bare title to it, plus, generally, a right to your rent.)

On the face of it, this arrangement is very like that which I create when I give you a life estate, then John—or more especially myself—a fee simple absolute in remainder. As we have seen, the law has concluded that the disadvantages of the latter arrangement make it unacceptable, and that it needs to take effect instead via a trust, with the latter's facility for overreaching the fragmentary interests so as to allow transfer of full ownership after all. The law continues to allow the creation of leases, however. If I have leased the house to you for 10 years, for that period I simply cannot transfer full

---

[39] This is the effect of the Law of Property Act 1925 ss 1(1) (for sequential estates) and 34 and 36 (for concurrent ones).

ownership. I can of course sell my own interest, but until the 10 years have elapsed the buyer will be bound by your rights, as a sitting tenant, just as I was.

Why does the law not insist on overreaching here too? Because the usefulness of leases in allowing temporary ownership of land, especially on a rental basis, is seen as outweighing the damage to the market that this entails. The usual presence of rent makes a difference. Someone might well want to buy the land even with a sitting tenant precisely so as to receive the income, in a way that could not occur if he acquired only a trustee's title to the land, with the trust obligations still attached: as we have seen, a trustee cannot personally benefit at all. At the same time, as we shall see in § 14.5.3, the susceptibility of trusts themselves to overreaching has varied over the years, and is nowadays less than it once was. This too is a reflection of the social value of the rights concerned: today, trusts of land commonly arise where a couple own their home, plainly a useful application. The suppression of the facility to create fragmentary estates occurred when the dynastic applications to which it was classically put ceased to be perceived as meriting the market damage that it entailed.

1.3.5 The Security of Ownership

As we saw in § 1.3.3, one aspect of the paradigm idea of ownership depicts an owner as having the right to exclude others from the asset in question. Thus, someone whom we see as the 'owner' of a piece of land has legal recourse against others who, lacking his permission to do so, seek to make use of it: as where I, the owner of a house, can sue you as a trespasser if you squat in it. If I had no recourse against trespassers, either (if we somehow otherwise knew that I owned the land) the law would be deficient, or we should have to conclude that I did not own the land in the first place.

Of course, I can allow you to be on the land, or indeed transfer it to you. That is consistent with, in fact an expression of, my ownership. But there exist a number of other ways in which you can lawfully use the land, or acquire a right in it, or indeed take the ownership of it from me, without my consent ... and yet the knowledge of this does not stop us saying that I own it. Part 2 of this book examines a variety of ways in which the law allows rights in rem to be acquired. Some of them rest on consent, as where I simply confer the right on you, but others have different bases, such as where my land is compulsorily purchased by the government in order to build a road over it. The fact that this is always a possibility does not prevent us from thinking of me as owner until it happens. The more commonly and unavoidably such things are possible, however, the less comfortable we are with thinking of me as owner. At the same time, we might still depict me as owner, as part of the rhetoric against the sort of provision in question. So, if I have to allow ingress to my land under the 'right to roam' legislation,[40] I have moved a step away from full ownership of it; and the view that I should be its full owner, so that such steps are improper, forms an argument against the legislation.

Traditionally,[41] English land law took a heavily qualified position on the matter. It did not even purport to operate a secure idea of ownership, in which I could ward off any intruder. To be sure, it has always offered remedies against trespassers. But it operated a set of rules whereby possessing land, even as a trespasser, itself gave you a claim to it. You could be defeated, but only by someone able to show that they likewise possessed it (or acquired it directly or indirectly from someone who possessed it) before you. And they could be defeated, but only by someone able to do the same to them. Since it was normally impossible to point to the first ever possessor of a piece of land, it followed that virtually all claims to land were relative in this way, and—certainly from the present point of view—not to be thought of as fully 'ownership'.

It is true that, within this culture, security was in one sense enhanced, by a doctrine known as 'adverse possession'.[42] If, despite being a trespasser against those with older claims, you behaved as though you owned the land for 12 years, their ability to defeat you became blocked. This left your claim safe against theirs, and so gave you more the kind of security we associate with ownership. But compared with the paradigm, it was striking that you had to wait 12 years before acquiring such an entitlement ... and, of course, that you could in turn be displaced by someone who adversely possessed against you. So the improved security afforded by adverse possession was of a highly unstable kind.

But eventually a new approach was developed, which prevails today. As a result, English law's idea of entitlement to land has moved much closer to the paradigm of ownership. The principal vehicles for this development have been the Land Registration Acts of 1925[43] and, replacing the latter, 2002. The new approach involves indicating on a government register that a piece of land is yours, and also (at least some of) the rights that bind you in respect of it. The aim is to produce greater stability of title, by stipulating that the

---

[40] Countryside and Rights of Way Act 2000.

[41] See further A Simpson, *A History of the Land Law* (2nd edn, Oxford, 1986) ch 2 and 150–55.

[42] Adverse possession is explored in greater detail in § 6.2.

[43] And before that, the Land Transfer Act 1875. For the context of these early statutes, see A Offer, *Property and Politics, 1870–1914: Landownership, Law, Ideology and Urban Development in England* (Cambridge, 1981); J Anderson, *Lawyers and the Making of English Land Law 1832–1940* (Oxford, 1992); A Offer, 'Lawyers and Land Law Revisited' (1994) 14 *OJLS* 269; J Anderson, 'The 1925 Property Legislation: Setting Contexts' in S Bright and J Dewar (eds), *Land Law—Themes and Perspectives* (Oxford, 1998) ch 4. These accounts explore the reasons why those involved in the development of the 1925 Act may have taken the positions they did. But the gist of the Act—and of other reforms made in the late 19th and early 20th centuries, eg in the area of fragmented ownership (§ 1.3.4)—was to the effect described in the text.

position regarding the title to the land is what the register says it is. The full working out of this idea has taken some time to evolve. It can certainly be seen in the 1925 Act, but in a noticeably inchoate form, with many remaining tensions between the position under the pre-existing rules and the new logic left unresolved.[44] It is more confidently embedded in the 2002 Act, which is said[45] to involve not 'registration of title' but 'title by registration'.[46] So, for example, under the 1925 Act it was still possible for you, despite being registered as owner of the land, to lose it to someone else by the old doctrine of adverse possession. Whereas under the 2002 Act, while some vestige of this possibility remains, the emphasis is much more firmly on the idea that if you are registered as owner, you are (therefore) secure.

Still not absolutely secure, however. There are rules whereby, under certain circumstances, the register's statements about a given piece of land—who owns it, and what rights obtain against it—can be amended, or (as the legislation terms it) 'altered'.[47]

Of course, the law would need to provide for alteration even if it operated a fully secure idea of ownership, so as to reflect changes occurring on the ground: as where I, owning the land, rent it to John, or give a right of way over it to Kate, or sell it to Liam, or die leaving it to Meg; or where a lease or a mortgage over it comes to an end. It is therefore wholly unsurprising, and not inimical to secure ownership, that the rules[48] allow for alteration of this kind.

But the rules provide for alteration also for the purpose of correcting mistakes, as where I am registered as owner but you ought to have been (though the mistake may be less dramatic than this).[49] Where correcting the mistake will not injure the registered owner, the rules provide for it to be done

---

[44] See also A Pottage, 'The Originality of Registration' (1995) 15 *OJLS* 371; and further, 'Evidencing Ownership' in Bright and Dewar, *ibid* ch 5.

[45] Law Commission, *Land Registration for the Twenty-First Century—A Consultative Document* (Law Com No 254, London, 1998) para 10.43. See also Law Commission, *Land Registration for the Twenty-First Century—A Conveyancing Revolution* (Law Com No 271, London, 2001) para 1.10.

[46] Indeed, the Land Registration Act 2002 s 58(1) declares: 'If, on the entry of a person in the register as the proprietor of a legal estate, the legal estate would not otherwise be vested in him, it shall be deemed to be vested in him as a result of the registration.' The unqualified nature of this provision is striking ... not least because it is essentially contradicted by the Act's provisions for alteration, explored below.

[47] The rules are contained in the Land Registration Act 2002 Sch 4.

[48] *Ibid* paras 2(1)(b), 5(b) and (d).

[49] The legislation is blithe in the way it invokes the concept of a 'mistake' without explaining what a mistake looks like. The state of the register will be 'mistaken' if it asserts something that is untrue ... but untrue by reference to what yardstick? The general assumption is—surely correctly—to that of the law relevant to registered land (whether stated in the land registration legislation or otherwise). See *Norwich and Peterborough Building Society v Steed (No 2)* [1993] Ch 116 (CA) for an exploration of the same difficulty as it arose under the (albeit superficially rather different) pre-2002 rules (Land Registration Act 1925 s 82), and apparent arrival at the same conclusion.

almost automatically.[50] But where correction will injure the registered owner, it is called 'rectification',[51] and then: if the registered owner is *not* in possession of the land, the correction must likewise be made almost automatically;[52] but if the registered owner *is* in possession of the land,[53] it must not be made unless the mistake was the registered owner's own fault,[54] or it would be unjust not to correct it.[55] So, if I am registered as owner but you ought to have been, correcting the mistake will plainly injure me: I will lose the land. If I am in possession of the land, I shall probably be safe, whereas otherwise I shall very probably suffer.[56]

Certainly in allowing a correction to be made despite injuring me, these rules lessen the degree of security that registration offers ... but by no means to an extent, or in a way, that makes us hesitate about viewing a registered owner as indeed owner. This is at least partly because mistakes are in practice very rare (the Registry claim that virtually all their entries are correct); the picture would be very different if registered 'owners' lost their land on a daily basis. It is partly, too, the result of the protection given to an owner in possession: a given correction would commonly injure such an owner more, because of the dimension added by the fact of possession, than the same correction would injure one not in possession. A further rule is also relevant: where rectification occurs and I do suffer (or indeed where it is refused and so you suffer), compensation—'indemnity'—will normally be payable out of state funds.[57] While the indemnity arrangements soften the blow, however, they do not quite bolster the degree of security that English law accords to land ownership, for by definition they become relevant only where the element of insecurity is more to the fore.

The registration regime applies to most pieces of land in England and Wales, but not all. When originally introduced, in 1925, it was made applicable only to certain areas. The number of areas was increased over time, until eventually the whole of the two countries was covered. Even when a

---

[50] Except in 'exceptional circumstances': Land Registration Rules 2003 (SI No 1417) r 126. This, however, relates only to alteration ordered by a court. The position regarding alteration at the Registry's own initiative appears not to have been so firmly settled.

[51] Land Registration Act 2002 Sch 4 para 1.

[52] '... unless there are exceptional circumstances which justify ... not doing so ...': *ibid* paras 3(3), 6(3).

[53] This has an extended meaning, additionally covering various situations where one is not personally in possession but permits another to be: *ibid* s 131.

[54] '... unless ... he has by fraud or lack of proper care caused or substantially contributed to the mistake ...'

[55] Land Registration Act 2002 Sch 4 paras 3(2), 6(2).

[56] See further D Fox, 'Forgery and Alteration of the Register under the Land Registration Act 2002', and P O'Connor, 'Registration of Invalid Dispositions' in E Cooke (ed), *Modern Studies in Property Law, Volume 3* (Oxford, 2005) chs 2, 3.

[57] The provision for this is contained in the Land Registration Act 2002 Sch 8: see especially para 1(1)(a) and (b). Exceptionally, if I suffer rectification because, despite being in possession, the mistake was wholly or partly my own fault, I lose my indemnity to the extent of that fault: Sch 8 para 5.

piece of land is located in an area to which registration applies, however, the registration regime becomes applicable to it only when its title has been entered on the register: and that need occur only when it is involved in some transaction, though it can also occur without such a transaction, being registered voluntarily.[58]

Land that has been registered, and to which the registration regime accordingly applies, is called 'land of registered title', or more commonly 'registered land', while land that has not yet been registered is called 'unregistered land'. Given the great and increasing preponderance of registered land, this book focuses almost exclusively on the rules regarding it. They differ from the unregistered land rules in other respects too: notably, in respect of the circumstances in which a right in rem relevant to the land in question, and so capable of binding a disponee of it, will in fact do so. In Chapter 2 we shall look at these circumstances, as the registered land rules define them.

1.4 Why Focus on Rights in Rem in Land?

Why should we concern ourselves, as in this book, with the rights in rem that can exist in respect of land?

To begin with the focus on *land*. From as long ago as we can see, English law's rules regarding land have been different from its rules regarding other entities. (A similar observation can probably be made about the rules of other legal systems.) Land is not unique in this: there are myriad differentiations between the rules relating to other classes of entity too. Such differentiations occur wherever the class of entity in question has some particular quality requiring regulation of human behaviour regarding it. Thus, for example, there are special rules detailing how we can or must behave towards animals, reflecting inter alia the fact that, as animate creatures, we should be concerned with their welfare, in a way that we are not in the case of inanimates; and there are special rules concerning firearms, reflecting their unusual potential for harmful use. So when we observe that land has in fact been made the subject of distinctive rules, we should be able to ascribe their distinctiveness to particular distinctive qualities that land possesses. What are these qualities?

---

[58] The details of the relevant rules have evolved over time, the trend being to increase the set of 'transactions' entailing a requirement of registering the land concerned. For the current law relating to initial registration, see *ibid* Part 2 and Sch 1.

Most basically, land is uniquely vital to sustaining animal, including human, life. Such life is ultimately powered by the consumption of plants, and nearly all plant life is in turn supported by nutrients extracted from the soil, ie land. Given the make-up of the planet, things could hardly have evolved otherwise. Also vital to plants and animals is a supply of suitable water, and by far the most accessible sources of water as principally needed (both directly and indirectly) by humans are those to be found on or in the ground, ie land.[59] So a legal system centred (as legal systems always are) on human fulfilment can hardly not seek to ensure that the land within its jurisdiction delivers these goods, and to address the conflicts to which securing them may well give rise. At not much less basic a level, and thus also attracting dedicated rules, land is the unique resource from which we extract most of our raw materials (timber, stone, clay, metals, oil), and upon which, given gravity, we must live our lives: make our homes, do our jobs, and so on. Much else follows: land is thus indirectly essential to economic activity and 'standard of living' (and via these, to the maximisation of human happiness), and also to power. Land is also special in perhaps less obvious ways. In particular, it is more or less indestructible, making it a basis for long-term or indefinite arrangements; and it remains for practical purposes in one place, which can be helpfully reassuring (rights connected with a piece of land are much less prone to frustration by its disappearance than those connected with other assets: a point vital to the supply of finance via mortgage arrangements). The latter feature in turn also means that any given plot of land has a fixed spatial relationship with any other plot, creating both opportunities (for joint exploitation) and problems (of nuisance) to which the law does well to react.

Now the interest in *rights in rem*. A right relating to land is essentially a mechanism for allowing humans to exploit that land in some way (such as to source food, water or other raw materials, or to provide a place to live, do work, etc). And a right in rem relating to land is such a mechanism, with the distinctive quality of remaining in force while other rights relating to the same land are reconfigured (ie of 'affecting disponees' of the land). Given the essential nature of many of the uses to which land can be put, it is unsurprising that rights with this quality should be wanted, and should be thought valuable enough to merit acceptance despite the damage to the market to they entail—this, as explained in § 1.2.2, being the condition for a right's ability to operate in rem. Rights in rem in land thus represent our most valued ways of facilitating the exploitation of our most valued resource. It is thus understandable that they—alias the subject of land law—should attract attention.

---

[59] On the rules developed around this, see J Getzler, *A History of Water Rights at Common Law* (Oxford, 2004).

This is not to say that everything in land law is unique, of course. As time has gone on, human inventiveness has developed new kinds of assets, and new ways of exploiting them, so creating a demand for rights—and in some instances a case for rights in rem—relating to them too. Certainly, most of the kinds of right in rem that can be created concerning land can also be created concerning at least some other types of asset. (Ownership, mortgages and trust rights in particular.) But land remains the pre-eminently essential resource, and the ideas developed for it—land law, again—largely act as the paradigm. Indeed, certain differences still remain, at least some of which follow from land's enduringly distinctive nature. In particular, the list of possible rights in rem concerning land includes easements and restrictive covenants. As will be explained in Chapters 9 and 10, these rights are specifically aimed at certain issues arising from the unalterable physical proximity of two pieces of land. We do not encounter this phenomenon with other assets: so these rights remain special to land, and land law.[60]

1.5 Law and Equity

By way of a preliminary to some of what appears in later chapters, we need to address one final issue. English law, together with other legal systems derived from it, has a peculiarity: it comes in two varieties, 'common law'—alternatively called simply 'law'—and 'equity'.[61]

Common law is the set of rules developed by the courts of King's (or Queen's) Bench, Exchequer and Common Pleas, and equity is the different set of rules developed by the court of Chancery, during the period when

---

[60] Some decisions have experimented with applying the restrictive covenant rules outside the land context: see eg *De Mattos v Gibson* (1858) 4 De G & J 276 (Ch); *Lord Strathcona Steamship Co Ltd v Dominion Coal Co Ltd* [1926] AC 108 (PC); *Port Line Ltd v Ben Line Steamers Ltd* [1958] 2 QB 146 (QBD); *Swiss Bank Corporation v Lloyds Bank Ltd* [1979] Ch 548 (Ch D). But the venture has never fully taken hold—unsurprisingly, for the reason given in the text. See S Gardner, 'The Proprietary Effect of Contractual Obligations under *Tulk v Moxhay* and *De Mattos v Gibson*' (1982) 98 *LQR* 279.

[61] There are two sources of confusion here. First, the word 'law' is also used—as in the phrase 'English law' at the start of the sentence in the text—to refer to the set of rules comprising *both* common law *and* equity: ie the entirety of English jurisprudence. Indeed, it is probably used more often in this sense than in contrast to equity. Second, 'common law' is also contrasted with 'statutory' law. In this sense, 'common law' means the law made by the judges in their decisions, while 'statutory' law is that enacted by Parliament. This meaning of 'common law' includes both common law, in the sense used in the text, and equity. (Conversely, both law and equity, as explored in the text, contain both judge-made and statutory rules.) Despite the manifest scope for confusion, it is usually clear from the context which meaning is intended.

these all existed as separate courts: the late middle ages to the end of the 19th century.[62] The different courts were merged by the Judicature Acts 1873–5, but the rules for which they were historically responsible continue to be identifiable by their distinct origins.

Equity operates as a supplement to the common law. That is, it takes the common law's answer to a given situation, and adjusts that answer if it seems inappropriate. So say the common law courts had a rule saying 'In situation *ABC* you must do *X*'. If the Chancery agreed, it added nothing, and the rule operated without complication. But if the Chancery disagreed, it ruled 'In situation *ABC*, you must *not* do *X*: instead you must do *Y*'. The Chancery did not pretend that the common law required anything but *X*, but it imposed its own requirement of *Y*. In concrete terms, if your adversary sought to enlist the help of the common law courts to make you do *X*—as was his right, in their eyes—you could have the Chancery order him not to, and to accept *Y* instead. The conflict between the two rules would have been intolerable unless one took priority over the other. In fact, it was the Chancery's rules that had priority[63]: so the law's overall bottom line was that you had indeed to do *Y*. And when the courts themselves were merged, that remained the case.

Sometimes, equity's answer will simply contradict the common law's, with the result that the latter will simply drop out of the picture altogether, and be forgotten about. For example, say you and I make what looks like a contract, but you mislead me about some relevant issue, though you do so innocently. The common law regards the contract as nonetheless valid, but equity regards it as invalid. Because the two answers simply contradict one another, there is no reason to recall the common law's: for the bottom line, we can—and do—refer simply to equity's.

But sometimes the relationship between the two answers is less straightforward, and then it will be right to continue to be aware of and to speak of both. So if, again, you and I have a contract, and you break it, I can certainly sue you for damages. That is the common law's rule. There is a different equitable rule. It does not however say that I cannot have damages. Instead, it allows me, in certain cases, to claim an injunction or an order for specific performance against you as an alternative: something that the common law does not.

The classic instance of this latter kind is the trust. We looked briefly at the idea of a trust in § 1.3.4, and shall explore it in greater depth in Chapters 13

---

[62] For the history, see eg A Simpson, *A History of the Land Law* (2nd edn, Oxford, 1986) ch 8.

[63] This rule is sometimes ascribed to the Judicature Acts 1873–5, but it is much earlier. King James I's ruling in favour of equity in connection with *The Earl of Oxford's Case* (1615) 1 Ch Rep 1 (Ch) reflects it, but again did not create it. In truth, though its universal acceptance took some time, it is a function of the essential relationship between common law and equity: equity cannot operate as a supplement to the common law without it.

and 14. For present purposes, the point is that if we say 'I hold this property on trust for you', we are saying that the common law regards me as owning the property, while equity obliges me to use it not for my benefit but for yours.[64] At first sight, the fact that I cannot use the property for my own benefit seems to leave me very far from owning it: as we saw in § 1.3.3, we think of an 'owner' as having the (personal) right to enjoy the property in various ways. Nonetheless, we do not simply omit all reference to the common law position, and say that you own the property, full stop. There are certain respects in which (equity agrees) the property does and should continue to rest in my hands. For example, I have to keep the property so as to look after and manage it; and if the property is to be sold to someone else, only I—not you—can make a valid transfer of it. Essentially, it is not that the ownership rights are simply taken away from me; rather, I continue to have them, *but must use them only for your benefit*.

Land law has a certain number of places where equity has an answer different from the common law's. Where the difference takes the form of a straightforward contradiction, little or no attention will be drawn to it in this book. For example, a restrictive covenant—explained in Chapter 10—is a right in rem recognised only ever by equity, simply overriding the common law's position that no such right can arise in the relevant circumstances. This lack of complication means that for almost all practical purposes, one can ignore the right's provenance.

Where the contradiction is less straightforward, however, this book will speak of the respective common law and equitable positions, though only to the extent needed to explain matters properly. For example, some such talk may be necessary when discussing trusts, as just explained. It will also be needed when we look at the conferral of rights. As the law stands, if I am to confer a right—say, an easement—on you so that both equity and the common law will recognise it, I must usually use a deed; while equity alone will recognise me as having done so also if I use only writing. (These rules are discussed in detail in Chapter 4.) So if I use a deed, you acquire a 'legal easement'; but if I use only writing, you acquire an 'equitable easement'. Given equity's claim to the last word, we might think of saying simply that you acquire an easement in both cases ... except that traditionally, the two kinds of easement have behaved somewhat differently as regards their effect on a subsequent disponee of the land to which they relate,[65] and although the differences have now been reduced by the registration rules, some still remain,

---

[64] For further discussion of the significance of trusts being equitable concepts, see S Gardner, *An Introduction to the Law of Trusts* (2nd edn, Oxford, 2003) 16–22.

[65] For example: historically, a legal right (eg a legal easement) normally bound a disponee without further ado, but an equitable right (eg an equitable easement) bound a disponee unless he was a bona fide purchaser of the land without notice of the right.

at any rate for the time being.[66] To this extent, then, it remains useful to make explicit reference to 'common law' and 'equity'. It would of course be possible to speak of the complex of rules we find in such cases (the exact position in trusts, and the different kinds of rights produced by a deed or writing) without using these terms; they are justified merely as a kind of shorthand.[67]

---

[66] Nowadays, as detailed in Chapter 2, both legal and equitable rights in rem can normally be registered so as to bind a disponee, and under certain circumstances (when they qualify as 'overriding interests') will bind a disponee despite not being registered ... but those circumstances can vary between legal and equitable rights. For example, while a legal easement can sometimes operate as an overriding interest in its own right, an equitable easement can do so only in the (rather unlikely) event that its holder occupies the land over which it obtains: § 9.3.

[67] The matters discussed in the text are details in a much larger picture, the question at stake being whether (or to what extent) the law's various 'common law' and 'equity' rules have been, or should be, 'fused'. The literature is voluminous. See perhaps especially A Burrows, 'We Do This at Common Law but That in Equity' (2002) 22 *OJLS* 1; S Degeling and J Edelman (eds), *Equity in Commercial Law* (Pyrmont NSW, 2005).

When are Disponees Bound?

In the previous chapter[1] we saw that, in English law, rights in rem are rights which are in principle capable of binding disponees ... but that commonly, they will actually bind a particular disponee only if certain conditions are present. This chapter looks at the rules telling us what those conditions are, when the rights are ones that concern land.

There are two sets of such rules: one for registered land and one for unregistered land. As we saw in § 1.3.5, most land in England and Wales is now registered land. The question whether a disponee of a piece of registered land is affected by a right in rem relating to it is decided solely by the rules contained in the Land Registration Act 2002. No other rules are relevant.[2] In the case of unregistered land the same question is decided partly by rules in the Land Charges Act 1972, and partly by some non-statutory rules. This book will go on to look in detail only at the provisions of the Land Registration Act 2002, relating to registered land.

---

[1] § 1.1.2.
[2] Sometimes a disponee will incur an obligation by reason of a rule not supplied by the Act, but this is an essentially different matter from becoming the subject of a pre-existing right in rem, which is our principal focus. A rule of the former kind is that generating a 'constructive trust' against a disponee who, as part of the disposition transaction, promises to do something he would not otherwise have to: see § 8.2.

2.1 The Registered Land Regime

2.1.1 The Principles

Under the Land Registration Act 2002, a right in rem will affect a disponee of the land in question in two sets of circumstances: if it is entered on the register, and if it operates as an 'overriding interest'.[3]

The Act makes detailed provision for the entering of rights in rem on the register.[4] Nearly all types of right in rem can be registered;[5] only a few are not registrable.[6] The most important of the non-registrable types is an ordinary lease for three years or less (including therefore a weekly, monthly or yearly tenancy[7]), which can therefore affect a disponee only via the alternative route, as an overriding interest.[8]

A right in rem that has not been registered (despite the fact that, usually, it could have been) will nonetheless bind a disponee if it operates as an overriding interest. And it will do so if it fits the description in Schedule 3 to the Act.[9] This lists 14 kinds of circumstances in which a right can be overriding.[10] In 13 of them, the right qualifies as overriding simply by being a particular kind of right, as named in the Schedule. The most generally important of such rights are ordinary leases of up to seven years' duration,[11] and some kinds of easement.[12] The 14th case is that described in Schedule 3

---

[3] Land Registration Act 2002 ss 28–30. The expression 'overriding interest' was used in the Land Registration Act 1925; the 2002 Act avoids it, coming closest with the phrase 'unregistered interests which override', but the shorter form remains in common usage and will be adopted here.

[4] Land Registration Act 2002 Part 4.

[5] ss 32, 40. The word 'interest'—meaning right in rem—is used to cover all such rights except those which are specifically excluded.

[6] s 33.

[7] See § 11.4.2.

[8] The rules about registering rights under trusts (ss 33(a), 40) are also special, reflecting a preference that such rights, though in some sense rights in rem and so capable of binding a disponee, do not actually do so, but instead are 'overreached': ie detached from the land at the moment of the disposition, and thenceforth attached instead to the purchase money. This phenomenon is explored more fully in § 14.5.

[9] Sch 3 explains when rights will count as overriding against a disposition of land, title to which is already registered. When the disposition is one as a result of which the land's title will become registered for the first time, rights against it will count as overriding under the slightly wider, but essentially similar, rules in Sch 1.

[10] A 15th is added by s 90, giving overriding interest status to PPP leases over the London Underground: a very specialised category.

[11] Sch 3 para 1: see § 11.7.1. So leases that cannot be registered, as being for three years or less, are thus covered, together with some that can be registered.

[12] Sch 3 para 3: see § 9.3. Easements are rights such as rights of way.

paragraph 2. By this, almost[13] *any* right in rem concerning a piece of land operates as an overriding interest if the person to whom it belongs is in actual and apparent[14] occupation of that land at the time of the disposition (though not if the disponee asks that person about the right, and they do not reveal it[15]). The idea of 'actual occupation' is explored in more detail in § 2.1.2.

So in theory, almost all rights in rem can be registered, which is one route by which they can bind a disponee; but, if not registered, they can almost all (so long as they are either one of the 13 named rights in Schedule 3, or accompanied by actual and apparent occupation) bind a disponee nonetheless, as overriding interests.[16] In practice, however, the range of overriding interests is not quite so wide. Some kinds of rights in rem do not themselves entitle their owner to occupy the land to which they relate, and will thus rarely, and coincidentally, satisfy paragraph 2. So unless they are among the 13, they will not normally qualify as overriding interests.[17] But many important rights can still be seen as realistically able to bind disponees *either* via registration, *or* by being overriding.

There is, however, no third alternative. This rule represents a choice: before 2002, there was a third alternative, but the 2002 Act has eradicated it. It can be seen in the pre-2002 case of *Peffer v Rigg*,[18] holding that a right which was neither registered nor overriding nevertheless bound a disponee who actually knew of it. This conclusion was reached on the basis of the wording of the then prevailing Land Registration Act 1925,[19] which certainly

---

[13] Two kinds of right are excluded (Sch 3 para 2(a) and (d)), namely beneficial rights under the Settled Land Act 1925 and leases with a start date three months or more after their grant, where the start date has not yet arrived; but the former type is not truly a right in rem anyway, and a tenant under the latter type would be unlikely to be in occupation.

[14] 'Obvious on a reasonably careful inspection of the land at the time of the disposition'.

[15] If 'inquiry was made [of him] before the disposition and [he] failed to disclose the right when he could reasonably have been expected to do so', unless the disponee actually knew about it anyway.

[16] At one time, some people seem to have thought that, under the Land Registration regime, any given type of right in rem could be capable *either* of registration, *or* of operation as an overriding interest, but not both. But there was never a basis for this view in the relevant statutory wording, and it was authoritatively denied in *Williams & Glyn's Bank Ltd v Boland* [1981] AC 487 (HL).

[17] For example, a restrictive covenant: a right that you may have, as my neighbour, forbidding me from say erecting additional buildings on my land (see Ch 10). When I sell my land to John, and the question arises whether he is bound by your right, it is unlikely that you will be able to rely on its operating against him as an overriding interest, because a restrictive covenant is not among the 13 named rights, and by the nature of it you are unlikely to have been in occupation of my land at the time, so as to bring it under Sch 3 para 2.

[18] [1977] 1 WLR 285, 293–4 (Ch D).

[19] ss 20(1) and 59(6). The two sections described the circumstances in which a disponee was bound and not bound in differing terms. The judge's ruling was one of a number of possible readings of their combined effect. Under s 59(6), read with s 3(xxi), a disponee took free of unregistered and non-overriding rights only if he was in good faith. The judge held that a disponee was not in good faith if he knew of the right but went on to buy the land ostensibly free from it.

id to this effect.[20] But it arguably also embodied a view that such ought to be bound, as a matter of general principle. That view ered by the Law Commission during the design phase of the 2002 rejected,[21] principally on grounds of its incompatibility with the idea a right in rem will not bind a disponee unless it is registered. The provisions for overriding interests are thus the only route by which rights in rem can bind despite not being registered. As part of our appraisal of those provisions, however, we shall consider whether the law is right to draw the line there, or whether another such route—the alternative here under discussion—ought to be added.[22]

2.1.2 'Actual Occupation'

As we have seen, Schedule 3 paragraph 2 gives overriding status to almost any right in rem whose owner is, at the time of the disposition of the land to which it relates, in actual and apparent occupation of that land. Say you have a right in rem over a house which I own, and that I transfer the house to John. If you are, and are discoverable as being, in actual occupation of the house at the time of that transfer, you can claim that your right binds John as an overriding interest in this way. This section looks at the idea of 'actual occupation'.

In many cases, applying the concept of 'actual occupation' poses no problem. (As a consequence, actual authority regarding these cases is sparse, but there appears no reason to doubt one's common sense instincts.) If you live in a house, you will normally be in actual occupation of it. This remains so notwithstanding that you may be physically absent from it at the precise moment of the disposition. You may be out for a few hours (at work, on a walk, shopping, etc), or away for a longer spell (on business, on holiday, in hospital,[23] etc). It probably need not be your main home (so you could be in actual occupation of our weekend cottage as well as our flat in town), or even your real home at all (as where you are living with me for the time being, but have no expectation that this will be a permanent arrangement). On the other

---

[20] This was the decision's second ratio decidendi. It had two others. The first pointed out that the rules (ss 20(1) and 59(6)) required the right to be registered or overriding only if the disposition was for valuable consideration, and held that, on the facts, the disposition in the particular case was not for valuable consideration. This is a narrow issue, on which the result would be the same under the Land Registration Act 2002: ss 29(1), 132. The third ratio was that the disponee was bound (not by the right itself, operating in rem, but) by a 'constructive trust' generated by the circumstances of the transaction. This involves an idea of considerable general importance, discussed in § 8.2.4.

[21] Law Commission, *Land Registration for the Twenty-First Century—A Consultative Document* (Law Com No 254, London, 1998) paras 3.44–3.46, and *Land Registration for the Twenty-First Century—A Conveyancing Revolution* (Law Com No 271, London, 2001) para 5.16; Land Registration Act 2002 ss 28, 29.

[22] See § 2.2.3.

[23] As in *Chhokar v Chhokar* [1984] FLR 313 (CA).

hand, 'mere fleeting presence' is not enough; 'some degree of permanence and continuity' is required[24]: so the fact that you happen to pay me a quick visit at the moment of the disposition will not avail you. There are, however, bound to be marginal situations, in which it will be impossible to give a confident answer either way. As, perhaps, where we have a number of homes, and move between them ... at the time of the disposition of one of them, you happen to be there ... this is your first visit to it for six months, and you plan to stay for a fortnight.[25]

Some of the pre-2002 interpretations of 'actual occupation' slanted it to cover only situations in which the disponee could readily discover the putative occupant, or perhaps in which the disponee could readily discover the occupant's right.[26] This tendency has now been institutionalised in the requirement of Schedule 3 paragraph 2 that the occupation be not only actual, but also apparent: 'obvious on a reasonably careful inspection of the land at the time of the disposition'. Under this formulation, it is not necessary (or sufficient) for the right itself to be obvious, or discoverable from the occupation alone. Rather, insisting that the occupation—and so the occupant—be discoverable, the formulation ensures that the disponee is in a position to make enquiries of the occupant, which in turn should lead to discovery of the right. Paragraph 2 rules that if the disponee makes such enquiries (they have to be addressed to the owner of the right, not merely say to the disponor), and the right is not disclosed when disclosure could reasonably be expected, the disponee is not bound by the right, unless he knows about it anyway.

Some decisions treat you as in actual occupation of a house on the strength of facts other than your own personal presence there. So you might qualify as in actual occupation, despite not being there yourself, on the basis that John is there ... and John is your employee, there to do his job for you,[27] or perhaps if he is your spouse[28] ... but apparently not if he is your tenant,[29] or your guest.[30] You might also qualify as in actual occupation on the basis

---

[24] *Abbey National Building Society v Cann* [1991] 1 AC 56, 93 (HL).

[25] In *Stockholm Finance Ltd v Garden Holdings Inc* [1995] NPC 162 (Ch D) the visit was the first for over a year, and was held *not* to represent actual occupation.

[26] *Epps v Esso Petroleum Co Ltd* [1973] 1 WLR 1071, 1080G–H (Ch D); *Kling v Keston Properties Ltd* (1984) 49 P & CR 212, 221 (Ch D); *Lloyds Bank plc v Rosset* [1989] 1 Ch 350, 379, 394, 405 (CA); *Abbey National Building Society v Cann* [1991] 1 AC 56, 88 (HL). See further P Sparkes, 'The Discoverability of Occupiers of Registered Land' [1989] *Conv* 342.

[27] *Lloyds Bank plc v Rosset* [1989] 1 Ch 350 (CA): occupation via builders.

[28] *Strand Securities Ltd v Caswell* [1965] Ch 958, 984–5 (CA). Would any other relationship suffice? Perhaps the presence of a child would amount to actual occupation by a parent ... but in that decision, the presence of a step-daughter was not regarded as actual occupation by her step-father.

[29] The Land Registration Act 1925 did treat a landlord as in actual occupation via his tenant (s 70(1)(g)), but this has not been carried forward into the Land Registration Act 2002 Sch 3 para 2.

[30] *Strand Securities Ltd v Caswell* [1965] Ch 958, 984–5 (CA).

that your belongings are there[31] ... but apparently not if they have been there for only a short time when the disposition occurs.[32] It is hard to understand why you should thus count as in actual occupation in circumstances where, in ordinary terms, you are not. Perhaps the thinking is that in these circumstances the disponee should be able to discover your right. This is problematic (as we saw in the previous paragraph, the legislation focuses not on discoverability of the right itself, but on the occupation of the right-owner, from whom information about the right may then be elicited), but even if it is correct, it does not fully account for the various distinctions. These seem not consistently to reflect the discoverability of the right, or even of the 'occupation'. The contrasting treatments of belongings may perhaps be understood in that way, but not those regarding the presence of other people.

Sometimes you do not count as in actual occupation of a house even if, without complication, you *are* present there at the relevant time, living in it as your home. In some old decisions, where a husband owned a house, and lived in it with his wife, she was nonetheless regarded as not in actual occupation of it.[33] In *Williams & Glyn's Bank Ltd v Boland*[34] this approach was abandoned, in favour of one whereby 'actual occupation' means what (or at any rate not less than) it appears to. But the earlier view has been revived, in a ruling that children under 18 living in their parents' house do not count as in actual occupation of it.[35] Perhaps this ruling too was intended to ensure discoverability (one certainly hopes that it rests on more than a mere sense that children do not count). If so, it ought not to prevail in the law as configured by Schedule 3 paragraph 2. As we have seen, the latter demands only discoverable occupation. A child's occupation is probably no less discoverable than an adult's, and certainly cannot be said always to be undiscoverable. After that, it is for the disponee to make appropriate enquiries. In the case of a young child, the disponee may not be protected by the rule whereby a right that is *not* disclosed on enquiry to its owner does not bind, because the rule demands that it be reasonable to expect such disclosure, and in the case of a young child it would often not be reasonable. But the disponee will normally be able to ensure that the right *is* disclosed, by enquiring of the child's parents.

The foregoing paragraphs focus on actual occupation of a house. Land put to other uses can of course be the subject of occupation too, and what counts as 'occupation' may vary with the use. For example, to show that you are in actual occupation of my warehouse, you would point out that you

---

[31] *Chhokar v Chhokar* [1984] FLR 313 (CA).

[32] *Abbey National Building Society v Cann* [1991] 1 AC 56 (HL), where the time between the arrival of the belongings and the disposition was 35 minutes.

[33] See especially *Bird v Syme-Thomson* [1979] 1 WLR 440 (Ch D).

[34] [1981] AC 487 (HL).

[35] *Hypo-Mortgage Services Ltd v Robinson* [1997] 2 FLR 71 (CA).

keep your goods there: no one would expect you to live there. Actual occupation of a garage would normally consist in keeping a car in it,[36] and actual occupation of a farm would presumably consist in farming it.

2.2 The Appropriateness of the Registered Land Regime

2.2.1 An Argument For Registration

The provision for rights in rem to bind when they are registered is generally welcome. Say I own some land, and you have a right affecting it (say, a right of way), then I transfer it to John. From your point of view, the advantage of being able to bind John by registering your right is that if you proceed in this way you cannot lose your right. (As you might under some other approaches, such as the old non-statutory rule whereby John was sometimes bound unless he was a bona fide purchaser without notice: this meant that John was not bound by your right if he was justifiably ignorant of it, and in that case you lost it.) And from John's point of view, the advantage is that he can discover the rights by which he will or may be bound (yours and others) relatively easily, by interrogating the register. The difficulty and cost of the transaction should therefore be diminished, and the market in land therefore lubricated.

But it is more controversial whether the law is right to allow rights in rem to affect disponees alternatively as overriding interests. Indeed, this alternative provision has been widely criticised. The central criticism is that it runs contrary to the key aim of a registration regime. This, it is asserted, is accurately to reflect all aspects of the title to a given piece of land. 'All aspects of the title' means all the legal rights by which a person acquiring an interest in the land could be affected: in short, all the rights in rem germane to the land. The idea that the register should display all these rights is generally referred to as the 'mirror principle'.[37] Evidence for its authoritative

---

[36] As in *Kling v Keston Properties Ltd* (1983) 49 P & CR 212 (Ch D). Apparently inconsistently, *Epps v Esso Petroleum Co Ltd* [1973] 1 WLR 1071 (Ch D) held that parking a car on an open but nonetheless defined piece of land did not amount to actual occupation of it.

[37] Reference is also made to the 'curtain principle'. In its original guise, this seems to have consisted in the idea that putative disponees should not have to concern themselves with beneficial interests under a trust on which the land might be held (that such interests existed 'behind the curtain'), because in the event of a disposition these interests would be overreached and so would not affect the disponee (see § 14.5). More recently, however, 'the curtain principle' seems to have become the counterpart of 'the mirror principle' in a composite thesis to the effect that a disponee is bound by all interests shown on the (mirror of the) register, but only by those interests (any others being curtained).

influence on thought in this field can be found in the words of judges,[38] in publications by those connected with the Land Registry,[39] and in Law Commission reports.[40] These texts (of course) acknowledge the provision for overriding interests, but not as something to be applauded. For it is clearly inconsistent with the mirror principle that rights in rem should—as they do with overriding interests—subsist, and be capable of binding purchasers, despite not being registered. From this perspective, overriding interests have been described as a 'cavernous crack' in the mirror.[41]

Historically speaking, this assertion about the key aim of a registration regime is mistaken. Before the land registration regime was introduced, some rights affecting land were generated in transactions on paper, and the collection of such pieces of paper was known as the 'deeds' to the land. But other rights arose in other ways, as where a right of way arose by prescription, ie on the basis of 20 years' usage.[42] When registration was first introduced, it was clearly understood that the register was to reflect only rights in the former of the two classes. That is, it was to be a 'mirror' of the paper title, but only the paper title.[43] Rights not shown on the paper deeds were to continue operating on a non-formalised basis: that is, as overriding interests.

This is not a full answer to the criticism, however. It remains arguable that in principle the aim should be for the register to reflect ('mirror') *all* rights in rem germane to the land. That is, that the old fact of life—that not all rights were shown on the papers—was a defect which registration should be calculated to cure: that a mature registration regime should be expected to deliver this aim. On this view, we return to the argument that providing for overriding interests is a bad thing, because it prevents the achievement of this aim.[44]

A full mirror can hardly be an end in itself, however. It must be desired as a means to some more fundamental end. The principal[45] argument is that a

---

[38] eg *Abbey National Building Society v Cann* [1991] 1 AC 56, 78 (HL) (Lord Oliver).

[39] eg J Stewart-Wallace, *Introduction to the Principles of Land Registration* (London, 1937) 32; T Ruoff, *An Englishman Looks at the Torrens System* (Sydney, 1957) ch 2.

[40] eg Law Commission, *Land Registration for the Twenty-First Century—A Conveyancing Revolution* (Law Com No 271, London, 2001) paras 1.5, 8.1, 8.6.

[41] D Hayton, *Registered Land* (3rd edn, London, 1981) 76.

[42] See § 6.3.

[43] Commission on Registration of Title, *Report* (1857) HCP xxi 245 (London, 1857) para 63.

[44] See C Harpum, 'Property in an Electronic Age' in E Cooke (ed), *Modern Studies in Property Law, Volume 1* (Oxford, 2001) ch 1.

[45] Another suggestion is transparency, ie a concern that as much information as possible should be in the public domain: Law Commission, *Land Registration for the Twenty-First Century—A Conveyancing Revolution* (Law Com No 271, London, 2001) para 2.9. This is a reasonable goal for a democratic society, as empowering individuals. But in broad terms, other potentially countervailing concerns, also ascribable to the empowerment of individuals, are also worthy of attention: in particular privacy, and the freedom not to have to bother. The accommodation between the two sets of concerns has to be worked out sensitively to the nature of the information in question. It has certainly never been demonstrated that the proper accommodation in this context demands a full mirror.

full mirror is needed so as to promote the market in land, by reducing the difficulty and cost of transactions involving it. As already noted, the fact that a right concerning a piece of land is recorded on the register has this effect. But the argument's logic requires *all* the relevant rights to be registered. If any can bind a disponee without being registered, as overriding interests do, costs will be reintroduced as the disponee seeks to discover whether this will occur in his case. And the costs involved in searching for even one such right are likely to be no less than those generated by having to search for many. So from the viewpoint of promoting the market, nothing would have been gained.

This argument for a full mirror, and so against overriding interests, must clearly be taken seriously. It would be wrong, however, instantly to conclude that the law must not provide for overriding interests. It is possible to point to a rival argument, in favour of providing for overriding interests.

2.2.2 An Argument For Overriding Interests

The argument is that the overriding interest provisions cater to those rights in rem that arise in disorganised ways, as a result of which it would be unrealistic to require their registration.

The rights in rem over land recognised by English law arise in two ways. The distinction between the two ways is not officially made, so there is no established pair of terms for referring to them. We shall call them 'organised' and 'disorganised'.

A right arises in an *organised* way when it is acquired as a result of someone intending, indeed planning, to confer it: as where I transfer my house to you in fulfilment of our contract for you to buy it, or grant you a mortgage,[46] or make a restrictive covenant in your favour.[47] When someone is involved in a transaction of this kind, he will know that he is dealing in rights in land. And, land being the valuable and notoriously sophisticated commodity that it is, he will use lawyers to ensure that everything is done properly. The lawyers will know what right is in play, will know the law's rules about how to create or transfer it, and will follow these rules. So if the law requires these rights to be registered, in the nature of things they normally will be registered. Indeed, they normally will be even if the law does not require them to be, ie even if the law does also allow for overriding interests. Except for a saving of the small registration fee, there is certainly no advantage in not registering them. And there is likely advantage in registering them, as cutting out all scope for argument over such matters as whether their owner was in actual and apparent occupation at the relevant time.

---

[46] Ch 12.
[47] Ch 10.

In contrast, however, English law also allows rights in rem concerning land sometimes to arise in *disorganised* ways. That is, they are acquired in circumstances where the parties do not realise, or have only a vague idea, that they are dealing in legal rights at all; or, if they do realise any of this, assume that the law itself will 'see them right'. As a consequence, they do not normally enlist the services of a lawyer. Rights of this kind include those arising by the doctrine of proprietary estoppel,[48] or under a constructive trust.[49] Take a characteristic example. I own some land adjoining yours. You believe that it too belongs to you, and cultivate it. I know all this, but do not bother to correct you. The law will probably award you some sort of right in rem over the land in question, under the doctrine of proprietary estoppel. But you will likely not realise this, or not with any clarity. Moreover, it is of the very nature of a situation like this that we are not using lawyers: otherwise, we would not have got into such a muddle. And without lawyers, there is nobody to know about, and comply with, any technical rules that the law may impose.[50] So even if the law were to require rights acquired in such a way to be registered, in the nature of things the requirement would not normally be complied with.

The law does not have to recognise both modes of generating rights. In a strongly individualistic political context, we should expect rights to arise only where people are organised enough to arrange them, with no support for people who do not look after themselves. On the other hand, in certain other kinds of political context, such as a strongly paternalistic one, the law would impose its own solutions, to the extent of taking no account of any efforts that people did make to settle their own rights. Unsurprisingly, English law supposes it appropriate to allow those who can to settle their own rights, and to support those who fail to do so but deserve them nonetheless. So it recognises both modes. In consequence, it produces the situation in which lawyers, who alone know about registration, will only sometimes be involved: and so, the situation in which only some of its rights in rem will in practice normally be registered. We shall look at the organised creation of rights (in effectuation of their creator's wish) in Chapters 4 and 5, and a variety of ways in which rights are recognised as arising in a disorganised fashion (for important reasons of justice or utility) in Chapters 6 to 8.

So whilst rights arising in organised ways typically will be registered, those arising in disorganised ways typically will not. If the latter are to survive, then, there must be provision for them to affect disponees without registration: that is, as overriding interests. This way of accounting for overriding

---

[48] Ch 7.

[49] Ch 8.

[50] It is sometimes suggested that campaigns should be undertaken to educate the lay public about land registration. The suggestion seems unpromising in itself, but moreover, education about registration would be useless without education also about the circumstances in which rights can arise requiring registration—which seems even less feasible.

interests underlies the Law Commission's apologia for them: that, owing to the nature of rights of this kind, it is 'neither reasonable to expect nor sensible to require any entry on the register'.[51] It also connects with the historical fact, noted above, that the register was originally intended only to reflect those rights which appeared in the paper title to the land in question. These would have been the rights created in an organised way. Those not shown in the paper title would have arisen in disorganised ways: so the decision not to require their registration was based on just the argument presently under discussion.

To understand the full strength of this argument for overriding interests, remember the fundamental point of this chapter: to look at the rules (including the provision for overriding interests, if one is to exist) establishing exactly when a right in rem, ie capable of binding a disponee, will actually do so. Given that they have this role, these rules are connected not merely adjectivally, but intrinsically, with the rights in rem themselves. The rules' design therefore must be sympathetic to the qualities of the rights in rem that the law maintains. (They are, if you like, the fuel on which the in rem engine runs ... it being obvious that the fuel and engine must work together.) As we have seen, the law in fact provides for rights in rem to arise in disorganised ways. It cannot properly then design the rules for the operation of rights in rem along such lines that rights arising in disorganised ways cannot fulfil their mission of binding a disponee. Rules sympathetic to these rights' qualities are required. That is, rules allowing them to bind despite not being registered; in other words, rules providing for them to operate as overriding interests.

2.2.3 A Compromise Between the Two Arguments

This argument in favour of providing for overriding interests is a powerful one. But we have not finished yet. In § 2.2.1 we noted the argument for promoting marketability, and so making no provision for overriding interests; and it too was impressive. What position should the law in fact take?

There is no difficulty about rights arising in organised ways. The market argument in favour of registration obviously operates here, but there is no opposition to it: as explained in § 2.2.2, those involved in the conferral of such a right—who will almost necessarily include lawyers—will know of the possibility of registering it, and will naturally do so, because of the advantages of improved security that this will bring. The question is what to do about rights arising in disorganised ways, where the market argument in favour of registration remains the same, but now runs up against the counter-argument we have identified.

---

[51] Law Commission, *Land Registration for the Twenty-First Century—A Conveyancing Revolution* (Law Com No 271, London, 2001) para 8.53.

One might contend for the complete victory of either argument over the other, so that such rights either always bound despite not being registered, or never did so. Such an outcome would be unsatisfactory, however, as failing to reflect the truth behind one argument or the other.[52] The best outcome has to involve some kind of compromise between them. The Land Registration Act 2002 has in fact adopted such a compromise. Its shape is to be found in the terms of the rules about overriding interests, in Schedule 3.

To be sure, Schedule 3 is not explicitly confined to disorganised rights (on the face of it, it allows almost any right in rem to become overriding, regardless of how the right arose[53]). But this is its scope in reality, for, as already noted, those involved in a right's organised conferral will in practice register it. However, the Schedule does not give overriding status to all disorganised rights under all circumstances. To qualify for overriding status, the right must meet the Schedule's stipulations. That is, it must fall within one of the 13 listed categories, or be accompanied by actual and apparent occupation.

This is the key point, the nub of the compromise: these stipulations are calculated to ensure that even disorganised rights achieve overriding status only if they are readily discoverable by a disponee. So, for example, certain leases and easements are allowed to be overriding, but certain others are not:[54] both sorts can be equally disorganised, but the former are thought more easily discoverable than the latter.[55] So too the rule that almost any kind of right will be overriding if its owner is in actual and apparent occupation of the land to which it relates: this fact, by definition unmissable in itself, should make it easy for a disponee also (by inquiries) to learn of the right, regardless of its discoverability otherwise.

This restriction of overriding status to those rights that are not only disorganised but also easily discoverable makes the compromise a soundly principled one. (In contrast, say, to a rule giving disorganised rights overriding status, but only on alternate days of the week.) The concern of the argument against overriding interests—in favour of demanding registration without exception—is, as we have seen, a worry about increasing disponees'

---

[52] Indeed, a regime which made no provision for disorganised rights to operate in rem without registration might infringe the European Convention on Human Rights, First Protocol, Art 1: it would deprive the rights' owners of their 'possessions', admittedly in a legitimate cause (protecting the market in land), but in a disproportionately vigorous manner.

[53] Exceptionally, the combination of the Land Registration Act 2002 ss 27(2)(d) and Sch 3 para 3 has the effect of preventing expressly granted—ie organised—easements from operating as overriding interests.

[54] Sch 3 paras 1 and 3. Briefly, the rights excluded under these provisions are a lease taking effect more than three months after its creation; a disorganised easement not 'obvious on a reasonably careful inspection of the land', unless actually known to the disponee, or used within the last year; and an equitable easement. See §§ 11.7.1 and 9.3.

[55] See Law Commission, *Land Registration for the Twenty-First Century—A Conveyancing Revolution* (Law Com No 271, London, 2001) paras 8.10 and 8.65. But withholding overriding status from equitable easements cannot be justified in this way, and appears ill-judged: § 9.3.

costs and so damaging the market in land. By accepting the case for having overriding interests at all, the law has brought this problem to life. But by ruling that a disponee need trouble only about those unregistered rights that are readily discoverable, it has ensured that he incurs only a limited amount of extra cost, and so has contained the extent of the problem.

It would be wrong, however, to think that this ruling firmly positions the law at some notional point mid-way between those advocated as ideals by the competing arguments. The concepts used in the ruling are often malleable.[56] A court especially impressed by the argument for or against overriding interests will thus find it easy to bend the compromise towards its preferred position.[57] The pre-2002 caselaw certainly shows this effect.[58] There is no reason to think that it will no longer occur.

One final point. Since the compromise aims to allow a disorganised right to bind a disponee, despite non-registration, when the disponee could easily (cheaply) discover it, one would expect it to contain a rule whereby a disponee who *actually knows* of such a right is bound by it, without more. Indeed, such a rule should be a stronger candidate for acceptance than the overriding interest rules themselves. As we have seen, the latter create an incentive for the disponee to incur costs in finding out about the right, though they are designed so as to limit the extent of these costs. But a rule reacting only to a disponee's actual knowledge creates no such incentive: if anything, the reverse. As we saw in § 2.1.1, a rule on these lines existed in the pre-2002 law,[59] but does not feature in the Land Registration Act 2002.[60] The reason is a concern that if disponees could be bound by actual knowledge, the law might drift into their being bound by less than actual knowledge, so reintroducing incentives to investigate.[61] This seems a weak argument: the concepts used for expressing such a rule would be no more malleable than those apparently found acceptable for stating the overriding interest rules.

---

[56] In § 2.1.2, for example, we discovered considerable instability in the idea of 'actual occupation'; and Sch 3 paras 2 and 3 both use the expression 'obvious on a reasonably careful inspection of the land', which is obviously highly indeterminate.

[57] See N Jackson, 'Title by Registration and Concealed Overriding Interests: The Cause and Effect of Antipathy to Documentary Proof' (2003) 119 *LQR* 660.

[58] Pro-market decisions, constructing their concepts on lines unsympathetic to the protection of disorganised rights, include *Abbey National Building Society v Cann* [1991] 1 AC 56 (HL). Decisions constructing their concepts more sympathetically to the protection of disorganised rights include *Williams & Glyn's Bank Ltd v Boland* [1981] AC 487 (HL). (Discussions of these and related decisions sometimes, however, overstate their room for conceptual manoeuvre and therefore their impact on the shape of the law. See M Conaglen, 'Mortgagee Powers Rhetoric' (2006) 69 *MLR* 583.)

[59] *Peffer v Rigg* [1977] 1 WLR 285 (Ch D).

[60] ss 28–29. (The sections do not explicitly deny the rule, but are phrased in such a way as not to admit it.) For discussion, see E Cooke and P O'Connor, 'Purchaser Liability to Third Parties in the English Land Registration System: A Comparative Perspective' (2004) 120 *LQR* 640.

[61] See Law Commission, *Land Registration for the Twenty-First Century—A Conveyancing Revolution* (Law Com No 271, London, 2001) para 5.16; *Land Registration for the Twenty-First Century—A Consultative Document* (Law Com No 254, London, 1998) paras 3.44–3.46.

2.2.4 The Future of Overriding Interests

There are plans to reduce the profile of overriding interests, by two principal strategies.[62]

First, the Land Registration Act 2002 provides that, of the 14 kinds of right on the current list of overriding interests, the five most esoteric shall remain on the list only for 10 years, after which they will bind disponees only if registered.[63] The case for this change is that, however unreasonable and unrealistic it may be to expect and require these rights to be registered, they are relatively difficult for a disponee to discover. So in terms of the accommodation we have identified between the arguments for a full mirror and those for overriding interests, their claim to overriding status is relatively weak. They were included in the Act's list merely so as to give their owners the benefit of a notice period before their (essentially merited) discontinuance.[64]

Second, it is planned that, at a point in the future, at least some rights which the current regime leaves as overriding will require registration for their very creation.[65] Thus registered in order to exist at all, there will be no question of their being able to bind disponees without registration.[66] So, at present a lease for more than seven years can be made only by a registered transaction,[67] but an ordinary lease for seven years or less can be overriding.[68] If the seven year threshold for compulsory registration is lowered, say to three years, leases only for less than that will be capable of being overriding.[69] Unless registered, a lease for more than three years will not exist, and so necessarily will not be able to form the basis of an overriding interest. The Land Registration Act 2002[70] provides for statutory

---

[62] A third consists in provisions requiring the Land Registry to register most hitherto overriding interests which do come to its attention (Land Registration Act 2002 s 37), and allowing it to require people applying for registration to disclose, for registration, overriding interests of which they are aware (s 71). These provisions are uncontroversial, but of limited impact.

[63] s 117. The rights in question are those in Sch 3 paras 10–14, namely: 'A franchise. A manorial right. A right to rent which was reserved to the Crown on the granting of any freehold estate (whether or not the right is still vested in the Crown). A non-statutory right in respect of an embankment or sea or river wall. A right to payment in lieu of tithe.'

[64] See Law Commission, *Land Registration for the Twenty-First Century—A Conveyancing Revolution* (Law Com No 271, London, 2001) paras 8.35–8.46 and 8.81–8.89. The Commission believes that immediate termination of their overriding status would have violated the European Convention on Human Rights (cf n 52 above), but that the notice period will prevent this result.

[65] On registration for a right's creation, see further §§ 4.4.4–4.4.5.

[66] Law Commission, *Land Registration for the Twenty-First Century—A Conveyancing Revolution* (Law Com No 271, London, 2001) paras 8.2, 8.74.

[67] Land Registration Act 2002 ss 4, 6 and 7.

[68] Sch 3 para 1.

[69] The significance of three years is that, below this duration, a lease can—under the present law—validly be made without any formality at all: Law of Property Act 1925 s 54(2) (§ 4.5).

[70] s 93.

instruments to be made adding rights to the list of those required to be registered, and so unable to operate as overriding interests, in this way.

It is envisaged that such instruments will be made once the Land Registry's IT arrangements have been further developed, allowing the introduction of 'electronic conveyancing'.[71] Whereas under present arrangements, parties' lawyers send physical paperwork concerning their transactions to the Registry for the Registry to make the appropriate entries on the register, under electronic conveyancing the lawyers will themselves make the entries online. In terms of the principles involved in the present compromise, why should this make a difference?

One can undoubtedly argue that it should *not* make a difference. The feasibility of registering organised transactions online does not in the least make it more reasonable to expect rights arising in disorganised ways to be registered too, whether online or otherwise. The disorganised nature of the ways in which they arise itself rules this out. Equally, the possibility of searching the register for organised (registered) rights online does not make it less easy to make the quite different inquiries that the design of Schedule 3 makes relevant to disorganised (unregistered) rights. So long as the law continues to have disorganised rights in land at all, the advent of electronic conveyancing should make no difference to the correctness of allowing them to operate as overriding interests.[72]

One might however challenge this view, by arguing that electronic registration is part of a wider social movement towards privileging online activity: towards arranging human affairs around the internet, and in the process abandoning, as a worthwhile sacrifice, modes of behaviour that are incompatible with the internet's configuration. Within this, one might view the disorganised creation of land rights, and informal regimes (such as overriding interests) for operating them, as among the required sacrifices. It is impossible to deny that some such movement is afoot. But it would surely be a mistake to perceive it as all-embracing, leaving no room for activities so conceived as to be conductable only in other ways. It is not hard to think of many such activities; it would be not at all aberrant to see as among them the continued recognition and operation of disorganised rights over land.

---

[71] On electronic conveyancing, see further § 4.4.5.

[72] At one time the Law Commission appeared to accept this, remarking 'rights that could arise without express grant or reservation or by operation of law, interests under trusts and short leases which were overriding interests would not be subject to the "creation by registration" requirement': *Land Registration for the Twenty-First Century—A Consultative Document* (Law Com No 254, London, 1998) para 2.47. But the Commission's more recent discussion of electronic conveyancing in *Land Registration for the Twenty-First Century—A Conveyancing Revolution* (Law Com No 271, London, 2001) pt XIII contains no such statement.

2.3 Registration More Generally

This chapter has been about the circumstances under which a right in rem, ie a right capable of affecting a disponee, will actually do so. Addressing only registered land, it has explained that those circumstances are defined by the rules in the Land Registration Act 2002 (and are that the right must either be registered, or qualify as an overriding interest under Schedule 3).

For clarity's sake, it is worth noting that this is not the only task at which the Act is aimed. In particular, it also makes provision regarding the circumstances in which rights can arise at all. It does so in two principal areas. Addressing the organised creation of rights, it contributes rules about the formalities that must be used in order for certain kinds of rights to be conferred at all (not simply for them to affect a subsequent disponee). These rules, including those contributed by the Act, are explained in Chapters 4 and 5. And addressing the circumstances in which rights may arise in a disorganised way, it makes large changes in one doctrine having this effect, namely adverse possession. This is covered in § 6.2. But these two sets of rules have a common theme with that discussed in this chapter, whereby a right capable of affecting a disponee must sometimes be registered in order actually to do so. It is that the legal facts relating to a piece of land should, *ceteris paribus* (the provision for overriding interests, and the continued existence of an adverse possession doctrine at all, being reminders of contrary considerations), be shown on the register. This is a desideratum because it fosters the market in land: the accessibility and reliability of the registered information reduces the costs involved in transacting with it.

At the same time, however, the Act provides also for abandonment of the information shown on the register where that information is in some way corrupt. The case for such a provision is easy to see: one would not wish people's substantive rights to be determined by clerical errors or indeed frauds. But even correcting corrupt information is troublesome to the project of ensuring that the facts relating to the land are those shown by the register. The Act accordingly allows such adjustment to the register (known as 'alteration', sometimes 'rectification') only in specified, quite narrow, circumstances, presumably where the harm done by allowing the corrupt information to stand is thought to be greater than that done by modifying it. This aspect of the Act was touched on in § 1.3.5.

3

Consenting Out of a Right

3.1 The Rule in *Bristol and West Building Society v Henning*

3.1.1 The Rule

Say you have a right over land which will in principle bind a disponee of that land, in one of the ways explored in Chapter 2: it is a right in rem, and either it is registered or it qualifies as an overriding interest. If however you consent to the disponee not being bound by the right after all, he will not be bound by it. This was established in *Bristol and West Building Society v Henning*,[1] a decision in the context of unregistered land which was soon applied to registered land in *Paddington Building Society v Mendelsohn*.[2]

Imagine, for example, that you and I live together in a house which I own, but in which, we have agreed, you should have an interest too. The law accords you that interest; it is a beneficial interest under a constructive trust,[3] and so a right in rem. You may have registered it, but if not (which is more probable), it will be an overriding interest on the basis of your actual and apparent occupation. Now I sell the house to John. If you were unaware of the sale, your interest will bind John.[4] But that is an unlikely scenario. More likely is that I sell the house because we have decided to move home, and you go along with the steps I take to that end. When the sale goes through, you cannot change your mind and claim to keep your right in the house after all. You consented to John not being bound by it, and must abide by that. Your interest is 'postponed' to his, meaning that you still have it, but instead of ranking ahead of his right, it ranks after his right. In a straightforward case,

---

[1] [1985] 1 WLR 778 (CA).
[2] (1985) 50 P & CR 244 (CA).
[3] See § 8.3.
[4] For the (complicated) law on the effectiveness of trust interests against buyers, see §§ 14.4–14.8.

this means simply that, now that the house belongs to John, you no longer have rights in the house.

The same principle applies if the transaction is not to sell the house, but to mortgage it. Say again that you and I live in a house which I own but in which you have an interest. Then, instead of selling the house, I 'release the equity' in it: ie borrow money against its value, by giving the lending bank a mortgage over it.[5] As your interest is in rem, and you are (let us suppose) in actual and apparent occupation at the time of the mortgage, your interest will in principle affect the bank as an overriding interest. Then, although I have purported to grant the bank a mortgage over the entire value of the house, your interest—binding the bank—has to be subtracted from what the bank actually gets. That is to say, the mortgage will be effective only to the extent of my interest in the house. This may well be discomforting for the bank.[6] But loans raised in this way are often used for purposes in which we are both involved, such as home improvements. In such a case you will normally know what is going on and consent to the mortgage, so postponing your right and allowing the mortgage to apply to the house's full value after all. On the other hand, such loans are also sometimes used for purposes in which you are not necessarily involved, such as to put extra money into my business. Then, it is not unknown for me to act without you realising it and thus without your consent,[7] meaning that your right will operate as an overriding interest and bind the bank after all.

3.1.2 The Underlying Analysis

In *Bristol and West Building Society v Henning*,[8] the court explained this rule in a particular way. This explanation was not satisfactory, however.[9] Although there has been no explicit discussion of the change in the cases, the more recent ones have replaced the original explanation with a new one. It is said now that, if you go along with my steps to sell or mortgage our house,

---

[5] For mortgages, see Ch 12.

[6] Say I have a 67% share in the house, and you have the other 33% share. The fact that the mortgage is effective only to the extent of my interest means that, if I default on the loan and the bank repossesses the house to recoup itself, the bank can take only 67% of the house's value, and must give the other 33% up to you. So if my loan was for more than 67% of the house's value, the bank will lose. For a more detailed account of the relevant law, see Ch 14, especially § 14.8.1.

[7] As apparently in eg *Williams & Glyn's Bank Ltd v Boland* [1981] AC 487 (HL).

[8] [1985] 1 WLR 778 (CA).

[9] It involved—in terms of the example given in § 3.1.1—recalling that you acquired your right in the house via an agreement with me, and continuing to assert that built into this agreement was an understanding that your right would be postponed as described in the text. This account had two deficiencies. First, the alleged understanding about postponement would be quite fictitious, aimed at fulfilling some other agenda, which had better be identified more transparently. Second, the consent principle should apply not only to rights arising from an agreement between us, but also to rights arising in other ways, which would be impossible under the explanation given.

you will be prevented from setting up against the disponee any interest that would otherwise bind him, on the basis that you are estopped from doing so.[10] By going along with my steps, you have impliedly represented to the disponee that you will not set up your right against him; and the disponee has relied on this representation to his detriment, by undertaking his part in the disposition; so you may not go back on your representation.

3.2 What Counts as the Necessary Representation?

To be estopped from setting up against a disponee a right of yours which would otherwise bind him, you must represent that you will not enforce it, and he must act in reliance on that representation in such a way that it would be inequitable for you to enforce it after all.

3.2.1 Finding the Necessary Representation

When will you be regarded as representing that you will not set your interest up against the disponee? The caselaw contains very little discussion of this question, but we can suggest some answers on the basis of general principles.

Fundamentally, whatever language or behaviour you use, whether it counts as the required representation depends on its objective appearance: ie whether it would be interpreted as such by a reasonable bystander.

An appropriate explicit statement will suffice, of course.[11] But so should an implication, such as going along with the steps I take to sell or mortgage the house, so giving the impression that you are not going to put obstacles in the way. Most of the cases involve a mere omission to object to the disposition, and treat it as enough. In principle, however, such an omission to object should suffice only if you could have been expected to object. Contrast two illustrative scenarios.

The first, which is the one addressed by the cases, is that where I sell to John—or mortgage to a bank—the house that I hold on trust for myself and you and that is our home. In this scenario, it normally would be reasonable for John or the bank to reckon that you know what I am doing, and to

---

[10] *Skipton Building Society v Clayton* (1993) 66 P & CR 223 (CA); *Woolwich Building Society v Dickman* [1996] 3 All ER 204 (CA).

[11] According to *Woolwich Building Society v Dickman, ibid*, the disponee can rely on your consent only if (presumably, your consent has been given explicitly, and) *it has been noted on the register*. There is no warrant for this view, however, and it has attracted no attention in other decisions.

interpret silence on your part as a promise to postpone your right. So your omission to object does qualify as the required representation. In the second scenario, however, I sell to John a piece of land over which you, living next door, have a right of way. Even if John has reason to think that you know of the sale, he has no reason to expect you to take an interest in it. So here your failure to object to the sale, or to assert your right, ought not to be seen as a representation that you will postpone your right.

The contrast between the two scenarios arises from the difference in the relationship between you and me. Crucial to the first scenario is the fact that the house is our shared home. This suggests that I am acting on behalf of both of us. It makes it reasonable to suppose that you share my aim of making the disposition on the basis that the disponee will be unconcerned with your right. In the second scenario, however, your position is quite independent of mine, so it is not reasonable to see you as aligning your position with mine: even though, evidently, I plan to make way for the disponee, there is no reason to suppose that you do too.

3.2.2 Vitiation

Even if your words or behaviour are read as the required representation in that way, this representation should as a matter of principle not bind you if, when you made it, you were under pressure, or did not know or understand what you were doing.

But the precise ground regarded as covered by these phenomena varies between different areas of law, to reflect variations in the policy consider-ations prevailing in them. The circumstances in which saying 'yes' to sexual intercourse fails to represent consent for the offence of rape,[12] for example, are clearly different from those in which someone's apparent agreement will be regarded as invalid for civil law purposes. The latter must normally qualify as 'duress', 'undue influence', 'misrepresentation' or 'mistake'. And there are differences within the civil law itself. A mistake will vitiate a *gift* whenever it causes the giver to make the gift,[13] but a *contract* only when it is shared by both parties, and is 'fundamental'.[14] The less sensitive contract rule tracks the concern that the more invalidity one finds among apparently valid agree-ments, the greater the damage to commercial certainty, and so to trade. The more sensitive gifts rule reflects the fact that commerce is less affected by the

---

[12] See the Sexual Offences Act 2003 ss 74–76.

[13] *Barclays Bank Ltd v WJ Simms Son & Cooke (Southern) Ltd* [1980] QB 677 (QBD).

[14] *Bell v Lever Bros Ltd* [1932] AC 161 (HL); *Great Peace Shipping Ltd v Tsavliris Salvage (International) Ltd, The Great Peace* [2003] QB 679 (CA). A mistake is 'fundamental' if it makes the thing, service, etc contracted for 'essentially different from the thing [etc] as it was believed to be': [2003] QB 679, [154].

treatment of gifts in this respect, so the law can afford to be readier to see the giver's consent as vitiated by the mistake.[15]

To turn to our context, exactly when will your consent to a disposition, so as to postpone your right, be regarded as vitiated? Probably, when you gave it in circumstances of duress, undue influence, misrepresentation or mistake; but what meanings do these concepts have here? The cases offer scant discussion of the matter, but a view can be deduced from their facts and outcomes. In the leading cases,[16] the person held to have given agreement seems to have been far from fully informed about what was at stake, and probably also had little real choice whether to go along with the disposition, if their family was not to disintegrate. But the courts treated the agreement as self-evidently valid, not even considering the contrary possibility. That is, they tacitly constructed the idea of valid agreement, for the purposes of the present context, on relatively insensitive lines. The likeliest reading of them is that your agreement to a disposition will be treated as vitiated only in the circumstances in which a contractual undertaking would have been.

At first sight, this is odd, because the contractual understandings of the phenomena apply—obviously—when the parties between whom they arise are the parties to a (putative) contract: which you and I are normally not. In the scenario we have been considering, you and I live together in a house that I own but which you have helped pay for. Our relationship is probably therefore a family one. If the question of my consent's vitiation arose purely between ourselves, then, a contractual construction of the relevant rules would be inappropriate. The key, however, is that this question does not arise purely between us. By definition, it is aimed at determining whether my right is to bind a third party, John: who very probably does come into the picture via a contract (the disposition from me). It is presumably to safeguard that contract that this rather insensitive reading of the vitiation concepts has been adopted.

Even if your consent does count as vitiated, however, John is not automatically affected by this, so as to be unable to rely on the apparent postponement. Some additional rules govern the question whether or not he is so affected.

3.2.3 Do Flaws in your Consent Affect the Disponee?

So imagine that your apparent consent to postpone your right to John's is vitiated—probably, as just noted, on the basis of mistake, misrepresentation,

---

[15] For duress, undue influence, misrepresentation and mistake in contract, see eg M Chen-Wishart, *Contract Law* (2nd edn, Oxford, 2008) chs 5, 6, 8, 9.

[16] *Bristol and West Building Society v Henning* [1985] 1 WLR 778 (CA); *Paddington Building Society v Mendelsohn* (1985) 50 P & CR 244 (CA).

duress, or undue influence, as these ideas are read in the law of contract. When exactly will this affect John?

If your consent to postpone is vitiated by a *mistake*, John will not be able to rely on it. The source of the mistake does not matter, but (assuming the contract approach) it must be shared between you and either me or John. Either way, it will prevent John from relying on your agreement, as the effect of a mistake is to make an agreement void, ie of no legal effect at all.[17]

It is different, however, if your consent is affected by misrepresentation, duress, or undue influence. These render an agreement voidable rather than void: that is, of legal effect until set aside ('rescinded'). It can normally[18] be set aside against the author of the misrepresentation, duress, or undue influence. In our context, this will usually be me, the disponor: it is I, rather than John, who am likely to have lied to you or put pressure on you to get you to agree to the disposition. But there is little or no gain for you in being able to set aside your consent as against me alone, certainly once the disposition has gone through and the question has therefore arisen whether or not your right binds John. Your concern will be rather that you can set your agreement aside as against John too, so that your apparent postponement of your right is reversed, and the right will bind him after all. The law is that if your consent to a disposition is vitiated by duress, undue influence or misrepresentation on my part, you will be able to set it aside also as against the disponee only if, when acquiring his interest in the land, he *had notice of* the duress, undue influence or misrepresentation.[19]

3.2.4 'Notice'

To say that someone has 'notice' of some fact means that a reasonable person would have known or discovered that fact. A 'reasonable person' is one who acts with the care and perspicacity required by the law in the context in question. In different contexts, and at different times, the law has, as a matter of policy, raised and lowered its required standard of care and perspicacity.

For the purposes of the rule under discussion, the authorities suggest that notice means actual knowledge: ie that John can rely on your apparent consent to the disposition, notwithstanding that I have obtained that consent by (say) misrepresentation, unless he actually knows that fact.[20] These

---

[17] *Great Peace Shipping Ltd v Tsavliris Salvage (International) Ltd, The Great Peace* [2003] QB 679 (CA).

[18] Unless a 'bar to rescission' is present: eg laches, impossibility of *restitutio in integrum*. For details, see M Chen-Wishart, *Contract Law* (2nd edn, Oxford, 2008) 227–32.

[19] *Bridgman v Green* (1757) Wilm 58 (Lords Commissioners); *Turnbull v Duval* [1902] AC 429 (PC).

[20] *Cobbett v Brock* (1855) 20 Beav 524, 528 (Rolls); *Kempson v Ashbee* (1874) LR 10 Ch App 15, 21 (CA in Ch); *Bainbrigge v Brown* (1881) 18 Ch D 188, 197 (Ch D); but cf *Bank of Credit and Commerce International SA v Aboody* [1990] 1 QB 923 (CA), which seems to contemplate notice in its more usual sense of 'the ability to discover'.

decisions are antique, and may not be reliable. But since their effect is largely to protect the disponee, it would be unsurprising if they were indeed adhered to, making this the general vision of notice for present purposes.

There is, however, a very important exception to that general vision. It consists in the special rule about notice that was developed in *Barclays Bank plc v O'Brien*[21] and *Royal Bank of Scotland plc v Etridge (No 2)*.[22]

This rule applies only where two conditions are met. First, the relationship between you and me must be a non-commercial one: we must be for example a married or unmarried couple, or parent and child. And second, the transaction—the disposition by me to which you have given (vitiated) consent—must be[23] 'not to your advantage'. A case clearly satisfying this condition would be that where I release the equity in our house to finance my gambling habit. On the face of it, releasing the equity so as to expand my business is to your advantage in that it may well produce a better standard of living for both of us, meaning that the condition is not met; but the courts disregard this indirect advantage, regarding such a transaction as to your advantage only if you play an active part in the business itself. It is however assumed that my simply selling our house to John, so that we can move for any of the usual reasons (say, for the sake of my new job: but why is this not equivalent to a mortgage for the sake of my business?), is a transaction to your advantage and so does not attract the rule. It can be seen that these conditions effectively limit the scope of the rule to (certain) dispositions in favour of banks and the like.[24]

Where your consent to postpone your right is flawed because I have obtained it by misrepresentation, duress or undue influence, and these two conditions are met, a disponee bank will *automatically* have notice of the flaw in your consent ... unless it arranges for you to receive independent, one-to-one legal advice before you commit yourself. The automatic nature of notice here is justified because the presence of the two conditions (the combined facts that you and I have a non-commercial relationship, and that the transaction in question is not to your advantage) should itself alert the bank to the possibility that my behaviour in obtaining your consent has been

[21] [1994] 1 AC 180 (HL).

[22] [2002] 2 AC 773 (HL). See further M Chen-Wishart, *Contract Law* (2nd edn, Oxford, 2008) 361–6.

[23] So far as appears to the disponee: *UCB Group Ltd v Hedworth* [2003] EWCA Civ 1717, [121] (CA).

[24] The rule was originally applied only to a guarantee given by you to my creditor, underwriting my debt (*Turnbull v Duval* [1902] AC 429 (PC)). It was extended to the case where you and I jointly own our house, and you join with me in mortgaging it so as to secure my debt (*Barclays Bank plc v O'Brien* [1994] 1 AC 180 (HL); *Royal Bank of Scotland plc v Etridge (No 2)* [2002] 2 AC 773 (HL)); or where you alone own the house, and mortgage it to secure my debt (*Castle Phillips Finance v Piddington* [1995] 1 FLR 783 (CA)). It was then applied also to the context with which we are concerned, where I own the house but you have an interest in it, and you agree to postpone your right so as to allow me to mortgage it (*Scottish Equitable Life plc v Virdee* [1999] 1 FLR 863 (CA)).

such as to render it flawed. But if the bank arranges for you to receive advice, it can assume that your consent is satisfactory after all, for the advice session should ensure that you know your legal position and have more space to reach your decision (though total freedom from pressure cannot be achieved).

3.3 Consent to a Replacement Mortgage

Say that I own a house in which you have an interest. With your valid consent, I mortgage it to secure a loan from bank *A*. But then I replace this mortgage with a new one from bank *B*. If you know about and consent to this replacement mortgage, you will of course be held to have postponed your interest to it in the usual way.

But say now that I have taken out the bank *B* mortgage behind your back, so that on the face of things you do not consent to it. So long as the bank *B* mortgage is on terms no more onerous than the bank *A* one, your consent to the latter is carried forward, and your interest is postponed to the bank *B* mortgage after all.[25]

This result was originally explained in the same unsatisfactory way as the basic rule,[26] but is now regarded as occurring on the basis of subrogation. By this, when *X* (me) owes money under a mortgage to *Y* (bank *A*), and *Z* (bank *B*) pays *Y* the sum in question, *Z* steps into *Y*'s shoes, ie becomes *X*'s creditor for the same amount and enjoys the same mortgage over *X*'s property—all regardless of *X*'s knowledge or consent.[27] The idea of stepping into the previous creditor's shoes is taken to mean that, when I replace the bank *A* mortgage with the bank *B* one, bank *B* can take advantage of your consent to the bank *A* one. Conversely, if your consent to the bank *A* mortgage was flawed, and the flaw affected bank *A* in the way explained in §§ 3.2.3–3.2.4, bank *B* is affected by it too.[28]

Now say instead that, in transacting the replacement mortgage with bank *B*, I not only acted without your knowledge, but also arranged more onerous terms. Most obviously, perhaps, the sum I borrow from bank *B* is larger than that which I owed to bank *A*: for example, I owed bank *A* £200,000, but my new loan from bank *B* is of £250,000. Your consent to the bank *A* mortgage

---

[25] *Equity and Law Home Loans v Prestidge* [1992] 1 WLR 137 (CA).
[26] See n 9.
[27] *Butler v Rice* [1910] 2 Ch 277 (CA).
[28] *Yorkshire Bank plc v Tinsley* [2004] 1 WLR 2380 (CA).

once again avails bank *B*, but only to the extent of the sum owed to bank *A*, ie £200,000.[29] Subrogation allows bank *B* to take advantage of your earlier consent because bank *B* is stepping into bank *A*'s shoes, but it is doing so only to the extent of the loan that it is taking over.[30]

3.4 A Summary

Chapters 1 to 3, which together make up Part 1 of this book, have explored the idea of a 'right in rem' and its significance. Some details have required considerable discussion. It may be helpful to end Part 1 by recapping the key points. We have seen that:

— to be *capable of* binding a disponee of the land to which it relates, a right must be a right in rem; but
— for a right in rem *actually* to bind a particular disponee, the rules in the Land Registration Act 2002 must be complied with, ie the right must either have been registered or qualify as overriding; but
— the disponee will nevertheless *not* be bound by the right if the right's owner validly consents to the transaction by which the disponee acquires his interest in the land.

---

[29] *Equity and Law Home Loans v Prestidge* [1992] 1 WLR 137 (CA).
[30] Analogously, in *Castle Phillips Finance v Piddington* [1995] 1 FLR 783 (CA), the wife mortgaged a house which she owned to secure her husband's debt, and although subsequent lenders increased the amount of the debt, their rights by subrogation against the wife were limited to the outstanding balance on the original mortgage.

PART 2
Acquisition

In Part 1, we saw what rights in rem are, and how they behave. In Part 2, comprising Chapters 4 to 8, we look at the rules controlling how a right in rem in a piece of land—whether the ownership of the land, or some narrower right—can be acquired.

Conferment

4.1 Two Methods of Acquisition

As the law stands, there are two broad ways in which you can acquire a right in rem in my land. One is on the basis that I, the owner of the land[1] hitherto, intend you to acquire the right, and set out to confer it on you. The present chapter and Chapter 5 are concerned with acquisitions of this kind. Chapters 6, 7 and 8 focus on the other way: acquisition on grounds other than the owner's intention. These grounds will be detailed in due course, but they include ideas such as 'squatter's rights', and the phenomenon where I lead you to believe that you have, or will get, a right in my land, and you rely on that belief to your detriment, giving rise to rights under the doctrine of proprietary estoppel.

These two ways of acquiring rights are respectively the 'organised' and 'disorganised' ways referred to in § 2.2.2. As was explained there, the law does not have to recognise both approaches. It does so because of a perception that there are important values behind each. The values behind the rules covered in Chapters 6, 7 and 8 will be explored there. Behind the subject-matter of this and the next chapter—acquisition on the basis of the hitherto owner's intention—is the idea that respecting my hitherto ownership of the land means, among other important things, allowing me effectively to confer some or all of my rights on you. That I am able to choose to do this is part of what it means to say that I am an 'owner' at all, and protecting this ability is therefore something that modern English law has signed up to in maintaining the idea of ownership (over land) at all.

---

[1] Or of some interest in it from which yours could be derived. For example, if I am the tenant of some land (the owner—my landlord—being John), I might intend to give you a sub-tenancy, or a right of way over it lasting only as long as my tenancy.

4.2 Expression and Formalities

My conferment[2] of the right on you is thus based in my wish that you should have the right. But the law does not treat my wish alone as sufficient. My wish certainly needs to be *evinced*: the law has no means of reading my mind, and even if it had, it ought not to attach consequences to what remains merely an internal thought—people need the space to think what they will, and if they like to unthink it again, without it having legal significance.

Moreover, in order for my wish to be effectuated, the law requires that in most cases, I must have evinced that wish *in a particular way*: using certain formalities. The required formalities vary from one context to another, and the detailed rules will be explained in a moment. But the main kinds of formality that the law uses in this area are:

— *Writing*, signed by the conferor (or on his behalf, by an agent), with or without a requirement of witnesses.
— A *deed*, which nowadays[3] means a piece of writing that declares itself to be a deed, and that is signed by the conferor (or, with certain caveats, by an agent), witnessed, and 'delivered' (essentially, accompanied by some overt acknowledgement of binding effect, either immediate or conditional).
— *Registration* at the Land Registry.

Like most legal formalities, those required for the conferment of rights in land serve a number of purposes.

One is the promotion of *certainty*. One aspect of this is certainty that the transaction has occurred at all. This is provided by its being recorded in permanent form. Another aspect is clarity as to what the transaction comprises. This is provided by its details too being recorded in permanent form, but also by the fact that having to make such a record will make those involved focus more sharply on just what these details should be, and so avoid contradictions, crucial omissions and so on.

A second purpose is to improve *the quality of the intention* on which the transaction is based. The need to use formality will encourage those involved to give serious thought to what they are about to do, and perhaps also—as

---

[2] This chapter uses the word 'conferment' or 'conferral' to denote a transaction by which I voluntarily cause you to have a right over land which has (at least hitherto) been mine. These words are not technical legal terms, and are chosen for that reason. The relevant technical terms, which include 'conveyance', 'grant', 'transfer' and 'disposition', all have particular connotations not relevant to the present discussion.

[3] Law of Property (Miscellaneous Provisions) Act 1989 s 1.

where the supplying of the formality is a semi-public event, eg when witnesses must be present—make it less likely that they are under objectionable pressure.

A third purpose is to make the transaction more *visible* to persons or bodies not involved in its making, but having an interest in knowing about it or its effects. These persons or bodies might include the tax authorities, as where the transaction or the interest conferred is dutiable, or the environmental authorities, who might need to discover the owner of a piece of land that is the source of pollution. They might include those considering subsequent dealings with the property or parties involved: where I am hoping to buy a piece of land from you, for example, I will want to be sure that you are indeed its current owner, and that there are no problems for me in the make-up of your rights. Perhaps they also include the general public: there may be a public interest in being able to discover the owner of every inch of the country, on the ground that the country's citizens all have a stake in its physical form ... and perhaps also in being able to discover the various rights less than ownership there might be over it, though this is less plausible.

The three kinds of formality used for conferring rights in land all deliver the first two of these purposes, though they do it to varying extents. Writing and deeds do not themselves provide visibility, however, though one who is on the brink of taking a right from someone claiming to have the means to confer it would naturally be normally able to demand to see the documents supporting that claim. Visibility has been much better promoted by registration, since the register became a public resource.[4]

Underneath these purposes are deeper-lying considerations explaining why they count as valuable. The first and second of them spring from the liberal concern to maximise autonomy: the concern that people should be neither prevented from achieving what they want to, nor made to be involved in transactions which they do not genuinely want. The considerations underlying the third purpose, promoting visibility, are more various, ranging from the desirability of an efficient market (where it is a question of visibility to those considering subsequent dealings with the property concerned), to the aims of whatever tax is at issue (where it is a question of visibility to the tax authorities), to the communitarian notions yielding the idea that a country's citizens all have a stake in its land.

At the same time, formality requirements can be injurious to these or other values. An interest in privacy is evidently sacrificed in achieving full visibility. And most especially, if a person wishes to achieve a certain end, but is prevented from doing so by his non-compliance with a formality

---

[4] Under the Land Registration Act 1988 s 1. Access was previously confined to registered proprietors and others authorised by them, which in practice obviously included those to whom they hoped to sell rights. In the case of conferrals on death, visibility is achieved by placing all wills on public display.

requirement, the frustration of his wish will offend the liberal desideratum that he should be able to do as he likes. Here, then, we find a paradox: formality requirements can cut both ways in liberal terms. As we saw above, they can help someone achieve an end; but as we see now, they can equally frustrate him.

Whether it is overall a good or a bad idea to require formality[5] therefore depends significantly on the likelihood of people complying with that requirement. It is fair to say that people will generally comply with formality requirements applying to transactions involving rights over land. There is a general understanding that land is 'special', such that a person, realising that he is conferring a right in his land, will actually expect to do so formally: and not merely in some formal way of his own devising, but as indicated by the law. He is unlikely to know the content of the relevant law, but his general understanding will lead him to consult a lawyer, who will supply what is needed. The same is true whether the conferral is to take effect during his lifetime ('*inter vivos*') or on his death, ie under his will. (Indeed, the same general understanding probably applies to all dispositions on death, even those not involving land.)

Certainly from this key point of view, then, the balance of advantage lies in favour of requiring conferrals of rights in land to be made using formality.[6] As we are about to see, the law reflects this. The relevant rules do, however, have some surprising features.

The rules differ according to whether I am seeking to confer the right on my death, or *inter vivos*.

4.3 Conferment on Death

If I try to give you a right in my land in a way that takes effect on my death, I must do so using a will. And in order for my will to be valid, it must normally be in writing, signed by myself, and by two witnesses.[7]

---

[5] See further P Critchley, 'Taking Formalities Seriously' in S Bright and J Dewar (eds), *Land Law—Themes and Perspectives* (Oxford, 1998) ch 20.

[6] It is of course quite different where the acquisition of rights in a disorganised way is concerned. By definition, in this case, those involved do not understand the legal significance of what they are doing. They would therefore not comply with a formality requirement, and the law, in providing for the right, would be self-defeating if it required them to do so. Unsurprisingly, then, it does not. But this chapter is concerned only with organised conferrals.

[7] Wills Act 1837 s 9, amended by the Administration of Justice Act 1982 s 17. (Further rules exist about the details of these requirements.) There is a well-known method of leaving property

These rules, which have prevailed for a long time, seem apt. They are well calculated to promote thoughtfulness on the testator's part about what he is doing, clarity in his description of it, and also freedom from immediate (though one cannot say more than that) pressure. A further element of the law of wills, 'probate', involves opening a deceased's will to public inspection, so additionally giving visibility to what he has done.

4.4 Conferment *Inter Vivos*

4.4.1 The Rules

If I am trying to give you the right *inter vivos*, the requirements vary according to the type of right in question.

— To give you a *legal* right in my land (ie one recognised by the common law),[8] I must usually[9] use a deed,[10] and (in the case of registered land) in most[11] such cases the conferral must also be registered with the Land Registry.[12]
— To give you an *equitable* right (ie one recognised by equity), I must do so in writing,[13] with no further requirement of registration.

So, say I wish to give you an easement or a mortgage over my land, or indeed to transfer the freehold ownership to you.[14] These are all legal rights, and their conferral requires a deed and registration. Whereas say I wish to give you a restrictive covenant or a beneficial interest under a trust I shall create

---

on death without using a will, and so without having to comply with these formalities: the 'secret trust'. Properly understood, however, secret trusts are in principle (though not necessarily in practice: there is a problem) a vehicle for the acquisition of rights on a basis other than intentional conferment. As such, they do not belong in this chapter.

[8] For the distinction between legal and equitable rights, see § 1.5.

[9] The main exception is a lease for up to three years, which does not normally require a deed, and can indeed be made orally: Law of Property Act 1925 s 54(2).

[10] *Ibid* s 52(1). This refers to 'legal estates'. The Act had already defined that term to include rights properly speaking less than estates, such as mortgages and easements: s 1(4).

[11] The main exception is a lease for up to seven years. If for more than three years (and sometimes if for less), the lease must be made by deed, but it need not additionally be registered. The special rules about leases are explained in § 4.5.

[12] Land Registration Act 2002 s 27.

[13] Law of Property Act s 53(1).

[14] For easements (eg rights of way), see Ch 9. For mortgages, see Ch 12.

in your favour.[15] These are equitable rights, and their conferral requires only writing.

Where a right's conferral requires not only a deed but also registration, its conferral is known as a 'registrable disposition'.[16] In the case of a registrable disposition, the conferral of the right must be registered *in order to take effect at all*.[17] All other kinds of rights in rem in land—rights which are not the subject of registrable dispositions—can be registered too, and ideally should be, so as to ensure that they bind a disponee of the land, as explained in § 2.2.1. But unlike the rights which are the subject of registrable dispositions, a failure to register them does not leave them simply ineffective. Even if, remaining unregistered, they fail to bind a disponee of the land (and that will depend on whether they can operate instead as an overriding interest), they will normally still be valid against the person who conferred them.

Take a restrictive covenant. As noted above, the conferral of a restrictive covenant is not a registrable disposition. Say I make a restrictive covenant in your favour over my land (using writing, as required), but you do not register it against my land; and then I transfer my land to John. Your failure to register the right means that you cannot use this route to enforce it against John. But you still have it, and can enforce it against me ... and against John too, if you can show that it operates as an overriding interest.[18] Contrast this with an easement, the conferral of which is a registrable disposition.[19] Say I purport to confer an easement on you (using a deed, as required), but we omit to register it; and then I transfer the land in question to John. This time, you cannot enforce the easement against John, even as an overriding interest: for, lacking registration, the law simply does not recognise the easement as existing at all. Nor can you enforce it even against me: again, lacking registration, the law simply does not recognise it as existing at all.[20] Registration is as much a pre-condition for its valid existence as the deed which is also required to confer it.

---

[15] For restrictive covenants (essentially, a restrictive covenant is a right enjoyed by you as my neighbour, preventing me from doing something—eg erecting further buildings—on my land), see Ch 10. For trusts, see Chs 13–14.

[16] Land Registration Act 2002 s 27.

[17] That is to say, in order for the conferral to take effect at all as the conferral of the *legal* right in question. If the conferral is not registered as required, it will usually operate instead to create the *equitable* version of the right, in the manner described in § 5.2.4—but criticised in § 5.2.5.

[18] In the case of a restrictive covenant, this would have to be on the basis that you are in actual and apparent occupation of my land at the time of the transfer to John: which is in practice rather unlikely. See § 10.4.

[19] Land Registration Act 2002 s 27(2)(d); § 9.2.8.

[20] These statements relate only, however, to the *legal* easement that we purported to create. As explained in n 17, although no legal easement has arisen, an *equitable* easement may well have done so. An equitable easement does not require registration in order to exist, so you will be able to enforce it against me; and also against John if you later register it, or as an overriding interest, in the again unlikely event that you are in actual and apparent occupation of my land at the time of my transfer to him: § 9.3.

4.4.2 The Distinction between the Legal and Equitable Rules

So the rules draw a marked distinction between legal and equitable rights, normally requiring a deed and registration for the former but only writing for the latter. Is this distinction supportable?

At one time, there were significant differences in the behaviour of legal and equitable rights. In particular, a legal right would bind any disponee of the land in question, without further ado, while an equitable right would bind a disponee only so long as he was not a 'bona fide purchaser for value without notice' of the land in question.

It is doubtful whether these differences ever justified the disparity in the formality rules for the two kinds of rights. This disparity arose historically, from other differences between the approaches of the common law and of equity.[21] The common law has always (that is, since mid-medieval times) demanded a deed. Indeed, to say 'demanded' may give a misleading impression of the original idea: early on, acts done in a certain stylised way, ie by deed, were seen as possessing an intrinsic dispositive significance, capable of production in no other way. As equity developed, however, it required no formality at all. (An oral expression, or even apparently a gesture, sufficed.) It took this position as a corrective to what it now constructed as the obtuseness of the common law in demanding a deed, appealing instead to conscience, ie how a person stood vis-à-vis divine justice: God, it was reckoned, neither needed nor was interested in formal proofs. The divergence was captured by the saying 'equity looks to the substance, not the form'. Eventually, however, it came to be thought that equity's preference for informality was doing more harm than good: transactions were apparently being falsely alleged on a substantial scale. So from 1677 the Statute of Frauds required the conferment of equitable rights in land to be proved in writing. Hence the modern rule (though the additional requirement for legal rights, alone, to be registered was introduced much more recently). Coming at the matter today, however, whatever we may think of the relative merits of the common law and equitable approaches to proof (formality), there is nothing in the difference between legal and equitable *rights* to imply that they should attract different kinds of formality.

Indeed, the substantive differences between legal and equitable rights have largely disappeared. In particular, in place of the old division over the need for 'notice', nowadays both legal and equitable rights in registered land will bind a disponee only if they have been registered, or qualify as an overriding interest. The rules about the possibility of registering a right and of its qualifying as an overriding interest preserve a few distinctions between legal and

---

[21] For their relationship, see § 1.5.

equitable rights,[22] but these are relatively few, largely unjustifiable, and surely destined for extermination.[23] At that point, the distinction between legal and equitable rights will have disappeared, and the idea that they should have different formality requirements will become wholly unsustainable.

Having concluded that the formality rules for the conferral of a right in land should certainly not differ according to whether the right in question is legal or equitable, we need to consider what shape they should actually take. As explained in § 4.2, it seems right to require that the conferral of a right in land be attended with some kind of formality. It would be possible to devise completely new kinds, but we shall confine ourselves to those currently in play, appraising the choice between a deed and writing, and the demand for completion by registration.

4.4.3 Deed or Writing?

Consider first the choice between a deed and signed writing.

A deed used to be a piece of writing 'signed, sealed and delivered' by the conferor. But since 1989,[24] the requirement of a seal has been dropped—instead, the writing must merely assert itself to be a deed—and although the requirement of 'delivery' remains, it adds little. A deed does have to be witnessed,[25] however, and this is therefore the principal contemporary difference between it and the kind of writing demanded by the law's current rule for equitable interest, which must be signed but need not be witnessed.

The involvement of witnesses does add a degree of assurance that the transaction supposedly underlying the formal documents actually took place, and perhaps that its maker was acting voluntarily. But the contrary possibilities seem not to be a significant problem in practice, and in any case, whenever the necessary writing is arranged by a solicitor, the solicitor will normally make sure it is indeed witnessed, precisely so as to provide this kind of assurance.

---

[22] For example, only legal leases (for not more than seven years) can be overriding interests under the Land Registration Act 2002 Sch 3 para 1 ... though an equitable lease accompanied by actual and apparent occupation will qualify as overriding under Sch 3 para 2. There is also a difference as regards easements: § 9.3.

[23] It is still just possible to assert that different remedies are available for the breach of a legal and an equitable right. Sometimes this difference may be warranted by the substantive nature of the specific kind of right, but often it springs solely from a historical disparity between the remedial equipment of the common law and equity courts. In the latter case, it too has become unsupportable and destined for extermination. (See further A Burrows, 'We Do This at Common Law but That in Equity' (2002) 22 *OJLS* 1.) In any event, it once again does not warrant a difference in the formality requirements for the two kinds of right.

[24] Law of Property (Miscellaneous Provisions) Act 1989 s 1.

[25] *Ibid* s 1(3)(a).

Today, then, the distinction between a deed and writing is very small indeed, and could very easily be collapsed into a single, uniform requirement. This uniform requirement might be of signed writing, which need not be witnessed but in practice very often would be.

4.4.4 Completion by Registration?

As noted in § 4.4.1, the current rule is that where the conferral of a right requires a deed (but not otherwise), it is usually also a registrable disposition, ie requires registration in order for the right to exist at all.

Is the law right to demand completion by registration in this way? Yes. In essence, the rule ensures greater visibility for the right: obviously, greater than if it were not registered at all, but also greater than if the right could come into existence without registration, and needed to be registered only before the moment of a subsequent disposition, so as to bind the disponee. If John is interested in buying my land, he will find it helpful to know the rights against it (including the fact that I am indeed its owner) not merely at the moment before it becomes his, but at a much earlier stage. In order to calculate the price he is willing to pay for the land, and more generally to decide whether it is suited to his needs at all, he needs to know about complications such as problematic rights from the moment he begins to contemplate his purchase. If he can only find out about them later, his time, and quite possibly his effort and money, could be wasted. It follows that a right should, as the registrable disposition regime has it, be made visible as part and parcel of its entry into existence.

But although it is thus essentially commendable, there are three weaknesses to this regime.

First, it applies only to conferrals of a limited set of rights, rather than to *every* conferral to which formality requirements are appropriate at all. Remember that it applies only to legal rights, such as easements, and not to equitable rights, such as restrictive covenants and trust rights. But visibility to potential disponees is just as important, and just as achievable, in respect of the latter as of the former. The regime ought to be applied to both.

Second, the registration of the conferred right is the responsibility of the conferee. So while it yields the desideratum of visibility, it does not provide the boons we expect[26] internally to the conferral process, such as clarity, and a good quality of intention on the part of the conferor. To address this deficiency, the law—rightly—requires that the conferral of the right not only be registered, but *also* done by deed (though, as we argued in § 4.4.3, writing should really be enough).

Third, the right's registration is something that happens in and through the actions of the Land Registry, some time after the transaction between the

---

[26] See § 4.2.

parties themselves: so even if there are no complications, a time-lag (known as the 'registration gap') occurs as the transaction queues in the Registry's in-tray.[27] During this time, the benefits that registration in principle delivers are not forthcoming. The continuing requirement of a deed removes part of the problem, giving the conferor and conferee themselves an immediate marker to the transaction. But the deed is far from guaranteed to make the right visible to third parties. So, to take an extreme case, having sold my land to you, I have during this period the opportunity to 'sell' it over again to John. Your right should nonetheless prevail against John;[28] certainly both you and John will have claims against me for any loss suffered; and I shall very likely have committed a crime. But at best I—aided and abetted by the registration gap—will have caused a great deal of trouble.

These three weaknesses of the current registrable disposition regime will, however, fall away with the introduction of electronic conveyancing.

4.4.5 Electronic Conveyancing

'Electronic conveyancing' means an arrangement whereby the parties—or more realistically their lawyers—effect the conferral of the right by registering it online, directly accessing the Land Registry computer files. The Land Registration Act 2002 contains enabling provisions, aimed at this system's introduction in the near future.[29]

With this system, the right's registration will be immediate, so removing the registration gap and the problems it gives rise to. It will also be under the conferor's control as much as the conferee's, so it will deliver the especial benefit of a formality rule to him, namely to safeguard the quality of his intention. Both the reasons for demanding a deed as well as registration will therefore vanish, and the law will no longer do so.[30] The 2002 Act does not

---

[27] A solution might be to rule that the conferral has no effect until registered, but that cannot be countenanced: it would smack of the bureaucratic tail wagging the substantive dog. The Land Registration Act 2002 s 27(1) nonetheless toys with the idea, making the right take effect *at law* only when the conferral is completed by registration: impliedly meaning, however, that in the meantime—from the moment it is given by deed—the right will take effect, but *in equity*, on the basis (as an 'estate contract') explained in § 5.2.4. This interim adjustment to the right's quality does not affect the right's operation as between conferor and conferee: for them, it has full immediate effect. It impacts only, and to a limited extent, on the circumstances in which the right will bind a subsequent disponee. Not being registered, it can bind only if it qualifies as an overriding interest: and some rights (leases and easements) qualify as overriding interests without more only if they are legal ... though their equitable forms will qualify if accompanied by actual and apparent occupation.

[28] Though the Land Registration Act 2002 itself does not make this clear.

[29] ss 91–95 and Sch 5. For a full description of what is envisaged, see Law Commission, *Land Registration for the Twenty-First Century—A Conveyancing Revolution* (Law Com No 271, London, 2001) paras 2.41–2.68 and pt XIII.

[30] Land Registration Act 2002 s 91(5), stating that the right's electronic registration will itself count as the deed which would otherwise be required: a roundabout way of saying that a deed will no longer be required.

itself state which rights will need to be conferred by electronic registration: they are left to be identified by future subordinate legislation ('rules').[31] But it may be anticipated that all the rights whose conferral is currently a registrable disposition will be subjected to this regime immediately it is introduced. The Act also allows for the application of the electronic regime to equitable rights,[32] and states that a right's electronic registration will count as any signed writing that would otherwise be required.[33] We noted in the previous section the inappropriateness of the existing registrable disposition regime's confinement to legal rights. Applying the new electronic registration regime to both legal and equitable rights will effect the assimilation between the two for which we argued in § 4.4.2, and will do so, as we have seen, on essentially[34] satisfactory lines.

4.5 The Special Case of Leases

We shall deal with leases in Chapter 11. The rules regarding their conferral have certain unique features, and so require a short account of their own.

4.5.1 The Formality Rules

Leases are legal rights. In accordance with the general rule stated in § 4.4.1 for legal rights, therefore, they must be conferred by deed and registration[35] ... save that:

---

[31] *Ibid* s 93(1).

[32] s 93(1) provides for the regime to be applied to 'a disposition of ... a registered estate'. At first sight, these words may seem to restrict it to the conferral of a legal right in rem (Law of Property Act 1925 s 1(4)). But the Land Registration Act 2002 uses the word 'disposition' to cover the conferral of any right in rem (this emerges from the phrasing and content of s 27(1) and (2)), so 'a disposition *of* ... a registered estate' means the conferral of any right in rem, legal or equitable, *over* a registered estate.

[33] s 91(4).

[34] In practice, it is hard not to have qualms about the robustness of the required IT arrangements, which will need to be accessible enough to guarantee operability by conveyancing lawyers up and down the country, but also secure against abuse. (My illicitly transferring your house into my name is only the most obvious of the manifold ways in which an insecure system could imaginably be misused.) See R Perry, 'E-conveyancing: Problems Ahead?' [2003] *Conv* 215. For further concerns, see R Smith, 'The Role of Registration in Modern Land Law' in L Tee (ed), *Land Law: Issues, Debates, Policy* (Cullompton, 2002) ch 2, 34–42.

[35] Law of Property Act 1925 s 52(1); Land Registration Act 2002 s 27.

— with certain exceptions, leases for up to three years do not require a deed, or even writing, but can be made orally;[36] and
— with certain different exceptions,[37] leases for up to seven years are not required to be registered.[38]

Note the way 'periodic tenancies' connect with these rules. Periodic tenancies are leases which nominally last only for say a week, or a month, or a year, but which are automatically renewed each week, month, year unless steps are taken to prevent this.[39] They thus have the potential to run on indefinitely. But for these purposes they count as lasting only for a week, month, year ... so, for less than three years (let alone seven) ... and can validly be made orally.

4.5.2 An Appraisal

The general idea behind these rules is that short leases are commonly made in a somewhat disorganised way, and so cannot appropriately be made the subject of formality requirements.

The stereotype is of a person renting residential accommodation from a private landlord, probably on a monthly or yearly basis. To be sure, the transaction will not be so markedly disorganised as some. English law recognises some rights as arising over land when the people involved might well not realise anything of the kind: rights arising under the doctrine of proprietary estoppel are of this type. Short leases are not like that: the parties to them undoubtedly realise that they are entering into a legal relationship, and can probably say a certain amount about its implications. But those making these leases commonly act without legal advice, and without a sense that this is a particularly stupid thing to do, probably assuming that the law will sort out any problems in a fair way. It is these leases' dissociation from legal advice that is the reason why they cannot aptly be subjected to a formality requirement. Without lawyers to relay it, the need for registration or a deed, perhaps even writing, would not very reliably occur to the parties.

That is the background idea, but where should the line be drawn between the leases that are to be regarded in this way, and so exempted from the

---

[36] Law of Property Act 1925 s 54(2). The exceptions are that a lease of less than three years requires a deed if it has a delayed start (is not 'taking effect in possession'), or if it is paid for by lump sum in advance or by a nominal rent (is not 'at the best rent which can be reasonably obtained without taking a fine').

[37] A delay of up to three months is allowed, but no longer; there is no stipulation as to rent; but there is an exception if the lease is 'discontinuous', ie giving the tenant a right to possess the land not every day, but only for certain days (as with a timeshare). There are further exceptions of more specialised significance.

[38] Land Registration Act 2002 s 27(2)(b).

[39] See further § 11.4.2.

formality requirements, and their more organised cousins, for which formality is rightly demanded?

A reasonable case could be made for restricting the exempt category to the very type of case just sketched, namely a periodic (up to yearly) tenancy of residential accommodation between two private individuals. Give one or both of the parties, or the nature of the premises, a business character, and it becomes more reasonable to expect that legal advice will be taken. Likewise, probably, if the tenancy is non-periodic, even if it does not exceed three years.

So even the current exemption from the deed requirement for most leases of up to three years is arguably over-generous, though perhaps that is the right side on which to err. The seven year exemption from the registration requirement, however, is hard to defend even in that way. It is best regarded as an interim arrangement. Before the Land Registration Act 2002, registration was required only of leases of 21 years and more. The 2002 Act substituted seven years. It was explained that the previous rule exempted even most business tenancies, which are commonly of up to 21 years,[40] but no positive justification for the choice of a seven year limit seems to have been offered. There is provision for reducing the limit further, however,[41] and the Law Commission has suggested that, with the advent of the electronic conveyancing regime (under which registration takes the place of a deed[42]), the line should be drawn for registration where it currently is for a deed, ie at three years.[43] That would make the law internally consistent, and, as explained above, more or less defensible.

4.5.3 Implied Periodic Tenancies

Say I purport to give you a 10 year lease of my land, but we fail to use a deed (as required for a lease above three years) or to register (as required above seven years). The upshot is that you do not acquire the lease I purported to give you. Say, however, that you go into possession of the land nonetheless, and begin to pay me rent. The law will often take you to be my tenant after all, with a periodic tenancy reflecting the basis on which you are paying rent.[44] As explained in § 4.5.1, this periodic tenancy, counting as one for less than three years, will be valid despite its lack of any formality.

---

[40] Law Commission, *Land Registration for the Twenty-First Century—A Conveyancing Revolution* (Law Com No 271, London, 2001) para 3.16.

[41] Land Registration Act 2002 s 118(1)(d).

[42] *Ibid* s 91(5): see § 4.4.5.

[43] Law Commission, *Land Registration for the Twenty-First Century—A Conveyancing Revolution* (Law Com No 271, London, 2001) para 3.17.

[44] If, for example, you pay on a monthly basis, you will be taken to have a monthly tenancy. But the presumption is that periodic payments are made on an annual basis, yielding a yearly tenancy, even if money actually changes hands at more frequent intervals.

But a periodic tenancy will be found in this way only if the parties believe themselves to be landlord and tenant. So if you and I know that our purported lease is ineffective (as may be shown, for example, by our continuing to negotiate over it), we will regard ourselves as *not* (yet) landlord and tenant. It will therefore be inappropriate to find a periodic tenancy instead, and one will not be found.[45] One should be found, however, where we are unaware of the invalidity of our original purported lease.

But while the periodic tenancy is thus used only where not incompatible with the parties' own perception of their position, it is a right imposed on a disorganised basis by the law, rather than transacted by the parties themselves. This is emphasised by the fact that the periodic tenancy found will not have the same content as the lease which I unsuccessfully purported to give you: obviously, it may be terminated earlier, and it will contain only such terms of that lease as make sense in the periodic context.[46] It serves to correct the unsatisfactory discrepancy that would otherwise exist between the parties' legal position and the way in which, in bona fide reliance on their assumed legal position, they conduct themselves in practice. In particular, if we both think our purported lease is valid, and you set yourself up in the premises on that basis, and I lend myself to this (especially by accepting your rent), it would be unfair to allow me, discovering the invalidity, to say you have no right at all to stay. The periodic tenancy that the law imposes is the minimum needed to prevent this unfairness.

So although the requirements of a deed and of registration for our purported 10 year lease are in a sense undercut by the finding of a valid periodic tenancy in its place, the undercutting is the result of the appropriate operation of a disorganised acquisition rule, and so is defensible.

---

[45] *Javad v Aqil* [1991] 1 WLR 1007 (CA).
[46] Covenants requiring the tenant to redecorate at intervals longer than a year would be dropped on this basis, for example.

Contracts to Confer

Chapter 4 described the ways in which I may confer on you a right in rem in my land, and the formality requirements relevant to those ways. But it is very common for the conferral to be something I am obliged to do under a contract I have with you. There are formality rules concerning such contracts too. This chapter looks at these rules. It looks also at an additional matter: a rule whereby a valid contract to confer a right can operate as a quasi-conferral of that right.

5.1 Pre-conferment Contracts

When you set out to buy a house, and have decided that you would like to buy mine, the ordinary sequence of events is this.

First, you and I agree on the sale orally, whether in person or through an estate agent. So far as the general law of contract goes, nothing more is needed to make a binding contract. But where the contract's subject-matter is land,[1] an oral contract will not be valid: the contract must be in writing, and signed by both of us (or by agents acting on our behalf).[2] At the oral agreement stage, then, you and I may regard ourselves as morally committed,[3] but no legal obligation will have arisen. The 'For Sale' board

---

[1] That is, it is 'a contract for the sale or other disposition of an interest in land': Law of Property (Miscellaneous Provisions) Act 1989 s 2(1).

[2] *Ibid* s 2.

[3] Or we may not. This is the point at which, in a rising market, 'gazumping' may occur: ie the seller, having accepted an offer from one buyer, now accepts a better offer from a second buyer—leaving the first buyer disappointed, or obliged to enter into a bidding war. Unless there is something unusual in the circumstances, there is nothing illegal about this practice.

outside my house will be changed to read 'Sold', but there will be the additional words 'Subject to Contract', meaning that we still await the making of a legally binding, ie written, agreement.

You and I now instruct our solicitors to prepare the necessary written contract. Our solicitors will commonly correspond with each other, but in order that these letters do not become the written contract before everyone and everything is ready, they too will contain the words 'subject to contract', which are recognised as preventing the letters from having contractual effect.[4] Eventually, everything will be settled, and the solicitors will have you and me sign the actual contract documents.

At this point, we are legally committed to the agreed sale; the 'Subject to Contract' rider should come off the board, though estate agents often do not get round to it. All that now remains is the stage known as 'completion', which means the actual transfer of the house from me to you (this is when you get the keys), and your payment of the price to me.[5] Completion is the fulfilment—performance—by each of us of the obligations which we undertook in the contract. It includes my conferring the ownership of the house on you, which is a transaction of the sort dealt with in the previous chapter. As explained there, to make it effective, I have to use a deed, and you have to register yourself as the new owner.[6]

That is the sequence of events leading up to the sale of a freehold, but essentially the same process generally occurs whenever someone buys any kind of right in another's land. If you want a right of way across my yard, for example, you will normally first agree on it with me orally; then have solicitors create an appropriate written contract; then proceed, with me, to the

---

[4] *Tiverton Estates Ltd v Wearwell Ltd* [1975] Ch 146 (CA). This decision disapproved another (*Law v Jones* [1974] Ch 112 (CA)) which had held that written memoranda 'subject to contract' could be turned into a binding contact by an oral agreement to that effect. The current, more recent, version of the formality requirement would itself make that reasoning impossible, as it requires the contract to be '*made* in writing': Law of Property (Miscellaneous Provisions) Act 1989 s 2(1). The oral agreement, if acted upon, might however be the basis of a claim in proprietary estoppel (as in *Waltons Stores (Interstate) Ltd v Maher* (1988) 164 CLR 387 (High Court of Australia)); but it is controversial whether that doctrine can be used to circumvent the formality requirements for contracts in this way: see § 7.4.3.

[5] Often you will have raised part of the price by way of mortgage. Mortgages are explained in Ch 12. Briefly, what technically happens is that you are loaned the money in question by bank A; you use this money to pay me; and you simultaneously give bank A a right over your new house, entitling it to repossess the house from you if you fail to keep up your repayments of the loan. But although in theory the loan is to you and the payment to me, in practice bank A will forward the money to your solicitor, who will pay it to my solicitor, who will use it to pay off the remainder of the mortgage I currently have on the house in question with bank B. Simultaneously, my solicitor will receive the new loan I have arranged with bank C, enabling me to pay for the new house I have contracted to buy from John: and so on.

[6] The process can evidently take some time. It can also be precarious, with the parties breaking away for all sorts of reasons. It is sometimes said that the former spawns the latter, and various reforms aimed at speeding matters up have been made or advocated. It seems likely, however, that the problem (if it is a problem) is deeper-rooted.

performance of this contract, by paying me the agreed price while I grant you the right of way, using a deed, and you register yourself as now having it.

The rule, then, is that a contract for the conferral of a right in land must usually[7] be made in writing, and signed by each of its parties, or agents on their behalf.[8] This formality requirement seems justified, as ensuring that the parties are helped—they are unlikely to want it otherwise—to take care over what is likely to be a very major (valuable, complicated, implication-laden) transaction for them, and that the transaction is given clarity for the benefit of others who may have to engage with its impact (other members of the 'chain', for example). Of itself, however, a requirement merely of signed writing does not give the transaction any external visibility, so outsiders who might be affected by it are not alerted. Under the current law, it is possible to register the effect of the contract with the Land Registry,[9] but this is not normally done, it presumably being felt that the effort is not worthwhile, given that the completion of the transaction, which must be registered (§ 4.4.1), should follow soon after. But there is a proposal to include the contract stage in the electronic conveyancing regime.[10] Then, the contract will have to be made (no longer by signed writing but) in the form of an electronic document, with electronic signatures, via the Land Registry website. Like the application of the regime to the completion stage, this will not only preserve the benefits of the current formality rule, but—assuming it works well—also give the contract the visibility that the current rule cannot deliver.

---

[7] One exception is a contract for a lease of up to three years: Law of Property (Miscellaneous Provisions) Act 1989 s 2(5)(a). This is justified on the same basis that formality is not required for the *conferral* of such a lease: § 4.5. Another exception is a contract made at a public auction: s 2(5)(b). It is in the very nature of an auction that the contract is made orally, and the stylised and public nature of the event is a kind of formality in itself, obviating the mischiefs that may otherwise beset oral contracts: participants should be fully focused on the implications of what they are doing, and there should be plenty of witnesses to what is agreed.

[8] Law of Property (Miscellaneous Provisions) Act 1989 s 2.

[9] As explained in § 5.2, the contract normally generates a right known as an 'estate contract', which is essentially an equitable anticipation of the right contracted to be conferred, and thus itself a right in rem, and capable of registration as such.

[10] Law Commission, *Land Registration for the Twenty-First Century—A Conveyancing Revolution* (Law Com No 271, London, 2001) para 2.54. (Para 2.52 depicts the Registry as facilitating the transaction more generally—eg by keeping the various members of a chain informed of each other's progress towards completion—but time will tell whether this aspiration is realistic.)

5.2 Estate Contracts

5.2.1 The Doctrine of Conversion

Say I validly (so, in writing) contract with you to confer on you a right in rem over land which I own. As explained in § 5.1, we are then supposed to perform ('complete') this contract by my actually conferring the right on you, using whatever formality (deed, registration) is required for this step.

In the meantime, our positions might be expected to be governed simply by the law of contract. So if, for example, I refuse to perform after all, you could claim an order for specific performance obliging me to do so, but you would still not actually acquire the promised right until I comply with this order and confer it on you. But this is not the case. Instead, the law applies a notion called the 'equitable doctrine of conversion', whereby 'equity looks upon as done that which ought to be done'. That is to say, we each *automatically* move into more or less the position we would occupy if we had already completed the contract: so you are regarded as acquiring the right as soon as the contract is made, and without me having actually to confer it at all.[11] Actual conferral remains a good idea and normally occurs, however, because (as we shall see in § 5.2.2) the right yielded by this automatic effect is only *more or less* the same as that which we contracted for: conferral is needed to put the finishing touches.

So say you and I have a contract obliging me to confer on you, and you to accept from me, a 10 year lease. Given this contract, actually conferring the lease (by deed and registration) is something that 'ought to be done'. Because of conversion, equity will look upon it as already done. That is, in the eyes of equity, I have already made myself your landlord, and you my tenant, under a 10 year lease.

The set of rights you acquire under this doctrine is known as an 'estate contract'. The term sounds most appropriate in the case of the conferral of a freehold or lease, but extends also to conferrals of other rights, such as easements and mortgages. In the case of a lease, there is an alternative term, having the same meaning: an 'agreement for a lease'.

In the abstract, the doctrine of conversion is rather baffling: *why* should equity look upon as done that which ought to be done?[12] But for all that

---

[11] For discussion of a recent move away from this position by the Australian courts, see R Chambers, 'The Importance of Specific Performance' in S Degeling and J Edelman (eds), *Equity in Commercial Law* (Pyrmont, NSW, 2005) ch17.

[12] There is in fact an answer, but it is obsolete. The effect that we call conversion was the reasoning by which, in the 15th century, the law began to think that a putative buyer of land could sue a seller for non-performance of the agreement: on the footing that the agreement made

estate contracts arise in this mysterious way, they are functionally valuable. They order our rights in the potentially problematic transition period (especially in the freehold case) between contract and completion, providing default rules on such matters as which of us must insure the property and which of us shall receive any profits it generates.[13]

5.2.2 The Nature of Estate Contracts

Your having an estate contract does not mean that you *actually have* the 10 year lease (or whatever) that we contracted for: that was a 10 year lease *recognised by the common law*. What you have is the position of *being treated by equity as* having that lease. This is usually translated into 'What you have is a 10 year *equitable* lease',[14] though as will be seen in a moment, on one view that slightly overstates the nature of your rights. What, then, is the difference between your having the intended (common law) lease or other right, and having instead this equitable version of it? Not a great deal, but enough to notice.

As we saw in § 1.5, where the common law and equity give conflicting readings of a situation, the equitable reading takes precedence. So when the common law says that you do not have a 10 year lease, but equity says you do, the bottom line is that you do. This is the basis on which it was said, a moment ago, that the difference between your having the original purported common law lease, and having instead this equitable version of it, is not great. As was also said a moment ago, however, a perceptible difference does remain.

This is partly because some statutory rules are expressed in terms which limit the rule's application to the relevant common law right, excluding its equitable counterpart.[15] More fundamentally, it is because equity itself may not regard you as having the relevant right (eg the 10 year lease) in absolutely every case where we have a valid contract for its conferral. It may regard you

---

the land in some sense immediately the buyer's. (See S Gardner, 'Equity, Estate Contracts and the Judicature Acts: *Walsh v Lonsdale* Revisited' (1987) 7 *OJLS* 60, 74–77.) Nowadays, of course, we allow the buyer to sue (for breach of contract) simply on the basis of the agreement itself.

[13] For details, see A Oakley, *Constructive Trusts* (3rd edn, London, 1997) ch 6.

[14] Or, as the case may be, 'equitable easement', 'equitable mortgage', etc. And where freehold ownership is involved, therefore, 'equitable ownership'. (If I am the legal owner of land but you are its equitable owner, I necessarily hold it on trust for you. So in this case, the freehold estate contract can also be described as a trust: *Shaw v Foster* (1872) LR 5 HL 321, 338 (HL); *Lysaght v Edwards* (1876) 2 Ch D 499, 506 (Ch D). But to say merely that it is a trust is to omit reference to some important aspects of it. See Oakley, *ibid.*)

[15] Especially the Law of Property Act 1925 s 62, regarding the implied grant of an easement (see *Borman v Griffith* [1930] 1 Ch 493 (Ch D)); and the Land Registration Act 2002 Sch 3 para 1, regarding a lease's operation as an overriding interest (see *City Permanent Building Society v Miller* [1952] Ch 840 (CA), considering the corresponding, and similarly worded, provision of the Land Registration Act 1925, s 70(1)(k)).

as having the 10 year lease only if the contract is not only valid, *but also capable of specific performance.* If this is not the case, equity may not regard you as having the lease after all.[16] Purists therefore assert that your right does not amount to an 'equitable *lease*' at all.[17] That expression would suggest a straightforward anticipation of the legal lease which was due to be conferred on you, but the effect of requiring the contract to be not only valid but also specifically enforceable is to leave your right a little short of that.

5.2.3 The Specific Enforceability Requirement

The demand is that, for conversion to occur, the contract must be one of which a court would grant specific performance, as between the parties to the dispute that has arisen, and in the current circumstances.

It must immediately be said that this will usually be the case, so equity will usually regard you as having the right. In particular, specific performance is the ordinary remedy associated with contracts to grant a right in land. It will be available in such a case unless there is some reason why not.[18]

Such a reason might be, however, that you have breached one of the terms of the purported lease: this would disable you from claiming specific performance against me ('he who comes to equity must come with clean hands', and yours would not be), and so from relying on conversion against me.[19] Though not vice versa: if *I* wanted to rely on an equitable lease against *you*, I should be able to do so, for your breach should not prevent me from claiming specific performance against you.

But notice that the account in § 5.2.2 says only that the unavailability of specific performance *may* lead equity not to regard you as having the right. That is because there is uncertainty whether such a requirement really exists, or whether equity will treat you as having the relevant right, full stop, as soon as a valid contract for its grant exists between us.

---

[16] In the case of a lease, you may then be able to fall back on a (common law) periodic tenancy, as explained in § 4.5.3. If the purported grant was of some other type of right, eg a freehold or mortgage or easement, you may be left only with an action for breach of contract. Depending on the surrounding facts, however, a disorganised acquisition doctrine such as proprietary estoppel (Ch 7) may be relevant.

[17] *Swain v Ayres* (1888) 21 QBD 289, 295 (CA).

[18] For discussion of a recent move away from this position by the Canadian courts, see R Chambers, 'The Importance of Specific Performance' in S Degeling and J Edelman (eds), *Equity in Commercial Law* (Pyrmont, NSW, 2005) ch 17.

[19] *Coatsworth v Johnson* (1886) 54 LT 520 (CA). It might be asked whether your inability to claim specific performance, and so rely on an equitable lease, makes any difference to the bottom line: even if you had been able to rely on the equitable lease, would not your breach have meant you lost ('forfeited') it? Not necessarily: the rules about forfeiture are complex (see § 11.5.2), but they do give tenants quite a lot of leeway before the whole lease is lost in the way that it is if your breach simply prevents you claiming specific performance.

There are certainly some well-known judicial statements saying that the specific enforceability condition is part of the law,[20] and few asserting that it is not.[21] But the alleged condition is often tacitly ignored, in that the law takes positions irreconcilable with it.[22] These include the fact that equitable leases (and other types of estate contract) are in rem at all. Take the scenario where I contract to grant you a 10 year lease. If I then transfer my freehold to John, can John be bound by your right? Not if you have to be able to claim specific performance of our contract against him, for he is not a party to it.[23] But it is quite clear that the law is to the contrary: your right is in rem, ie can bind John (and will do so if you have registered it or are in actual and apparent occupation of the land). This is explicable only on the basis that the right arises as an equitable lease *at the outset*: its nature as a lease makes it in rem (for leases are in rem), and thus capable of binding John when the land in question is later transferred to him.[24]

5.2.4 'Discovered' Contracts

So far, we have supposed the contract from which the estate contract arises to be a real one: the contract to confer a right that normally precedes the actual conferral. But there is another possibility.

As explained in § 5.1, the conferral of the right commonly represents the completion of a preceding contract. If the conferral is made using the required formalities, it will take effect; otherwise, the conversion of the preceding contract will normally give you an estate contract, in the way described in § 5.2.1. But sometimes the conferral will not be preceded by any contract: the conferral itself will represent the totality of the transaction between us. That is often the case with leases, in particular: we may omit the contract stage (at any rate, the written contract stage) and instead declare ourselves there and then to be giving and taking the lease itself. Again, if the conferral is made using the required formalities, it will take effect; but if not, on the face of it there in this case appears to be no contract to be converted so as to produce an estate contract.

---

[20] See eg *Coatsworth v Johnson, ibid*; *Swain v Ayres* (1888) 21 QBD 289, 295 (CA); *Manchester Brewery Co v Coombs* [1901] 2 Ch 608, 617 (Ch D).

[21] Perhaps the only explicit statement unequivocally to this effect (as opposed to loose talk where greater precision was unnecessary) is by Denning LJ in *Boyer v Warbey* [1953] 1 QB 234, 245 (CA).

[22] See further S Gardner, 'Equity, Estate Contracts and the Judicature Acts: *Walsh v Lonsdale* Revisited' (1987) 7 *OJLS* 60.

[23] This was recognised in *Purchase v Lichfield Brewery Co* [1915] 1 KB 184 (KBD), holding that the obligations in an equitable lease cannot therefore be enforced against an assignee from one of its original parties.

[24] Note too how the Landlord and Tenant (Covenants) Act 1995 s 28(1), governing some central aspects of the law of leases, expressly defines 'tenancy' as including 'an agreement for a tenancy', ie an equitable lease. In the relevant respect, this makes an equitable lease operate in the same way as a legal lease.

The law, however, supposes otherwise. In such a case it will after all 'discover' (the discovery is by definition fictitious) in the failed conferral a contract to make the conferral.[25] Of course, to be of further help, this contract must itself be valid. So it—that is, the purported conferral in which it is 'discovered'—must have the formality necessary to contracts for the conferment of rights in land, ie (as explained in § 5.1) be in writing, signed by each of us.[26] But given such validity, the contract can be sued upon for damages, or for specific performance, ordering the conferral actually to be made, properly. And it will also be the subject of conversion, so as immediately to create an estate contract over the land, corresponding to the right with whose actual conferral, failing for want of formality, we began.

So, for example, if I purport to confer on you a legal lease for 10 years, but we do not use a deed or register the lease, the purported conferral will fail as such but will be treated as a contract to confer. And, so long as the purported conferral is in writing,[27] this contract will be converted so as to give you an 'equitable lease' on the same terms. This combination of conversion with the 'discovery' of the required contract in a failed conferral is known as 'the doctrine in *Walsh v Lonsdale*'.[28]

5.2.5 Estate Contracts as Undercutting Legal Formality Requirements

To sum up what we have learned about estate contracts. The relevant situation is one in which a legal conferral has not taken place, for want of a deed or (where relevant) registration. This may be the case either where the transaction has not yet reached the stage requiring a deed or registration at all; or where it has reached that stage, but the required deed has not been used, or the required registration has not occurred. So long as there is an underlying contract (genuine or 'discovered') in writing, an equitable right—an estate contract—will arise; and although its effect will not be quite the same as that of the intended legal right, it will be similar.

As we saw in § 5.2.1, estate contracts are functionally valuable devices, for the structure they give to the parties' rights in the transition period between contract and completion. But this role is more or less confined to the case where the contract in question is a genuine one, and the parties are proceeding to a proper completion. If the parties do not proceed to a proper completion, which will almost certainly be the case where the required

---

[25] *Parker v Taswell* (1858) 2 De G & J 559 (Ch).

[26] Law of Property (Miscellaneous Provisions) Act 1989 s 2.

[27] If it is merely oral, it may nonetheless ground the finding of a periodic tenancy, as explained in § 4.5.3.

[28] (1882) 21 Ch D 9 (CA). This decision involved a lease. Other decisions, on the same lines, apply to further kinds of right whose conferral requires a deed, and nowadays also registration: eg *Shaw v Foster* (1872) LR 5 HL 321 (HL) (freehold); *McManus v Cooke* (1887) 35 Ch D 681 (Ch D) (easement); *Mason v Clarke* [1955] AC 778 (HL) (profit à prendre); *Ex parte Wright* (1812) 19 Ves 255 (Ch) (mortgage).

contract is 'discovered' in the manner explained in § 5.2.4, estate contracts instead operate (to the large extent that the equitable right does replicate the intended legal right) in lieu of the right purportedly conferred. They thus undercut the formality requirements that the conferral does not meet, making it the law's bottom line that the right's conferral requires only writing, not a deed and (where relevant) registration, after all.

Is this undercutting effect acceptable? It might be if the generation of estate contracts were a disorganised mode of creating rights, for then it would rightly proceed without reference to the formality rules that would otherwise apply. It is fair to regard the generation of an estate contract as disorganised in the sense that the parties do not always intend specifically this right, as opposed to the legal right whose conferral has not (yet) occurred. But estate contracts arise only within the context of an organised transaction for the conferral of a legal right, and they operate substantially to effectuate that conferral. The effect must therefore count as an essentially organised one. In principle, therefore, the law ought to demand formality in respect of it. Indeed, it does so, by requiring the contract from which they arise to be in writing. It ought also, however, to make that formality no less than it properly demands for the conferral of the legal right itself, as discussed in Chapter 4.

'Properly' is important, however. Consider first the contrast between the requirement of writing for the estate contract, and that of a deed for the conferral. Although the undercutting is unacceptable, it is the demand for a deed that is misplaced. As was argued in § 4.4.3, there is insufficient justification for the respects in which a deed requires more than writing. Writing ought therefore to be enough for both the estate contract and the grant.

Consider then the contrast between the requirement of writing for the estate contract, and that of registration (under the registrable disposition regime) for the conferral. Again, the undercutting is unjustified in principle. But this time, it is the estate contract's lack of a registration requirement that is unsatisfactory. As was argued in § 4.4.4, a requirement of registration is justified because it makes the right visible to prospective disponees of the land to which it relates, enabling them not to waste time and resources exploring transactions in which, discovering the full picture, they lose interest. From this point of view, writing alone—which does not deliver such visibility—is not enough. Registration should in principle be required for estate contracts just as much as for conferrals.

There are practical reasons why such a rule could not be expected under the land registration arrangements that have existed hitherto. Registration is too sluggish a process to be sensibly required in respect of transitory rights, which estate contracts arising from genuine contracts (though not 'discovered' ones) are: they exist only until the performance of the contract by the conferral proper. But this problem will fall away when electronic conveyancing comes into operation, with its feature that registration will take place simultaneously with—indeed, as a very component of—the transaction itself.

As noted in § 5.1, the enabling legislation for electronic conveyancing[29] clearly envisages that contracts for the conferral of rights in land will need to be made via the register, just as the conferral itself will. Estate contracts will continue to arise from the contract, and this is all to the good, for the sake of the valuable transitional effects that we have noted. But because the formality requirements for estate contracts will be aligned with those for conferral, the latter will no longer be undercut by the arising of estate contracts. Many centuries of dysfunction will have come to an end.

---

[29] Land Registration Act 2002 s 93(2).

Adverse Possession and Prescription

6.1 Disorganised Acquisition

In Chapters 4 and 5, we focused on the possibility of your acquiring a right in my land for the reason that I intend you to, and set out to confer it on you. We are calling acquisition in this way 'organised'. But at the outset,[1] we noted that this is not the only way in which you may acquire a right in my land. Factors of other kinds may equally mean that you ought to have such a right. In fact the law has a number of rules giving you a right in this alternative—what we are calling 'disorganised'—way. This chapter looks at some of these rules; Chapters 7 and 8 look at some others.

6.1.1 'Factors of Other Kinds'

When it is said, above, that 'factors of other kinds' may mean that you ought to have a right in my land, what might these factors be?

There is certainly no pre-ordained template for them. But, on the plane of principle, nor is there simply a blank page on which any idea may be written as validly as any other. To merit acceptance, and implementation by the law, a possible factor needs a satisfactory moral or political justification. Recognising this does not, of course, constrain the answer very tightly, for there is room for debate over what moral and political arguments are satisfactory. This book will not attempt to engage with that issue. It will confine itself to identifying some of the main arguments reflected in English law, and explaining the rules in which they are reflected.

---

[1] § 4.1.

Some useful basic mapping can be done. First, there is a distinction between arguments about justice and those about other forms of good, often utility. Many rules exist, or have existed, based on considerations of the latter kind. The law on compulsory purchase is a major example. This permits land to be acquired by bodies of various kinds, to allow them to pursue purposes regarded by Parliament (which creates the facility) as of value to the nation. Thus, land can be compulsorily purchased to create new roads: this being thought valuable for such ends as giving citizens more freedom to get about, and lubricating trade.

Rules aimed at doing justice work to correct unfairness between individuals (or groups). The unfairness may be an embedded one: that is, one which was not, or not at all directly, the result of events for which an identifiable person is responsible. In this case, the unfairness will lie simply in the fact that two people ought (there is a lot of baggage beneath this 'ought', of course) to enjoy equivalent or in some other way comparable advantages, but do not. A rule may then be made aimed at delivering such equivalence or comparability. A project of this kind is said to promote 'distributive justice'. English law's taxation rules are partly of this kind: although the reason for raising the money at all is generally a utilitarian one (to finance the NHS, etc), the incidence of the liability to pay varies with wealth, identifying and seeking to redress an unfairness in the way this is distributed.

But such a broad mission cannot be pursued between two parties at a time, as in the sort of litigation we are accustomed to. If distributive justice is to be done in such litigation, it must be on the basis that the parties' relationship requires equality (or some other goal) *specifically between the two of them*. So, when a couple are divorced, and the judge is called upon to make a 'fair'[2] redistribution of their property between them,[3] the approach is to minimise the material impact of the divorce on any children, to secure the parties' 'reasonable requirements', and to divide any remaining assets equally between them.[4] The theory underlying these operations seems to be that the parties owe each other and their children the level of wealth in question, by virtue of their marriage and their status as parents. I might be ordered to transfer my house, or a share in it, to you on this basis.

Or the unfairness may have come about as a result of events for which an identifiable person (or group) is responsible. Then, achieving justice—

---

[2] *White v White* [2001] AC 596, 599 (HL).

[3] Matrimonial Causes Act 1973 ss 24, 25. These provisions require the judge 'to have regard to all the circumstances', and list some which are not to be overlooked. The majority of these consist in the problems that the divorce may cause for the parties' future standard of living. So although it expresses no particular goal, the statute does seem to hint that the parties' assets should be reallocated so as to secure their future material well-being in some way.

[4] *White v White* [2001] AC 596 (HL); *Miller v Miller, McFarlane v McFarlane* [2006] 2 AC 618 (HL).

redressing the unfairness—will consist in transferring goods[5] from the person (or group) responsible to the person (or group) whose position has suffered through those events. Adjustments of this kind pursue 'corrective justice'.[6] An example of corrective justice is the relief given for torts or breaches of contract. Rights in land are conferred on this type of basis under the doctrine of proprietary estoppel. Say you believe that you have, or are going to have, a right in my land, and I am in some way responsible for that belief, most notably because I told you so. Then you act (perhaps you spend some money) in reasonable reliance on your belief, and suffer a detriment as a result. Because I am responsible for your belief, I am also responsible for this detriment you have suffered. There is thus an unfairness between us. The law may correct this unfairness by conferring on you a right in my land.[7]

So these three—utility, distributive justice and corrective justice—are the main bases on which the law may confer on you a right in my land for reasons other than the fact that I intended you to have such a right. In this and the following two chapters, we shall look at a collection of doctrines which, between them, exhibit all three of these bases. These doctrines are adverse possession; prescription; proprietary estoppel; and two doctrines said to give rise to constructive trusts. They are selected for coverage here simply because they commonly feature in the syllabus of the subject called land law, at which this book is directed. There is no essential difference between them and the areas of compulsory purchase and allocation of assets upon divorce, referred to above as instances of the general phenomenon at which this chapter is aimed. These latter areas of law are not discussed further here simply because they are not normally included in the land law syllabus.

6.1.2 Disorganised Acquisition and Formality

In Chapters 4 and 5, we saw how, if a right in rem over land is to be acquired in an organised way, its conferral must normally be effected using some

---

[5] Generally property (especially money, but also for example rights in land), but sometimes alternatively liberty (as with imprisonment) or bodily well-being (as where, if I am responsible for injuring you, you are permitted to injure me in return). At first sight, a regime of this alternative kind seems not to *transfer* anything, but that may be an insensitive appreciation. Where you and I exist in close proximity, or where I have harmed the overall well-being of society (a group), levelling my position down may be a way of restoring fairness between us.

[6] The division of justice-based claims between 'distributive' and 'corrective' in this way was first suggested by Aristotle. A considerable literature has grown up discussing what exactly Aristotle meant by 'corrective'; in particular, whether he wished to say that non-distributive claims are justifiable only in certain circumstances, narrower than we might otherwise think. In this book, the word 'corrective' is used simply to refer to all non-distributive claims, the question of their justifiability to be addressed independently of Aristotle's views.

[7] For proprietary estoppel, see Ch 7. As we shall see there (§ 7.4), however, this doctrine is a protean one, arguably representing more than one corrective project, and indeed a distributive one.

degree of formality (writing, deed, registration). What happens in this respect if such a right is to be acquired in a disorganised way?

As we saw in § 4.2, the goals of a formality requirement include improving the quality of the intention behind its conferral. This is irrelevant to the disorganised generation of a right, as this does not rest on intention. But the other goals we discussed were promoting certainty that the right has been acquired at all, clarity as to its details, and its visibility to the outside world. These goals are in principle no less important if the right arises in a disorganised than in an organised way. In particular, being in rem, the right is no less capable of binding disponees, so those contemplating a deal involving the land will certainly be helped if they can easily find out where they stand regarding it.

So there is a case for saying that rights arising in disorganised ways should be given some kind of formal mark. But in general, the law does not take this position. It allows them to arise quite informally, and this is indeed the more appropriate answer. If a formality requirement were imposed in the disorganised sector, it would hardly ever be complied with. Since, by definition, a disorganised right arises against the (hitherto) owner of the land for reasons other than his wanting it to, one certainly could not rely on him to register it. Nor, however, could one rely on the person acquiring the right, for in the nature of disorganised acquisition, he might well not even realise that he is acquiring it; and even if he does, he will not have the help of a lawyer, and so access to information about the formality rule. (If it were otherwise, the story would not have been a disorganised one in the first place.) So if formality were required, the law's very object in generating the right would normally be immediately frustrated by the invalidity attendant upon the predictable failure to comply with that requirement.

Visibility remains an issue, of course. Although a right in rem arising in a disorganised way can be registered (not as a pre-condition to its existence but) in order actually to bind a disponee, it commonly will not be, for the reason just discussed: the person holding it will often neither personally know that the right exists or can be registered, nor have reason to discover this via a lawyer. Rightly, therefore,[8] its route to binding a disponee will normally be as an overriding interest. But as we found in § 2.2.3, the law permits it to operate as an overriding interest only where, in its own nature, it is reasonably visible.

One could get past the difficulty preoccupying us, and require formality for disorganised rights after all, by arranging for them to arise only when declared to do so by an official organ, such as a court. (The court would obviously know to comply with a formality rule, such as a demand to register the right.) Something of this kind is in fact now the case where a right in

---

[8] § 2.2.2.

registered land arises by adverse possession (§ 6.2): in this case, the right is only clinched through an alteration of the register, by the Land Registry.[9] It is also the case where the property of former spouses or civil partners is reallocated under the Matrimonial Causes Act 1973. It is not the case,[10] but on one view should be, where a right arises under the doctrine of proprietary estoppel.[11]

The argument against such an approach—that is, in favour of allowing the right to arise from the key facts themselves, rather than requiring an official order—is that the latter seems to give the people concerned more autonomy (treating their rights and obligations as in essence theirs, to be recognised rather than conferred by the court). But taking the latter position can be counter-indicated if the rule under which the right arises needs to take account of a complex set of factors, such that its result in a given case can only be satisfactorily elicited by the exercise of a discretion by a judge ... or, even without this complication, if the desirability of formality is thought too important to allow the right to arise without an official order.

6.2 Adverse Possession

You can acquire the freehold ownership of my land[12] via the doctrine of 'adverse possession'.[13] This doctrine has two elements. The first is that you must take adverse possession of the land. This is considered in § 6.2.1. Before 2002 (and still today, in the case of unregistered land), the second was that you had to remain in adverse possession for 12 years. Since the Land Registration Act 2002, however, the second has become (so far as registered land is concerned)—roughly speaking—that your adverse possession must have lasted for 10 years, and must either be followed by certain proofs of my having abandoned the land, or have occurred on land adjoining our common boundary, with you reasonably believing it to be yours throughout. We shall explore this second element in § 6.2.2.

---

[9] Land Registration Act 2002 Sch 6 paras 1–9.

[10] *Ibid* s 116(a).

[11] See § 7.5.1.

[12] Or a lease over it, if that is the interest I myself have. Certain complications arise in this case, which are not detailed in this book.

[13] See further A Clarke, 'Use, Time, and Entitlement' (2004) 57 *CLP* 238; A Goymour, 'The Acquisition of Rights in Property by the Effluxion of Time' in E Cooke (ed), *Modern Studies in Property Law, Volume 4* (Oxford, 2007) ch 8.

6.2.1 The First Element: 'Taking Adverse Possession'

To acquire an interest by adverse possession, then, the first thing you have to show is that you have taken adverse possession of the land in question. What counts as 'taking adverse possession'?

'Possession' is essentially the set of things that an owner has the right to do with the land.[14] These can be instanced, but cannot be exhaustively enumerated, for the set is open-ended: it comprises everything that is physically possible, minus those things that are prohibited.

The idea of 'taking' possession means *behaving as though* you have this set of rights.[15] This has two aspects.

The first is that you must have the mindset known as *'animus possidendi'*, ie intention to possess. That is, you must envisage yourself doing, not necessarily all the things an owner might do (obviously), but as many of them as you may fancy, rather than a limited class of them.[16]

So in principle, you should need to envisage excluding anyone unwelcome, including me, and living in the land gratis; these being two of the things an owner can do. But it has also been ruled that you can have *animus possidendi* even though you realise and concede my ownership, and, therefore, even though you concede the possibility of not excluding me, or of needing to pay me rent in order to stay.[17] It is hard to see how this ruling can co-exist with the fundamental idea of *animus possidendi*. The courts have fudged the difficulty. They have decided that you have animus possidendi so long as you reckon to exclude me 'so far as is reasonably practicable and so far as the processes of the law will allow',[18] ie so far as you can get away with it. Likewise as regards rent: you have *animus possidendi*, despite a mere mental

---

[14] The Latin root of 'possession' means something like 'having power over', and one judicial rendition speaks (losing something of the true amplitude?) of the exercise of 'custody and control': *JA Pye (Oxford) Ltd v Graham* [2003] 1 AC 347, [40] (HL). The most illuminating paraphrase is perhaps 'dealing with the land in question as an occupying owner might have been expected to deal with it': *Powell v McFarlane* (1977) 38 P & CR 452, 471 (Ch D), approved in *JA Pye (Oxford) Ltd v Graham* at [41].

[15] 'Using the land in the way one would expect [you] to use it if [you] were the true owner': *JA Pye (Oxford) Ltd v Graham, ibid* [71].

[16] That is, you must have 'an intention to occupy and use the land as [your] own': *JA Pye (Oxford) Ltd v Graham, ibid*. A claim to adverse possession failed on this ground in *Powell v McFarlane* (1977) 38 P & CR 452 (Ch D), where the claimant, aged 14 at the relevant time, used the land to graze his cow: especially given his age, he probably did not aspire to a broader range of use.

[17] *JA Pye (Oxford) Ltd v Graham, ibid* [42]–[43]. Regarding an argument for the contrary view, see L Tee, 'Adverse Possession and the Intention to Possess' [2000] *Conv* 113; O Radley-Gardner and C Harpum, 'Adverse Possession and the Intention to Possess—A Reply' [2001] *Conv* 155; and L Tee, 'Adverse Possession and the Intention to Possess—A Rejoinder' [2002] *Conv* 50. This argument would narrow the scope of adverse possession substantially. As we shall see in § 6.2.2, it is now reflected in the only case where, in registered land since 2002, you can rely on your adverse possession alone, rather than your adverse possession together with my failure to object.

[18] *Powell v McFarlane* (1977) 38 P & CR 452, 472 (Ch D), approved in *JA Pye (Oxford) Ltd v Graham* [2003] 1 AC 347, [43] (HL).

preparedness to pay, so long as you do not actually offer to do so.[19] The distinctions being made here are clearly unstable, so will be difficult to apply in practice, making the law unpredictable in its effect.

Then, as the second aspect of taking possession, you must put your *animus possidendi* into effect. Since (as explained above) the set of an owner's rights is open-ended, you necessarily can be found to have done so even though your actual deeds fall short of the entire set. Something fairly substantial is nonetheless demanded, presumably in that it would be unsafe to extrapolate too narrow a base of behaviour to the required conclusion that you rule out nothing. So the question is whether you are 'dealing with the land in question as an occupying owner might have been expected to deal with it',[20] ie whether you are making reasonably full use of the particular piece of land concerned. You can take possession of a house by living in it; of a garden by tending it; of an arable field by ploughing it; and so on.[21] But your use of the land need not match the use to which I previously put it, or to which someone else might put it.[22] Judgments on this issue are often impressionistic. This, combining with the difficulties over *animus possidendi*, leaves the law in this area highly discretionary.

Finally, you must take—and retain—possession in an 'adverse' manner. There are two aspects to this too.[23] First, you must be a trespasser: your possession cannot be adverse if I consent to it, permit it.[24] (So there is no

---

[19] *JA Pye (Oxford) Ltd v Graham, ibid* [46]; cf *Pavledes v Ryesbridge Properties Ltd* (1989) 58 P & CR 459 (Ch D). For unregistered land, there was a statutory manifestation of this rule in the Limitation Act 1980 s 29. In a further fudge of the principle at stake, s 29 could however be invoked only if you put your acknowledgement in writing: s 30.

[20] *Powell v McFarlane* (1977) 38 P & CR 452, 471 (Ch D), approved in *JA Pye (Oxford) Ltd v Graham, ibid* [41].

[21] *Powell v McFarlane, ibid.* Fencing the land in, or locking its gates, is sometimes treated as conclusive (see eg *Seddon v Smith* (1877) 36 LT 168, 169 (CA)), but this seems implausible, if you do nothing further.

[22] So in *Buckinghamshire County Council v Moran* [1990] Ch 623 (CA), where the council left the land alone, intending to use it for road improvements, the defendant took possession by using it as a garden. But in *Boosey v Davis* (1988) 55 P & CR 83 (CA), where the land in question had development potential, the grazing of goats on it was held to be too limited to amount to taking possession of it.

[23] There is no further requirement that you forcibly evict me—*JA Pye (Oxford) Ltd v Graham* [2003] 1 AC 347, [35]–[38] (HL)—though I must be excluded or at any rate absent from the land, otherwise it will remain in my possession, rather than come into yours. Nor need your user actually incommode me: *ibid* [44]–[45].

[24] *JA Pye (Oxford) Ltd v Graham, ibid* [35]–[38]. So, in *BP Properties Ltd v Buckler* (1987) 55 P & CR 337 (CA) the owner stopped the possession from being adverse by writing a letter to say that it was permitted. The permission may of course be implied as well as express. But it cannot be inferred from the mere fact that, despite being aware of your presence on my land, I fail to evict you: Limitation Act 1980 Sch 1 para 8(4), reversing a contrary position taken in *Wallis's Cayton Bay Holiday Camp Ltd v Shell-Mex & BP Ltd* [1975] QB 94 (CA). It is difficult to fault the logic of the latter decision (a licence would readily be found under such circumstances if adverse possession were not at stake), and its statutory reversal seems a (possibly ill-advised) policy initiative aimed at restoring the potency that would otherwise have drained from the doctrine of adverse possession.

question of adverse possession if you possess my land by virtue of a lease I have given you.) Second, before your possession without my consent can tell against me, I must have had the opportunity to give concrete effect to my lack of consent, by suing to evict you ... and have failed to do so.[25] So if your possession is undetectable,[26] or I have only a future interest in the land,[27] or I am disabled from attacking your possession for a number of other reasons,[28] I lack the necessary opportunity, and you should fail. But if I am merely absent, or take no interest in the land, the law regards me as still having the necessary opportunity, and your possession as therefore adverse.

6.2.2 The Second Element

Before the Land Registration Act 2002, you acquired my land if, having taken adverse possession of my land, you remained in possession of it for 12 years.[29] Under that Act, however, the 12 year rule no longer applies.[30] Instead, you acquire my land only if, in addition to taking adverse possession of it:

— after remaining in adverse possession for at least 10 years,[31] you apply to be registered as owner;[32] then, when the Registry notify me of your application:
— *either* I fail to object;[33] *or* I do object, but two further years pass without my proceeding to evict you;[34] *or* (whether I object or not) we own neighbouring pieces of land, and the area in question, while hitherto part of my land, adjoins our boundary, and you reasonably thought it yours.[35]

---

[25] To prevent you relying on adverse possession, before the end of the qualifying period I must either (obviously) actually evict you, or have a court judgment not more than two years old entitling me to do so, or be suing you to this end: Land Registration Act 2002 Sch 6 para 1(3). It is not however enough if within the last six months I evict you otherwise than through court proceedings: Sch 6 para 1(2).

[26] *Rains v Buxton* (1880) 14 Ch D 537 (Ch D).

[27] Land Registration Act 2002 Sch 6 para 12.

[28] *Ibid* para 8.

[29] Limitation Act 1980 s 15, following the Real Property Limitation Act 1874, before which the law used longer periods.

[30] Land Registration Act 2002 s 96.

[31] The change from 12 to 10 years reflects a general proposal to reduce limitation periods: see Law Commission, *Limitation of Actions* (Law Com No 270, London, 2001).

[32] Sch 6 para 1.

[33] Sch 6 para 4.

[34] Sch 6 para 6.

[35] Sch 6 para 5(4). Paras 5(2) and (3) purport to add two further cases: where you deserve the land in question under the doctrine of proprietary estoppel, and where you are entitled to it for some other reason. These, however, are free-standing reasons why you can claim the land, nothing of substance being added by your having also adversely possessed it.

Put shortly, these additional requirements mean that, having adversely possessed my land for 10 years, you now become owner of it in only two scenarios. One is where I have in effect abandoned the land—as shown by my failure to object, or to press my objection. The other is where the land lies on our boundary, and you reasonably believed it yours.[36] (The latter scenario's restriction to boundary land and its demand that you reasonably believe yourself owner are in fact connected. In general, the register shows me as owner, so a contrary belief cannot be reasonable. But the register does not indicate exactly where a property's boundaries lie, so in this respect a reasonable error can occur.)

Where one of these two scenarios is made out, you are entitled to be registered as owner of the land in place of me.

6.2.3 The Pre-2002 Doctrine's Basis and Acceptability

We now turn to consider why the law should make you owner of the land in these circumstances, if indeed it should at all.

Before the changes in 2002, the doctrine achieved its effect in the following way. The first element, the demand for adverse possession, represented English law's traditional position[37] that taking possession of land itself gave you an entitlement to it.[38] You became owner of the land except to the extent that someone else could show a better entitlement. This would be someone who, or whose title derived from someone else who, had possession before you. As it was normally impossible to know the first person ever to possess a piece of land, this relative kind of entitlement was as good as you or anyone else could hope to have: unqualified ownership did not exist. But if in reality, for one reason or another, you were reasonably safe from such eviction, for practical purposes your relative entitlement was not too different from the non-existent unqualified ownership. Picking up on this last reflection, the law added the doctrine's second element: the rule whereby, if you stayed in possession for 12 years, all who might otherwise have evicted you lost the ability to do so,[39] and indeed lost their own rights in the land.[40] The invulnerability this gave you to earlier claims meant that you acquired something

---

[36] In order to apply to be registered as owner, you must of course have discovered your error. The demand is thus that you must have been in adverse possession for 10 years before doing so.

[37] See § 1.3.5.

[38] Hence the demand that you 'take possession', ie behave like an owner: if you presented yourself as anything less than an owner, the law would have no reason to treat you as one. (Though initially, the key idea was not possession but the similar though not identical concept of seisin.) For an account, see eg A Simpson, *A History of the Land Law* (2nd edn, Oxford, 1986) ch 2 (especially 37–40), and also 150–55. For the assumptions embedded in the construction of 'possession', see further K Green, 'Citizens and Squatters: Under the Surfaces of Land Law' in S Bright and J Dewar (eds), *Land Law—Themes and Perspectives* (Oxford, 1998) ch 9.

[39] Limitation Act 1980 s 15.

[40] *Ibid* s 17.

even more like unqualified ownership of the land (though of course you in turn could lose the land to someone who later adversely possessed against you).

At any rate from the 19th century on, the basis for the doctrine seems to have been a desire to facilitate the marketability of land, to utilitarian ends.[41] If in due course you found yourself trying to sell the land to John, John would want to feel reasonably sure that he was not wasting his money, as he would have been if someone with a better right to the land than you could show up and evict him. And if John could not feel reasonably sure of this, he would be less eager to engage in land transactions at all … to the detriment of the nation's economy, for then land would not find its way to the person valuing it highest, and the projects for which they so valued it would never be put into operation, and so on. From this point of view, the idea behind the first element, that entitlement rests upon possession, posed a problem as much as it offered a solution. The solution lay in the second element. This operated to reassure John and so correct all this. So long as you had been in possession for the relatively short period of 12 years, or you derived your title from one who had, John had no need to concern himself with what might have gone before.

This utilitarian project may have provided a sufficient justification for the original form of the second element, given the problem created by the first. But any such justification disappeared when the law simultaneously[42] set about stabilising land titles in a different way. This involved eradicating the first element—the idea that possession in itself gives someone a title to the land—and replacing it with registration: the idea that title belongs to the person registered as having it.[43] Given the latter, a rule transferring title to someone who adversely possessed the land for 12 years was no longer needed to provide stability, and indeed in general (we shall note an exception in a moment) had the opposite effect. John, wanting to buy land registered in your name, would actually be injured by the possibility that some other person had acquired title to it by having adversely possessed it. Certainly in its then form, therefore, the doctrine of adverse possession was no longer needed for the utilitarian task which had previously justified it, and indeed from the point of view of that basis had in general become positively malign.

For a time, it was thought that, in thus giving uncompensated transfers without sufficient justification, the doctrine violated Article 1 of the First Protocol to the European Convention on Human Rights, whereby 'No one

---

[41] See M Dockray, 'Why Do we Need Adverse Possession?' [1985] *Conv* 272.

[42] But not coincidentally: the 19th and 20th centuries saw many new rules aimed at the same end. Most were complementary, however, rather than mutually antagonistic, in the manner of those explained here.

[43] Though of course the initial registration would naturally be made on the basis of the traditional possession theory.

shall be deprived of his possessions except in the public interest ...', and in a manner proportionate to the particular interest in question.[44] That position was later reversed, it being held that the doctrine's infelicities did not exceed what was allowable under the margin of appreciation.[45] The doctrine was nonetheless unsatisfactory, and was given the overhaul it needed in the Land Registration Act 2002.

6.2.4 The Post-2002 Doctrine's Basis and Acceptability

The doctrine was not, however, simply abolished by the 2002 Act. Instead, as we have seen, it was retained, but narrowed by adjustments to its second element. In its new form, it comprises two distinct rules, each having its own basis.

The first of these rules is that whereby you can acquire boundary land by adversely possessing it for 10 years, even if I object. The basis for this continues to be the stabilisation of titles. Remember how, above, it was said that adverse possession is *in general* inimical to this goal. There is an exception. The register is not designed to give an accurate statement of properties' boundaries. When you offer land for sale, then, there is still a need to ensure that the exact area you are offering is indeed yours to sell, to the market's benefit. Hence the rule. The rule's demand that you should have reasonably believed the land to be your own is a new one, however: as we saw in § 6.2.1, the traditional view of adverse possession involves no such demand.[46] But the demand is appropriate—an improvement on the old approach—as ensuring (very properly, for a utilitarian project) that the good done by stabilising title is not outweighed by a countervailing harm. There would be such a countervailing harm if you could acquire boundary land despite knowing or suspecting it to be mine, for then there would be an incentive to the theft of such land.[47]

The other of the new law's rules is that whereby you acquire my land if you adversely possess it for 10 years and I then abandon it. The consideration behind this version of the rule seems to be a different utilitarian goal: promoting the active use of land. This is seen as desirable because, certainly

---

[44] *JA Pye (Oxford) Ltd v United Kingdom* (2006) 43 EHRR 3 (ECtHR). *Beaulane Properties Ltd v Palmer* [2006] Ch 79 (Ch D) rescued the pre-2002 rules by reinterpreting them (under the Human Rights Act 1998 s 3(1)) so as in effect to demand the original owner's consent to the transfer, thereby giving a transfer under them the additional, legitimising, support of that consideration.

[45] *JA Pye (Oxford) Ltd v United Kingdom* (2007) 46 EHRR 1083 (Grand Chamber of the ECtHR); *Ofulue v Bossert* [2008] EWCA Civ 7 (CA) (affirmed, without argument on this point, [2009] UKHL 16 (HL)).

[46] *JA Pye (Oxford) Ltd v Graham* [2003] 1 AC 347, [42]–[43] (HL).

[47] For other ways of dealing with mistakes about boundaries, see P O'Connor, 'An Adjudication Rule for Encroachment Disputes: Adverse Possession or a Building Encroachment Statute?' in E Cooke (ed), *Modern Studies in Property Law, Volume 4* (Oxford, 2007) ch 9.

in England, land has become a rather scarce resource, relative to the size of the human population and to that population's aspirations, so that the common good requires its reasonably intensive exploitation.[48] The rule's first element—adverse possession itself—tracks this goal only in the crudest way. In two fairly recent decisions, the original owner, while not using the land at the time, intended it for road improvements[49] or house-building,[50] while the squatter used it for a garden or for grazing respectively. Transferring the land on this basis alone (as the pre-2002 rule did, after 12 years) does not intensify the land's use, except in the short term. Crucially, however, the rule now demands that I must also have abandoned the land, as shown by my failure to oppose its transfer to you, or to evict you. This element makes it highly likely that transferring the land to you will intensify its use. Under the new arrangements, the original owners in the two decisions just mentioned, for example, would surely oppose the transfer and evict the squatter. The same element also ensures that the good done by promoting more intensive use is not outweighed by the harm involved in creating an incentive to land theft: even if you take adverse possession of my land deliberately so as to acquire it, you will rarely succeed, for I will normally oppose the transfer.

The post-2002 rules thus rest upon arguments from utility that are respectable, and indeed, given the rules' design, significantly stronger than before. A problem may remain, however. The rules continue to take my land away from me without compensation. Although the argument from utility alone may justify this in the case of boundary land, it is probably insufficient where the whole area is at stake: if the public interest demands taking the land from me so as to put it to better use, I should at least be compensated. The argument's deficiency may be corrected, however, by the element of consent that must also be present under the new rules concerning this case. The requirement that I be given the opportunity to oppose the transfer to you, and fail to take it, tends to show not only that I have abandoned the land in question, so as to confirm the advantage in transferring it to you, but also that I accede to the transfer. The degree of consent thus displayed is insufficient to justify an uncompensated transfer on its own (it shows that I do not object to the transfer, rather than that I positively will it), but it and the argument from utility together may claim to do so.

One final point. Strictly, there is no reason why the post-2002 rules should continue to use the concept of 'adverse possession' at all. In unregistered land, the concept was key because, as explained in § 1.3.5, it encapsulated

---

[48] This is not beyond challenge, of course. One might argue that a fuller understanding of the common good (or some higher value, capturing more than the human common good alone) demands that land be exploited less intensively. If adverse possession has the opposite effect, this argument might require its abolition.

[49] *Buckinghamshire County Council v Moran* [1990] Ch 623 (CA).

[50] *JA Pye (Oxford) Ltd v Graham* [2003] 1 AC 347 (HL).

English law's traditional basis for the ownership of land. Given your adverse possession, you had a claim to the land only one degree less strong than mine: so extinguishing mine, as policy was thought to require, necessarily left yours in its place. In registered land, however, this is not the case. Title to land is more a function of the state of the register. If policy requires provision for sometimes adjusting title for utilitarian reasons (as we have seen it may), the adjustments can be shaped in whatever way the same policy indicates. They do not have to proceed from adverse possession. At the same time, however, the concept of adverse possession formed the traditional basis of title not accidentally, but because the happenings covered by it—'behaving like an owner'—generated reasons for the effects the law ascribed to it. It is reasonable for today's rules to find what is significant for them in broadly the same sorts of happenings: that is, for the projects of stabilising boundary titles and of promoting the intensive use of land likewise to focus on someone's behaving like the owner of the land in question.

6.3 Prescription

Prescription[51] is a means of acquiring easements.[52] Easements are explained fully in Chapter 9, but to explain prescription let us take one instance of an easement, namely a right of way: a right entitling you to cross my land on your way to and from yours. You can acquire an easement by my conferring it on you;[53] or by prescription, on the basis, roughly speaking, that you have behaved as though you had it—ie you have crossed my land—over a period of 20 years.

Prescription can occur under three different rules, or families of rules. They are 'prescription at common law', 'lost modern grant', and prescription under the Prescription Act 1832. Each rule was developed not so as to reform its predecessors, but to allow prescription in meritorious cases which it was thought fell outside the earlier rule(s). The result, however, is at best unnecessary complexity.

---

[51] See further J Getzler, 'Roman and English Prescription for Incorporeal Property' in J Getzler (ed), *Rationalizing Property, Equity and Trusts—Essays in Honour of Edward Burn* (London, 2003) ch 11.

[52] With some differences, it is also a means of acquiring two other kinds of rights—profits and commons—but we shall focus only on easements.

[53] In the context of easements, the law on conferral has some special features (some striking rules regarding especially *implied* conferral), which require extended treatment: see § 9.2.

The rules of prescription at common law and lost modern grant ask us to suppose that your behaviour occurs under an easement that was conferred at some time in the past (hence the very label, 'lost modern grant'), and to overlook the fact that no (other) evidence can be found to show this. But the supposition is a fiction:[54] in truth, both these rules and the 1832 Act generate rights on the basis of your behaviour, and my reaction to it.

Your behaviour—your crossing my land, say—must have been '*nec vi, nec clam, nec precario*'. That is, you must have crossed my land peacefully, rather than by the use of force against me; openly, rather than in a manner which I could not detect; and on your own account, rather than with my permission.[55] Your behaviour must also have been 'as of right', meaning that, to external appearances, you seemed to be acting lawfully (though neither of us need have believed that you actually were[56]). And your behaviour cannot be prescriptive if you commit an offence while you are about it.[57]

The crux here is the demand that you should have acted as though you already had the easement in question. Your having behaved in this way is taken to create a reason why you should in future have the right to do so. That reason seems to be a utilitarian one: a desire, as in one version of adverse possession,[58] to promote the more intensive use of land. As explained in § 9.1.6, easements allow for the cross-exploitation of land, precisely so that it can be used more intensively than would otherwise be possible. Your having used my land in the manner in question for an extended period suggests that this particular instance of cross-exploitation may in fact be valuable.

But an easement might be equally valuable even without such prior user, yet not arise, except under some statutory provision, having its own more specific utilitarian basis. This suggests that the argument from utility is insufficient on its own to warrant your acquiring an easement against me. That is plausible. The cross-exploitation in question may be valuable, but it is unlikely to be vital, as would be needed to justify such a confiscation of my property without compensation (which a statutory provision would normally provide). Hence the need for prior user on your part. When such prior user is of the kind required for prescription, there can additionally be found an

---

[54] In the context of lost modern grant, the courts have said explicitly that the question whether there really was an express conferral cannot be entered into: *Dalton v Angus & Co* (1881) 6 App Cas 740 (HL); *Tehidy Minerals Ltd v Norman* [1971] 2 QB 528, 552 (CA). As a result, this rule, which has the fewest other pitfalls of the three, is nowadays the one most commonly resorted to.

[55] The caselaw goes into considerable detail about the exact meaning of these demands, in particular dealing with the hazy borderlines that each possesses.

[56] *R v Oxfordshire County Council, ex p Sunningwell Parish Council* [2000] 1 AC 335 (HL), concerning the analogous context of commons.

[57] *Cargill v Gotts* [1981] 1 WLR 441, 446 (CA).

[58] That which applies where you adversely possess my land for 10 years, apply to have it transferred to you, and I do not effectively oppose this: § 6.2.4.

element of consent[59] on my part to your acquiring the easement, which—as in adverse possession—combines with the argument from utility, and may justify the prescription.

This element of consent is relatively weak, compared with the case where I willingly confer the easement on you; so (as in the corresponding aspect of adverse possession) it is not enough to warrant your acquiring the easement on its own. But it is discernible. One of its ingredients is the demand that your behaviour must be open. This means I can know what you are doing, so as to have a fair opportunity to stop you before you acquire an easement.[60] Another is the demand that you must not have used force or committed an offence against me: such factors may not quite deprive me of a fair opportunity to stop you, but they colour my failure to do so, making it less consent than submission. Another again is the requirement that your behaviour must not be permitted by me. At first sight this cannot be right: surely I consent the more if I do permit your behaviour? Not so. Our focus is on my consent not to your behaviour, but to your acquiring an easement against me. That is suggested by my failing to oppose behaviour of the kind in question when I do not consent to it in its own right.

Is the combination of this degree of consent and the argument from utility sufficient to warrant your acquiring the easement? Quite possibly not. The problem lies in the relative weakness of the argument from utility. As we have seen, it takes your protracted use of my land in the manner in question as evidence that such a use is a valuable instance of cross-exploitation. But unlike the rule about adverse possession in the context of abandonment, which we saw in § 6.2.4 also to operate on the combined basis of utility and consent, prescription is not actually confined to the case where giving you the right will fairly clearly mean a more advantageous use of the land. Some other rules[61] generating easements on the same combined basis are so confined, demanding that the new easement be needed or at least useful.

---

[59] *Oakley v Boston* [1976] QB 270, 284–5 (CA) refers to it as acquiescence.

[60] There is a difficulty, however. It is wrong to assume that the openness of your behaviour necessarily gives me a fair opportunity to stop you. The assumption works if your behaviour involves a tort against me—a trespass or nuisance—such as where you go to and from your land across mine. Then I can stop you by legal action against you, or perhaps self-help. But some easements ('negative easements') involve only your passive and entirely legal reliance on a state of affairs prevailing on my land: such as where your building's foundations, while contained within your own land, would collapse if I excavated my neighbouring land. The only way for me to stop such 'behaviour' is actually to negative the state of affairs on which you rely, eg to excavate my land. My failure to do so can hardly be regarded as acquiescence in your reliance. Responding to this, where your reliance is on the light reaching your window across my land, the law has created a special way for me to stop it, by notice under the Rights of Light Act 1959; and the courts have strictly limited the kinds of negative easements that can exist (*Phipps v Pears* [1965] 1 QB 76 (CA); *Hunter v Canary Wharf Ltd* [1997] AC 655 (HL): see § 9.1.4). But otherwise the problem remains.

[61] See §§ 9.2.2, 9.2.4. But one such rule, that in the Law of Property Act 1925 s 62, suffers from the same weakness as prescription, and is similarly criticised: § 9.2.5.

Without such a restriction, even with a modicum of consent, the prescription rules seem to provide insufficient reason to impose the easement on me. If prescription is not to be abolished outright,[62] therefore, it should be restricted to cases where some degree of need for the easement can be shown.[63]

---

[62] As proposed by the Law Reform Committee, *Acquisition of Easements and Profits by Prescription* (14th Report, 1966); but cf Law Commission, *Easements, Covenants and Profits à Prendre: A Consultation Paper* (Consultation Paper No 186, London, 2008) paras 4.151–4.256. See further S Bridge, 'Prescriptive Acquisition of Easements: Abolition or Reform?' in E Cooke (ed), *Modern Studies in Property Law, Volume 3* (Oxford, 2005) ch 1; F Burns, 'Prescriptive Easements in England and Legal "Climate Change"' [2007] *Conv* 133.

[63] See further C Sara, 'Prescription—What Is it For?' [2004] *Conv* 13; A Clarke, 'Use, Time, and Entitlement' (2004) 57 *CLP* 238; A Goymour, 'The Acquisition of Rights in Property by the Effluxion of Time' in E Cooke (ed), *Modern Studies in Property Law, Volume 4* (Oxford, 2007) ch 8.

7
Proprietary Estoppel

7.1 An Outline

This chapter looks at your acquiring a right in my land via the doctrine of proprietary estoppel.[1]

There is no definition of proprietary estoppel that is both comprehensive and uncontroversial (and many attempts at one have been neither), but the following outline of the doctrine is offered. As will emerge over the course of the chapter, however, there is uncertainty, at some level, about virtually all of its aspects.

If I encourage you to believe—or if I acquiesce in a belief you already hold—that you have a right over my land, or else that I will confer such a right on you; and you then, in reliance on that belief, act to your detriment; you will be entitled to relief. This entitlement is itself a right in rem, capable of binding any subsequent disponee of the land in question.

An illustration will help. Say you and I are neighbouring landowners. Included in my land is a strip in which I take no interest (perhaps it is cut off from the remainder by a hedge). You, however, see value in it. In a conversation with you one day, I tell you that you can have the strip, or even that I believe it to be yours already. You, taking me at my word, begin to cultivate it. Under the doctrine of proprietary estoppel, you thereupon become entitled to a remedy against me. And if, before you in fact claim the strip, I transfer it to John, then so long as your entitlement is registered or counts as an overriding interest, you will be able to claim your remedy from him instead.

---

[1] There is a considerable literature about the fundamental ideas involved here, including M Spence, *Protecting Reliance* (Oxford, 1999) and E Cooke, *The Modern Law of Estoppel* (Oxford, 2000).

7.2 The Requirements for an Estoppel

7.2.1 The Requirements

The requirements for claiming an estoppel are thus:

— You must firmly believe either that you already have a right over my land, or that I will confer such a right on you.
— You must act to your detriment.
— You must suffer your detriment in reasonable reliance on your belief, which in turn must be the reasonable product of an assurance (whether by way of encouragement or acquiescence) on my part.

We must now examine these requirements in more detail.

7.2.2 Your Belief

According to the statement above, you must firmly believe that you either already have, or are going to acquire, a right over my land or other property.[2]

So you must believe that you *definitely* have the right, or that I shall *definitely* confer it on you.[3] This requirement is easily explicable. If you act upon what you realise is only a possibility, I am not responsible for your doing so: it is for you to clarify matters first, or to decide to take the risk anyway. A claim can readily fail on this basis, especially where your belief is as to the future. You will have no claim if I promise to give you the right but you think 'I'll believe it when I see it'. For example, if I say I shall leave you the right in my will, that might well be what you think (or at any rate what the court will be persuaded you think). You surely know that, even if I make a will to this effect, I can always revoke it.

A contrary tendency is visible in some cases about wills, however. A leading decision is *Gillett v Holt*.[4] The court there concluded that the claimant's belief was sufficiently definite. In favour of this answer was the fact that the defendant not only promised the claimant that he would leave certain

---

[2] In most cases the right has been over land, but there is authority that it can be over any form of property: *Re Basham* [1986] 1 WLR 1498 (Ch D); *Jennings v Rice* [2002] EWCA Civ 159 (CA); *Cobbe v Yeoman's Row Management Ltd* [2008] 1 WLR 1752, [14] (HL), *Thorner v Majors* [2009] UKHL 18 (HL).

[3] *Ramsden v Dyson* (1866) LR 1 HL 129 (HL); *A-G for Hong Kong v Humphreys Estate (Queen's Gardens) Ltd* [1987] AC 114 (PC); *Cobbe v Yeoman's Row Management Ltd* [2008] 1 WLR 1752 (HL).

[4] [2001] Ch 210 (CA). *Re Basham* [1986] 1 WLR 1498 (Ch D), *Jennings v Rice* [2002] EWCA Civ 159 (CA) and *Thorner v Majors* [2009] UKHL 18 (HL) are similar.

property to him by will: he also announced this promise to his family on important family occasions, which was especially significant as they would have expected to inherit the property otherwise. Yet this did not quite prove that the claimant believed his inheritance to be in the bag: 'I'll believe it when I see it' would still have been a natural reaction. The court tried to bolster its reading with more general reasoning. It asserted that the law itself, in the shape of the estoppel doctrine, would make the promise irrevocable and so definite. But this argument is circular: it tries to use the estoppel doctrine to make the promise be definite, when correctly, the doctrine does not bite in the first place unless the claimant's understanding is definite in itself. The decision's conclusion, that the claimant's belief was sufficiently definite, therefore seems questionable. The case really stands for an attenuation of the very requirement that you have a definite belief.

According to *Cobbe v Yeoman's Row Management Ltd*,[5] your belief must be in a 'certain interest'[6] which is also a 'proprietary right'.[7] But this does not accurately state the law.

A 'certain interest' seems to mean a defined right over defined property. The suggestion therefore seems to be that if, in the illustration in § 7.1, I had said merely 'we'll sort something out for you', an estoppel would not have arisen in your favour: I should have needed to say something more focused, such as 'you can have the strip', or 'you can use the strip'. This requirement is overstated, however. You must certainly believe in a right *over my property*, but greater specificity than that seems not to be required:[8] even 'we'll sort something out for you' should be enough, if it implies that you should have a right over my land.[9] Nor need the right in question be identified with any precision;[10] and it commonly will not be, for by definition, estoppel cases will not normally involve formal documentation, so the particular words used are likely not to have been carefully chosen, and also to be difficult of proof.

---

[5] [2008] 1 WLR 1752 (HL).

[6] *Ibid* [18]–[23].

[7] *Ibid* [14]. Or 'proprietary claim': [16].

[8] In *Thorner v Majors* [2009] UKHL 18 (HL), the claimant's belief seems to have been that he would inherit the defendant's 'farm'. There was obviously room for debate as to what, if anything, the 'farm' comprised, beyond the land itself. The judge took it to cover the farm buildings, live and dead stock, other assets of the farming business, and £24,000 in the defendant's business account. The House of Lords had no difficulty with this; see especially at [98].

[9] There is, however, a potential difficulty where I promise to leave you some asset in my will (eg 'my farm') ... it being understood that, in view of the time-lag before you are due to have it, I may in the meantime lose the asset, or alter its substance (eg I may expand or shrink my farm, or exchange it for a new farm altogether). This difficulty is noticed, and some lines of approach suggested, in *Thorner v Majors* [2009] UKHL 18, [9], [18], [20], [62], [88], [95] (HL).

[10] *Ramsden v Dyson* (1866) LR 1 HL 129, 171 (HL); *Plimmer v Mayor &c of Wellington* (1884) 9 App Cas 699, 713 (PC); *Thorner v Majors* [2009] UKHL 18, [64], [97] (HL). Likewise, in *Crabb v Arun District Council* [1976] Ch 179 (CA), the defendant promised the claimant a right of way over its land for a price to be agreed; the court awarded the claimant the right of way, untroubled by the indeterminacy as to its price.

When *Cobbe v Yeoman's Row Management Ltd*[11] demanded that you must believe in a 'certain interest', it did so as a proxy for the requirement that you must (reasonably) believe in a right over my property.[12] That decision involved commercial parties. They did not precisely specify the right in question because they never settled that the claimant should have any right at all; fundamentally, it was for the latter reason that the claimant could not establish an estoppel claim. If you and I are non-commercial parties, however, it is perfectly possible, and reasonable, for you to believe in a right over my property, yet for that right to remain vague.[13]

The further demand that your belief be in a 'proprietary right' is not to be taken very literally. This phrase ordinarily means 'right in rem'. So, apparently, an estoppel can arise if I say you can live in my house on your own, since the right to do this is in rem;[14] but an estoppel cannot arise if I say you can live there with me, since the right to do that is in personam.[15] But a demand for a belief in a right in rem would run counter to established authority.[16] It seems clear that an estoppel can indeed arise if I say that you can live in my house with me, or, to revert to our original illustration, that you can make use of my strip of land alongside me. The requirement thus seems to be that you believe in a right, whether in rem or in personam, over some piece of land (or other property) of mine, as opposed to a right that I will do something for you. A belief in a right to live in my house would therefore be enough; but a belief in a right to be housed by me, in some unspecified location, would not.[17]

7.2.3 Your Detriment

According to the account in § 7.2.1, you must then act to your detriment. Actions of any kind will suffice.

To show 'detriment', it is not enough that you are worse off (unless you win redress from me) than my assurance led you to expect to be. That will

---

[11] [2008] 1 WLR 1752, [18]–[23] (HL).

[12] *Thorner v Majors* [2009] UKHL 18, [96]–[99] (HL).

[13] Indeed, the author of the 'certain interest' requirement—Lord Scott—subsequently indicated that, while cases failing it may not succeed in proprietary estoppel, they should succeed by way of 'remedial constructive trust': *Thorner v Majors* [2009] UKHL 18, [20] (HL). For discussion of this proposal, see § 7.5.1.

[14] It is a lease: § 11.2.1.

[15] It is a licence: *ibid*, and § 15.1.

[16] *Plimmer v Mayor &c of Wellington* (1884) 9 App Cas 699 (PC); *Inwards v Baker* [1965] 2 QB 29 (CA)—decisions cited, with apparent approval, in *Cobbe v Yeoman's Row Management Ltd* [2008] 1 WLR 1752 (HL). See also eg *Greasley v Cooke* [1980] 1 WLR 1306 (CA).

[17] Likewise, a right to a particular investment, owned by me, would be covered; but a right to be paid some sum of money from my assets at large would not. Thus in *Re Basham* [1986] 1 WLR 1498 (Ch D), the claimant successfully relied on proprietary estoppel in a case where she believed that she would inherit the defendant's entire estate, ie believed in a right over his specific property.

necessarily be the case. The idea is rather that your reliance on your belief has left you worse off (unless you win) than you were *before you acted in reliance on my assurance*: as in the illustration in § 7.1, where you believe the strip of land is now yours, and (expend money and labour to) cultivate it.

There are plenty of cases where this requirement has been applied uncontroversially. In *Gillett v Holt*,[18] however, the Court of Appeal indi-cated[19] that it is to be applied loosely. The court held the claimant to have suffered detriment when, believing he would inherit the defendant's land, he remained in the defendant's employment; continued living, rent-free, in a house owned by the defendant rather than buying or renting a house for himself; and paid for his younger son to attend boarding school, the defendant having paid for the claimant's elder son to do so.[20] It is not impos-sible that the claimant became worse off as a result, but concluding to this effect involves speculation about how the claimant would have fared if he had not remained in the defendant's employment and housing, and the taking of the surely dubious view that paying for the younger son's schooling was a 'loss' at all.[21] The best way to see the decision is as, having attenuated the requirement of belief, doing the same to the requirement of detriment.

7.2.4 My Responsibility

The remaining requirements are that I must encourage or acquiesce in your belief; that your belief is a reasonable conclusion for you to draw from that encouragement or acquiescence; that you suffer your detriment in reliance on your belief; and that this reliance too was reasonable. This set of require-ments operates to make me responsible for what has occurred. That is: if, but only if, all these requirements are present, a thread of responsibility can be followed through from your detriment, via my encouragement or acquies-cence, to me.

The two ideas of encouragement and acquiescence cover the spectrum between your developing your belief because of what I say; and your conceiving it for yourself or because of something you pick up elsewhere, and my not correcting it. The former scenario is straightforward, but in the latter, I must be aware that you hold the belief:[22] otherwise, my failure to

---

[18] [2001] Ch 210 (CA).

[19] *Ibid* 232: 'The detriment need not consist of the expenditure of money or other quantifiable detriment, so long as it is something substantial. The requirement must be approached as part of a broad inquiry as to whether repudiation of an assurance is or is not unconscionable in the circumstances.' The same approach was taken in *Campbell v Griffin* [2001] EWCA Civ 990, [23]–[24] (CA), though on the facts there the conclusion reached was less controversial.

[20] [2001] Ch 210, 234–5 (CA).

[21] For discussion of the decision's approach to 'detriment', see R Wells, 'The Element of Detriment in Proprietary Estoppel' [2001] *Conv* 13.

[22] And aware also that you do not already have the right in question: *Taylors Fashions Ltd v Liverpool Victoria Trustees Co Ltd* [1982] QB 133n (Ch D). There is no such requirement if I actively encourage your belief (*ibid*), for in doing so I take the risk of any mistakes.

correct it cannot make me responsible for it. The law's very acceptance of acquiescence is surprising, however. If you and I were negotiating towards a contract, it would not be enough: you normally[23] have no relief for mistakes which you make and which, even knowingly, I fail to correct.[24] Estoppel is more generous to you: it is unclear why it should be.[25]

I can encourage or acquiesce in your belief in any way that produces the necessary result, ie a belief that you already have the right in question, or a belief that I will confer it on you. Remember the illustration in § 7.1, involving the strip of land. I can encourage or acquiesce in your belief that you own the strip by giving you to think either that the strip has been yours all along, or that I am there and then giving you it. I can encourage or acquiesce in your belief that I will give you the strip either by giving you to understand that we have an enforceable contract to that effect, or else by firmly promising you it. The caselaw includes decisions and statements showing that proprietary estoppel reacts to assurances of all these kinds,[26] and that is unsurprising, because my assurance could very easily be ambiguous between them: as for example if I simply say, referring to the strip, 'It's yours.'

But my encouragement of or acquiescence in your belief does not make me responsible for the detriment you have suffered unless the two are linked: that is, unless you suffer the detriment 'in reliance on' your belief,[27] and that reliance is reasonable.

---

[23] It is otherwise where our relationship is a special kind, such that I have a duty to look after your interests: but relationships in estoppel cases are not normally of this kind, any more than they are in contract cases.

[24] *Smith v Hughes* (1871) LR 6 QB 597, 607 (QB).

[25] The point could be readily explained if, in estoppel, I were always enriched by your loss: the law does treat receipt of an enrichment as creating a duty to correct any mistake under which that enrichment is being given. (Though this differentiation between the rule where I am enriched, and that where you merely lose, requires justification in its turn. The key is probably that stronger reasons are required to say that I must compensate your loss than to say that I must reimburse you for a gain that I have made at your expense.) But that is not the case: your estoppel claim does not depend on my being enriched: sometimes I will be, sometimes not.

[26] For example, representation that the right is already yours: *Taylors Fashions Ltd v Liverpool Victoria Trustees Co Ltd* [1982] QB 133n (Ch D); purported conferral: *Dillwyn v Llewelyn* (1862) De GF & J 517 (Ch); assurance that we have a contract entitling you to the right: *Ramsden v Dyson* (1866) LR 1 HL 129, 170 (HL); promise of the right: *ibid*, *Crabb v Arun District Council* [1976] Ch 179 (CA); *Thorner v Majors* [2009] UKHL 18 (HL). (A statement in *Cobbe v Yeoman's Row Management Ltd* [2008] 1 WLR 1752, [14] (HL) describes proprietary estoppel as 'a sub-species of "promissory" estoppel'. Promissory estoppel certainly reacts only to promises; so taken literally, this statement suggests that in proprietary estoppel too, the assurance must be a promise. This cannot however be reconciled with the decisions just cited, involving other forms of assurance. Indeed, the statement is more fundamentally ill-conceived. A promissory estoppel arises where I promise not to treat certain behaviour on your part as the breach of your obligation to me that it would otherwise be: a domain which is quite separate from that of proprietary estoppel, where I say that you have, or can have, a right over my property. See further *Thorner v Majors, ibid* [67].)

[27] See further S Nield, 'Estoppel and Reliance' in E Cooke (ed), *Modern Studies in Property Law, Volume 1* (Oxford, 2001) ch 5.

According to the courts' traditional reading of the requirement of reliance,[28] you suffer your detriment 'in reliance' on your belief if your belief is at least a *but for* cause of what you do. Say I promise you that you can be a part-owner of my house, and you act to your detriment by home-making for us. On this reading, you act 'in reliance' on your belief if your mindset is either 'the only reason I'm doing this washing is my share in the house,'[29] or 'I'm doing the washing because the clothes are dirty, but I wouldn't be doing it if I didn't think I had a share in the house'. It would not be enough if you would have done the washing anyway.

Wayling v Jones[30] shows a wider reading, however. According to it, you also act in reliance if you say to yourself 'I'm doing the washing because the clothes are dirty, and having a share in the house is neither here nor there to that. But you *promised* me a share, and that makes a difference: I'm not washing for someone who breaks his promises to me.' This wider reading represents another attenuation of the traditional requirements for an estoppel claim. It allows you to ascribe your detriment not to your belief in *having a right over my property* at all, but instead to your belief in my trustworthiness. So it works equally well if my promise has nothing to do with you having a right over my property: say, if it is to marry you.

In a further attenuation of this requirement, too, the usual onus of proof is reversed in regard to proving reliance. If a detrimental action by you might plausibly have been made in reliance on the belief in question, it is for me to prove that you did not in fact rely on that belief, rather than for you to prove that you did.[31]

If I say something to you and you put a silly interpretation on it (one which a reasonable person would not have put), that is your problem: I am not responsible for a loss you suffer as a consequence. Likewise if, although your belief is sensible, you decide to take some silly actions on the strength of it. So the traditional position is that your belief and your reliance on it must be reasonable products of my encouragement or acquiescence. Once again, however, the courts' decisions show that this rule is not being taken completely seriously.[32] Take *Gillett v Holt*[33] again. If the claimant there really

---

[28] Found in *Greasley v Cooke* [1980] 1 WLR 1306 (CA), and probably many other cases.

[29] According to *Coombes v Smith* [1986] 1 WLR 808 (Ch D), this alone qualifies as 'in reliance'. But this approach appears excessively narrow (you would rarely do the washing *solely* because of your belief), one of several devices adopted by the judge to defeat the claim in that case. The decision seems an isolated one.

[30] (1993) 69 P & CR 170 (CA), followed in *Campbell v Griffin* [2001] EWCA Civ 990 (CA) and *Ottey v Grundy* [2003] EWCA Civ 1176 (CA).

[31] *Greasley v Cooke* [1980] 1 WLR 1306 (CA); *Wayling v Jones* (1993) 69 P & CR 170 (CA); *Campbell v Griffin* [2001] EWCA Civ 990 (CA).

[32] This is pointedly so where you believe that I have in fact validly conferred the right on you, or that I am enforceably contracting with you to do so. In both cases, the law sometimes imposes formality requirements, but the courts have never said that your belief could therefore not have been reasonable.

[33] [2001] Ch 210 (CA): n 4 above.

did believe that his bequest from the defendant was in the bag, he very arguably should not have done. Promises of bequests are notoriously unreliable, however loudly, publicly and frequently they are made (indeed, perhaps the more so for being made loudly, publicly and frequently, as showing a manipulative streak in the testator). Yet the court gave the issue no real attention at all.

7.2.5 A Summary

In this group of sections, we have seen that, for an estoppel claim to arise, the official approach requires that you firmly believe you have a right over my land, or that I will confer such a right on you; that you act to your detriment; and that you do these things in reasonable reliance on my encouragement or acquiescence. But we have also seen that each of these requirements has been compromised, so that an estoppel claim can in fact arise in their substantial absence.

This discussion has not used the word 'unconscionability'. It is more common for accounts of proprietary estoppel to use and indeed emphasise this word. While acknowledging the elements of belief, encouragement or acquiescence, detriment, reliance, they tend to wrap everything in the question of whether it is 'unconscionable' for me to see you suffer in this way. In *Gillett v Holt*,[34] for example, it is said: 'the fundamental principle that equity is concerned to prevent unconscionable conduct permeates all the elements of the doctrine.' Statements such as this confirm the impression that the courts are ready to allow estoppel claims where the traditional requirements are less than fully met—or, equally, to disallow them even where those requirements are fully met.[35]

This raises the question: if the courts are allowing or denying estoppel claims for reasons other than those embedded in the official approach, what are these reasons? We shall come to this question in § 7.4, after taking stock

---

[34] *Ibid* 225. See too *Taylors Fashions Ltd v Liverpool Victoria Trustees Co Ltd* [1982] QB 133n, 151–2 (Ch D): the question is 'whether, in particular individual circumstances, it would be unconscionable for a party to deny that which, knowingly or unknowingly, he has allowed or encouraged another to assume to his detriment rather than to inquiring whether the circumstances can be fitted within the confines of some preconceived formula serving as a universal yardstick for every form of unconscionable behaviour'. But compare Lord Walker's depiction of unconscionability as 'unifying and confirming, as it were, the other elements. If the other elements appear to be present but the result does not shock the conscience of the court, the analysis needs to be looked at again' (*Cobbe v Yeoman's Row Management Ltd* [2008] 1 WLR 1752, [92] (HL)). This seems a little more hesitant, though also less clear.

[35] See perhaps *Sledmore v Dalby* (1996) 72 P & CR 196 (CA), where an estoppel right arose which would ordinarily have entitled Mr Dalby to remain in a house—but the court regarded this entitlement as having already ended, on the ground that Mrs Sledmore, the owner of the house, needed it more than he did. For disapproval of this kind of approach, however, see *Cobbe v Yeoman's Row Management Ltd, ibid* [17], [28]; *Thorner v Majors* [2009] UKHL 18, [98] (HL).

of the courts' approach to relief, which also needs to be factored into our answer.

7.3 Estoppel Relief

7.3.1 Estoppel Relief is Discretionary

If all these requirements are satisfied, so that you have the benefit of the estoppel doctrine against me, what does that entitle you to? That is, what is your relief?

It is reasonably firmly established that the outcome of a successful estoppel claim lies in the court's discretion.[36] For a moment, a non-discretionary view—requiring the outcome always to be the vindication of the claimant's belief—seemed recently to be espoused by the House of Lords in *Cobbe v Yeoman's Row Management Ltd*,[37] but the discretionary position was reaffirmed in *Thorner v Majors*.[38]

In the exercise of this discretion, the courts have arrived at a variety of outcomes. It is not easy to account for these,[39] not least because the courts themselves have commonly made little effort to explain them. But Robert Walker LJ in *Jennings v Rice*[40] made an important attempt to illuminate the issue.

[36] Decisions highlighting such a discretion included *Pascoe v Turner* [1979] 1 WLR 431 (CA); *Sledmore v Dalby* (1996) 72 P & CR 196 (CA); *Jennings v Rice* [2002] EWCA Civ 159 (CA). But it is spoken of and/or visible in very many more.

[37] [2008] 1 WLR 1752, [14] (HL), Lord Scott: proprietary estoppel 'bars [me] from asserting some fact or facts, or, sometimes, something that is a mixture of fact and law, that stands in the way of some right claimed by [you].' This formulation might even have been thought to mean that proprietary estoppel would operate only where the defendant was estopped from denying the existence of a valid contract to the effect for which the claimant contended (as in estoppel *in pais*: *Amalgamated Investment & Property Co Ltd (in liquidation) v Texas Commerce International Bank Ltd* [1982] QB 84, 131–2 (QBD and CA)). That this was not, however, Lord Scott's intention was shown by his apparent approval of earlier proprietary estoppel decisions where a claims succeeded not via contract in this way, but directly on the basis of the estoppel: notably *Plimmer v Mayor &c of Wellington* (1884) 9 App Cas 699 (PC); *Inwards v Baker* [1965] 2 QB 29 (CA); *Crabb v Arun District Council* [1976] Ch 179 (CA).

[38] [2009] UKHL 18, [66] (HL). The latter seems even to have been substantially accepted by Lord Scott, the author of the *Cobbe* position, though he preferred to badge it 'remedial construct trust' rather than proprietary estoppel (*Thorner v Majors, ibid* [20]–[21]). For discussion of this suggestion, see § 7.5.1

[39] See S Gardner, 'The Remedial Discretion in Proprietary Estoppel' (1999) 115 *LQR* 438.

[40] [2002] EWCA Civ 159 (CA); see S Gardner, 'The Remedial Discretion in Proprietary Estoppel—Again' (2006) 122 *LQR* 492.

7.3.2 *Jennings v Rice*

According to Robert Walker LJ,[41] the court's award has to be 'proportionate' to the value of the detriment suffered by the claimant in reliance on the defendant's assurance, while also taking account of his expectation. In 'bargain' cases, where the parties had agreed upon the claimant's expectation and how he had to earn it, the claimant's detriment is to be regarded as equivalent to his expectation, and the 'proportionate' outcome is thus the award of that expectation. Otherwise, it is at large.

Robert Walker LJ went on to say that, as well as 'proportionality', the outcome has also to reflect—as and when relevant—the parties' conduct (eg reducing your award if you have been gratuitously horrible to me); the need for a clean break between us (deciding against an order that we share my house, because we now hate each other); alterations in the defendant's circumstances (reducing your award because of my impoverishment); the effect of taxation (choosing between two styles of award on the basis that one would be taxed more heavily, and so be worth less to you, than the other); other claims on the defendant or his estate (reducing your award because I have significant responsibilities, legal or perhaps also moral, to other people too); and possibly other considerations too.[42]

Robert Walker LJ's judgment is an important one, but it is also difficult, for two main reasons. First, it is hard to say what the key notion of 'proportionality' means. The idea is apparently to take some account of both the claimant's expectation and his detriment, but (except in 'bargain' cases) not to give either pure and simple.[43] But that rather negative information is all we have. The suspicion is that, so long as they stay somewhere in the region between the value of the claimant's detriment and that of his expectation, judges are left to decide for themselves on the aim to be pursued. But giving judges discretion to decide the law's very aim, and to do so afresh in each case, would be antithetical to the Rule of Law. Unsurprisingly therefore, Robert Walker LJ stated that he envisaged no such thing.[44] But we remain unclear what he did envisage.

Secondly, there is a puzzle over the significance of the other factors—the parties' conduct, the need for a clean break between them, alterations in the defendant's circumstances, the effect of taxation, other claims on the

---

[41] *Ibid* [45]–[56].

[42] On a strict reading of Robert Walker LJ's judgment (*ibid* [52]), these factors were to be taken into account only in 'non-bargain' cases. This was probably a slip, however. *Burrows and Burrows v Sharp* (1989) 23 HLR 82 and *Gillett v Holt* [2001] Ch 210 (CA) appeared to be 'bargain' cases in which relief took account of such factors. Say we had bargained for you to live with me in my house, in return for services. If we now hated each other, a clean break would be just as necessary as in a non-bargain case.

[43] cf A Robertson, 'The Reliance Basis of Proprietary Estoppel Remedies' [2008] *Conv* 295, arguing that relief was indeed focused purely on detriment.

[44] [2002] EWCA Civ 159, [43] (CA).

defendant or his estate, and possible further considerations. The problem is that none of these affects the extent to which estoppel's actual requirements are present—the extent to which your reliance on your belief has injured you, and the extent to which I am responsible for that. If they are relevant, it can only be because, despite appearances, estoppel is not (or not only) about those requirements. In § 7.4, we shall consider what (else) it may be about.

7.3.3 More about the Discretion

In practice, in the exercise of the discretion, awards have been made by reference frequently to the claimant's expectation,[45] and occasionally to his detriment.[46] There has also been a hint that, where the claimant's action in reliance has enriched the defendant, the award may involve the return of that enrichment.[47] Of particular interest, however, is a group of cases in which the award seems to reflect more than anything (the court's perception of) the implications, in the circumstances that had come about, of the personal relationship between the parties.[48]

In several of these cases, the claimant had provided live-in care for the defendant after being promised the defendant's house in the latter's will. The awards in these cases were of money, rather than a right *in specie*. In their quantum, they did not track the claimant's expectation (the promised house itself), nor his detriment, nor his enrichment of the defendant (these were not normally even quantified); their basis was in fact never specified. But they may have reflected the cost to the claimant of finding substitute accommodation, of the standard he had enjoyed in the defendant's house before the latter's death, and to which (it was assumed) he continued to be entitled as a

---

[45] As in *Dillwyn v Llewelyn* (1862) De GF & J 517 (Ch); *Plimmer v Mayor &c of Wellington* (1884) 9 App Cas 699 (PC); *Inwards v Baker* [1965] 2 QB 29 (CA); *Greasley v Cooke* [1980] 1 WLR 1306 (CA); *Re Basham* [1986] 1 WLR 1498 (Ch D); *Thorner v Majors* [2009] UKHL 18 (HL). Some of these can be regarded as 'bargain' cases within Robert Walker LJ's analysis, but by no means all of them.

[46] As in *Dodsworth v Dodsworth* (1973) 228 EG 1115 (CA) (though this was criticised as insufficiently generous in *Griffiths v Williams* (1978) 248 EG 947, 950 (CA)); *Burrows and Burrows v Sharp* (1989) 23 HLR 82 (CA); *Baker v Baker* [1993] 2 FLR 247 (CA) (though in the latter the claimant's reliance loss exceeded his expectation interest, and his award was capped at the latter). *Crabb v Arun District Council* [1976] Ch 179 (CA) can also be seen this way. The claimant sold off part of his land, leaving the remaining part with no road access. He did this in reliance on the defendant's promise to give him such access through its own adjoining land. He was awarded the promised access. This could be seen as a vindication of his expectation, but alternatively as a correction of his reliance loss, ie his loss of the opportunity to secure such access more effectively before his sale.

[47] This was the nature of the award sought in *Blue Haven Enterprises Ltd v Tully* [2006] UKPC 17 (PC). The claim failed on the facts, but no objection was taken in principle. See further N Hopkins, 'Estoppel and Restitution: Drawing a Divide' in E Cooke (ed), *Modern Studies in Property Law, Volume 2* (Oxford, 2003) ch 8.

[48] The importance of the parties' relationship is also highlighted by Lord Scott in *Thorner v Majors* [2009] UKHL 18, [12] (HL).

result of his estoppel. In *Jennings v Rice*,[49] for example, it was the trial judge's view, approved by the Court of Appeal, that to award the claimant the promised house itself, valued at £420,000, would have been excessive, for he was single, and merely the defendant's employee. He needed only £150,000 to buy a suitable house, and £200,000 sufficed to 'see him all right'.[50] Similarly in *Campbell v Griffin*,[51] where the claimant was awarded £35,000, the court explaining: 'It would not be right to confer on [the claimant] (who began as a lodger with one out of four bedrooms) a right in respect of the whole house ... [£35,000] will not by itself enable him to buy a freehold house in [the town in question], but it will assist him with rehousing himself.'[52]

The group extends more widely. It includes *Pascoe v Turner*,[53] in which a claimant was awarded the defendant's house not because he had promised her it, but because it was the best way of giving her a secure future following the breakdown of their relationship as lovers; and *Sledmore v Dalby*,[54] in which, while the claimant was granted a right to remain in the house which the defendant (his mother-in-law) had promised he could occupy, this right was truncated in its duration because the defendant, now an impoverished old lady, needed the house more than he did.

7.4 What is Estoppel About?

This chapter depicts proprietary estoppel as one of the rules by which the law gives one person rights in the land of another. But what is the theoretical basis on which it does so?

---

[49] [2002] EWCA Civ 159 (CA).

[50] *Ibid* [15].

[51] [2001] EWCA Civ 990 (CA).

[52] *Ibid* [36]. Likewise perhaps *Ottey v Grundy* [2003] EWCA Civ 1176 (CA). The claimant had a role similar to that of a wife to the defendant for many years. They separated shortly before his death, and he left her nothing. Not having been married to the defendant, she was unable to use the provisions of the Inheritance (Provision for Family and Dependants) Act 1975 aimed at securing an appropriate share in a deceased's estate for his spouse. Having been rejected by the defendant at the time of his death, she was also unable to use that Act's provisions aimed at securing the reasonable needs of dependants and intimate cohabitants. She succeeded however in her estoppel claim, the award being £100,000.

[53] [1979] 1 WLR 431 (CA).

[54] (1996) 72 P & CR 196 (CA).

7.4.1 The Problem

A doctrine's theoretical basis—its aim—should, obviously, be reflected in the rules controlling what it does: the situations to which it applies, and the outcomes it yields. To see the aim of proprietary estoppel, therefore, we need to reflect on what we have learnt in §§ 7.2 and 7.3.

Take the rules about outcomes. We have seen that some decisions have granted expectation relief (you get the interest in which you believed). These decisions therefore suggest that the doctrine's aim is to uphold assurances. But we have also noted some other decisions yielding various other outcomes, notably the recoupment of your detriment, and the vindication of our relationship's implications for the circumstances in question. Such decisions must assert that the doctrine's aim is to deliver these goals. In short, the cases about outcomes allow for more than one account of proprietary estoppel's theoretical basis.

Commentators have responded to this diversity by arguing that one basis or another is the true one, and that the others are false (from which it would follow that the courts should not order outcomes in their terms).[55] These arguments can always readily point to aspects of the doctrine evincing the view that they support: unsurprisingly, given the range of views that the cases stand for, as we have seen. In presenting the doctrine's basis as one thing rather than another, however, they all ask us to disregard—or regard as mistakes—other things we know about it.

Another approach is possible, however. Each of the arguments accounts for some but not all of the things we know about estoppel. That need be a problem only if we assume, as the arguments do, that the term 'proprietary estoppel' denotes a single legal project. If the term in fact refers to a collection of different projects, the problem disappears. We need only see whether we can assemble, and justify, accounts of what those different projects are.

7.4.2 The Projects

The projects apparently in play include the following:

— The effectuation of otherwise ineffective conferrals of interests in land, or contracts or promises to confer such interests, or representations of the existence of such interests.
— The correction of reliance loss on your part for which I am responsible.

---

[55] See eg P Birks, 'Equity in the Modern Law: An Exercise in Taxonomy' (1996) 26 *University of Western Australia Law Review* 1, 60; S Bright and B McFarlane, 'Proprietary Estoppel and Property Rights' [2005] *CLJ* 449; A Robertson, 'The Reliance Basis of Proprietary Estoppel Remedies' [2008] *Conv* 295.

— Distributive justice, requiring me to put you into a satisfactory material position, in a context where a fair distribution between us is called for.

We shall look at each in turn.

7.4.3 Enforcement of Otherwise Ineffective Conferrals Etc

The first suggestion, then, is that proprietary estoppel has a project to effectuate otherwise ineffective conferrals of interests in land, or contracts or promises to confer such interests, or representations of the existence of such interests.

Remember the illustration given in § 7.1, and suppose that I say 'OK, have the strip', thus purporting to confer the strip on you. Or that I say 'You can have the strip if you'll do such-and-such for me in return', thereby (if you accept) purporting to contract to confer the strip on you. Or that I say 'I'll give you the strip', thus making a non-contractual promise to confer the strip on you. Or that I say 'The strip's already yours', so representing that this is the case. None of these utterances is in itself enough to give you the strip, or an entitlement to it. The conferral and the contract would have been enough if they had been supported by the necessary formalities, but cannot be effectively made by my spoken words.[56] The bare promise and representation could never have been enough: the law does not give dispositive force to such utterances at all. The first suggested project, however, depicts proprietary estoppel as, in all these cases (so long as you reasonably believe me, and rely on your belief to your detriment), operating to give you the strip nonetheless.

This suggestion connects with some of the courts' estoppel decisions. Certainly, utterances of all these kinds, when accompanied by belief, reliance and responsibility, give rise to estoppel claims.[57] (We should expect the belief, reliance and responsibility to be real, if they are to justify your claim. This project therefore strikes no chord with the attenuation of those requirements, which we noticed in § 7.2; but that may turn out to be evidence of another project.) And the relief required by this project is the effectuation of my utterance: which, as we have seen, is one of the measures of relief used in proprietary estoppel.

So it is certainly possible to perceive such a project in what we know about proprietary estoppel. But there are two problems of principle.

First, if my assurance takes the form of a conferral or contract, it will, as noted above, normally be ineffective in itself for want of formality.[58] If—as this project proposes—proprietary estoppel can operate to effectuate my

---

[56] §§ 4.4.1 and 5.1.
[57] § 7.2.4.
[58] §§ 4.4.1 and 5.1.

assurance after all, the law appears to its subvert own formality rules.[59] It is hard to see that this can be proper.

In *Cobbe v Yeoman's Row Management Ltd*,[60] Lord Scott took a curious position over this issue. He expressed the opinion (without firmly deciding) that proprietary estoppel cannot be used to effectuate a *contract* despite its informality in this way, since to use it thus would indeed contradict the relevant formality requirement.[61] But the remainder of his reasoning assumes that the doctrine can be used to effectuate an informal *conferral*: I am estopped from setting up my own right against your assertion of the right in which I gave you to believe. There seems no reason why the two should be treated differently in this way: if there is a contradiction in the case of contract, then there is too in the case of conferral.[62] More usually, the courts have not differentiated between informal conferrals and contracts in this way, allowing proprietary estoppel to effectuate both.[63] This avoids the inconsistency of Lord Scott's position, but at the expense of an even greater subversion of the formality rules. If proprietary estoppel is to avoid subverting formality rules in this way, it must not seek to effectuate assurances that fall foul of them: that is, it must not carry on the first project.

The second problem with this project is more fundamental. It is hard to see why estoppel claims should yield expectation relief at all. To be sure, vindicating an *effective* assurance on my part would require such relief, by definition. But the assurances in question here are by definition (estoppel apart) *ineffective*: either (in the case of conferrals or contracts) for want of formality, or (in the case of bare promises or representations) because in themselves they simply lack legal significance. The basis for estoppel intervention, then, lies not in the assurance itself, but in the belief, reliance and

---

[59] See further M Dixon, 'Proprietary Estoppel and Formalities in Land Law and the Land Registration Act 2002: A Theory of Unconscionability' in E Cooke (ed), *Modern Studies in Property Law, Volume 2* (Oxford, 2003) ch 9.

[60] [2008] 1 WLR 1752 (HL).

[61] *Ibid* [29].

[62] Although worded slightly differently, the relevant statutory provisions suggest no such difference. Regarding contracts, the rule (Law of Property (Miscellaneous Provisions) Act 1989 s 2(1)) reads: 'A contract for the sale or other disposition of an interest in land can only be made in writing ...' Regarding conferrals, the principal rule (Law of Property Act 1925 s 52(1)) reads: 'All conveyances of land or of any interest therein are void for the purpose of conveying or creating a legal estate unless made by deed.'

[63] As well as *Ramsden v Dyson* (1866) LR 1 HL 129, 170 (HL), see (in the context of the current contractual formality rule, in the Law of Property (Miscellaneous Provisions) Act 1989 s 2(1)) *Yaxley v Gotts* [2000] Ch 162 (CA); *Kinane v Mackie-Conteh* [2005] EWCA Civ 45 (CA); *Oates v Stimson* [2006] EWCA Civ 548 (CA); and—even after *Cobbe v Yeoman's Row Management Ltd* [2008] 1 WLR 1752 (HL)—*Brightlingsea Haven Ltd v Morris* [2008] EWHC 1928 (QB). The approach generally adopted in these decisions is to the effect that the estoppel claim, rather than effectuating the contract directly, gives rise to a 'constructive trust', to which no formality requirement applies (Law of Property (Miscellaneous Provisions) Act 1989 s 2(5)). It is hard to see that the outcomes in question amounted to trusts at all, so this reasoning seems fallacious: surely the estoppel claim is operating in its own right. Either way, however, the de facto outcome remains the effectuation of the informal contract via an estoppel award, as discussed in the text.

responsibility that the doctrine requires. And these afford no reason for the effectuation of your expectations. If I give you to think that you have or shall have my strip of land, and you, believing me, expend money and/or effort in cultivating it, you certainly deserve a claim against me. But if the basis of your claim is your detrimental reliance, rather than my assurance itself, your remedy ought to be compensation for the loss entailed by this detrimental reliance.[64]

In short, while evidence of this project can be found in the way the courts have used proprietary estoppel, it is unsustainable in principle.

7.4.4 Correction of Reliance Loss

The second project with which proprietary estoppel may be identified is one aimed at correcting your reliance loss: that is, at making me compensate you for the loss you suffer when you rely to your detriment on your belief, for which I am responsible.

The occasional awards of compensation for reliance loss in proprietary estoppel[65] can of course be ascribed to this project. The project also connects well with estoppel's traditional requirements of belief, reliance and responsibility, using these to show that I ought to compensate your reliance loss.[66] By the same token, this project cannot account for decisions yielding other outcomes; nor for many of the attenuations of the traditional rules regarding 'belief', 'detriment' and 'reliance' that we noticed in § 7.2. But on the supposition that 'proprietary estoppel' refers to more than one project, these points need not be evidence against the present suggestion, merely evidence for some other project(s).

This second project is in broad terms intelligible in principle. It is readily understandable that I should have to compensate you for the loss you suffer in reasonable reliance on a belief for which I am responsible—in short, loss for which I am, therefore, responsible. There are two points requiring discussion, but they turn out not to leave this project unsupportable.

First, the loss you suffer in a proprietary estoppel case is always economic. If we take the law as a whole, economic loss is recoverable only in rather special circumstances. Among these are the cases where you incur the loss in reasonable reliance on an incorrect statement that I negligently make within

---

[64] Compare the old (abolished in 1989) doctrine of 'part performance'. In the context of a contract that had not, as required, been put in writing, but given facts similar to those generating an estoppel, this doctrine too gave you a claim against me ... which was always met by enforcement of the contract. There is the same puzzle as to the remedy.

[65] *Dodsworth v Dodsworth* (1973) 228 EG 1115 (CA); *Burrows and Burrows v Sharp* (1989) 23 HLR 82 (CA); *Baker v Baker* [1993] 2 FLR 247 (CA); perhaps *Crabb v Arun District Council* [1976] Ch 179 (CA). See § 7.3.3 above.

[66] Proprietary estoppel is also depicted in this way by Lord Walker in *Cobbe v Yeoman's Row Management Ltd* [2008] 1 WLR 1752, [48] (HL).

an appropriately close relationship,[67] or a contractual promise that I break. It is appropriate to limit recovery in this way to cases where I have undertaken a particular responsibility towards you, on the basis of which you rely on me; if you could recover whenever you were my 'neighbour',[68] without such encouraged reliance, liability for economic loss would proliferate too widely. The project under discussion could well be seen as aligned with these other special cases, by recalling that in it too, you suffer your loss in reasonable reliance on something I tell you, or at least allow you to believe.

Second, the traditional understanding of proprietary estoppel, confirmed in *Cobbe v Yeoman's Row Management Ltd*,[69] limits it to the case where your belief is in (my statement is about) *an interest over my property*. This limitation appears inapt to a project aimed at redressing reliance loss. It could be explained if it helped show that I have allowed you to rely on me, in the way just discussed: but it obviously does not. Remember however the attenuation of the 'reliance' requirement in *Wayling v Jones*,[70] allowing your reliance to be not on your belief in a right over my property at all, but instead on your belief in my trustworthiness. This sidelines the requirement of such a belief, leaving it an arbitrary restriction on estoppel's scope. The logical next step would be its abandonment, leaving an unproblematic fit with the current project.

So a project to correct reliance loss can be discerned in the positions that the judges have sometimes (remember, that is all that is needed) taken regarding proprietary estoppel. It can also be supported in principle, as compatible with what we otherwise want to say about the correction of economic loss suffered by a claimant in reliance on the defendant's statements. This project is thus a possible one. Fully accepting it does however require some violence to the traditional understanding of proprietary estoppel as focused on rights over property: for a project on these lines, such a focus would be out of place.

7.4.5 Distributive Justice

The third of the projects that can be identified with proprietary estoppel is one aimed at doing distributive justice: that is, at requiring me to put you into

---

[67] *Hedley Byrne & Co Ltd v Heller & Partners Ltd* [1964] AC 465 (HL).
[68] cf *Donoghue v Stevenson* [1932] AC 562, 580 (HL), Lord Atkin: 'The rule that you are to love your neighbour becomes in law, you must not injure your neighbour; and the lawyer's question, Who is my neighbour? receives a restricted reply. You must take reasonable care to avoid acts or omissions which you can reasonably foresee would be likely to injure your neighbour. Who, then, in law is my neighbour? The answer seems to be—persons who are so closely and directly affected by my act that I ought reasonably to have them in contemplation as being so affected when I am directing my mind to the acts or omissions which are called in question.'
[69] [2008] 1 WLR 1752 (HL): see § 7.2.2.
[70] (1993) 69 P & CR 170 (CA): see § 7.2.4.

a certain material position, on the ground that our (previous or continuing) relationship itself requires that outcome.

The idea of distributive justice was explained in § 6.1.1. An example of a distributive jurisdiction is that providing for the reallocation of a couple's property upon their divorce,[71] which focuses on minimising the material impact of the divorce on any children, securing the parties' 'reasonable requirements', and dividing any remaining assets equally between them: all on the basis that the parties owe each other and their children the level of wealth in question, *by virtue of their marriage or civil partnership and, where relevant, their status as parents*. There is evidence that the courts sometimes do work of this kind via proprietary estoppel. That is, they use estoppel to reallocate property from me to you where, and to the extent that, this is what our relationship itself requires.

So, the third project provides the best explanation for the treatment of quantum in a number of important decisions.[72] As we saw in § 7.3.3, these decisions appeared to reflect the implications of the parties' relationship, in the circumstances that had occurred. For example, where a claimant had been the defendant's resident carer, and had been promised the defendant's house in the latter's will but had in fact been disappointed, he was then awarded not the house itself, nor his reliance loss, but the cost of finding accommodation of a standard similar to that which he had enjoyed when living with the defendant, before the latter's death.

The third project also helps make sense of Robert Walker LJ's judgment in *Jennings v Rice*,[73] considered in § 7.3.2. As we saw there, this judgment was problematic, for the lack of fit between on the one hand the central idea of 'proportionality', and the various additional discretionary considerations (the parties' misconduct, etc), and on the other hand estoppel's ostensible requirements of belief, reliance and responsibility. This lack of fit becomes explicable if Robert Walker LJ was creating space for a project to do something, such as to achieve distributive justice between the parties, that is unconnected with estoppel's ostensible structure.

In the same way, this project can account for the attenuations we have observed in the requirements for an estoppel claim. For a distributive jurisdiction, it simply does not matter whether you act to your detriment in reliance on a belief in a right over my property, for which I am responsible. Attenuating these requirements allows a claim to succeed despite their real absence.

---

[71] Matrimonial Causes Act 1973 s 24; *White v White* [2001] AC 596 (HL); *Miller v Miller, McFarlane v McFarlane* [2006] 2 AC 618 (HL).

[72] *Campbell v Griffin* [2001] EWCA Civ 990 (CA); *Jennings v Rice* [2002] EWCA Civ 159 (CA); *Ottey v Grundy* [2003] EWCA Civ 1176 (CA); *Pascoe v Turner* [1979] 1 WLR 431 (CA); *Sledmore v Dalby* (1996) 72 P & CR 196 (CA).

[73] [2002] EWCA Civ 159 (CA).

It is especially noteworthy that the main decisions in which the attenuation took place—*Gillett v Holt*[74] and *Wayling v Jones*[75]—were in cases where the parties had been in long-term relationships which could plausibly be regarded as *in themselves* creating obligations on the defendants in favour of the claimants; and that the courts attached importance to this. So, in *Gillett v Holt*,[76] the court refers to a number of episodes which, since they antedated any relevant belief on the claimant's part, could not have amounted to detrimental reliance, even in that concept's attenuated form. What does emerge, however, is the establishment of a relationship of patronage between defendant and claimant, in the course of which the defendant promised to bequeath his property to the claimant, before eventually fracturing the relationship and letting the claimant down. And in *Wayling v Jones*,[77] where there was a similar relationship and a similar promise, the claimant had difficulty showing that the services he rendered the defendant were 'in reliance' on the promise: for in his relationship with the defendant, he would have done the same anyway, out of love and loyalty. Reading 'in reliance' however as focused not on the content of the promise but on the promisor's trustworthiness,[78] the court turned it from a requirement likely to be defeated in such a context to one positively likely to be met: it is in a committed relationship that trustworthiness matters most of all.

A project of delivering the distributive implications of personal relationships is evidently supportable in principle. And there thus seems to be evidence that the judges have treated proprietary estoppel as having such a project, in addition to the first two projects. This evidence consists in the approach some decisions have taken to quantum, and their attenuation of proprietary estoppel's official requirements. But attenuation is not really enough. The project cannot operate coherently without the requirements' complete removal from the picture, and replacement by explicit reference to the relevant relationship(s). At which point, the jurisdiction will cease to warrant the title 'estoppel' at all.

---

[74] [2001] Ch 210 (CA). As noted in §§ 7.2.2 and 7.2.3, this decision attenuated the requirements of belief and detriment.

[75] (1995) 69 P & CR 170 (CA). As noted in § 7.2.4, this decision attenuated the requirement of reliance. The same comment can also be made of *Greasley v Cooke* [1980] 1 WLR 1306 (CA), holding (§ 7.2.4) that the onus of proof regarding 'in reliance' rests on the defendant rather than the claimant.

[76] [2001] Ch 210, 234–5 (CA).

[77] (1995) 69 P & CR 170 (CA). The pattern is similar in the other two decisions taking the same line on 'in reliance', *Campbell v Griffin* [2001] EWCA Civ 990 (CA) and *Ottey v Grundy* [2003] EWCA Civ 1176 (CA).

[78] § 7.2.4.

7.4.6 A Summary

Let us summarise this group of sections. We have found that each of the three suggested projects succeeds in describing some of what we know about proprietary estoppel, but beyond that the picture is not encouraging.

The first project—the effectuation of otherwise ineffective conferrals etc—has the closest fit with the traditional vision of proprietary estoppel. On the other hand, we found it unsupportable in principle. When you rely to your detriment on my assurance, doubtless you deserve relief. But there is no reason why that relief should be the fulfilment of the assurance.

The second and third projects—relieving your reliance loss, and doing distributive justice between us—are more readily supportable in principle. But while they do strike some chords with what the judges have done in the name of proprietary estoppel, they both demand a substantial rewriting of that doctrine. The second project requires the abandonment of the traditional requirement that you believe in a right *over my property* (if the aim is to correct your reliance loss, there is nothing special about beliefs of that kind). The rewriting required for the third project goes even further, amounting to the abandonment of all reference to belief, detriment and responsibility: the proper driver being simply the implications of our relationship in the circumstances in question.

The conclusion is that none of the three suggested projects provides an adequate justification for what the law has been doing under the name of proprietary estoppel. It follows that, unless it is engaged in some further project(s) more convincing than those uncovered here, the doctrine of proprietary estoppel should be abolished. The second and third projects would be better carried on under their own names, while the first should be seen as unsustainable, and aborted.

7.5 The Estoppel 'Equity'

One last question requires attention. What is the nature of your rights, under the estoppel doctrine, between the time when the doctrine's requirements are met (you act to your detriment in reliance on a belief, encouraged or acquiesced in by me, in a right over my property), and the judgment of the court to which you bring your case?

7.5.1 When do Estoppel Rights Arise?

Section 116(a) of the Land Registration Act 2002, applying to registered land, declares that 'an equity by estoppel ... has effect from the time the equity arises ...'.

Although the wording is circular, this provision seems to mean that you have an 'equity by estoppel' immediately the requirements for establishing an estoppel claim have been met. We need, however, to decide what the phrase 'equity by estoppel' means—what in fact you are entitled to from that moment. The message is surely not merely that, from that moment, you can have whatever outcome a court ultimately awards you, effective from the time it does so. That would be too obvious to require special statement. Nor can it be merely that, from that moment, you have a right to bring your claim to court at all:[79] this is a quite general right, applicable to all the law's substantive areas,[80] and requiring no particular mention in the context of estoppel. The message seems rather to be that you are entitled to a retrospective award: that is, to the court's eventual award taking effect from the time when the facts creating your claim occurred. So, for example, if the court eventually awards you a right entitling you to occupy my land, you are treated as having had the same right since the moment your claim arose. So if you did occupy without my permission during that period, I cannot sue you for having been a trespasser. Your 'equity', which section 116(a) describes (albeit woollily) as arising simultaneously with your claim, is a reified representation of your entitlement to this eventual backdating.

Rights, by definition effective from the operation of a rule on the facts, are a good idea. Furthering a liberal vision operating through the precepts of the Rule of Law, they allow people to organise their lives without going to court. But this is possible only where, without going to court, one can nevertheless know what the relevant rights are. Where this is not the case, rights are positively dangerous. For they mean that the legal situation between us is structured along lines that we cannot discover. We are thus obliged to conduct our affairs in the dark, at risk of later learning that we have transgressed. For example, take again the situation where you occupy my land,

---

[79] The position prior to the 2002 Act was presented in this way in P Ferguson, 'Constructive Trusts—A Note of Caution' (1993) 109 *LQR* 114, 121–3 and D Hayton, 'Equitable Rights of Cohabitees' [1990] *Conv* 370, 372 and 'Constructive Trusts of Homes—A Bold Approach' (1993) 109 *LQR* 485. But this analysis was probably incorrect: cf *Crabb v Arun District Council* [1976] Ch 179 (CA), where the claimant's remedy included compensation for the loss he suffered when the defendant denied his claim for the seven years between the requirements being met and the case reaching court; *Voyce v Voyce* (1991) 62 P & CR 290 (CA), where time began to run against the claimant as soon as the requirements were met, for the purposes of prescription; *Birmingham Midshires Mortgage Services Ltd v Sabherwal* (2000) 80 P & CR 256 (CA), where the beneficial interest to which the court eventually declared the claimant entitled was overreached by a disposition occurring between the time the requirements were met and that of the judgment.

[80] European Convention on Human Rights, Arts 6 and 13.

without my permission, between the time of the facts generating your estoppel claim and that of the court award. If the nature of the award lies in the court's discretion, there is a problem. If the court eventually awards you a right entitling you to occupy, the backdating of this outcome means that you were entitled to occupy all along: so if I have evicted you, I shall be additionally liable for the loss the eviction causes you. But if the court gives you some other form of relief, you will have had no right to occupy in the meantime: so if you have occupied, you will be liable to me in damages for trespass. If an award is unpredictable, then, it is better that it *not* be backdated.

In proprietary estoppel, as we saw especially in § 7.3.1, the decision of the House of Lords in *Cobbe v Yeoman's Row Management Ltd*[81] momentarily presented the courts' approach as non-discretionary. On that view, section 116(a)'s backdating of the award—alias the proposition that you have a right to it in the meantime—is appropriate. But the majority of decisions, now including *Thorner v Majors*,[82] take a discretionary approach. On this view, then, section 116(a) is dangerous, in the way explained in the previous paragraph; it would be better to have the opposite rule, namely that your award takes effect only from the time it is made, generating no rights in the meantime.

Better still, use could be made of a 'remedial constructive trust'. Despite their name, 'remedial constructive trusts' do not have to be trusts, which estoppel outcomes may or (usually) may not be. They are outcomes of any sort, awarded and profiled (eg backdated or not) by the court in an ad hoc discretionary determination.[83] So the court, in fixing your estoppel relief, would also choose whether or not it should be backdated, as a matter of discretion. If it felt, in the particular circumstances, that you deserved to have the outcome backdated and that this could safely be done, it would so order; otherwise your remedy would have prospective effect only.

Remedial constructive trusts are controversial, and indeed the Court of Appeal has rejected their use in English law.[84] But the argument against them is not so much that they cannot be usefully applied in this way to discretionary jurisdictions, as that discretionary jurisdictions should not exist: that there should be rights (necessarily arising from the relevant facts, rather than from court determinations), and nothing else.[85] So long as the law does in

---

[81] [2008] 1 WLR 1752 (HL).

[82] [2009] UKHL 18 (HL).

[83] For a full account, see D Waters, 'The Nature of the Remedial Constructive Trust' in P Birks (ed), *The Frontiers of Liability, Volume 2* (Oxford, 1994) ch 13; D Wright, *The Remedial Constructive Trust* (Sydney, 1998).

[84] *Re Polly Peck International plc (in administration) (No 2)* [1998] 3 All ER 812 (CA).

[85] See eg P Birks, 'Proprietary Rights as Remedies' in P Birks (ed), *The Frontiers of Liability, Volume 2* (Oxford, 1994) ch 16, and 'The End of the Remedial Constructive Trust' (1998) 12 *Trusts Law International* 202; cf S Gardner, *An Introduction to the Law of Trusts* (2nd edn, Oxford, 2003) 121–6.

fact have discretionary jurisdictions,[86] remedial constructive trusts create useful alternative possibilities with regard to backdating.

More recently, in *Thorner v Majors*,[87] Lord Scott has suggested that the term 'proprietary estoppel' should be applied only to cases where the response is the non-discretionary effectuation of the claimant's belief;[88] but that the more discretionary responses often associated with that term should be seen as emerging instead, and perfectly properly, via remedial constructive trusts. This suggestion involves a different perception of remedial constructive trusts to that put forward above. It treats the expression 'remedial constructive trust' as referring not to a jurisdiction to fine-tune outcomes emerging under established causes of action, such as proprietary estoppel, but to a cause of action in its own right, with its own components and underlying rationale. The cause of action being 'remedial', however, these components and underlying rationale would themselves be a matter for the courts' discretion, and that is how Lord Scott appears to see them, for he makes no attempt to describe them. The resulting position would be utterly at odds with the Rule of Law.[89]

7.5.2 Estoppel Equities as Rights in Rem

Section 116(a), besides thus declaring that your 'equity' will take effect from—ie your award will be backdated to—the time when the relevant facts occurred, also rules that your equity will be a right in rem, capable of binding anyone who takes a disposition of the land from me during the period between the facts occurring and the award.[90] Say the facts on which you rely occurred in January; in July, the court gives judgment, making an award in your favour; but in April, I transferred the land in question to John. Your equity binds John, so long as the usual conditions for that are met.[91] So you can now enforce your award against John.

This rule is a problematic one, for two reasons. One is that it may not make sense for your entitlement to be in rem. Depending on the particular facts and the court's exercise of its discretion, your remedy can take a number of forms. I might for example be ordered to transfer the land in question to

---

[86] Their value to the law is explored in K Hawkins (ed), *The Uses of Discretion* (Oxford, 1992).

[87] [2009] UKHL 18, [14], [20]–[21] (HL).

[88] That is, the material which he identified as the proper domain of proprietary estoppel in *Cobbe v Yeoman's Row Management Ltd* [2008] 1 WLR 1752 (HL).

[89] cf *Jennings v Rice* [2002] EWCA Civ 159, [43] (CA).

[90] 'An equity by estoppel … has effect from the time the equity arises *as an interest capable of binding successors in title*' (emphasis added). This replicates what was probably the rule anyway, it being taken thus in a number of cases, including *Inwards v Baker* [1965] 2 QB 29, 37 (CA); *Lloyds Bank plc v Carrick* [1996] 4 All ER 630, 642 (CA); *Campbell v Griffin* [2001] EWCA Civ 990, [37] (CA); *Lloyd v Dugdale* [2001] EWCA Civ 1754, [39] (CA).

[91] That is, either the right is registered (unlikely, as proprietary estoppel is a disorganised way of generating rights), or it operates as an overriding interest (probably via your actual and apparent occupation of the land).

you,[92] or to give you a lease[93] or an easement[94] over it; in other words to give you a right in rem over the land. On the other hand, you might be awarded only some right in personam against me, such as the right merely to occupy the land alongside me,[95] or the right that I pay you a sum of money.[96] Where your remedy turns out to be in rem, it makes perfectly good sense for your entitlement to that remedy to be likewise in rem, so here section 116(a) comes as no surprise. But where your remedy turns out to be in personam, your entitlement to that remedy should surely be likewise in personam, and section 116(a)'s statement to the contrary (that your entitlement is in fact in rem) is surprising and absurd. The quality—in rem or in personam—of your 'equity' should track the quality of your relief.

The other problem with the rule that the estoppel 'equity' operates in rem arises from the discretionary natue of estoppel relief. To see this problem, remember the observation in the previous section, that backdating a discretionary award is dangerous, as it means that people's legal position will be affected in ways that they cannot yet know. There, we focused on the position between the parties to the estoppel claim themselves: you and me. Now, we see that the rule means afflicting others, such as John, in the same way. For John personally, the problem is no worse than it is for you and me, as already discussed. But John also represents the class of disponees generally. All rights in rem are essentially disadvantageous to disponees, and so damaging to the marketability of land and the further policy concerns lying behind that. The level of damage is limited by maximising the visibility of the right's existence and content. Since estoppel 'equities' anticipate relief that is discretionary, this cannot be done. In short, since estoppel awards are discretionary, it is bad enough to backdate them; but to backdate them and make the backdating effective in rem is worse still. Again, the remedial constructive trust may offer a better solution, allowing the court to bind disponees only where the necessary predictability is present.

---

[92] As in *Thorner v Majors* [2009] UKHL 18 (HL).
[93] As in *Dodsworth v Dodsworth* (1973) 228 EG 1115 (CA).
[94] As in *Crabb v Arun District Council* [1976] Ch 179 (CA).
[95] As in *Inwards v Baker* [1965] 2 QB 29 (CA).
[96] As in *Jennings v Rice* [2002] EWCA Civ 159 (CA).

Constructive Trusts

8.1 Two Constructive Trust Doctrines

This chapter looks at two further doctrines whereby you may gain a right in my land, in an essentially disorganised way. These are the doctrines whereby a constructive trust arises against me if I acquire the land after giving an undertaking to allow you to benefit from it; or in some circumstances when you and I are family members together.

Both doctrines thus announce themselves as yielding you a constructive trust. Saying that the trust is 'constructive' means that it arises for reasons other than that I intend it to: which is another way of saying that it arises on a disorganised basis. Our task will be to see what these reasons are, and to assess their merit.

8.1.1 The Doctrines' Limitation to Trusts

Before going on, however, let us look at the stipulation that these doctrines generate *trusts*, and only trusts.

We looked at the idea of a trust briefly in §§ 1.3.4 and 1.5, and will explore it fully in Chapters 13 and 14. In outline, a trust is 'a situation in which property is vested in someone (a trustee), who is under legally recognised obligations, at least some of which are of a proprietary kind [ie in rem], to handle it in a certain way, and to the exclusion of any personal interest.'[1] Take the case where I own some land but hold it on trust, for you as the beneficiary of that trust. The land will remain vested in me (ie registered in my name), but I will be obliged to let you, as beneficiary, have all the benefit from it, retaining none for myself ('to the exclusion of any personal

---

[1] S Gardner, *An Introduction to the Law of Trusts* (2nd edn, Oxford, 2003) 2.

interest').[2] This distinguishes a trust right from all other rights in rem short of ownership itself. Where you have such another right over my land it does not absorb all the benefit. All the benefit not absorbed by the right remains with me, as owner. For example, if you have a right of way over my land, you can cross it by the route in question, but nothing else. In all respects not inconsistent with this, the land is mine to enjoy.

Contrast the disorganised acquisition doctrine which we looked at in Chapter 7, namely proprietary estoppel. The latter can generate any kind of right in rem over land:[3] a trust (so that you take all the land's benefit) or some other right (so that you take some benefit, but I keep the rest), as the circumstances warrant. It is striking that the doctrines we shall look at in this chapter purport to generate only trust rights. Assuming we find that they should generate you a right at all, we shall want to think why it should have to be a trust right, and cannot be anything else. In fact, we shall find that the first of this chapter's two doctrines can, despite assertions that it generates only constructive trusts, generate any kind of right. The second of the two doctrines, however, is actually defined in such a way that it produces specifically trust rights—though the fundamental ideas involved could perhaps yield other outcomes.

8.2 Transfer Subject to an Undertaking

The first of our two doctrines is this. Say I acquire some land from John, promising John that I will allow you to use the land in some way (commonly, to continue to use it as you did in John's time, but this is not essential). The law obliges me to keep my promise, saying that I now hold the land on constructive trust for you.[4]

8.2.1 The Principle

This doctrine originated in two groups of decisions.

[2] I can of course hold the land on trust for you and John together, meaning that all the benefit goes to the two of you. And indeed, I can hold it on trust for you and me together, in which case I share the benefit with you: that is to say, while I can derive no benefit *in my capacity as trustee*, I can do so as co-object of the trust with you. This matters especially for the second of our two doctrines, which most commonly operates so as to produce such an outcome.

[3] As well as some other outcomes, including a right in personam over land, a right in rem or in personam over other kinds of property, and a money award.

[4] See further B McFarlane, 'Constructive Trusts Arising on a Receipt of Property *Sub Conditione*' (2004) 120 *LQR* 667.

One[5] deals with the case where my acquisition of the land is *inter vivos*, and I make John an oral promise to hold the land on trust for you (or indeed him). The *inter vivos* creation of trusts of land requires writing,[6] so at first sight my oral promise is ineffective. But John relied on my promise in transferring the land to me, or at any rate doing so without putting the trust in writing. If I were now to go back on my promise, John would have been injured by this reliance. My obligation to keep my promise arises so as to prevent this injury.

The other group[7] deals with the case (involving what is known as a 'secret trust') where John transfers the land to me on his death. John does not stipulate in his will that I should hold the land on trust for you, which is what the Wills Act 1837 requires if he is to make an express trust effective upon death.[8] But he takes a promise from me that I will do so. Again, John's reliance on my promise (failing to use the proper form to make his trust for you) means that he will suffer detriment if I go back on my promise, and, to prevent that, the law obliges me to keep my promise.

The effect seen in these cases is sometimes put as 'equity will not permit a statute [the Wills Act or the *inter vivos* formality requirement] to be used as an instrument of fraud', my failure to keep my promise, so injuring John, being the (actual or potential) fraud. But this view of the matter suggests that the court is able to abort the application of the statutory rule, which is hard to understand. It is more intelligible to see the statutory rule as stopping any express trust from arising, but the need to prevent my fraud as requiring relief against me, on the corrective grounds just described. As it happens, this relief needs to take the same shape as the express trust would have had, ie an obligation requiring me to keep my promise. It would not suffice merely to return the land to John, so as to give him the chance to impose the trust—using the proper form—for himself. That is because returning the land to John in this way, even if John is still alive, would not allow him to establish the trust *from the moment he wanted it*. The only way to achieve that outcome is for the law, straight away, to hold me to the trust. So the best view of the matter is that the law imposes the promised trust on me[9] as a constructive trust.[10]

---

[5] *Rochefoucauld v Boustead* [1897] 1 Ch 196 (CA); *Bannister v Bannister* [1948] 2 All ER 133 (CA).

[6] Law of Property Act 1925 s 53(1)(b): see § 13.3.3.

[7] The principal decision of this kind is *Blackwell v Blackwell* [1929] AC 318 (HL), but there is much other authority.

[8] § 4.3.

[9] That is, the trust arises not from John's stipulation alone, but from the combination of that stipulation, my agreement, and John's reliance. The trust so generated is therefore appropriately said, in the secret trust context, to arise 'outside the will'. That truth is sometimes, however, misunderstood as connoting that the trust arises from John's stipulation alone, but is exempt from the Wills Act's requirements: an impossible idea. See further S Gardner, *An Introduction to the Law of Trusts* (2nd edn, Oxford, 2003) 86–93.

[10] *Rochefoucauld v Boustead* [1897] 1 Ch 196, 208 (CA) treats the trust as express, but does so only for limitation purposes (under *Soar v Ashwell* [1893] 2 QB 390 (CA)): this does not signify that it *is* express.

8.2.2 Must the Outcome be a Trust?

In the original decisions, my promise was always to hold the land *on trust*. Following the reasoning above, my obligation is thus also a trust, and correctly labelled as such. Some further decisions, however, hold that a constructive trust arises in this way also if the promise I make to John is not to hold the land on trust for you, but to allow you to enjoy it in some other way. Say John owns a stately home, and you have a contract with him allowing you to sell refreshments to his visitors. John transfers the house to me. Your rights under your contract are not rights in rem, capable of binding me automatically.[11] But if John takes a promise from me that I will continue with the same arrangement, the cases say that I will be obliged to do so, my obligation being a constructive trust in your favour.[12]

It is correct that I should come under the obligation described, for the reason given above: otherwise, John will have suffered the detriment of failing to provide for you in the way he wished. But calling my obligation a trust is incorrect. As we saw in § 8.1.1, saying I hold land *on trust* for you denotes that, although I am the land's legal owner, I have no rights to enjoy it myself. That is not the case here. In our example, I must allow you to continue with your refreshment business, but I have the right to enjoy the land in all other respects myself. So if I resell the land, I keep the proceeds. I do not give the proceeds to you, as I would have to if I truly held the land on trust for you.[13]

If my obligation really is a trust, as in the original decisions, it will—as such[14]—be a right in rem, so as potentially to bind someone to whom I in turn transfer the land. If it is not a trust, its character as in rem or in personam should in principle depend on its content. My obligation to allow you to sell refreshments should be in personam, because there is no such recognised right in rem. But say I promised to allow you a lease or a right of

---

[11] You have a contractual licence, which operates in personam: see § 15.3.3.

[12] *Binions v Evans* [1972] Ch 359, 368–9 (CA); *Lyus v Prowsa Developments Ltd* [1982] 1 WLR 1044 (Ch D); *Ashburn Anstalt v WJ Arnold & Co* [1989] Ch 1, 22–27 (CA).

[13] Can it be argued that I hold not the land as whole, but the specific right (your right to sell refreshments) on trust for you? No, because this right has no separate identity in my hands, so as to allow it to be something that I can hold on trust. It exists only as *your* right *against* John or me. Alternatively, can it be said that I hold the land as a whole on trust for you (to the extent of your refreshment right) and myself (as to the remainder) together? This is a more interesting suggestion. But the conventional wisdom is that where two or more people have trust rights entitling them to benefit from the asset simultaneously, the benefit must remain a single package to be enjoyed on a shared basis (ie on the basis of 'unity of possession'). That is to say, the benefit may not be divided, in the manner of the suggestion, so as to give the different people different pieces of it.

[14] More strictly, at least some obligations under every trust are in rem (see § 14.4), but this leaves it fair to say for present purposes that 'a trust is a right in rem'.

way over the land. These are recognised rights in rem, so my obligation, reproducing them, ought to be in rem too.[15]

8.2.3 Proving the Promise

So if, on acquiring the land in question from John, I promise him that I will let you use it in some way, the law protects John's reliance on my promise by imposing on me an obligation to adhere to it.

In principle, the promise I make to John in your favour can be either express or implied. Whether it is sufficiently evidenced will require a judgment on individual facts.[16]

A word is needed, however, about one type of case: that where John transfers the land to me, and I agree to accept it, 'subject to' your right. These words could in principle have two different meanings, only one of which involves the promise on my part needed to create the obligation under discussion.

The contract under which John sells me the land will normally oblige John to give me 'vacant possession' of the land. So—continuing with the example above—if you are still running your refreshment business on the land when it becomes mine, the possession I receive will not be vacant, and John will find himself in breach of contract ... unless we have agreed that he will give me possession that is vacant in all respects except your presence. Making the contract 'subject to' your presence will do that.

The words 'subject to' will always operate in this way. In the first of their two possible meanings, however, that is all they do. Then, they do not oblige me to let you remain: I can evict you, but I cannot recoup the losses I suffer in the process by suing John. But in their second meaning, the words *additionally* denote a promise by me to let you remain. Then, an obligation to that effect will arise against me in the manner currently under discussion.

---

[15] The cases have not yet addressed this issue properly; the most that can be said is that they contain nothing inconsistent with the proposition suggested in the text. In *Chattey v Farndale Holdings Inc* (1998) 75 P & CR 298 (CA) the undertaking was to honour a lien, which is a right in rem, and the resulting obligation seems to have been treated as in rem (*ibid* 313–17). No decision has yet been required on the position where the undertaking is to honour a right in personam. There is, however, a hint in *DHN Food Distributors Ltd v Tower Hamlets London Borough Council* [1976] 1 WLR 852 (CA) and, following it, *Re Sharpe (a bankrupt)* [1980] 1 WLR 219 (Ch D) that the obligation in that case is, contrary to the argument here, in rem. But the right in personam in question in those decisions was a contractual licence, which some judges wished to reclassify as a right in rem (§ 15.3.3). The decisions may be seen as influenced by that project, and were (therefore) disapproved in *Ashburn Anstalt v WJ Arnold & Co* [1989] Ch 1, 24 (CA).

[16] *Ashburn Anstalt v WJ Arnold & Co* [1989] Ch 1, 26 (CA) asserts that it should not be found by 'inferences from slender materials'. In the secret trust context, there is some authority that a higher than usual standard of proof is required—*Re Snowden* [1979] Ch 528 (Ch D)—but the statement is confused.

How do we tell which meaning the words have in a given case? The short answer is that we cannot always know for sure. But, it is sometimes said, if the land is priced below the figure that it could command with vacant possession, that shows I am promising to let you stay. This is insufficiently sophisticated, however. Certainly, if I have to let you stay, the value of the land is less than it would be if it were wholly vacant, and its price will normally reflect that. But even if I can evict you, the fact that I cannot reclaim any associated losses should also impair the value of the deal and show up in a reduced price. The reduction in the latter case should be smaller than in the former, as my right to evict you allows me to eradicate the reason for the diminution in the land's value. But it will sometimes be hard to be confident which of the two levels of impaired value is reflected in an admittedly reduced price. That approach aside, remember also to think about the contractual language itself, in its context. If the relevant term stipulates that I will take the land from John 'subject to your *right*', rather than merely to 'your presence', it seems to indicate that I am promising to let you stay.[17]

8.2.4 An Alternative to a Promise?

So far, we have discussed this doctrine in terms of my *promising* John to allow you to use the relevant land in some way. This is certainly the standard account of it.[18]

But some decisions[19] suggest that such an obligation also arises against me if you have a right against John to use the land in the way in question, and I

---

[17] In *Ashburn Anstalt, ibid* 25–26, it is said that John's making the transfer 'subject to' your right could alternatively be a performance by John of the duty, normally found in his contract with me, to disclose to me any 'incumbrances' affecting the land that are known to him. Explained in this way, the words would again not amount to a promise by me to let you stay. The argument is not clean, however. 'Incumbrances' are properly speaking rights in rem already extant against the land, which *will* bind me, even without a promise. *Ex hypothesi*, the kind of right presently under discussion is not an already extant right in rem, so will not bind me on that basis (only if I promise that it should). So it does not require disclosure as an incumbrance anyway.

[18] The statement of the principle in *Ashburn Anstalt v WJ Arnold & Co* [1989] Ch 1, 22–27 (CA) does not commit itself univocally to the requirement for a *promise*, instead demanding an inquiry whether, in all the circumstances, it would be 'unconscionable' for me not to owe you the obligation in question. However, *IDC Group Ltd v Clark* [1992] 1 EGLR 186 (Ch D) and *Lloyd v Dugdale* [2001] EWCA Civ 1754, [50]–[56] (CA) appear to regard this unconscionability as arising from John having transferred the land to me on the basis of my promise, as described in the text.

[19] *De Mattos v Gibson* (1859) 4 De G & J 276, 282 (LJJ); *Catt v Tourle* (1869) 4 Ch App 654 (CA in Ch); *Luker v Dennis* (1877) 7 Ch D 227 (Ch D); *Binions v Evans* [1972] Ch 359, 369 (CA); *Peffer v Rigg* [1977] 1 WLR 285, 294 (Ch D). (The proposition under discussion forms the third ratio of *Peffer v Rigg*. It is quite distinct from the first and second ratios, which address the possibility that the right in question bound the transferee as a right in rem. For discussion of the latter issue, see § 2.1.1.)

buy the land from John *knowing of* this right. Other decisions reject this extension, however.[20] Which view is right?

It must of course be assumed that your right will not bind me of its own accord—that is, as a right in rem, effective against me either through having been registered, or as an overriding interest.[21] In traditional unregistered land law, an equitable right in rem would affect me unless I was a bona fide purchaser of the land in question for value and without notice of the right. In that context, then, if your right was in rem, and I knew of it, it would bind me. But that is quite different from the hypothesis under discussion. This concerns the case where a right will *not* bind me of its own accord, either because it is in personam, or because, though in rem, it has not been registered and does not qualify as overriding. The hypothesis is that I will put myself under a new obligation ('constructive trust') to honour the right if I know about it, just as if I promise to honour it, when I buy the land.[22]

As we saw in § 8.2.1, when I acquire land from John promising John to honour your right, I am bound because an obligation arises to correct the detriment (loss of opportunity for John to protect you) for which I would otherwise be responsible. But there seems to be no reason why I should incur an obligation merely because I know about your right. If John suffers detriment in such a case, my awareness of it is insufficient to ascribe it to me: in the absence of a promise from me to honour your right, any expectation on his part that I would do so is not of my making. The correct decisions are therefore those[23] which hold that knowledge of a non-binding right does *not* oblige me to honour it.

Sometimes, however, on top of my knowledge of your right, there is a possible further factor. Does this make a difference? Two kinds of further factor may be considered.

---

[20] *Formby v Barker* [1903] 2 Ch 539 (CA); *London County Council v Allen* [1914] 3 KB 642 (CA); *Ashburn Anstalt v WJ Arnold & Co* [1989] Ch 1, 26 (CA). *Midland Bank Trust Co Ltd v Green* [1981] AC 513 (HL) is sometimes added to these, but incorrectly. The discussion there was solely of the terms of the Land Charges Act 1925 s 13. That section ruled that I was not bound by a right in rem to which the Act applied if you had not registered it. The question was whether the section contained an exception if I nonetheless knew about your right. The answer was no.

[21] So distinguish the present discussion from the argument, in § 2.2.3, that a disponee of land should be bound by a right in rem against it if he knows of the right, as an alternative to it being registered or counting as overriding under the Land Registration Act 2002 Sch 3. The point of that argument is that the right is in rem—ie exists to bind the disponee—and, given his knowledge, there is no reason why it should not do so.

[22] There is thus no analogy with the obligation which arises under the doctrine known as 'knowing receipt of trust property'. If I acquire trust property and, knowing that it is not mine, lose it again, so causing a loss to the trust, this doctrine makes me liable to the trust for the loss. Properly understood, this doctrine depends on my being bound, as I acquire the property, by the rights in rem which make it trust property: so I become its trustee: and when I lose it, I break my duty as trustee to keep it safe, and so am liable in that way. See S Gardner, *An Introduction to the Law of Trusts* (2nd edn, Oxford, 2003) 281–2.

[23] n 20.

First, where not only do I know about your right, but also John charges me a reduced price for the land, because he believes I will honour your right. Unless my acceptance of the price reduction suggests that I am making an implicit promise after all, this should make no difference:[24] I have done nothing to mean that John's erroneous belief should be ascribed to me, and his acceptance of a lower price on the strength of this belief is simply a mistake on his part.

Second, where not only do I know about your right, but also John transfers the land to me deliberately so as to destroy your right (though this will normally give you a right to compensation from John). If I am merely the innocent instrument of John's scheme, I should not be affected by it any more than by my knowledge alone. But if I co-operate with John in his scheme (and going ahead knowing of the scheme seems necessarily to amount to co-operating in it), I become responsible for the detriment you have suffered, because I lend myself to the wrong by which John brings that about.[25] Correcting that detriment by imposing a corresponding obligation on me appears right.[26]

8.3 Family Property

8.3.1 An Outline

We now turn to the second of our constructive trust doctrines.

Say I own a house, and I wish to give you a share in it. I can do so by intentional conferral. As the creation of a beneficial interest in land, this operation will require writing.[27] If I use writing, however, the upshot will be an *express* trust of the house, I being the trustee, for you and myself in the intended proportions.[28]

Say, on the other hand, that I own a house; that you and I are members of a family, probably living together in the house; and that you and I

---

[24] Compare *Tulk v Moxhay* (1848) 2 Ph 774, 778 (Ch), where it is said that such facts do generate an obligation against me. The obligation is better understood as a right in rem, the restrictive covenant, newly created by that case: see Ch 10.

[25] There is perhaps a connection with the wrongs of inducing a breach of contract, and dishonest assistance in a breach of trust.

[26] Whereas (the third ratio in) *Peffer v Rigg* [1977] 1 WLR 285, 294 (Ch D) apparently imposed an obligation on the basis of knowledge alone (see at n 19), the facts of the case suggest that the true explanation may be the analysis now under discussion.

[27] Law of Property Act 1925 s 53(1)(b); § 4.4.1.

[28] For express trusts, see § 13.3.1.

agree—have a 'common intention', as the cases in this area generally put it—that you should have a share in it, but I do not put this in writing. No express trust can arise, but the law gives effect to our intention nonetheless, recognising it as generating a *constructive* trust. Under this constructive trust, I again become trustee of the house for you and myself, in the intended proportions. It is this constructive trust that is the focus of the present discussion.

This sketch has so far focused on the simple case, where I am the sole registered owner of the house (the 'sole name' scenario). The same principles apply also where you and I are registered as joint owners of the house (the 'joint names' scenario). Unless the registration or other paperwork indicates otherwise, the law assumes that we hold the house for our own benefit, in 50:50 shares.[29] If I wish you to have a larger share, I can confer it on you expressly, by the use of writing.[30] But even without such writing, if it is our common intention that you should have a larger share, the law will again rule that we hold the house on constructive trust in the intended proportions.

In both scenarios, then, our (unwritten) common intention—that the house should belong to us in such-and-such proportions—gives rise to a constructive trust to that effect. But this statement is only an initial outline of this type of constructive trust, providing a point of departure for a fuller treatment. We shall encounter a number of complexities and difficulties. In particular, 'common intention' will turn out not to mean what it appears to.

8.3.2 Two Questions

At the outset, it is necessary to separate two questions with which the doctrine deals. The first question is whether to depart from the prima facie position. In the 'sole name' scenario, the prima facie position is that the house is entirely mine, so this question is in effect whether you should have a share in it at all; while in the 'joint names' scenario, the prima facie position is that the house belongs to us in 50:50 shares, and the question is whether you should have a larger fraction. If the answer to this first question is 'yes', we continue to the second question: how large should your share then be?

In principle, there is no reason why these two questions should be treated differently. They could and should be condensed into the single question of whether you ought to have such-and-such a share; this being—obviously—a larger share than that, if any, to which you would otherwise be entitled (ie than the prima facie position). But as the cases currently stand, they require separate discussion. We shall take them in turn.

---

[29] *Stack v Dowden* [2007] 2 AC 432, [54]–[58] (HL).
[30] Law of Property Act 1925 s 53(1)(c).

8.3.3 Departure from the Prima Facie Position

First, then, the question whether to depart from the prima facie position, so that in the 'sole name' scenario you can claim a share at all, and in the 'joint names' scenario you can claim more than 50 per cent.

As stated in the outline above, your ability to do so depends on whether you and I have a common intention that you should. Two points require further examination: what this 'common intention' involves; and whether anything further is needed.

In *Gissing v Gissing*[31] and *Lloyds Bank plc v Rosset*,[32] the House of Lords held that the common intention had to be a genuine one, rather than one invented by the court.[33] It could be either express (where you and I had actually spoken about the matter and agreed that you should have more than your prima facie share) or implied (where, though we had not actually spoken about the matter, it is nonetheless discoverable that we had such an intention).[34] But whereas an express common intention could be proved by all relevant evidence, an implied common intention could be proved by only one kind of evidence: 'direct contributions to the purchase price [of the house in question] by the partner who is not the legal owner, whether initially or by payment of mortgage instalments'[35]—often abbreviated to 'direct financial contributions'. So activities such as home-making and child-raising could not be treated as evidence of an implied common intention; nor even could indirect financial contributions: as, say, where you use your earnings to meet our day-to-day costs, leaving me to pay the mortgage.

To the requirement of a genuine common intention, discovered according to these rules, was added a requirement that you should act in reliance on that intention, and suffer detriment as a result.[36] There were no special rules about what counted as this detrimental reliance.[37]

This set of rules was in important respects ill-conceived. The 'direct financial contributions' rule was economically naïve, since enabling me to pay the mortgage is tantamount to paying it yourself. It also discriminated against family members (predominantly women) contributing in other ways, no less essential to the family's well-being and prosperity than paying the mortgage.[38] Unsurprisingly, then, the judges sometimes found it too uncomfortable to apply the 'direct financial contributions' rule, and strove to escape

[31] [1971] AC 889 (HL).
[32] [1991] 1 AC 107 (HL).
[33] *Gissing v Gissing* [1971] AC 889, 904 (HL). More strictly, the requirement was that *a reasonable bystander would have thought* there was a genuine common intention: *ibid* 906.
[34] *Lloyds Bank plc v Rosset* [1991] 1 AC 107, 132–3 (HL).
[35] *Ibid* 133.
[36] *Ibid* 132.
[37] *Grant v Edwards* [1986] Ch 638, 656–7 (CA).
[38] It may thus have infringed the European Convention on Human Rights, as discriminating on grounds of sex and property (relative income) (Art 14) with regard to the right to respect for family life and one's home (Art 8(1)).

it, usually[39] by purporting to find an express common intention where in truth there probably was none.[40] In reality, moreover, they were going further than finding implied but genuine common intentions in breach of the 'direct financial contributions' rule. They were surreptitiously *inventing* common intentions, contrary to the original prohibition on doing so.[41]

It came as no surprise, then, when the law was altered by the House of Lords in *Stack v Dowden*.[42] Under the new approach introduced by that decision, the common intention can be:

— Genuine and express, proved by all relevant evidence.
— Genuine and implied, proved not merely via 'direct financial contributions', but by reference to the parties' 'whole course of conduct in relation to [the property]',[43] which in effect means all relevant evidence.
— Invented ('imputed') by the judge,[44] again on the basis of the parties' 'whole course of conduct in relation to [the property]'.

The wide scope of the parties' 'whole course of conduct in relation to [the property]' was emphasised. It extends all the way from the parties' contributions to the acquisition of the property to the nature of their relationship itself, with all the latter's ramifications.[45] Further, no reference was made to a requirement of detrimental reliance, and it must logically have been dropped. One can only rely on an agreement that in fact exists, not—as is sufficient under the new approach—one invented by a judge.

It is arguable, however, that the first question is approached in this new way only in the 'joint names' scenario. *Stack v Dowden*[46] itself was concerned with that scenario, and it contains a statement suggesting that it was not intended to reform the way the first question should be addressed in the 'sole name' scenario.[47] Other passages, however, suggest that the new approach

---

[39] But cf *Le Foe v Le Foe* [2001] FLR 970 (County Court), where the judge simply found an implied common intention in breach of the 'direct financial contributions' rule. The rule was also aspersed by the Law Commission: *Sharing Homes* (Law Com No 278, London, 2002), para 4.27.

[40] As especially in *Eves v Eves* [1975] 1 WLR 1338 (CA) and *Grant v Edwards* [1986] Ch 638 (CA). In each, the defendant refused to agree that the claimant should have a share in the house, but gave an excuse—a lame reason—for so refusing. The courts treated the defendant's excuse as proving that there was an express agreement, whereas in truth it showed merely that, while the defendant refused to agree, he may have been ashamed of this. See also *Hammond v Mitchell* [1991] 1 WLR 1127 (Fam D) and *Stokes v Anderson* [1991] FLR 391 (CA), where express agreements were found on the basis of very thin evidence.

[41] S Gardner, 'Rethinking Family Property' (1993) 109 *LQR* 263.

[42] [2007] 2 AC 432 (HL). The decision was shortly afterwards reviewed and applied by the Privy Council in *Abbott v Abbott* [2008] 1 FLR 1451 (PC).

[43] *Stack v Dowden, ibid* [60].

[44] *Ibid* [17]–[22], [60]–[61].

[45] *Ibid* [69]–[70] (HL). Contrast the dissenting view of Lord Neuberger, *ibid* [131]–[136], especially [133].

[46] *Ibid.*

[47] *Ibid* [63].

governs the first question in both scenarios.[48] Certainly, there is no reason to treat the two scenarios differently as a matter of principle, and even if as a matter of technical authority they attract different rules today, it seems highly likely that the courts will correct this in the near future.

8.3.4 Quantum ... And a Single Rule

If the first question is answered in the affirmative—that is, it is decided that the claimant deserves more than his prima facie share, if any—the second question arises: how large a share should he in fact have?

Over the years, the courts have experimented with a number of different approaches to this question.[49] *Stack v Dowden*[50] has now established that the approach it applies to the first question (at any rate in the 'joint name' scenario) is to be used here too. So the size of the claimant's share is determined by reference to the parties' common intention.[51] Once again, this common intention may be a real one (express or implied), but may equally be one invented ('imputed') by the judge.[52] And it can be shown by reference to the parties' 'whole course of conduct in relation to [the property]',[53] encompassing many different kinds of behaviour.[54]

So far as this second question is concerned, it is already quite clear that the same approach is taken in both the 'joint names' and the 'single name' scenarios.[55] Which is perhaps an additional reason for thinking that it also covers both scenarios so far as the *first* question is concerned. That would leave us where we should be, with a single rule governing both questions in both scenarios. Where I or we own a house, and it is our common intention (whether genuine or invented) that you should have a certain share in it greater than that (if any) to which you are prima facie entitled, a constructive trust will arise giving you a right to that share. (Notice that the rule thus necessarily gives you a share in the house. To say that you have a 'share' in the house is to say that you have the entire benefit of the fraction in question. So your right is necessarily a trust right; the doctrine's very configuration means that its outcome is thus always a trust.)

---

[48] *Ibid* [20]–[21], [25]–[26]; also *Abbott v Abbott* [2008] 1 FLR 1451, [5]–[6] (PC). The passages in question amount to a *quite general* rejection of the old rules forbidding invention and permitting reference (outside express agreement cases) only to 'direct financial contributions'. The decisions which introduced these rules (*Gissing v Gissing* [1971] AC 889 (HL) and *Lloyds Bank plc v Rosset* [1991] 1 AC 107 (HL)) were addressed to the 'sole name' scenario.

[49] For the most striking efforts, see *Midland Bank plc v Cooke* [1995] 4 All ER 562 (CA) and *Oxley v Hiscock* [2005] Fam 211 (CA).

[50] [2007] 2 AC 432 (HL).

[51] *Ibid* [61].

[52] *Ibid* [17]–[22], [60]–[61]; *Abbott v Abbott* [2008] 1 FLR 1451, [5]–[6] (PC).

[53] *Abbott v Abbott, ibid* [6].

[54] *Stack v Dowden* [2007] 2 AC 432, [69]–[70] (HL).

[55] *Stack v Dowden, ibid* itself applied it in the 'joint names' scenario; immediately afterwards, *Abbott v Abbott* [2008] 1 FLR 1451 (PC) applied it in the 'sole name' scenario.

For all that this rule may sound clear and straightforward, however, there are two major problems with it.

8.3.5 The First Problem

The first problem concerns cases in which we have a genuine common intention, the effect of the rule being that we are entitled to shares in accordance with that intention.

The difficulty is this. As we saw at the outset, if I had intended you to have more than your prima facie right in the house, and had put this in writing, it would have yielded an express trust in the intended proportions.[56] According to the rule we have just examined, however, if I share that intention with you, the law gives effect to it in exactly the same way, but via a constructive trust, without need of writing. There seems no reason why this should be. Your concurrence in my intention provides no distinct basis for relief. If the law demands writing to effectuate my unilateral intention, it should demand it as much in the case of a common intention.

Remember how the rule stood before *Stack v Dowden*.[57] You and I had not only to agree that you should have the share in question; in addition, you had to act to your detriment in reliance on that agreement.[58] Your loss, and my responsibility for it via our agreement, did afford an additional reason why the law should intervene in your favour (there is a similarity with proprietary estoppel,[59] which many judges and commentators remarked upon). But we saw earlier how the requirement of detrimental reliance was dropped in that decision, as a necessary concomitant of its acceptance of invented common intention: you cannot rely on an agreement that never existed. As a result, a genuine common intention can no longer be the basis for the imposition of a constructive trust.

So this type of constructive trust cannot properly arise on the basis of a genuine but unwritten common intention after all. Parties can indeed agree their own arrangements, but only by using writing so as to produce an express trust. If common intention is to provide a satisfactory basis for a constructive trust at all, it must be via the phenomenon of judicial imputation.

8.3.6 The Second Problem

The second problem concerns that phenomenon.

---

[56] Nn 27–28.
[57] [2007] 2 AC 432 (HL).
[58] *Lloyds Bank plc v Rosset* [1991] 1 AC 107, 132 (HL).
[59] Ch 7. And also with the constructive trust doctrine discussed in § 8.2, which likewise revolves around the correction of a reliance loss.

Under the current rule, a genuine common intention can be proved from all relevant evidence, alias (especially where it is implied rather than express) from the parties' 'whole course of conduct in relation to [the property]',[60] which in turn means by reference to many different aspects of their behaviour.[61] Where the parties do not have a genuine common intention, however, the judge may impute—invent—one, again referring to the parties' 'whole course of conduct in relation to [the property]'.

Notice that the parties' 'whole course of conduct in relation to [the property]' plays a quite different role in the two contexts. In the finding of a genuine common intention, it is used simply to show, in an evidential way, the intention the parties actually had. In the imputing of a non-genuine common intention, however, it is used to indicate, in a normative way, the intention they should be treated as having had. But the courts have provided no explicit guidance as to how it does this; that is, as to the significance to be ascribed to the various possible kinds of behaviour.

Imagine, for example, that you and I were unmarried partners for 10 years, but have now separated. Our former home together is registered in my name alone, but you are now claiming a share in it. We had no genuine common intention on the matter, so you are asking the court to invent one by reference to our behaviour. I was always the sole wage-earner, and so all our outgoings, including the mortgage repayments on the house, came from my earnings—though we operated a joint account, as you needed to draw on my earnings too, for the shopping that you did. You kept house for us, and indeed redecorated the house and remodelled the garden.[62]

Stack v Dowden[63] allows reference to all these facts for the purposes of inventing a common intention. But a court might respond to them in a number of ways. Consider two, though it is possible to imagine others. First, it might give you a half share in the house, on the basis that you and I shared our lives: pooled our efforts and resources, making different but equally valuable contributions, in a way that suited our particular relationship best. For this perspective, it is in your favour that you were not a wage-earner, but depended financially on me: this helps confirm that we must have seen ourselves as sharing. Second, the court might give you a share reflecting your contribution to the acquisition of the house. Directly, in the form of actual mortgage repayments, you contributed nothing; but you could be seen as

---

[60] *Stack v Dowden* [2007] 2 AC 432, [60] (HL).

[61] *Ibid* [69]–[70].

[62] This example involves the 'sole name' scenario, and assumes that the question whether you have a right at all is governed by *Stack v Dowden, ibid*. For discussion whether this is correct, see § 8.3.3. If it is incorrect, it is easy to adjust the facts so as to put it beyond doubt that you have a right, eg by saying that for a brief period after moving in with me you went out to work, your earnings going into our joint account and so helping to repay the mortgage. Either way, *Stack v Dowden* certainly governs the issue of quantum; and, as we are about to see, this is the area of principal difficulty.

[63] *Ibid*.

contributing indirectly. By undertaking your work in and around our home, you saved me the cost of hiring a house-keeper, cook, personal shopper, decorator, gardener (therapist, escort, …), allowing me to put the saved sums towards repaying the mortgage.

It is easy to find problems with each of these perspectives, or at any rate their view of the facts to which they point. But there is a more fundamental difficulty: neither in *Stack v Dowden*[64] nor in any other decision have the judges explicitly said how we are to choose between them, and indeed any others that might suggest themselves. That is, they have not articulated the rationale behind the imputation of common intention—what goal it is aimed at achieving.

8.3.7 A Possible Solution to the Second Problem

This goal may, however, be identified by considering the way in which the courts have drawn particular outcomes from particular fact situations. As yet there is little to go on. *Stack v Dowden*[65] is itself illustrative, however, and so is *Abbott v Abbott*,[66] decided shortly afterwards by the Privy Council. In *Stack v Dowden*,[67] the claimant was found entitled to at least[68] a 65 per cent share, apparently on the basis that this reflected the contribution her earnings had made to the acquisition of the property in question, relative to that made by the defendant.[69] In *Abbott v Abbott*,[70] the claimant emerged with a 50 per cent share. Although she had made a financial contribution, it was much smaller than this. The outcome seems to have reflected the fact that she was married to the defendant, and that they had pooled their financial resources through a joint bank account[71]—in contrast to *Stack v Dowden*,[72] where the parties were unmarried, and had kept their financial affairs sharply separate.[73]

Even given this slender evidence, it is possible to detect a pattern. The key question appears to be whether the parties have a materially communal relationship: ie one in which, in practical terms, they pool their material resources (including money, other assets, and labour). If they do (as in *Abbott v Abbott*[74]), the claimant will be entitled to a 50 per cent share (as

[64] *Ibid*.
[65] [2007] 2 AC 432 (HL).
[66] [2008] 1 FLR 1451 (PC).
[67] [2007] 2 AC 432 (HL).
[68] She claimed a 65% share, and was awarded it. Her true entitlement may have been higher.
[69] [2007] 2 AC 432, [86]–[88] (HL).
[70] [2008] 1 FLR 1451 (PC).
[71] *Ibid* [9], [18].
[72] [2007] 2 AC 432 (HL).
[73] *Ibid* [90]–[92].
[74] [2008] 1 FLR 1451 (PC).

there[75]). This seems to be a defensible distributive operation: the law follows the relationship's own implication that the house, like the parties' other assets, should likewise be pooled. If, however, the parties' relationship is not materially communal (as in *Stack v Dowden*[76]), the relationship itself will have no particular message as regards the allocation of the property. Instead (again, as there), the claimant will be entitled to the share that reflects his contribution, if any, to the acquisition of the house.[77] Such an outcome is aimed—again defensibly—at correcting what would otherwise be the claimant's unjust enrichment of the defendant, who would otherwise be left with a share in the property, wholly or partly paid for by the claimant.[78]

This division between materially communal and non-materially communal relationships also accounts for a statement of the House of Lords, in *Stack v Dowden*,[79] that only in a 'very unusual' joint names case will unequal contributions to the acquisition of the property yield unequal shares in it. 'Very unusual' may or may not be a correct prediction of the relative incidence of the two kinds of relationship in litigated cases. The key point is that unequal contributions will sometimes matter, sometimes not: by the argument here, only in non-materially communal cases.

In the illustration given in the last section, therefore, we should expect the first of the two suggested outcomes: that is, you and I are entitled to equal shares in the house. The second outcome (shares reflecting our respective contributions to the acquisition of the house) was driven by unjust enrichment, and would have been apt if you and I had not had a materially

---

[75] And also as in *Fowler v Barron* [2008] 2 FCR 1 (CA). There, the house was registered in the parties' joint names, so prima facie they had 50:50 shares in it. But the claimant's earnings alone had paid for it, and he now argued that he should therefore be seen as solely entitled to it. The court rejected his claim. He and the defendant had lived as a couple for 23 years, and had had two children together. Although they each worked, and although they did not have a joint account (though they had made mutual wills), they depended on each other's contributions (in particular, most expenditure was funded by the claimant's higher earnings, while the defendant spent most time with the children). Given this relationship (one which the text calls materially communal), a 50:50 entitlement was (therefore) the correct outcome: so the prima facie position was left undisturbed (*ibid* [46]).

[76] [2007] 2 AC 432 (HL).

[77] This outcome is the same as that which will ensue if the property in question is not a 'family home' at all, as for example where the parties' relationship is a commercial one. Then, the doctrine discussed in the text will not apply, and instead there will be a 'presumed resulting trust'. But this too means that, unless the parties intended otherwise, they will have shares in the property corresponding to their respective contributions to the cost of acquiring it (though it is unclear whether mortgage repayments count as such a contribution: cf *Stack v Dowden* [2007] 2 AC 432, [118]–[120] (HL)). See *Laskar v Laskar* [2008] EWCA Civ 347 (CA) (where the parties were mother and daughter—ie in a family relationship—but had acquired the house in question as a commercial venture); N Piska, 'Two Recent Reflections on the Resulting Trust: Revisiting Resulting Trusts' [2008] *Conv* 441.

[78] For further discussion, see S Gardner, 'Family Property Today' (2008) 124 *LQR* 422.

[79] [2007] 2 AC 432, [68] (HL). See too *Fowler v Barron* [2008] 2 FCR 1, [18] (CA).

communal relationship; but in fact we did have a materially communal relationship, warranting equal shares.[80]

8.3.8 Some Remaining Difficulties

This analysis thus fills out the otherwise empty idea of imputation, and offers a defensible reason why constructive trusts should arise in this way at all. There are, however, problems with it, including the following.

Take first the response by way of correcting unjust enrichment. Consider a case where you run our home and care for our children, while I go out to work. It is possible to present this, as we saw in § 8.3.6, as saving me the money that I would otherwise have to pay to hire a housekeeper and a nanny, thus as entitling you to a share in the house corresponding to that fraction of its value. But thinking in this way has weaknesses. Work of this kind is generally not well paid, so your entitlement, calculated on this basis, may well be smaller than you could have gained by going out to work and making a financial contribution.[81] And the market price of your efforts is only one aspect of their full significance: done by you, work of this kind will have qualities different from those brought to it by others, which cannot be well expressed in pounds and pence. It is, however, some comfort that such difficulties are likely to arise most pressingly in cases where the parties' relationship is materially communal, requiring treatment on that basis, anyway.

If the law is to predicate rights upon the implications of materially communal relationships, moreover, it must be able to identify such relationships. In some instances, that will be possible; but this will not always be the case. Even if the parties themselves are both clear about and happy with the nature of their individual relationship, the set of possible relationships will form at best a spectrum, and drawing the required line between those that are materially communal and the rest will entail treating quite similar relationships strikingly differently, bringing about substantive injustice. And, of

---

[80] There are some more recent decisions, broadly consistent with the argument in the text. They generally proceed by reference to the parties' contributions, in contexts that were non-materially communal, though sometimes only subtly so. See eg *Holman v Howes* [2007] EWCA Civ 877 (CA) (where a divorced couple bought a house together in an abortive attempt at reconciliation); *Kali and Burlay v Chawla* [2007] EWHC 2357 (Ch D) (where although the parties were married when they bought the house, they soon separated and divorced, only the husband continuing to live in it and meet the outgoings); *Morris v Morris* [2008] EWCA Civ 257 (CA) (where, although the parties were married, the question was as to their shares not in their home but in the husband's farming enterprise, in which the wife was little involved). There is, however, an exception in *James v Thomas* [2007] EWCA Civ 1212 (CA), where the parties' relationship was apparently materially communal, but the court proceeded by reference to their respective contributions.

[81] You might do better by pointing not to the value of your contribution to me, but to the cost to you of making it—notably, the loss of your career prospects. But an unjust enrichment analysis privileges the former, as capturing the extent to which *I am enriched*.

course, it is highly optimistic to suppose that people will always be both clear about and happy with the nature of their relationship, leaving this at best an uncomfortable determinant of the law's response.[82]

8.3.9 Other Approaches

Given such difficulties with the constructive trust doctrine, we find ourselves considering alternatives.

In one context, indeed, the doctrine has been disapplied. Where the parties' relationship is marriage or a civil partnership and this has broken down, the Matrimonial Causes Act 1973 allows the courts to redistribute their property between them having regard to 'all the circumstances of the case'.[83] In practice, this means covering their needs and those of their children, then (normally) dividing any remaining property between them equally.[84] In our terms, the relationships in question here will almost inevitably be materially communal. The focus on needs aims to reflect the distributive implications of the relationship for the particular situation in which that relationship is now over. With its likewise distributive regime of otherwise equal division, the Act tracks the way that our doctrine too deals with property held within such relationships. It escapes the objection raised earlier, however, that it may be impossible satisfactorily to label many relationships as materially communal: for the relationships with which it is concerned— marriage or a civil partnership—are by definition materially communal, and people opt into them with that in mind.

So far so good, then; but that leaves the question what to do in the case of other relationships. The Law Commission[85] has addressed itself to some of these: those where the parties have lived as a couple in a joint household and have either had children or lived together for a defined period (probably of somewhere between two and five years),[86] and, again, the relationship has now broken down. The Commission's proposed scheme would aim to share the economic advantages and disadvantages arising from the parties' contributions to the relationship and experienced on its breakdown. Say, for example, a man and a woman lived together (without marrying); initially, both were employed, and had similar incomes; but after they became parents

---

[82] See A Bottomley, 'Women and Trust(s): Portraying the Family in the Gallery of Law' in S Bright and J Dewar (eds), *Land Law—Themes and Perspectives* (Oxford, 1998) ch 8.

[83] ss 24, 25.

[84] The Act does not itself lay down this regime, but it is established by the caselaw, notably *White v White* [2001] AC 596 (HL); *Miller v Miller, McFarlane v McFarlane* [2006] 2 AC 618 (HL).

[85] *Cohabitation: The Financial Consequences of Relationship Breakdown* (Law Com No 307, London, 2007). In March 2008, the government announced that it would not seek to legislate on the basis of these proposals, pending a review of the impact of a similar scheme recently introduced in Scotland: Family Law (Scotland) Act 2006.

[86] *Ibid* paras 3.4–3.63.

the woman ceased working, or worked part-time or at a lower level, so that she could look after the children. As a result of her move, she can no longer hope for employment at the level of income she could have expected without this interruption, ie she has a reduced earning capacity; while the man was enabled to maintain his career progression unaffected by the impact that child-rearing would otherwise have had, ie he has an enhanced earning capacity. The relationship has now broken down. The scheme would perceive the woman as entitled to redress from the man for the loss and gain caused by their joint life choices, and brought to the surface by the breakdown.

This proposed scheme thus takes a corrective rather than a distributive approach, so it escapes the difficulties which we identified in the previous section as attending the latter. This comes at the cost, however, of overlooking the truths that such an approach in fact captures: some of the relationships to which it applies will certainly be materially communal, but will not be treated on that basis. Its corrective approach could suffer from problems as great as those which the previous section identifies in the present law's unjust enrichment approach. And cases not covered by the scheme but left to the existing law—such as where adult siblings or platonic companions make their home together, an elderly person lives with his next-generation relatives, or an adult child stays at home to care for his aging parents—could well thus be treated differently from cases to which the scheme applies, for no good reason.[87]

So, although, as we have seen, *Stack v Dowden*[88] does not shape the law regarding family homes in a fully satisfactory way, this alternative structure offers no panacea either. Perhaps in fact there is no panacea to be had; this may be an area where the law simply cannot solve all the problems.

8.3.10 The Rule's Effect

The rule in *Stack v Dowden*[89] requires that you and I have a (real or invented) common intention that you should have such-and-such a share in the house. If we do, you emerge with that share as a trust right. This right takes effect from the time of the facts required to generate it, ie from the time of the formation of our (real or invented[90]) common intention. This proposition is implicit in many decisions[91] where the issue at stake was whether your right

---

[87] For further criticisms, see D Hughes, M Davis and L Jacklin, '"Come Live with Me and Be my Love"' A Consideration of the 2007 Law Commission Proposals on Cohabitation Breakdown' [2008] *Conv* 197.

[88] [2007] 2 AC 432 (HL).

[89] *Ibid.*

[90] When is the time of the formation of an invented common intention? The point has not yet been explored, but it is presumably the time of the behaviour by the parties on which the imputation is based.

[91] For example, *Williams & Glyn's Bank Ltd v Boland* [1981] AC 487 (HL); *Lloyds Bank plc v Rosset* [1991] 1 AC 107 (HL).

(which, being a trust right, is in rem[92]) binds a subsequent disponee of the land in question.

In taking this position, however, the law is additionally problematic. In § 7.5, when we discussed the equivalent issue in the context of proprietary estoppel, we saw that a strongly discretionary approach to relief is not properly compatible with a rule that the resultant right takes effect from the time of the underlying facts, especially as a right in rem: the discretion means that the outcome is not sufficiently predictable to operate satisfactorily as a *right* in this way. We encounter the same problem in the present context. Here the law is undoubtedly discretionary. This will especially be so if the courts maintain the opacity of *Stack v Dowden*[93] regarding the principles controlling when, and to what effect, a common intention is to be invented, as discussed in § 8.3.6. But it will also be the case even if the courts articulate those principles along the lines suggested in § 8.3.7, for these do not necessarily deliver sharp results. As we have already seen, it will not (and should not) always be easy to say whether a particular relationship counts as materially communal; and a finding of unjust enrichment could be marginal, especially where the claimant's contribution takes the form of work, and it is disputed whether the defendant actually wanted it, at any rate at the price of a share in what was otherwise his house.[94]

In the context of proprietary estoppel, the solution to such concerns was suggested (in §§ 7.5.1–7.5.2) to be the use of the 'remedial constructive trust', enabling the court, in making its award, to decide whether to backdate its effect to the time of the facts or to impose it only prospectively, from the time of the decision. The same solution would be as appropriate here.[95]

---

[92] While trust rights are in principle in rem (§ 14.4), however, in practice there are many impediments to their actually binding a disponee, leaving them not far off rights in personam. See § 14.8.2.

[93] [2007] 2 AC 432 (HL).

[94] Cf P Birks, *Unjust Enrichment* (Oxford, 2003) 47–8.

[95] T Etherton, 'Constructive Trusts: A New Model for Equity and Unjust Enrichment' [2008] *CLJ* 265 contends that *Stack v Dowden* [2007] 2 AC 432 (HL) has already introduced remedial constructive trusts to this area. In so saying, he appears to focus on the discretionary state in which that decision has left the law, as outlined in the text. The argument here, however, is that that is the problem, rather than the solution. There is nothing in the decision to suggest that an award under it can be fine-tuned as to its impact in the way that a true remedial constructive trust can.

PART 3
The rights

In Part 1, noting that this book sets out to focus principally on certain rights in rem that can exist in respect of land, we considered the essential nature and behaviour of such rights. In Part 2 we explored the ways in which such rights can arise. Part 3, which occupies the remainder of the book, now looks at the individual rights themselves.

It deals with easements (Chapter 9), restrictive covenants (Chapter 10), leases (Chapter 11), mortgages (Chapter 12), and beneficial interests under trusts (Chapters 13 and 14). It also looks at licences (Chapter 15), some of which are seen as in rem, and some others of which once were, but which are otherwise in personam. The treatment of licences serves partly to illuminate the border that licences share with leases, but also as a context in which to look closely at the way in which the law answers the question whether a right should be in rem.

9

Easements

9.1 What is an Easement?

The label 'easement' covers an assortment of rights in land, whose content varies but which are covered by the formula in *Re Ellenborough Park*,[1] explored below. Important examples are rights of way (entitling you to cross my land, on a particular route, going to and from your own land); rights of water (entitling you to the water flowing through a channel or pipe which crosses my land before reaching yours, meaning that I must not divert the water away from you); rights of light (entitling you to the supply of light that reaches your windows via my land, meaning that I may not build on my land so as to block them); and rights of support (entitling you to the support my land gives your buildings; I must not do anything to my land that compromises that support).[2]

Lest the possibility of there being such rights against my land seem simply unfair on me, it should be understood that in principle they arise when I grant them to you (commonly for money), or my predecessor did so and, as I acquire the land, I am bound by them as the rights in rem they are (which will be reflected in my paying a lower price than I would have paid if there were no such disadvantage to me). We shall look at the issues of grant, and operation in rem, in §§ 9.2 and 9.3.

---

[1] [1956] Ch 131, 163, 170 (CA).

[2] Cousins to easements are profits à prendre (profits, for short), which differ from easements in entitling you to take something from my land, which until that moment counted as part of my land. Examples of profits are thus the right to excavate (and remove for your own benefit) the stone in my quarry or the coal in my mine ... and, because these things also count as 'land', to cut the trees in my wood or to graze your cattle on my grass, or to catch the fish in my lake or the game in my forest.

9.1.1 The Rule in *Re Ellenborough Park*

The instances of easements given above are not regarded as a series of individual rights in rem. They are treated as particular manifestations of a generalised concept.

The concept's most famous formulation was induced from earlier caselaw by a commentator,[3] and adopted by the court in *Re Ellenborough Park*.[4] According to this formulation, for a right to qualify as an easement '(1) there must be a dominant and a servient tenement: (2) an easement must "accommodate" the dominant tenement: (3) dominant and servient owners must be different persons, and (4) a right over land cannot amount to an easement, unless it is capable of forming the subject-matter of a grant'.

Although this formula is so inadequate that a fresh start might be preferable, its privileged status means that we must continue to pay attention to it. What follows is an attempt to describe the rules defining easements which follows the formula in *Re Ellenborough Park*,[5] but challenges this where necessary.

9.1.2 Elements (1) and (3): Two Pieces of Land, Two Owners

The formula demands two pieces of land, with different owners. Although the formula leaves it unexplained, the point behind this is that an easement is a right:

— requiring that one piece of land (the 'servient tenement': my land, in the examples above) be used in a certain way, and
— belonging to another piece of land (the 'dominant tenement': your land, in the examples).

That you and I must be different people is obvious: unless it existed between two people, giving one (you) entitlements against the other (me), an easement could not be a right at all. But we need to take a closer look at the two points just isolated.

First, the demand that an easement relate to the use of my land. In the abstract, your right against me could be a right that I behave in a certain way *in my personal capacity*. To be an easement, however, the right must control not merely what I do in my personal capacity, but what I do *on my land*. Otherwise, it could not rationally be attached to the land, as rights in rem regarding land necessarily are, so as to be capable of binding disponees of the land. Say I am a builder, and I undertake to do work to shore up your

---

[3] G Cheshire, *The Modern Law of Real Property* (7th edn, London, 1954) 456 *et seq.*
[4] [1956] Ch 131, 163, 170 (CA).
[5] *Ibid.*

buildings. My obligation does not affect my use of my own house or builder's yard, several miles away, and will not bind someone to whom I sell that house or yard. So there is no easement in this case: merely a contract. Whereas if I live next door to you, and my obligation is not to take away the support that my land gives your buildings, my obligation does connect with my use of my land, and so can be an easement. Hence the formula's statement 'there must be ... a servient tenement'.

Then, the demand that an easement must belong to your land. In the abstract, again, a right dictating what I do on my land could belong to you personally. Some rights in rem over land are like this: for instance, leases and mortgages. But to qualify as an easement, your right must (we shall explore this further in § 9.1.3) belong to you *in your capacity as owner of your land*. And to do this, it must benefit you in this capacity, ie connect with the use you make of your land: as where it is a right for you to cross my land, *so as to access your adjoining land*. And that in turn presupposes that you have some such land: 'there must be a dominant ... tenement'.

The idea that an easement 'belongs' to the dominant land (or 'appertains' to that land; so an easement is an 'appurtenant right') is of course a figure, since English law supposes that rights can only belong to humans. But it stands for the truth that, when you have an easement in your capacity as owner of some piece of land, and you transfer that land to John, the easement will automatically pass to John with it.

9.1.3 Element (2): 'Accommodating' the Dominant Land

As we have just seen, not only must you have some land: in addition, and as the reason for this rule, the right (if it is to be an easement) must benefit you in your capacity as that land's owner. The formula in *Re Ellenborough Park*[6] records this requirement in its separate assertion that 'an easement must "accommodate" the dominant tenement'. This section looks more closely at this requirement.[7]

Say you have the right to come onto my land so as to enjoy the views. This right benefits you in your personal capacity: the views are equally valuable to you regardless of whether, or where, you have land of your own. So, even if you live adjacent to me, it cannot be an easement: it can only be a licence. Licences are looked at in Chapter 15. Essentially, whereas easements are rights in rem, licences are only in personam. By contrast, a right to cross my land *so as to access yours* benefits you in your capacity as owner of your land, because you would have no reason to cross my land if you did not live in the adjoining land. So it can be an easement. Easements of this kind, called rights of way, are very common. Other rights benefiting you in your capacity

---

[6] *Ibid.*
[7] See further M Sturley, 'Easements in Gross' (1980) 96 *LQR* 557.

as owner of your land, and so capable of existing as easements, include those where you run a pub, and have the right to erect your sign on my nearby wall[8]; or where you have a farm, and have the right to a supply of water piped through my land to your farm, so as to irrigate your crops; or where you live in a house, and have the right to make use of my neighbouring garden.[9]

This requirement that the right benefit you as owner of your land is, however, often paraphrased, or glossed, in ways which make it more exacting. The effect is that rights which otherwise could be easements—they benefit you as owner of your land, and fulfil the other requirements—are prevented from existing as easements after all, meaning that they must be only licences. Several examples of this can be found.

First, some accounts demand that your land should be *close to* mine. Most easements are put under no pressure by this view, but it would rule out a right entitling you to let clients coming to your city-centre hotel land their helicopters in my field at the edge of the city, even though this right certainly benefits you in your capacity as owner of your hotel. Essentially, the effect is to privilege the more down-to-earth, traditional ways in which a right over my land can benefit you as the owner of yours.

Second, in the *Re Ellenborough Park*[10] formula itself, the requirement that you benefit as owner of your land is put in the form of the demand that the right 'must "accommodate" the dominant land'. This is a bad choice of paraphrase. In our culture,[11] to speak of benefiting the land itself is fundamentally unintelligible. The 'accommodation'—that is, benefit—has to be to the human who has the land, rather than to the land itself. But it is possible to make some sense of the idea. Farmers, especially, speak of some practice or happening as being good for the land. What they mean is that the practice or happening assists the work which some or all humans think the land should do. So salvaged, however, the rule that the right 'must "accommodate" the dominant land' makes it easiest to find easements in agricultural and similar contexts, where the focus is on working the land itself. Our original statement, that the right must benefit you in your capacity as owner of your land, is wider, allowing the easement to engage with any use to which you may put your land.

The difference can be seen in *Hill v Tupper*.[12] The claimant had a small piece of land on the bank of a canal. This was the base for his business, running pleasure boats on the canal. The canal company gave him the

---

[8] *Moody v Steggles* (1879) 12 Ch D 261 (Ch D).

[9] This was the situation in *Re Ellenborough Park* [1956] Ch 131 (CA) itself.

[10] *Ibid.*

[11] Contrast cultures, such as the native American, which ascribe animate quality to a wider range of natural entities and phenomena. Some, too, ascribe animate quality to man-made entities such as buildings, but perhaps this is no more than a metaphor.

[12] (1863) 2 H & C 121 (Ex).

exclusive right to do this. The court held that this right was not an easement over the canal. The boat business did not 'accommodate' the claimant's land in the sense of 'facilitate a working of the very soil of the land'. But it did benefit the claimant in his capacity as owner of the land, for this was the place which he in fact used to bring his boats to shore.

Third, further passages in the judgment in *Re Ellenborough Park*[13] assert that a right cannot be an easement unless it is 'connected with the normal enjoyment' of your land. Say your land is a farm, but you bought it not to farm it, but because you are a druid and the land contains part of a Neolithic henge where you wish to perform rituals. The remainder of the henge is on my adjoining land. You buy from me the right to come onto my land so as to visit all parts of the henge during your rituals. The right benefits you in your capacity as owner of your land, but it is not connected with the 'normal' enjoyment of that land. Or say I create a small development of houses, and, selling them off, grant their purchasers—including you—a right to use some tennis courts which I continue to own myself, but have created as a communal facility for the houses. You certainly have your right in your capacity as owner of your house. But if we list the features needed for the normal enjoyment of a house, they probably do not include tennis courts (whereas they do include a garden).

A right which *is* connected with the normal enjoyment of your land will almost certainly also be one which benefits you in your capacity as the owner of that land. So the fact that houses normally have gardens was a reason why the right to use a neighbouring garden has been accepted as an easement.[14] But it does not follow that a right should not be an easement *unless* it is connected with the normal enjoyment of your land. Such a rule requires justification in its own right. In fact, there is a major argument against it. The alleged rule would give easements an ephemeral quality, depriving them of the stability and visibility they should have as rights in rem. This is because it makes the question whether your right is an easement depend on the precise use you make of your land, and upon the application of the normality test to that use. A garden is a normal adjunct to a house ... but to flats, or an office? And does the right's identity as an easement come and go as the use of your land changes? And as ideas of normality vary (say, one day tennis courts become normal, or gardens cease to be)?

A fourth gloss is a view that a right cannot be an easement if the benefit it gives you is in the nature of 'mere recreation and amusement'. This view was raised as an argument against the possibility of an easement over a garden in *Re Ellenborough Park*.[15] The argument was rejected, making it hard to see

---

[13] [1956] Ch 131, 170, 173, 174 (CA).
[14] *Ibid.*
[15] *Ibid*, 177–9.

what purchase the alleged rule could have, but the court stopped short of denying the rule itself.

In comparison with the demand simply that you benefit as owner of your land, these various paraphrases and glosses allow your right to count as an easement in a restricted range of cases. As we have seen, they tend to privilege rights that are traditional, ordinary ('normal'), agricultural, and about business rather than recreation, over those benefiting you in other ways. But their treatment by the courts leaves their status and precise meaning far from clear.

9.1.4 Element (4): A Right 'Capable of Forming the Subject-matter of a Grant'

The formula in *Re Ellenborough Park*[16] ends with the statement that 'a right over land cannot amount to an easement, unless it is capable of forming the subject-matter of a grant.'

The mention of a 'grant' refers to the possibility of your acquiring an easement by my conferring it on you, using a deed. For this to be possible, you must be clearly enough identified, but that has nothing to do with the quality of the right, which is the focus of element (4). The right's content must also be clearly enough identified, but that is not confined to acquisition in this way rather than otherwise, or indeed to easements: it is intrinsic to your being recognised by the law as having any kind of right.

In truth, element (4) is an inept shorthand for three rules which impose further restrictions on the rights, of all those acceptable under the rules as explained so far, that are allowed to count as easements. These rules bar from existence as an easement rights which otherwise satisfy the law's requirements, but which:

— *require me actively to do something*, except to maintain a fence between our two pieces of land; or
— *benefit you without activity on your part* ('negative easements'), except those requiring me not to remove the support that my land gives your buildings, or not to impede a flow across my land of water through an artificial channel to your land, or of air or light to a particular aperture on your land; or
— *give you excessively extensive rights over my land*, rather than allow you to use it in some more restricted way.

As to the first of these rules, the law recognises as an easement the obligation on me to maintain a fence between my land and yours.[17] But that

---

[16] *Ibid.*
[17] *Jones v Price* [1965] 2 QB 618 (CA); *Crow v Wood* [1971] 1 QB 77 (CA).

apart, the traditional view is that an obligation requiring me actively to do something for you (even assuming it needs to be done on my land, and benefits you in your capacity as owner of your land) cannot be an easement.[18] So a right allowing you to take water through a pipe crossing my land cannot be an easement if, the pipe being metered as it enters my land, I have to pay for what you use.[19] This traditional view cannot be altogether right, however. If you foreseeably come onto my land, I owe a duty of care under the Occupiers' Liability Acts 1957 and 1984 to save you from injury. The discharge of this duty may well oblige me to take active steps. And this obligation is not merely a quite general one, having no particular association with easements: on the contrary, your having a right to enter my land—such as an easement—makes it particularly foreseeable that you will do so. Yet no one suggests that, on account of my obligation, your right cannot be an easement after all.[20]

The second rule limits the existence of 'negative easements'. A positive easement is one whose enjoyment involves you encroaching on my land, as for example by coming onto it yourself, or allowing fumes from your land to blow over mine. (So positive easements are those affording you a defence to trespass or nuisance against me.) A negative easement, on the other hand, is one which does not involve you encroaching on my land. Four kinds of negative easement are well established: those obliging me (1) not to impede a flow of water through an artificial channel[21] from my land to yours, or (2) a flow of air or (3) one of light across my land to a particular aperture[22] on your land; and (4) not to remove the support that my land gives your buildings.[23] In *Phipps v Pears*[24] it was held that no other kinds of negative

---

[18] *Moncrieff v Jamieson* [2007] 1 WLR 2620, [47] (HL). If the easement requires upkeep, this is your responsibility. So if you have a right of way along my track, but the track has become boggy, you have the right to enter and do the necessary work, at *your* expense.

[19] *Rance v Elvin* (1985) 50 P & CR 9, 13 (CA). The principle was distinguished, perhaps questionably, on the facts.

[20] See further A Waite, 'Easements: Positive Duties on the Servient Owner?' [1985] *CLJ* 458.

[21] You are entitled to the water in a natural river or stream as a 'natural right': that is, your entitlement comes automatically with your ownership of your land, and you do not need to point to an additional right—easement—against me.

[22] There is no natural right to the flow of light or air to your land over mine (as opposed to vertically down). The only rights of this kind are easements, and they can exist only in respect of light or air entering your land through a particular aperture such as a window, located on the boundary between your land and mine, which I would otherwise be free to block, say by building on my land. A particular aperture is required because otherwise, an easement could arise against me by prescription (§§ 6.3, 9.2.7) without my having a proper chance to prevent it.

[23] You are entitled to have my land support your bare land as a natural right. But this right does not entitle you to the additional support you may need for the buildings on your land. To obtain the latter, you need an easement against me.

[24] [1965] 1 QB 76 (CA); likewise *Hunter v Canary Wharf Ltd* [1997] AC 655 (HL). The two decisions (at 83 and 726 respectively) explain that further negative easements are embargoed because negative easements unduly restrict what I can do on my own land. This cannot be the point, however, because positive easements are no different from negative ones in this respect (I

easement can exist. There cannot, therefore, be an easement not to remove the protection from the weather that my building gives yours.[25]

This rule is not what it seems, however. An obligation which it prevents from being a negative easement can be created instead as a 'restrictive covenant'.[26] But restrictive covenants can be created only by conferral, whereas easements can arise alternatively by prescription: broadly, from the mere fact that you have behaved as though you had the easement in question for the past 20 years.[27] So the real effect of *Phipps v Pears*[28] is that although further rights in the nature of negative easements can be acquired by conferral (as restrictive covenants), they cannot be acquired by prescription. This makes sense. Prescription cannot be an acceptable basis for the generation of rights unless I have the opportunity to prevent the usage on which it is based.[29] In the nature of things, I normally do have the opportunity in the case of a positive easement, where you encroach on my land in some way. But the reverse is true in the case of a negative easement, where you do not encroach on my land. You merely arrange matters on your own land in a manner dependent on the configuration of mine—say, you build your house so that its windows' source of light and ventilation is across an open area of my adjoining land. I might well not even realise that I have any reason to react, and even if I do, the means of doing so will be awkward and possibly even detrimental to me: I might, say, have to build an otherwise unwanted wall purely so as to block your windows.[30] In truth, this problem is an argument against allowing *any* rights in the nature of negative easements to be acquirable by prescription. Yet *Phipps v Pears*[31] applied its embargo only to such rights beyond the established four. Presumably, the law's recognition of those four was too firmly entrenched to be reversed.

The third rule withholds the status of easement from an obligation giving you excessively extensive rights over my land, rather than allowing you to use

---

cannot build across your right of way any more than I can across your window), and because preventing me from doing things on what is otherwise my own land is the very *raison d'être* of easements.

[25] *Ibid.* But you apparently can have easements obliging me to allow your electricity, gas and so on to come through my cables, pipes etc up to your boundary, and such easements are negative too. Presumably they are analogous to the undoubted easement obliging me to allow your water to come through my land. Moreover, I can certainly have an easement to send my drainage out through your land, because it is positive: it would be bizarre if I could not have one to bring these other utilities in. Perhaps the point is that, unlike the negative easements discussed in the text, those noted here are highly unlikely to arise by prescription, in the way the text identifies as the true source of the embargo on further negative easements.

[26] For restrictive covenants, see Ch 10.

[27] For prescription, see §§ 6.3, 9.2.7.

[28] [1965] 1 QB 76 (CA).

[29] See § 6.3.

[30] In the case of light, however, the Rights of Light Act 1959 allows me to 'obstruct' your windows by registering a notice against you.

[31] [1965] 1 QB 76 (CA).

it in some more restricted way.[32] Obviously, the question arises 'What counts as excessively extensive?' The familiar kinds of easement, such as a right to cross my land, evidently do not infringe this rule: many of them certainly allow you some use of my land, but their familiarity tells us that this use does not count as excessively extensive. At the other extreme, if you and I own adjoining farms and I give you the sole right to use mine, everyone agrees that it is not an easement that I have created: it is a lease.[33] Between these well-established instances, however, lies a considerable area of doubt. In particular, the judges have struggled to decide whether—or in what circumstances—your right to store things on my land, or to park vehicles there, can be an easement.

It seems now to be accepted that your right can certainly be an easement if it allows you only the use of an unspecified part of my land, as where you have the right to park one car, in no particular space, on my large car park.[34] It has been doubted that a more extensive right, such as an exclusive right to park in a specified part of my land, can be an easement.[35] But if it cannot, the law seems arbitrary. Why should it matter whether we specify where you should park? And if my land as a whole is larger than the car park, why should you not have the whole car park? Yet on the other hand, why is it even relevant that I have land other than the car park?[36] Such reflections have prompted the suggestion that your right should count as too extensive only if it deprives me of the very possession and, subject to your reasonable use of your right, control of the land in question: that is, only if it means that I cannot myself use that land in any way at all.[37] This suggestion too is problematic,[38] however. It implies that a right allowing you to share the very occupation of my land can be an easement, which is a right in rem; when conventional thinking treats it as a licence,[39] a right in

---

[32] The rule is examined by P Luther, 'Easements and Exclusive Possession' (1996) 16 *LS* 51; but see, more recently, *Moncrieff v Jamieson* [2007] 1 WLR 2620 (HL). See too Law Commission, *Easements, Covenants and Profits à Prendre: A Consultation Paper* (Consultation Paper No 186, London, 2008) paras 3.34–3.55.

[33] See § 11.2.1.

[34] *London & Blenheim Estates Ltd v Ladbroke Retail Parks Ltd* [1992] 1 WLR 1278 (Ch D); *Batchelor v Marlow* [2003] 1 WLR 764 (CA); *Moncrieff v Jamieson* [2007] 1 WLR 2620, [137]–[138] (HL).

[35] *Batchelor v Marlow* [2003] 1 WLR 764 (CA). But such a right was held capable of being an easement in *Virdi v Chana* [2008] EWHC 2901 (Ch D).

[36] *Moncrieff v Jamieson* [2007] 1 WLR 2620, [54]–[59], [138]–[143] (HL).

[37] *Ibid* [47], [59] (Lord Scott), approving A Hill-Smith, 'Rights of Parking and the Ouster Principle after *Batchelor v Marlow*' [2007] *Conv* 223. A previous formulation asked whether the right would leave me 'without any reasonable use', or only an 'illusory' use, of my land: *London & Blenheim Estates Ltd v Ladbroke Retail Parks Ltd* [1992] 1 WLR 1278, 1288 (Ch D); *Batchelor v Marlow* [2003] 1 WLR 764, [15], [18] (CA). In *Virdi v Chana* [2008] EWHC 2901 (Ch D) this formulation was taken still to represent the law, the more recent discussion of the issue in *Moncrieff v Jamieson* [2007] 1 WLR 2620 (HL) being said (surely questionably) to have been only obiter.

[38] *Moncrieff v Jamieson* [2007] 1 WLR 2620, [144] (HL).

[39] § 11.2.1.

personam.[40] But this objection can itself be challenged. If your right to the sole use of my land is a right in rem (a lease[41]) and the right to the sole occupancy of some unspecified part of it is also in rem (an easement), why should the right to share all of it be only in personam (a licence)? It is apparent that this rule has not yet reached a stable form.[42]

9.1.5 Intention to Create a Right in Rem

Say we have created a right that satisfies the above rules. It will still not be an easement unless we want it to be. The *Re Ellenborough Park*[43] formula makes no reference to this point.

The presumption is probably that we do want such a right to be an easement, and usually we will. But if we prefer, we can make it a licence instead.[44] The difference is that an easement is a right in rem, and so capable of binding disponees of my land, whereas a licence is a right in personam, and so effective only between you and me.

In allowing us to choose whether or not our right should be in rem, the law takes a position different from that which it takes when the right is in the nature of a lease.[45] As explained in § 11.4.3, there we have no option to make it an in personam licence instead. But the rule for leases rests on a consideration special to them, namely a desire to prevent exclusion of the Rent Acts, which apply to leases but not licences.

9.1.6 Why do Easements Take this Form?

Summarising the foregoing sections: to be an easement, a right must therefore:

— not normally require me to do anything active; merely limit the use I can make of my land ...

---

[40] Ch 15.

[41] § 11.2.1.

[42] The judgments establishing this rule sometimes hint that they too proceed from a concern about acquisition by prescription: see *Dyce v Lady Hay* (1852) 1 Macq 305 (HL); *Copeland v Greenhalf* [1952] Ch 488, 498 (Ch D); *Batchelor v Marlow* [2003] 1 WLR 764, [4]–[6] (CA). But this makes no sense. A right depriving me of 'any reasonable use' of my land is not especially unsuitable for acquisition by prescription, in the way that, as we have seen, a right in the nature of a negative easement is. On the contrary, such a right ought to be highly visible to me, giving me a good opportunity to prevent its acquisition if I want to. The unhappiness about rights of this kind being acquired by prescription seems merely to reflect a dissatisfaction with prescription as a mode of acquisition in general.

[43] [1956] Ch 131 (CA).

[44] *IDC Group Ltd v Clark* (1992) 65 P & CR 179 (CA).

[45] See J Hill, 'Intention and the Creation of Proprietary Rights: Are Leases Different?' (1996) 16 *LS* 200.

—... though not too extensively (certainly, it must not give you exclusive possession of the land, and perhaps it must stop some way short of that); and

— be for your benefit, in your capacity as owner of your land ... though perhaps only in certain (traditional, ordinary, agricultural, business) ways.

But why should the law insist on this delineation?

Remember the *numerus clausus* principle, considered in § 1.2.2. As we saw there, in order to decide whether a right should be in rem, we need to see whether the damage this would do to trade in land is outweighed by the good that would follow in other respects. And this links with the question whether your enjoyment of the right ought to be protected in specie, or whether it is good enough that you lose the right and have to accept compensation instead. After I have alienated the land in question to John, a right in personam will still deliver the latter, but only a right in rem will deliver the former.

The footing on which easements exist as rights in rem should therefore be that their delineation gives them a nature requiring in rem status in this way. The core idea is for you, in doing what you do on your land, to be able to take limited advantage of my land too. Why should we regard this as meriting protection in specie, so as to affect someone to whom I transfer my land? Because it allows the exploitation of land to have the best of both worlds between division into sealed packets—mine and yours—and a more communal approach.

Division into sealed packets has a great merit: at a basic level, it gives the owner of each packet the maximum opportunity and incentive to exploit his own packet to the full. But a given packet of land may in practice not be self-sufficient in the things required for its optimal exploitation. It may lack efficient access, for example. Greater benefit can be extracted by running the land in question co-operatively with neighbouring packets, from which such additional requirements can be sourced. Say you decide that you can best exploit your land by growing crops, but your land lacks water to irrigate them when necessary: the solution could be to pipe water in from my nearby lake. Or say you want to build houses, but cannot come right to the edge of your land, for fear that I will block your houses' light and air by building right to the edge of my land too: the problem is solved if you can rely on my not doing so.

You could contract with me for a water supply or against activity inimical to the houses on your land. But a contract alone, being in personam, will not affect John, to whom I soon transfer my land: if John refuses to repeat my deal with you, you will be left with parched fields or uninhabitable houses. As you will be entitled to compensation (damages for breach of contract) from me, you yourself may emerge reasonably unscathed. But the common good will suffer: that food, or those houses, which would otherwise have become available for further use by others, will become unavailable after all. To allow your exploitation of your land to stick, therefore, you need to be able to secure what you need in a way that is enforceable not only against me, but also against John after me: that is, in the form of a right in rem—an easement.

The English law on easements thus developed most during the 19th century.[46] During the first three quarters of that century, English agricultural land was being divided into sealed packets, in a process known as 'enclosure'. Previously, the land had been operated much more communally. Enclosure was born of a realisation that the old communal approach impeded the land's maximal exploitation. But easements were developed out of a realisation, in turn, that even greater exploitation was possible if one could have it both ways.[47] At about the same period, too, intensive building was taking place, centred on the mills, factories and so on which were perceived as the most effective tools by which to exploit downstream resources. Maximum intensity was achieved by introducing easements to allow the collaborative use of neighbouring plots of land.

Care is needed, of course. Cross-exploitation does harm as well as good, for it erodes the benefits to be had from dividing land into sealed packets. The less *my* land becomes simply 'mine' because there are obligations such as easements affecting its use, the further *I* shall be from having the maximum opportunity and incentive to exploit it, by growing crops myself, or building houses, or whatever. So the establishment of easements needs to be restricted to the situations in which unsealing the packets does more good than harm. The law does this with its rules that limit the forms of benefit that can be associated with easements, favouring those that are traditional, ordinary, agricultural, and a matter of business rather than recreation, and its rule limiting easements to rights that do not intrude excessively into my own rights over my land. But the situations where unsealing the packets does more good than harm can be only imprecisely identified, so it comes as no surprise that we found the courts lacking in confidence as to the status and exact meaning of these rules.[48]

All this goes only to show the argument that does exist for having rights in rem in the shape of easements. It is by no means an argument against having rights in rem of other shapes. One such right is worth mentioning here, for it is a sister to the easement.

---

[46] The leading specialist book on the subject, *Gale on Easements*, was first published in 1839. Its preface speaks of both the need for, and the dearth of, law on the area.

[47] See generally A Simpson, *A History of the Land Law* (2nd edn, Oxford, 1986) 261–4. The connection between easements and enclosure may explain the possibility of creating an easement requiring me to maintain a fence (see at n 17 above).

[48] The Law Commission (*Easements, Covenants and Profits à Prendre: A Consultation Paper* (Consultation Paper No 186, London, 2008)) is similarly confused. At times it seems to think that only certain kinds of rights can be easements (eg paras 3.11, 15.12–15.13, 15.32); at other times, it seems to demand only that they should not be 'capricious and personal benefits' (paras 3.20–3.33).

Individual feeds of water, electricity, gas, data and so on to individual properties, if they have to cross other people's land, will count as easements. But the companies supplying these utilities also need to run their main distribution pipes and cables through other people's land,[49] and the rights under which they do so cannot be easements, because they do not benefit the company in its capacity as owner of its own land.[50] Nor can they easily be leases: these could arise only if the company had exclusive possession of the area in question,[51] and it would be hard satisfactorily to define the precise 'area' of the pipe or cable.[52] These rights clearly need to be in rem: the nation's utility distribution arrangements would collapse unless protected in specie through changes in ownership of the land over which they run: another facet of the truth that land cannot be maximally exploited if it is literally divided into sealed packets. But there is no other common law type of right in rem that these rights can be.[53] Instead, however, they are established as in rem in their own right, under statutory provisions aimed specifically at their context.[54]

9.2 The Creation of Easements

In principle, we should expect it to be possible to acquire easements in the sorts of organised and disorganised ways discussed in Part 2 of this book, and at one level that is the case: they can, in particular, certainly be acquired by conferral, prescription and proprietary estoppel.

In this context, however, 'conferral' is not a straightforward idea. It can be implied as well as express. Nevertheless, one might suppose that both forms depended on consent. As we shall see, however, only express conferral depends purely on consent, while implied conferral depends, like prescription, on a blend of an argument from utility and an attenuated form

---

[49] Or airspace, which counts as land.

[50] Though this statement may assume that the dominant and servient land must be adjacent, and that the idea of 'benefit' is limited as held in *Hill v Tupper* (1863) 2 H & C 121 (Ex) (see at n 12). As explained in § 9.1.3, neither of these assumptions is unchallengeable.

[51] See § 11.2.1.

[52] Whereas a road or railway can be put across my land using a lease, or (more usually) a purchase, for these require a more definable area.

[53] They can certainly be licences, for these can take any shape the parties wish, but they operate only in personam, not in rem: see § 15.1.1.

[54] For example, the Electricity Act 1989 Sch 4 para 6. They are described as 'wayleaves', though that word can probably also be used for rights to pipes and cables which are easements.

of consent. We shall see too that in some cases, the basis on which the easement arises provides insufficient justification for its doing so.

9.2.1 Express and Implied Conferral

If I intend to confer an easement on you, there are fewest problems if I do so expressly. Express conferral could occur in an ad hoc transaction. You and I are neighbours: you would like an easement over my land: you obtain my agreement, usually in return for payment: and I give you the easement. Often, though, conferral occurs when I own a piece of land and, splitting it in two, sell one part to you, keeping the other for myself. Reckoning that your part will be more attractive (so, I can charge you more for it) if it has some right over mine, I 'grant'[55] you an easement over my part as a term of the transfer to you of the land itself. Or—conversely—I might reckon that I want a right over your part, for the benefit of the part I keep (at the cost of being able to charge you less): as a term of the transfer of your part to you, I will 'reserve' an easement for myself.

But as well as being an express term of a transfer in this way, a conferral or reservation can be implied into the transfer. An argument can be made that this should not be possible, especially for the sake of certainty. But that position would sacrifice deserving cases.

The law might have sought to detect an implied easement merely by asking whether its creation was probably intended by the parties, as a matter of fact. This does seem to be one of its approaches,[56] but additionally, it allows implication to be found through a number of special rules.[57] We shall explore the details of these in a moment, but in outline they will generate an easement on the basis that it is 'necessary'; that it is needed for the use of the land in a way which the parties commonly intended when making the transfer; or that it reflects a pre-existing usage of the two pieces of land in question, via the 'rule in *Wheeldon v Burrows*'[58] or section 62 of the Law of Property Act 1925.[59]

---

[55] The word 'grant' is strictly applicable only to the valid conferment of a legal easement, using the formalities that the law requires for this. See § 9.2.8.

[56] *Re Webb's Lease* [1951] Ch 808 (CA); *Moncrieff v Jamieson* [2007] 1 WLR 2620, [52] (HL); but very few cases seem to have been decided on this basis.

[57] For discussion, see A Lawson, 'Easements' in L Tee (ed), *Land Law: Issues, Debates, Policy* (Cullompton, 2002) 74–96; as regards possible reform, see Law Commission, *Easements, Covenants and Profits à Prendre: A Consultation Paper* (Consultation Paper No 186, London, 2008) paras 4.107–4.150.

[58] (1879) 12 Ch D 31 (CA).

[59] Some commentators depict easements created by s 62 as expressly granted, in that the section operates by inserting words apt to create an easement into a transfer (see § 9.2.5). This, however, is a good description of implied grant: the word 'inserting' can be changed to 'implying', making the point exactly. Functionally, too, easements created by s 62 are relatives not of those created expressly, but of those created by (other) implied grant rules: the key point being that expressly granted easements are organised rights, while those created by s 62 and (other) implied grant rules are disorganised. So when the Land Registration Act 2002

Where the facts needed to trigger one of these special rules are present, the law does not ask whether the parties probably meant to create the easement. Rather, it *imputes* the easement: that is, it finds the easement automatically, unless the parties have decided and stipulated against creating it. (In other words, the law presumes the easement's creation, leaving it to me to rebut this presumption.) When you acquire an easement under one of these rules, therefore, you do so not simply for the reason that I intend you to. Nor do these rules connect to any corrective issue between us.[60] In fact, they seem to reflect a desire in legal policy, for utilitarian reasons, to achieve the most effective use of the resource that is land, by actively promoting the kind of cross-exploitation identified in § 9.1.6 as easements' raison d'être.[61]

Since implied easements depend on utility in this way, should they not be imposed wherever utility so indicates, rather than by imputation into my transfer of part of my land to you? The usefulness of cross-exploitation between two pieces of land could be just as great when their respective owners have had no dealings as when they have. In fact, easements do sometimes arise outside a transaction in this way, under statutory schemes in the nature of compulsory purchase.[62] It remains the case, however, that imputation into a transfer is privileged as a mode of creation on grounds of utility, if only because it involves no question of compensation. This is probably defensible[63] on the basis that in such cases, utility does not operate alone. There is at least a degree of consent, in the sense that if I wish to prevent an easement from being imputed into the transfer, I can always have the terms of the transfer so stipulate. This creates a close similarity between

---

s 27(2)(d) rules that the express grant of an easement must be completed by registration, but naturally does not apply this rule to easements created by implied grant, it goes on (s 27(7)) to include easements created by s 62 with the latter. It follows too that, like (other) impliedly granted easements, those created by s 62 can operate as overriding interests under Sch 3 para 3: see § 9.3.

[60] Where, however, there is such an issue, it may yield an easement under the doctrine of proprietary estoppel (Ch 7). *Crabb v Arunn District Council* [1976] Ch 179 (CA) may be an example of this.

[61] Lord Neuberger in *Moncrieff v Jamieson* [2007] 1 WLR 2620, [113] (HL) may take insufficient account of what the special rules owe to utilitarian considerations when he identifies them with the general principle 'that the law will imply a term into a contract, where, in the light of the terms of the contract and the facts known to the parties at the time of the contract, such a term would have been regarded as reasonably necessary or obvious to the parties' (see too *ibid* [130]).

[62] On this and analogous phenomena, see further S Grattan, 'Proprietarian Conceptions of Statutory Access Rights' in E Cooke (ed), *Modern Studies in Property Law, Volume 2* (Oxford, 2003) ch 18.

[63] A defence is required not only in principle, but also under the European Convention on Human Rights, First Protocol, Art 1, since in granting you the easement, the law deprives me of my possessions. This can be defended if the grant is a proportionate means of implementing a legitimate public interest. Given what has been said about utility, the need for a legitimate public interest seems to have been met, but the lack of compensation puts proportionality in doubt. The (albeit attenuated) ingredient of consent may meet that problem.

implied grant and prescription, which likewise operates on the basis of a combination of utility and low-grade consent.[64]

The approach to finding that an easement has been impliedly *granted* is somewhat different from that to finding that one has been impliedly *reserved*. We shall look at the former first, then, in § 9.2.6, consider the differences.

9.2.2 Necessity and Common Intention

The first two implication rules look at the situation that has come about as a result of my transferring part of my land to you, deduce from it that you should have an easement against me, and 'discover' the conferral of that easement as an implied term of the transfer.

The first rule operates where the piece of land I have transferred to you is landlocked, and—unless excluded by contrary intention[65]—finds an easement over my retained land so as to give you access to it. So an easement will not be found on this basis if there is a footpath, or even access by water, to your land.[66] Easements arising in this way are called 'easements of necessity'.

The second rule operates where we made the transfer with a common intention that you should use the transferred land for a particular purpose, and that purpose is feasible only if you have an easement over the land I retain. That easement will be found.[67] (You are *not* required to produce direct evidence that we commonly intended the easement itself: that is what the law infers from the fact of our commonly intending the *purpose*.) Say I own a building, and lease you the basement to use as a restaurant, retaining the higher floors. We never considered the issue, but it turns out that you cannot have a restaurant there without a ventilation duct, and that this will have to run up the outside wall of the higher floors. It will be inferred that the transfer (lease) contains an implied term giving you the easement you need to do so,[68] unless it stipulates to the contrary.[69]

The two rules operate only cautiously. Easements of necessity are used only so as to give you the bare minimum of access to your land,[70] and easements arise under the common intention rule only where they are

---

[64] See §§ 6.3, 9.2.7.

[65] *Nickerson v Barraclough* [1980] Ch 325 (CA).

[66] *MRA Engineering Ltd v Trimster Co Ltd* (1988) 56 P & CR 1 (CA); *Manjang v Drammeh* (1991) 61 P & CR 194 (PC). The courts seem not yet to have considered whether the possibility of access by air (eg by helicopter) likewise rules out an easement of necessity. In *Sweet v Sommer* [2004] 4 All ER 288n (Ch D), affirmed [2005] 2 All ER 64 (CA), however, a piece of land was regarded as landlocked even though its owner could have accessed it from his adjoining land by demolishing a building forming the boundary between the two.

[67] *Pwllbach Colliery Co Ltd v Woodman* [1915] AC 634 (HL).

[68] *Wong v Beaumont Property Trust Ltd* [1965] 1 QB 173 (CA). The court confuses matters by speaking, incorrectly, in terms of an 'easement of necessity'.

[69] *Pwllbach Colliery Co Ltd v Woodman* [1915] AC 634 (HL).

[70] *Corporation of London v Riggs* (1880) 13 Ch D 798 (Ch D).

essential to the sole use(s) to which we contemplated you would put the land.[71] Given this, the rules will generate an easement only where there is a high degree of utility. When this high degree of utility is combined with the element of consent that the rules also demand (in their limitation to a transfer from me to you, as part of which I can exclude the easement), the rules' effect in generating the easement seems justified.

9.2.3 Implication on the Basis of Prior Usage

The third and fourth rules by which implied easements are found are the rule in *Wheeldon v Burrows*,[72] and that arising under section 62 of the Law of Property Act 1925.

Like the first and second rules, these two rules operate to discover an easement implied in my transfer of part of my land to you. But the first and second rules focus on the present and future, generating an easement where this seems right in the situation that the transfer has created. The third and fourth rules, by contrast, primarily look back to the situation before the transfer. They see whether, at that time, the land was used in a way suggestive of an easement; and treat this as a basis on which to say that the transfer impliedly gives an easement allowing the use to continue after it.

Under these two rules, the new easement will have the shape of the prior usage. It follows that the prior usage must itself have been easement-shaped. This means, in particular, that the prior situation involved the use of one piece of land (that which will now become the dominant land) *identifiably for the benefit of another* (which will now become the servient land). Reproducing this situation, the new easement will—as it must—'accommodate' the dominant land.

The two rules thus both demand a prior situation of this kind. Beyond this, however, they diverge. The rule in *Wheeldon v Burrows*[73] deals with the case where, before the transfer which is alleged to contain the implied easement, I both owned and occupied the two pieces of land in question (ie there was 'unity of occupation'); while that in section 62 deals with the case where I owned both but occupied only one (ie there was 'diversity of occupation').[74] If in other respects the two rules were the same, this would be merely a technical dividing up of the territory, and we could nonetheless discuss them together. But as we shall see, there are other differences too, so we shall need to consider them individually, and compare their approaches.

---

[71] *Pwllbach Colliery Co Ltd v Woodman* [1915] AC 634 (HL).
[72] (1879) 12 Ch D 31 (CA).
[73] *Ibid.*
[74] *Kent v Kavanagh* [2006] 2 All ER 645, [45]–[46] (CA).

9.2.4 *Wheeldon v Burrows*

By the rule in *Wheeldon v Burrows*,[75] where I own two pieces of land, and transfer one to you, an easement over the piece I retain is implied into the transfer of the other piece to you where:

— before the transfer, there was a quasi-easement over the retained piece in favour of the transferred piece, in the shape of the easement that you now argue should be implied;
— at the time of the transfer, this quasi-easement was 'continuous and apparent'; and[76]
— it is 'necessary for the reasonable enjoyment' of the transferred piece that you now have an easement in the shape of this earlier quasi-easement.

The first of these requirements is that, before the transfer, there was a 'quasi-easement' corresponding to the easement that you now claim. A 'quasi-easement' is an easement-shaped practice that I have, as both owner and occupant of two pieces of land.[77]

Say I own and occupy a farm, which includes fields *A* and *B*. I keep cows in field *A*. When I need to bring cows in or out by road, I take them through field *B*. (Field *A* has road access of its own, but of a more dangerous nature.) This use of field *B* is easement-shaped. In particular, it benefits me as owner of field *A*. At this stage, as I own and occupy both fields, it cannot be an actual easement. But, being thus easement-shaped, it counts as a 'quasi-easement'. (Field *A* is called the 'quasi-dominant land', and field *B* is the 'quasi-servient land'.) Now I transfer field *A* to you, retaining field *B*. If my usage of field *B* before the transfer was also 'continuous and apparent', and if the ability to continue with it is 'necessary for the reasonable enjoyment' of field *A* after its transfer to you, this rule will imply into that transfer an easement entitling you too to cross my retained field *B* with your cows.

---

[75] (1879) 12 Ch D 31, 49 (CA), Thesiger LJ: '[O]n the grant by the owner of a tenement of part of that tenement as it is then used and enjoyed, there will pass to the grantee all those continuous and apparent easements (by which, of course, I mean quasi-easements), or, in other words, all those easements which are necessary to the reasonable enjoyment of the property granted, and which have been and are at the time of the grant used by the owners of the entirety for the benefit of the part granted.' For the provenance of this rule, see A Simpson, 'The Rule in *Wheeldon v Burrows* and the Code Civile' (1967) 83 *LQR* 240.

[76] This 'and' is controversial, however, as explained below.

[77] *Kent v Kavanagh* [2006] 2 All ER 645, [45], [73] (CA). The term 'quasi-easement' has in the past also been used to describe an easement-shaped usage of one piece of land for the benefit of another, where I own both but occupy only one (renting the other to a tenant): see eg *Hansford v Jago* [1921] 1 Ch 322 (Ch D). According to the account given here, however, that situation is addressed not by the rule in *Wheeldon v Burrows* but by the Law of Property Act 1925 s 62 (§ 9.2.5). If the account given here is wrong, so that a quasi-easement can exist also where there is diversity of occupation, it should make little difference: *Wheeldon v Burrows* will not normally be relied on in that situation, for s 62 applies to it, and involves less demanding requirements than *Wheeldon v Burrows*.

By contrast, say that before the transfer I move my cows using the route through field *B* purely because I enjoy the exercise. Or that I operate fields *A* and *B* as a single unit, leaving the gate between them open and letting my cows roam across both fields as they will. In these instances, in different ways, my use of field *B* does not benefit me in my capacity as owner of field *A*. It therefore does not count as a quasi-easement, and the rule will not give you an easement to do likewise when I transfer field *A* to you.

The rule's second requirement, that the quasi-easement must have been 'continuous and apparent', is fairly undemanding. It seems to mean merely 'always discoverable', often—though not necessarily—from permanent clues on the land rather than from the quasi-easement's actual exercise. The use of a made-up road will therefore count, even if the use itself is intermittent,[78] as will the use of drains beneath the quasi-servient land.[79] So my use of field *B* to take my cows to and from the road will count as 'continuous and apparent' if the cows' passage has worn a discernible track,[80] or perhaps even on the strength of the presence of gates at either end of the field. Taken thus, the requirement helps to ensure that an easement can arise under this rule only from a rather clearly identifiable quasi-easement. That is useful: without it, so that any quasi-easement existing before the transfer could yield an easement after it, arguments might proliferate over what quasi-easements there had been.

The rule's third requirement is that the easement in question be necessary for the reasonable enjoyment of the land transferred—field *A* in our example. This requirement is more exigent than the demand that, to be an easement at all, the right must 'accommodate' the land, ie benefit the transferee in his capacity as the land's owner. So in one case,[81] the court held that it was *not* necessary for the reasonable enjoyment of a business annexe at the back of a house for the transferees of the annexe to have access to it through the house, as well as by a path down the side of the house. On the other hand, a right can be 'necessary' for the land's 'reasonable enjoyment' without being 'necessary' in the way that an easement of necessity is: so the existence of alternative means of access will not always preclude an easement arising under the present rule.[82] This requirement attaches significance to the situation that has arisen since the transfer. It thus parts company with the

---

[78] *Borman v Griffith* [1930] 1 Ch 493 (Ch D).

[79] *Schwann v Cotton* [1916] 2 Ch 120 (Ch D).

[80] A track made by human traffic was accepted in *Hansford v Jago* [1921] 1 Ch 322 (Ch D). Such a case would be excluded by the formulation adopted in *Ward v Kirkland* [1967] Ch 194, 225 (Ch D), that there must be 'a continuous and apparent feature *designed or appropriate for* the exercise of the easement on the servient tenement' (emphasis added). But this seems too narrow.

[81] *Goldberg v Edwards* [1950] Ch 247 (CA).

[82] An easement was found in *Borman v Griffith* [1930] 1 Ch 493 (Ch D), where the alternative access was inadequate for heavy traffic, including that associated with the transferee's business as a poultry farmer. Compare *Wheeler v JJ Saunders Ltd* [1996] Ch 19 (CA), where an easement was not found, because the route in question was only 10 cm wider than the alternative access available.

first two requirements, which relate to the state of affairs existing before the transfer. On their own, they would generate an easement purely so as to replicate a usage that had previously gone on between the two pieces of land in question. The third requirement means that such replication occurs only where the right in question is now *needed*.

The third requirement is welcome. The previous existence of a continuous and apparent quasi-easement alone can provide evidence of a genuine implied intention to confer the easement, though it will only rarely suffice to prove it on the balance of probabilities. But that is not how the rule in *Wheeldon v Burrows*[83] operates. Instead, as explained in § 9.2.1, it actually creates the easement, by imputing an intention to confer it. And the existence of a continuous and apparent quasi-easement alone is an inadequate basis on which to do this. The imputation is acceptable only when the additional utilitarian argument for it is sufficiently powerful. The fact that I visibly did something in the past may contribute to the making of such an argument, by giving a prima facie indication that the alleged easement would be useful. But to complete the argument, the easement must be positively needed: as the law has it, 'necessary for the reasonable enjoyment' of the land transferred. Perhaps for this reason, although the relevant caselaw is in disarray,[84] the majority of commentators agree that this third requirement is essential.

9.2.5 Law of Property Act 1925 Section 62

We now turn to the final rule whereby the law discovers the implication of an easement into a transfer. This rule is rooted in section 62 of the Law of Property Act 1925.[85]

Like the rule in *Wheeldon v Burrows*,[86] this rule applies where I used to own an area of land, and have now transferred part of it to you, retaining the other part myself: and operates to imply into that transfer, as an easement in your favour over my retained land, a right modelled on the way in which the

---

[83] (1879) 12 Ch D 31 (CA).

[84] The statement of the rule in *Wheeldon v Burrows* (1879) 12 Ch D 31 (CA) itself (see n 75 above) treats the demands that the quasi-easement be continuous and apparent, and that the alleged easement be necessary for the reasonable enjoyment of your land, as synonymous. That is an impossible position, but it was repeated in *Wheeler v JJ Saunders Ltd* [1996] Ch 19, 31 (CA). *Ward v Kirkland* [1967] Ch 194 (Ch D) is sometimes read as asserting that the third requirement is part of the rule, but it in fact seems to take that for granted. Its insistence is rather on the second requirement, which, given the original statement, could hardly have been in doubt. *Kent v Kavanagh* [2006] 2 All ER 645, [43] (CA) firmly demands the third requirement, but does so without discussion.

[85] s 62(1) reads: 'A conveyance of land shall be deemed to include and shall by virtue of this Act operate to convey, with the land, all buildings, erections, fixtures, commons, hedges, ditches, fences, ways, waters, watercourses, liberties, privileges, easements, rights, and advantages whatsoever, appertaining or reputed to appertain to the land, or any part thereof, or, at the time of the conveyance, demised, occupied, or enjoyed with, or reputed or known as part and parcel of or appurtenant to the land or any part thereof.'

[86] (1879) 12 Ch D 31 (CA).

two pieces of land were used before the transfer. But there are two ways in which section 62 differs from *Wheeldon v Burrows*.[87]

First, as noted in § 9.2.4, *Wheeldon v Burrows*[88] applies only where there was unity of occupation before the transfer, as in the example of fields *A* and *B*. Section 62, on the other hand, applies only where there was diversity of occupation.[89] That is to say, although I owned both the pieces of land in question,[90] I occupied only the piece that I now retain: the piece that I have transferred to you was occupied by someone else (possibly you, as my tenant). The required prior use accordingly takes the form of a licence which I allowed that person over my retained land.[91] This difference merely means that the two rules divide the relevant territory between them. Second, however, *Wheeldon v Burrows*[92] demands additionally that the prior use be 'continuous and apparent' and that the easement now claimed be 'necessary for the reasonable enjoyment' of the transferred land. Section 62 does not make these demands, and indeed has no further requirements at all. This difference is more striking, and will be discussed further once we have a firmer idea of how section 62 operates.

So, say I own two adjoining houses, *C* and *D*. I rent *C* to a tenant—let us say you, but it might be someone else—while continuing to occupy *D* myself. *C* is heated by a wood-burning stove. Since *C* has no shed, however, I allow you (give you a licence) to keep your wood in a shed attached to *D*. I then transfer[93] *C* to you. By virtue of section 62, and regardless of whether your previous use of the shed was 'continuous and apparent' and whether it is necessary for your future enjoyment of *C* for this use to continue, the law regards the transfer as conferring on you an easement to that effect.[94]

Section 62 produces this effect in the following way.[95] By section 62, 'all ... rights ... appertaining ... to the land' are included in the transfer of the land,

---

[87] *Ibid.*

[88] *Ibid.*

[89] *Long v Gowlett* [1923] 2 Ch 177 (Ch D); *Sovmots Investments Ltd v Secretary of State for the Environment* [1979] AC 144 (HL). The rule was overlooked in *P & S Platt Ltd v Crouch* [2004] 1 P & CR 18, [42], [59] (CA), suggesting that s 62 applies in both situations, but reaffirmed in *Kent v Kavanagh* [2006] 2 All ER 645, [46], [73] (CA).

[90] The rule is sometimes expressed as a requirement for diversity of occupation *or ownership*. That is incorrect. Unless I owned both pieces of land at the moment of the transfer, I could not simultaneously transfer the one to you and grant you an easement over the other. The reference to ownership must refer only to the possibility that the diversity of occupation arose through your having (not strictly ownership but) a lease from me.

[91] For licences, see Ch 15.

[92] (1879) 12 Ch D 31 (CA).

[93] Give you the freehold ownership, or a new lease.

[94] The example given is similar to the leading decision on this rule, *Wright v Macadam* [1949] 2 KB 744 (CA). The other main authority is *International Tea Stores Co v Hobbs* [1903] 2 Ch 165 (Ch D) (concerning not the Law of Property Act 1925 s 62 but its similarly worded predecessor, the Conveyancing Act 1881 s 6).

[95] See further L Tee, 'Metamorphoses and Section 62 of the Law of Property Act 1925' [1998] *Conv* 115.

unless a contrary intention appears.[96] Your licence to use the shed attached to *D* was a 'right appertaining to' *C*, ie belonging to you in your capacity as the tenant of *C*. Applying section 62, it is therefore included in, and thus reiterated by, the transfer of *C* to you. No problem so far, but also no mention of an easement. The crucial step comes next. The supposition is that an easement-shaped licence is an easement *manqué*, in the sense of an easement in substance, lacking only the formality of a deed that is needed for its valid creation as such.[97] Then, the reasoning continues, the transfer of *C* is (necessarily) made by deed;[98] when section 62 reiterates the licence, it therefore implies this into that deed; so the lack of a deed is repaired, and the easement *manqué* blossoms into an easement proper.[99]

This reasoning could work. It does so if the licence was easement-shaped *in every particular*, including that it was intended by us to be an easement (§ 9.1.5), so that the lack of a deed was truly the only reason for its not taking effect as such. Otherwise, and even if the licence had all the other characteristics of an easement, putting it in a deed should make it not an easement, but simply a licence in a deed. But in practice, the courts seem not to restrict section 62 in this way, to licences that are easement-shaped *in every particular*. They apply it to licences which, while having some of an easement's characteristics, fall short of easements by more than just the lack of a deed. They may not be intended to be easements, or even not be easement-shaped in some other way.

Unsurprisingly, there is no explicit dissension from the proposition that, to be turned into an easement by section 62, the licence must be easement-shaped. But there is a degree of carelessness over ensuring this to be the case. So, for example, to become an easement, the right over my land given by the previous licence must not be too extensive.[100] But the leading case on section 62[101] fails even to consider the issue, despite having facts which certainly made it relevant. Likewise, to be easement-shaped, the licence must benefit the prior occupant of the dominant land in his capacity as owner of that

---

[96] s 62(4). The provision seems to require that the contrary intention be expressed, but *Birmingham, Dudley and District Banking Co v Ross* (1888) 38 Ch D 295 (CA) holds that it can be implied from the circumstances prevailing at the time of the transfer.

[97] § 9.2.8.

[98] § 4.4.1.

[99] *Wright v Macadam* [1949] 2 KB 744, 751 (CA). There is a similarity with the reasoning in *Wood v Leadbitter* (1845) 13 M & W 838 (Ex): see § 15.3.2. In this decision, the court held that a licence could be terminated ahead of its promised duration. It seemed to ascribe this conclusion to the fact that the licence was not a legal property right, such as an easement or lease, and proved this by pointing out that it had not been granted by deed. The implication seems to be that, if it had been granted by deed, it would have been such a property right, and could not be terminated.

[100] § 9.1.4.

[101] *Wright v Macadam* [1949] 2 KB 744 (CA). The facts involved the use of a shed, on similar lines to those of the example used in this section.

land, rather than in his personal capacity.[102] So, if I let you use the shed attached to *D*, not to store wood for your stove but to play your drum kit, an easement should not arise. But the cases have apparently treated section 62 as operating where, although the usage might by its nature have been for the benefit of the future dominant land, it was in fact enjoyed in a personal capacity: as where, say, I allow you to use my shed to keep your wood, but only because I want to do you a favour as an individual.[103] Again, a licence is not easement-shaped unless it is intended to be irrevocable.[104] So if I give you permission to use my shed on an open-ended but not necessarily permanent basis, this ought not to be enough. But the courts have expressly held section 62 to apply on such facts.[105] The breadth that this approach gives section 62 has been criticised as unfair,[106] but the more fundamental objection is that it is unprincipled.

But even if section 62 were applied properly, ie to fully easement-shaped licences alone, it would be problematic. As we saw in § 9.2.1, the implied grant rules in fact operate to *impute* easements, rather than on the basis of a genuine implicit intention, and section 62 is certainly no exception. To justify the imputation requires a utilitarian argument for the easement in question, bolstered by the degree of consent discernible in my failure to stipulate against it. Even given the prior usage, the rule in *Wheeldon v Burrows*[107] demands that the claimed easement be 'necessary for the reasonable enjoyment' of the transferred land, but section 62 has no such requirement, nor anything equivalent. Without such a requirement, the section demands only a lesser degree of utility in order to operate. That degree is surely insufficient, even given the element of consent.

---

[102] § 9.1.3. There is another reason why s 62 should not turn such a usage into an easement. The section implies into the conveyance only rights that 'appertain to' the land being conveyed. A usage that benefits only in a personal capacity does not 'appertain' to the land, and so should not be implied into the conveyance *even to be reiterated as a licence*.

[103] The issue might have been relevant, but was ignored, in *International Tea Stores Co v Hobbs* [1903] 2 Ch 165 (Ch D), *Wright v Macadam* [1949] 2 KB 744 (CA) and *Green v Ashco Horticulturist Ltd* [1966] 1 WLR 889 (Ch D).

[104] The important point is the intention. Unless given by contract, a licence is necessarily revocable (§ 15.2.2), but this would not prevent its being easement-shaped if it was nonetheless intended to be irrevocable.

[105] *International Tea Stores Co v Hobbs* [1903] 2 Ch 165, 172 (Ch D); *Wright v Macadam* [1949] 2 KB 744, 751–2 (CA); *Green v Ashco Horticulturist Ltd* [1966] 1 WLR 889, 896 (Ch D). But a distinction is drawn, so that s 62 does not apply, if I make my permission explicitly temporary (*Wright v Macadam* at 751), or conditional on its exercise not inconveniencing me (*Green v Ashco Horticulturist Ltd* at 897). It is correct to regard s 62 as inapplicable in the latter cases, as such licences are clearly not easement-shaped. But the distinction between them and the open-ended case, to which s 62 does apply, is unsustainable.

[106] *Wright v Macadam, ibid* 755; *Green v Ashco Horticulturist Ltd, ibid*. The Law Commission has provisionally proposed the abolition of this method of implied grant: *Easements, Covenants and Profits ˆ Prendre: A Consultation Paper* (Consultation Paper No 186, London, 2008) para 4.104.

[107] (1879) 12 Ch D 31 (CA): § 9.2.4.

There is less difficulty, however, about the fact that section 62 has no requirement that the prior usage be 'continuous and apparent', ie always discoverable, in the way that *Wheeldon v Burrows*[108] does. Such a requirement is in principle useful, as it enables the parties to the transfer to identify the rights that the transfer will create. But as we have seen, for section 62 to apply, the two pieces of land in question must previously have been occupied by different people, with a licence for one over the other. Under these circumstances, the right is likely to be discoverable in its very nature.

9.2.6 Implied Reservation

So far, the discussion has been about the four rules operating to impliedly *grant* you an easement, ie to give you an easement over the land that I retain, for your benefit as owner (or tenant) of the land that I have transferred to you. The question addressed in the present section is: do the same rules operate also to *reserve* an easement—to create an easement over the land that I have transferred to you, for my benefit as owner of my retained land?

The rule arising from section 62 of the Law of Property Act 1925 cannot operate to reserve an easement. This follows from the section's wording: it applies where I transfer some land to you, to give you the rights—not the obligations—belonging to that land.

The other three rules involve no statutory text. As we have seen, they depend principally on the existence of a utilitarian case for an easement. As a matter of principle, such a case can arise as much for reserving as for granting an easement. So if my transfer to you leaves me with a piece of land that is inaccessible, there is an argument for creating a right of way for me across your piece. Likewise if I lease you the upper part of my building, keeping the basement for myself so as to open a restaurant, and discover that I need to fix a ventilation duct to your part; or if I used to take my cows to and from field *A* over field *B*, and after transferring field *B* to you it is necessary for the reasonable enjoyment of field *A* that I should continue to be able to do so.

As we have seen, however, the law does not treat the argument from utility as sufficient to generate easements in these ways. Instead, it additionally requires a degree of consent. In the case of implied grant, this degree of consent is found in my transferring the dominant land to you without ruling out the easement, as I could have done. And there is a difference between grant and reservation in this respect. The person most in control of the transfer is me, the transferor. From my previous ownership of the two pieces of land, I will also have the greater sense of what easements might be useful between them. Your lack of previous acquaintance with the two pieces of land leaves you in the converse position. So your failure to rule the easement

---

[108] *Ibid*: § 9.2.4.

out does not so clearly bespeak a degree of consent to it on your part. The argument for implied reservation is thus weaker than that for implied grant.

According to the cases, the law will reserve as well as grant an easement where it is necessary[109] and where the parties commonly intended that the reserved land be used for a particular purpose and the easement is needed for this to occur;[110] but only grant, not reservation, is possible under the rule in *Wheeldon v Burrows*.[111] This division between the rules is understandable. The utilitarian case for an easement is stronger under the first two rules, with their requirement of necessity, than under *Wheeldon v Burrows*,[112] which accepts the lower standard of 'necessary for the reasonable enjoyment' of the land, together with a visible prior usage. It is right that the difficulty in pointing to consent on the transferee's part in a reservation case should fatally undermine the generation of an easement under the latter rule.

9.2.7 Prescription

Prescription is a means of acquiring an easement on the basis, broadly speaking, that for 20 years you have acted as though you already had it. For example, if you have gone across my land to and from your own for 20 years, you will generally acquire an easement against me entitling you to continue to do so.

The law about prescription was explained in § 6.3. For present purposes, recall that this method of acquisition is founded on a combination of utility and consent. However, it runs into the same criticism as is to be made of the imputation of easements under section 62 of the Law of Property Act 1925. Unlike the other grounds for imputing easements, section 62 does not require the easement to be in any way necessary, and nor does prescription. Instead, these grounds look to the prior usage alone. Their basis in utility is thus relatively weak. Even with the help of my consent, it may not be enough to warrant depriving me of my rights by giving you an easement.

9.2.8 Formalities

The express grant or reservation of an easement has to be made using the correct formalities. Formalities in general are discussed in Chapters 4 and 5. Briefly, to create a legal easement (ie a right recognised by the common law as an easement[113]), the grant or reservation has to be effected using a

---

[109] *Corporation of London v Riggs* (1880) 13 Ch D 798 (Ch D).

[110] *Pwllbach Colliery Co Ltd v Woodman* [1915] AC 634, 646 (HL).

[111] (1879) 12 Ch D 31, 49 (CA); *Kent v Kavanagh* [2006] 2 All ER 645, [47] (CA).

[112] (1879) 12 Ch D 31 (CA).

[113] Another condition must be satisfied before an easement can be recognised by the common law: the easement must be equivalent in duration to either a freehold or a lease: ie be either indefinite or for a 'term', as that concept is understood in the context of leases (see § 11.4.2).

deed,[114] and (since it counts as a registrable disposition) has to be registered.[115] To create an equitable easement (ie a right recognised by equity, though not the common law, as an easement), writing must be used:[116] there is no requirement of registration.[117]

An implied grant or reservation, though dependent on utilitarian considerations, is regarded as a deemed express grant or reservation, and so attracts the same formality requirements. At first sight, it fails to meet them. But the implication is into the transfer,[118] and the easement is seen as having been made with the formality that was used for the transfer. In particular, the transfer will usually be made by deed, so an easement implied into it will be regarded as made by deed too.[119] It is unclear whether the registration of the transfer[120] would likewise count as the registration of an easement implied into it. But the issue is avoided thanks to a rule—reflecting the utilitarian flavour of implied easements—lifting the requirement of registration from the creation of implied easements.[121]

The prescription rules generate easements by imagining (fictitiously, of course) that these easements were originally conferred by an express grant, which can no longer be discovered. That grant would need to have been made using the appropriate formalities. If there were any reason why the imagined grant *could not* have validly occurred, prescription under these rules will fail.[122] But although it is sometimes possible to point to other reasons why there could not have been a proper grant, it is hard to see any reason why the supposed grantor could not have used the relevant formalities. So the issue is unlikely to pose a problem in practice. That is as it should be, for prescription is, as we have seen, based not on intention, but on utility, subject to exclusion: it is therefore a disorganised way of generating the easement: so a formality requirement is counter-indicated, as explained in § 6.1.2.

Most easements meet this requirement (an easement for life would not, for example, but is uncommon), so in practice the distinction between legal and equitable easements usually depends on the formality issue.

[114] Law of Property Act 1925 s 52(1).

[115] Land Registration Act 2002 s 27(2)(d).

[116] Law of Property Act 1925 s 53(1)(a); or, if the equitable easement is the result of conversion (§ 5.2), Law of Property (Miscellaneous Provisions) Act 1989 s 2.

[117] But as equitable easements are not normally overriding interests (§ 9.3), they will have to be registered if they are to bind disponees.

[118] Implication under the Law of Property Act 1925 s 62 is specifically into a 'conveyance', which is the transfer of a legal estate. This rule cannot therefore imply an easement into an estate contract: *Borman v Griffith* [1930] 1 Ch D 493 (Ch D).

[119] The trick seems not to work, however, where an easement is implied in an oral lease for three years or less. Such a lease is itself valid: Law of Property Act 1925 s 54(2). But an easement implied into it has not been granted by deed.

[120] Under the Land Registration Act 2002 s 27. By s 27(2)(b), a lease need not be registered if it is for seven years or less, so an easement implied in such a lease would be in difficulties if it were not for the rule explained next.

[121] Land Registration Act 2002 s 27(2)(d).

[122] *Dalton v Angus & Co* (1881) 6 App Cas 740 (HL); *Tehidy Minerals Ltd v Norman* [1971] 2 QB 528, 552 (CA); *Oakley v Boston* [1976] QB 270 (CA).

The other main method of acquiring an easement is proprietary estoppel. The formality rules are simply inapplicable to this method: it does not even pretend to rest purely on an intentional conferral, so, again, any requirement of formality would be misplaced.

9.3 Easements' Effectiveness against Disponees

Say you have acquired an easement over my land. Will your easement bind a disponee of the land from me? Easements are rights in rem, so it is certainly capable of doing so. Whether it actually does, in the case of registered land, depends on the rules in the Land Registration Act 2002. It can bind either through registration or as an overriding interest. The details are, however, complex.

The rules distinguish between legal and equitable easements. An easement will be legal—ie recognised by the common law—if it is expressly or impliedly granted or reserved by deed, or created by prescription.[123] Otherwise it will be equitable. Equitable easements thus arise where the easement is expressly or impliedly given or reserved in a transaction that is recognised by equity but not the common law, such as an estate contract.[124] Easements generated by proprietary estoppel are also equitable, as this is an equitable doctrine. Then:

— The *express* grant or reservation of a *legal* easement is a registrable dispo- sition, so an easement created in such a way must be registered, in order to exist as a legal easement at all.[125] Being registered, it will necessarily then bind a disponee of the servient land. (If an easement would otherwise be legal but is not registered in this way, it becomes an equitable easement: for it is given by a transaction which equity recognises, but the common law does not.)
— A *legal* easement arising in any other way (ie by implied grant or reser- vation, or prescription) does not have to be registered in order to exist as a legal easement at all. However, it can be registered, so as to bind disponees of the servient land.[126] It can also operate as an overriding interest. But it will do so only if, at the time of the disposition, (i) the disponee knows of

---

[123] The easement must also be equivalent in duration to either a freehold or a lease: see n 108.
[124] § 5.2.
[125] Land Registration Act 2002 s 27(2)(d).
[126] *Ibid* s 34.

it; or (ii) it would have been obvious on a reasonably careful inspection of the land; or (iii) it has been exercised in the past year.[127]

— An *equitable* easement need not be registered in order to exist at all, but can be in order to bind a disponee.[128] It cannot, however, operate as an overriding interest.[129]

As explained in §§ 2.2.2–2.2.3, the general approach of the Land Registration Act 2002 is to require registration, except where it is 'neither reasonable to expect nor sensible to require' registration and the right is, despite not being registered, readily discoverable by a disponee.

The rules regarding legal easements broadly track this approach. Where an easement is created expressly, it will have arisen in an organised way, so it will be reasonable to expect and sensible to require its registration. Otherwise, it will have arisen in a disorganised way. It would therefore not be reasonable to expect or sensible to require its registration, so it is a candidate for overriding interest status. But the further desideratum of ready discoverability by the disponee is covered by the Act's insistence that one of the three conditions explained above be present. (Or is it? The third condition, that the easement has been exercised in the past year, does not quite secure its discoverability, and may reflect a loss of confidence in the Act's overall approach.)

The position regarding equitable easements—the rule that these cannot be overriding interests—is however ill-judged. These easements too will often have arisen in a disorganised way, so that it is not reasonable to expect or sensible to require their registration. And they should be no less readily discoverable by a disponee than their legal counterparts. So their inability to operate as overriding interests cannot be ascribed to the Act's own values. Rather, they seem to have been sacrificed so that the Act can be seen as lubricating trade in land by sweeping away a number of kinds of overriding interests entirely.[130]

The very distinction between legal and equitable easements is an unnecessary complication, moreover. It arises principally from the fact that the two systems historically applied different formality rules. The resulting situation is criticised in § 4.4.2.

---

[127] *Ibid* Sch 3 para 3.

[128] *Ibid* s 34.

[129] The overriding interest provision relating to easements (Sch 3 para 3) is limited to legal easements, as detailed above. An equitable easement could nevertheless count as an overriding interest under the provision relating to rights in rem generally (Sch 3 para 2), but only if the person entitled to the easement—the dominant owner—is in actual and apparent occupation of the servient land, which (in the nature of easements) is unlikely.

[130] Under the 2002 Act's predecessor, the Land Registration Act 1925, equitable easements (as well legal easements) could operate as overriding interests: *Celsteel Ltd v Alton House Holdings* [1985] 1 WLR 204 (Ch D) (though the relevant statutory wording itself was garbled).

Restrictive Covenants

The next kind of right in rem over land we shall consider is that known as a 'restrictive covenant'.

10.1 The Idea of a Restrictive Covenant

Say you and I have next-door houses. The law automatically imposes certain obligations on me requiring me to respect your amenity as my neighbour. It will be a tort of nuisance, for example, if I inflict an excessive amount of noise or smoke on you. On top of these automatic obligations, we can create additional ones as we wish. So we can oblige me not to use my house for business purposes (which might lead to annoyance for you), or not to erect further buildings on its garden (which might interrupt your view), or to keep my hedge trimmed to a certain height (again, so as to preserve your view).

We can create such additional obligations as contractual duties. In this case they will bind only me, as contractual obligations are only in personam; the benefit could in theory be personal to you too, but in practice will usually be extended to others living in your house (with you or after you) under the Contracts (Rights of Third Parties) Act 1999, or be capable of assignment. Alternatively, we can create such obligations as rights in rem. In this case, they will bind not only me, but also (so long as the relevant rules in the Land Registration Act 2002 are satisfied) disponees of my land from me; and the benefit of them will in principle belong first to you, but then to your successors in your house. More than one type of right in rem can be used for such purposes, but the principal type is the 'restrictive covenant'.

Restrictive covenants were developed by the Court of Chancery, and so are equitable rights. That is, the common law continues to assert that there are no such rights in rem, but they obtain because equity says the contrary, and equity takes precedence over the common law.[1] As rights in rem go, they are also relatively young. They emerged only in the 1840s,[2] and even then only with the benefit of hindsight: early accounts tended to say that disponees were bound not by the covenant's own power, but because they took the land with notice:[3] assertions that the covenant itself has in rem status are made confidently only from 1882.[4]

Perhaps for these reasons, treatments of the subject often present the relevant common law rules first, then go on to explain the difference that restrictive covenants make. This approach is confusing, however, and gives an unrealistic impression of the law (just as if one talked in this way about trusts, which likewise do not form part of the common law). It is better to focus primarily on the law's main right in rem of this kind, namely the restrictive covenant.

Let us familiarise ourselves with the terminology: the person first undertaking the obligation (me, in our example) is called the 'covenantor'; the person first holding the right (you) is the 'covenantee'; my land is the 'servient' or 'burdened' land, and yours is the 'dominant' or 'benefited' land.[5]

10.2 What Counts as a Restrictive Covenant?

A restrictive covenant is an obligation that I undertake in your favour and which:

---

[1] See § 1.5.

[2] The earliest traces of the relevant rules seem to be in *Whatman v Gibson* (1838) 9 Sim 196 (Ch) and *Mann v Stephens* (1846) 15 Sim 377 (Ch), followed by the better known *Tulk v Moxhay* (1848) 2 Ph 774 (Ch).

[3] See especially *Tulk v Moxhay* (1848) 2 Ph 774, 777–8 (Ch). The idea seemed to be that this generated a new obligation against the disponee, in the manner canvassed, though not accepted, in § 8.2.4.

[4] See *London & South Western Railway v Gomm* (1882) 20 Ch D 562, 583 (CA), followed by *Rogers v Hosegood* [1900] 2 Ch 388, 407 (CA), *Formby v Barker* [1903] 2 Ch 539 (CA) and *Re Nisbet and Potts' Contract* [1905] 1 Ch 391 (Ch D), affirmed [1906] 1 Ch 386 (CA). Earlier examples can be found, however: eg *Coles v Sims* (1854) 5 De G M & G 1, 7–8 (LJJ).

[5] Though as explained in the context of easements (§ 9.1.3), the idea of 'benefited land' cannot be taken literally: the benefit must necessarily be to humans' use of the land.

— 'touches and concerns' *my* land: ie affects the use I make of my land, and is intended to bind not only me, but also disponees of my land;

— 'touches and concerns' *your* land: ie is, and is intended to be, beneficial to you in your capacity as the owner of your land, rather than your personal capacity; and

— operates in a *negative* way: ie limits the things I may do on my land, rather than requiring activity from me.

10.2.1 The First Requirement: 'Touching and Concerning' the Servient Land

The first requirement—that the obligation must 'touch and concern' my land—has two aspects.

The first is that the duties created by the obligation must affect me *as regards the use I make of my land*. For example, an undertaking requiring me to refrain from competing with your business at all does not meet this requirement; but one requiring me *not to use my land* so as to compete with your business does. You and I can of course make a contract requiring me to refrain from competition with you at all,[6] but this cannot be a right in rem in the way that an undertaking not to use my land so as to compete with you thus can.

But even if an obligation does apply to the use of particular land in this way, it does not follow that the obligation must be in rem. The second aspect of the requirement that the obligation must 'touch and concern' is that we should additionally *intend* it to be in rem, rather than operating only in personam. But if the first aspect is present—that is, if the undertaking does in fact relate to the use of my land—the law presumes that the second is too, ie that the undertaking is intended to operate in rem, unless the contrary intention appears.[7]

10.2.2 The Second Requirement: 'Touching and Concerning' the Dominant Land

So the first requirement is that the undertaking must 'touch and concern' the servient land. The second requirement[8] is that it must also 'touch and concern' the *dominant* land. This requirement likewise has two aspects: the undertaking must benefit you in your capacity as owner of your (the dominant, or benefited) land, rather than in your personal capacity; and we must create it with the intention that it should do so.

---

[6] Subject to the allowability of such a contract under competition law.

[7] Law of Property Act 1925 s 79.

[8] Definitively recognised in *Formby v Barker* [1903] 2 Ch 539 (CA) and *London County Council v Allen* [1914] 3 KB 642 (CA).

Say I contract with you not to erect a religious building on my land. This undertaking touches and concerns my land. But it cannot qualify as a restrictive covenant, so as to operate in rem and bind John to whom I transfer my land, if it merely benefits you personally. Even if you live next door to my land, for example, you might want the undertaking because you yourself are a fervent atheist, and wish not to live cheek by jowl with the faithful. But it can qualify if it benefits you in your capacity as owner of your land (for example, if your aim is to preserve your house's access against the parking of church-goers' cars, or its tranquillity against the ringing of bells), and if we intend it to do so (ie if we intend it to benefit not merely you, but also your successors: those who take the land in question after you).

It will sometimes be obvious whether an undertaking touches and concerns the covenantee's land in this way; but sometimes less so.[9] But if it is clear (either from the words in which we make the covenant, or from the circumstances[10]) that we intend the covenant to benefit you as owner of your land, the law assumes that it also does so in fact, unless this seems unbelievable.[11] Equally, if an undertaking in fact benefits you as owner of your land, it is a likely inference that it is also intended to benefit you in that capacity.

A scenario in which this inference is especially easy is that known as a 'building scheme', or 'scheme of development'. Here, I sell a number of properties, and as I sell each property, I impose obligations regarding its use. The nature of the properties is such that they form an overall entity, such as a square, or terrace, or close, so that the use made of each property affects the others: the obligations regarding each property will thus benefit the others de facto.[12] The sale documents will probably say that the obligations are also *intended* to benefit the other properties, in which case this point too will be established. But even if there is no such statement, that is the natural inference, and the courts will draw it.[13]

---

[9] And careful thought will also be needed where, some time after the covenant is made, the covenantee's land is split up. The fact that it originally touched and concerned that land as a whole does not mean that it will necessarily touch and concern every one of the parts into which it has now been divided.

[10] *Renals v Cowlishaw* (1878) 9 Ch D 125 (Ch D); *Rogers v Hosegood* [1900] 2 Ch 388 (Ch D and CA). See too *Nottingham Patent Brick and Tile Co v Butler* (1885) 15 QBD 261, 268–70 (QBD) and (1886) 16 QBD 778, 784 (CA).

[11] *Marten v Flight Refuelling Ltd* [1962] Ch 115 (Ch D); *Earl of Leicester v Wells-next-the-Sea Urban District Council* [1973] Ch 110 (Ch D).

[12] The expression 'building scheme' originally referred specifically to the case where the properties are empty lots, the plan being for each purchaser to build his own house on the property he purchases. In that case, each purchaser's covenant contributes to the overall scheme by controlling the very design of the houses. But the expression has been extended to the case where the properties are sold with houses already built on them, and the covenants operate to maintain the overall entity in other respects, eg by preventing further building. The legal significance, as described in the text, is the same either way.

[13] In *Elliston v Reacher* [1908] 2 Ch 374, 385 (Ch D) inference from a building scheme was said to be possible only when the scheme has certain characteristics. Taken together, the list of these

10.2.3 The Role of the First and Second Requirements

These first two requirements, that the covenant should touch and concern land owned by the covenantor and by the covenantee, reflect the context in which these covenants began to be made, and their legal effectiveness urged and accepted.[14] It is such covenants' usefulness in this context that provides the argument for their acceptance by the law as rights in rem.

They date from the first half of the 19th century, a time of rapid growth of English towns.[15] Many inhabitants were poor, but there was also an affluent urban middle class, which aspired to a high standard of living. The prevailing environment of slum housing, factories and so on was inimical to this: even if a middle class family's home was inwardly agreeable, stepping outside the front door could entail a quite different experience. Things could be improved, however, by creating enclaves of middle class housing, producing a more pleasant external as well as internal environment. The techniques by which this was done included the architectural (eg the terrace; and the square was an especially useful way of creating such an enclave, especially if the rear rooms of the houses, facing the squalor beyond, were made the servants' quarters), and the horticultural (eg creating a pleasant garden in the middle of the square, a larger space than each individual house could command, and a place for socialising with persons similarly circumstanced).

But the trick would work only if it was possible to secure the enclave's integrity over time, ie to ensure that those inhabiting the enclave respected its standards. This was a task for the law. Restrictive covenants are best understood as the new rights in rem developed to perform it.

So, those buying houses in the enclaves were placed under obligations in this respect, requiring them not to use their premises for 'noxious trades', etc. It was essential—part of their job specification—that these obligations should operate in rem: the enclaves would not have been secured by obligations against the original inhabitants personally, ineffective against their

---

characteristics amounts to little more than a long-winded statement of the obvious ('there is a building scheme when there seems to be a building scheme'), but the details can occasionally pinch: *Lund v Taylor* (1975) 31 P & CR 167 (CA); *Emile Elias & Co Ltd v Pine Groves Ltd* [1993] 1 WLR 305 (PC). To approach the matter in this formulaic way, however, is to lose sight of the essential point: we are seeking evidence that the covenant is intended to benefit you as owner of your land rather than personally, and this evidence can come from any source: see at n 10 above. The latter approach was favoured in *Baxter v Four Oaks Properties Ltd* [1965] Ch 816 (Ch D), *Re Dolphin's Conveyance* [1970] Ch 654 (Ch D), *Brunner v Greenslade* [1971] Ch 993, 1006 (Ch D) and *Whitgift v Stocks* [2001] EWCA 1732, [85]–[87] (CA).

[14] *Tulk v Moxhay* (1848) 2 Ph 774 (Ch) itself involved facts of the kind about to be described, as did its precursors (*Whatman v Gibson* (1838) 9 Sim 196 (Ch); *Mann v Stephens* (1846) 15 Sim 377 (Ch)), and very many of its successors.
[15] The population of London rose from 957,000 in 1801 to 2,362,000 in 1851.

successors. Hence the first requirement, that such covenants should touch and concern land owned by the covenantor.

And it was equally part of such covenants' job specification that they should touch and concern land owned by the covenantee, as demanded by the second requirement. This is because their very *raison d'être* was to secure the integrity of the enclave *as between its inhabitants at a given time*—specifically, between a claimant occupying one of its houses and a defendant occupying another. Their effect on these lines was described at the time as 'local law'. So it is no coincidence that the law treats the existence of a building scheme as almost conclusively probative of this requirement's elements. The idea of a building scheme captures the very project for which this kind of right in rem was created: the establishment and preservation of an agreeable enclave for the mutual benefit of its inhabitants.

So the first two requirements reflect restrictive covenants' alignment to a certain social task, the perceived importance of which justifies their acceptance into the *numerus clausus* of rights in rem.[16] But in principle, there might be other social tasks, of equal importance, to which restrictive covenants might also be applied. The first requirement, that the obligation should touch and concern *servient* land, would remain: regardless of context, the restrictive covenant could not exist as a right in rem without it. (It does not make sense for the undertaking to affect a disponee of my land—this being the significance of its being a right in rem—unless it relates to the use of that land, rather than to my personal activities.) But the second requirement, that it should touch and concern *dominant* land, is a different matter. This requirement fits restrictive covenants to the task just described. But it might disable covenants from other tasks, also meriting admission to the *numerus clausus*. If so, covenants should be applicable to such other tasks without the second requirement.

Restrictive covenants have in fact been used for other tasks, and in the course of this the requirement for dominant land has indeed been questioned. One such task has been to protect you against business competition. The idea might be to prevent me and my successors from doing business with your competitors, by imposing on us an undertaking known as a 'solus tie'. In this case, I (say, a pub landlord) agree to buy my supplies exclusively from you (a brewery company).[17] The benefit of such an agreement is evidently to you yourself, not you as owner of your land. So if the law is to count such an agreement as a restrictive covenant (so as to bind not only me, but also disponees of my pub), it needs in this context to drop

---

[16] For the *numerus clausus*—the idea that a type of right cannot exist in rem unless the good involved in its doing so outweighs the harm—see § 1.2.2.

[17] Solus ties upon pubs were normally imposed in a *lease* of the pub by the brewery to the landlord. In that context, they were certainly in rem, and remain so. The development discussed in the text concerned some unusual cases in which such ties were created independently of a leasehold relationship.

the demand for dominant land. The courts experimented with using restrictive covenants in this way,[18] before ending the experiment by affirming that demand as a universal requirement.[19]

While preventing solus ties from operating in rem, however, this affirmation did not prevent the use of restrictive covenants for all business protection purposes. Say you and I own nearby shops, you run yours as a baker's, and I agree with you not to run mine as a baker's too. Here, the demand for dominant land is met, in the shape of your shop, so my undertaking can count as a restrictive covenant.[20] But this is not a sensible state of affairs. Whereas dominant land is crucial to the project of preserving urban enclaves, and so demanded in that context, it is essentially irrelevant to business protection. So the law needs to ask itself whether the task of business protection is so valuable as to warrant in rem status for agreements undertaking it;[21] and to give effect to its answer regardless of the presence or absence of dominant land.[22,23]

10.2.4 The Third Requirement: The Obligation Must be Negative

The remaining requirement is that the obligation must be negative, or 'restrictive' (hence the name, 'restrictive covenant').[24] So an obligation

---

[18] While solus ties were initially held in personam only (*Keppell v Bailey* (1834) 2 My & K 517 (Ch)), they were later held in rem (*Catt v Tourle* (1869) 4 Ch App 654 (CA in Ch); *Luker v Dennis* (1877) 7 Ch D 227 (Ch D)).

[19] *London County Council v Allen* [1914] 3 KB 642 (CA).

[20] See eg *Jay v Richardson* (1862) 30 Beav 563 (Rolls); *Stuart v Diplock* (1889) 43 Ch D 343 (Ch D and CA) (though the Court of Appeal expresses doubts); *Wilkes v Spooner* [1911] 2 KB 473 (KBD and CA); *Newton Abbott Co-operative Society Ltd v Williamson & Treadgold Ltd* [1952] Ch 286 (Ch D).

[21] This question arises, of course, only if such agreements are acceptable in themselves (ie in personam), as a matter of competition law.

[22] There is a further distinct task to which the courts have applied restrictive covenants. Where a lease contains a negative obligation against the tenant for the benefit of the landlord, this obligation binds all those deriving their interests from the tenant (assignees and sub-tenants) on a restrictive covenant basis: *Hall v Ewin* (1887) 37 Ch D 74 (CA). Nominally, this application complies with the requirement for dominant land, the landlord's freehold title to the leased property being regarded as that land. But this is unconvincing (the landlord's freehold title is quite different from the physical dominant land intrinsic to the original context of restrictive covenants), and either way, this application likewise requires its own justification. If it exists, that justification lies in considerations within the realm of leases, and the rule will be further discussed in that context: see § 11.7.3.

[23] The Law Commission (*Easements, Covenants and Profits à Prendre: A Consultation Paper* (Consultation Paper No 186, London, 2008)) regards it as proper for parties to be able to make rights in rem of any content they like, so long as they are appurtenant to dominant land (paras 8.16–8.24, 8.64. 8.71–8.73). Although the Commission seems to deny it (para 15.14), this view would have the startling result of allowing a contractual licence, a right only in personam (§ 15.3.3), to be made as a right in rem, so long as it was for the benefit of neighbouring land. The Commission offers no argument for its view.

[24] *Haywood v Brunswick Permanent Benefit Building Society* (1881) 8 QBD 403 (CA); *London & South Western Railway Co v Gomm* (1882) 20 Ch D 562 (CA); *Austerberry v Corporation of Oldham* (1885) 29 Ch D 750 (CA); *Rhone v Stephens* [1994] 2 AC 310 (HL).

requiring me not to erect buildings on my land can qualify as in rem in the present manner, for it is negative; whereas one requiring me to cut my hedge cannot, as it is positive.

Whether an obligation is positive or negative depends on its effect (whether it requires me to do something, including spend money), not on its wording. So, a covenant 'not to let my wall fall into disrepair' is as positive as one 'to keep my wall in good repair'; while one 'to keep my field as an open space' is as negative as one 'not to build on my field'. Sometimes a covenant has both positive and negative elements, for example 'to maintain the area in front of my house as a garden', which obliges me both to refrain from using the area for any other purpose and to keep it in good shape. Then, the law treats the negative aspect as a right in rem, leaving the positive aspect in personam (as a contractual obligation) only.

10.2.5 The Role of the Third Requirement

The requirement that the obligation be negative was established in *Haywood v Brunswick Permanent Benefit Building Society*.[25] The judgments offer little by way of argument for it, but perhaps do convey a sense that to allow disponees to be affected by positive as well as negative obligations would be to burden them excessively.

That disponees would be *burdened* is self-evident: it is the whole point of a right in rem. Why the burden would necessarily be *excessive* is less clear. An individual disponee should have nothing to complain about, for he will be bound only if the obligation is registered,[26] making it easily discoverable by him; and the price he pays for the land should reflect the obligations encumbering it, so the greater the burden, the lower the price. The worry may be at the level of the land market in general: not so much on the basis that such burdens would make land unsellable (the price correction mechanism should prevent this), as that they would chill its subsequent exploitation. This concern, however, seems as relevant to negative covenants, regarding which it is evidently seen as outweighed. But perhaps the concern was felt not in economic terms at all, but rather on a class basis. Positive covenants were entirely familiar, and seen as fully acceptable, in leases, where they affected tenants: but maybe freeholders could not be expected to render service in the same way, except on an in personam basis, ie with their personal consent.

The alleged drawbacks to positive covenants thus seem illusory. Indeed, positive covenants may sometimes actually benefit those who are subject to

---

[25] (1881) 8 QBD 403 (CA). The later decision confirming the requirement, *Rhone v Stephens* [1994] 2 AC 310 (HL), asserts that it is *doctrinally impossible* to recognise positive covenants as rights in rem, but this is a baseless view: see S Gardner, 'Two Maxims of Equity' [1995] *CLJ* 60.

[26] § 10.4.

them, as with the garden in the centre of the square described in § 10.2.3. The ban on positive covenants means that covenants cannot be used to require the householders around the square to contribute to its upkeep: so it is the more likely to degenerate, to the householders' detriment. Applied thus, the ban seems perverse.

It is no accident, therefore, that the law has introduced alternative ways of giving in rem effect to positive obligations *calculated to secure communal facilities*. The most notable[27] of these is 'commonhold'.[28] Say a set of flats, houses or other units has communal areas, such as the entrance, stairs, lifts and roof of a block of flats. The units (flats etc) can be sold to their individual owners on the basis that the communal areas are vested in a 'commonhold association' (a form of company, whose members are the owners of the units), having the duty to look after them for the unit-holders. The commonhold association's work is financed by contributions from the unit-holders. The unit-holders each have an obligation to make these contributions. These obligations are inherent in their ownership of their unit: in traditional terms, effective in rem. Commonhold associations are however controlled by arrangements that are bureaucratic, but even then arguably fail to give the unit-holders sufficient protection.

In any event, however, a commonhold arrangement makes sense only where there are communal facilities in this way. Otherwise—for example, where the owners of two semi-detached houses each covenant with the other to maintain their roof, against the damage that incoming rain could otherwise do to the other house—the need appears to be for a facility to undertake a positive obligation, pure and simple.[29]

---

[27] But as regards gardens in squares, see the Town Gardens Protection Act 1863 (and certain similar legislation), allowing a garden committee, elected by the square's residents, to levy a charge on the residents in order to maintain the garden.

[28] Commonhold was introduced by the Commonhold and Leasehold Reform Act 2002. This additionally provides for sets of units currently held on a leasehold basis, with their communal parts vested in the landlord, to be moved onto a commonhold basis. For discussion, see C van der Merwe and P Smith, 'Commonhold—A Critical Appraisal' in E Cooke (ed), *Modern Studies in Property Law, Volume 3* (Oxford, 2005) ch 11.

[29] The Law Commission provisionally favours allowing the creation of positive covenants: *Easements, Covenants and Profits à Prendre: A Consultation Paper* (Consultation Paper No 186, London, 2008) paras 7.39–7.66 (this passage does not, however, offer any argument for the move). The question would arise, against whom would such covenants be enforceable? Whereas a restrictive covenant requires everyone on the servient land to abstain from the act proscribed, a positive covenant needs performance only from one person associated with the servient land: the law would need to identify who this should be. This issue is discussed *ibid* paras 9.11–9.21.

10.3 The Creation of Restrictive Covenants

10.3.1 General

Restrictive covenants normally arise from an intentional conferral.

They are often created as part of a transaction whereby I transfer a piece of my land to you, retaining another piece for myself. Sometimes it is I who undertake the obligation, restricting the use to which the retained land can in future be put, for the benefit of you and your successors as owners of the land transferred. This will enable me to charge you a higher price for the transfer, as the benefit of my covenant will make the transferred land more valuable. Alternatively, I may (in what in the context of easements is called a 'reservation') extract the obligation from you, restricting the use of the transferred land, for the benefit of me and my successors as owners of the retained land. This will mean a lower price for the transfer, as the transferred land, burdened with the obligation, will be less valuable.

Equally, however, the covenant could be made not in the context of a transfer, but ad hoc. For example, we are neighbours; you, seeking to secure the view from your house, ask me to enter into a covenant not to erect further buildings on my land; and I agree, usually for a price.

An undertaking generating a restrictive covenant is normally express. Presumably, it could in principle be implied, for example an implied term of a transfer of one piece of my land to you. But such a thing is rarely, if ever, encountered in practice. There is no evidence of implied covenants being found in the way that implied easements are, for predominantly utilitarian reasons.[30] Nor can covenants arise via anything in the nature of prescription, on a similar predominantly utilitarian basis.[31] Given restrictive covenants' usefulness, such a thing might be contemplated in principle. But it would be rare for a covenant to be *needed*, to the degree required so as to warrant its creation on such a basis. It is, however, possible to imagine a restrictive covenant arising via proprietary estoppel.

---

[30] § 9.2.1.

[31] That is why the law is content to allow obligations to be created as restrictive covenants which it will not allow to arise as easements. If they could be easements, they could arise by prescription, and that is regarded as unsatisfactory. See the discussion of *Phipps v Pears* [1965] 1 QB 76 (CA) in § 9.1.4.

10.3.2 Conferral on a Third Party

So a restrictive covenant will normally arise from an intentional conferral. In the examples just given, I conferred a covenant on you, or vice versa, in a transaction between the two of us. But a covenant can also be conferred *in* a transaction between two people, but *on* a third person.

It is in fact very common for covenants to be created in this way. Say I build a pair of houses—call them *A* and *B*—and plan to sell each of them with a restrictive covenant in favour of the other. First I sell *A* to John, who undertakes the covenant. John's covenant is for the benefit of *B*, which I still own. So when I later sell *B* to you, you in turn acquire that benefit.[32] At the same time, you undertake your covenant, for the benefit of *A*. But I no longer own *A*: John already does, and you have no direct dealing with him. Nonetheless, he acquires the right to your covenant.

John can acquire the right to your obligation in this way because the rights and duties involved in restrictive covenants are not merely contractual.[33] As explained in § 10.3.1, and as seen in the example of you undertaking your covenant in buying house *B* from me, they are often created in contractual transactions; but that does not constrain their own essential nature. One aspect of this is familiar: the fact that the obligation is in rem, so that the duties can bind not only you but also your successors in *B* (contractual obligations operate only in personam). The phenomenon currently under discussion is less familiar, but it is another aspect of the same point. Despite your obligation being created in a contract between you and me, the right to that obligation belongs to the person(s) at whom it is aimed: namely John and his successors in *A*.[34]

It is a question of fact whether the covenant you make with me is meant for some third person such as John in this way, or whether it is meant merely as a contract between you and me. But it is essentially the same question as that whether, when you covenant with me in a case where I retain the benefited land myself, your obligation is meant to benefit me in my capacity as owner of my retained land, or merely in my personal capacity. As we saw in § 10.2.2, only if the former is the case does the covenant take effect as a right in rem between the two pieces of land, rather than as a mere contract between the two of us personally. Like the intention to benefit me in my

---

[32] The benefit of a restrictive covenant normally 'runs with' the benefited land: § 10.5.

[33] The Contracts (Rights of Third Parties) Act 1999 allows you to enforce a contract John makes with me but for your benefit. The Law of Property Act 1925 s 56 operates somewhat similarly. But these provisions operate only to widen the class of people (from me alone, to you too) having the right to John's *contractual* obligation. They have nothing to say about rights to obligations in rem, which are our concern.

[34] Other rights in rem can be created in the same way. Say John, in a contract with me, makes himself trustee of some property for you. The contract with me is irrelevant: John has thereby created an obligation in rem in your favour.

capacity as owner of my retained land, the intention to benefit third persons can be shown by the terms of the documentation,[35] or from the surrounding circumstances, especially the existence of a building scheme.[36]

10.3.3 Formalities

The making of a restrictive covenant by intentional conferral attracts a formality requirement of writing,[37] which—this being an organised mode of creation—is unproblematic and indeed appropriate.[38]

Strictly speaking, the word 'covenant' denotes an undertaking given by deed: a reflection of the fact that, as explained in § 10.3.1, these obligations are often created by the terms of a transfer, and transfers do have to be made by deed.[39] But the rule for restrictive covenants themselves requires only writing—not a deed or registration—because, as noted in § 10.1, restrictive covenants are equitable rights. In § 4.4.2, however, we criticised this differentiation between legal and equitable rights.

But intentionally made restrictive covenants will make good candidates for electronic conveyancing, ie the future system allowing the rights to which it applies to be made solely by electronic entry on the register.[40]

10.4 Restrictive Covenants' Effectiveness against Disponees

The obligation arising under a restrictive covenant is in rem, and so capable of binding disponees of the servient land. Under the Land Registration Act 2002, it will bind if it is registered.[41] There is no provision for restrictive

---

[35] *Rogers v Hosegood* [1900] 2 Ch 388 (Ch D and CA); *Baxter v Four Oaks Properties Ltd* [1965] Ch 816 (Ch D); *Re Dolphin's Conveyance* [1970] Ch 654 (Ch D).

[36] *Nottingham Patent Brick and Tile Co v Butler* (1885) 15 QBD 261, 268–70 (QBD); (1886) 16 QBD 778, 784 (CA).

[37] Law of Property Act 1925 s 53(1)(a).

[38] § 4.2.

[39] Law of Property Act 1925 s 52.

[40] See § 4.4.5. Meanwhile, the Law Commission (*Easements, Covenants and Profits à Prendre: A Consultation Paper* (Consultation Paper No 186, London, 2008)) provisionally recommends the replacement of restrictive covenants by (the very similar) 'Land Obligations' (para 8.13), and envisages that the intentional creation of these would count as a registrable disposition, ie (§ 4.4.4) require completion by registration (paras 8.29, 8.45).

[41] Restrictive covenants can be registered under s 34.

covenants to operate as overriding interests.[42] That is broadly as it should be: as we have seen, restrictive covenants normally arise only in an organised way, so it is sensible to expect them to be registered.

10.5 The Passing of the Benefit

If you have rights against me under a restrictive covenant, these rights can be enforced not only by you, but also by your successors on the land that the covenant benefits.[43] Unlike the parallel issue in easements (where the right passes to the successor automatically), this is a matter of some complexity. First we shall absorb the standard account of it, but then we shall criticise that account, seeing that its complexity is in fact unwarranted.

10.5.1 The Standard Account

According to the standard account, if I enter into a covenant in favour of you, then you transfer the land it benefits to Kate, Kate will acquire the covenant rights if one of three conditions is satisfied:

— the original transaction between me and you *annexed* the covenant to your
　land; or
— while it was not originally annexed to your land, you *assigned* the benefit
　of the covenant to Kate when you transferred the land to her (and Kate
　assigned it to anyone to whom she in turn transferred the land, and so on
　down to the present owner); or
— I entered into the covenant in your favour in the context of a *building
　scheme.*

Take first *annexation*. There are said to be two kinds. The first, 'express annexation', occurs if the original transaction not only creates the

---

[42] Your restrictive covenant against my land would bind my disponee as an overriding interest under Sch 3 para 2, if you were in actual and apparent occupation of my land. But that is unlikely.

[43] This account deals only with the passing of the benefit of a restrictive covenant, as part of our consideration of restrictive covenants as rights in rem. If I give you an undertaking that does not satisfy the requirements explained in § 10.2, and so counts not as such a right in rem but only as a contractual obligation (as for example a positive undertaking), the benefit of it may nonetheless enure to others besides you, especially by assignment or under the Contracts (Rights of Third Parties) Act 1999.

covenant, but additionally states—whether in express words or by necessary implication[44]—that the covenant is for the benefit not merely of you,[45] but of you in your capacity as owner of the land in question, or of you and your successors in that land.[46] Then, the right becomes fixed to your land, so when Kate acquires your land, she automatically acquires the covenant right too.[47]

The second kind of annexation, 'statutory annexation', was recognised in *Federated Homes Ltd v Mill Lodge Properties Ltd*,[48] which points—controversially[49]—to section 78 of the Law of Property Act 1925[50] as implying into the covenant the words which the express annexation rules present as necessary to effect an annexation. For the section to apply, the covenant must in fact benefit you in your capacity as owner of your land, and must be intended to do so (which can apparently be evidenced in any way). But this demand simply reproduces the second requirement for the existence of a restrictive covenant, discussed in § 10.2.2. This, and the first and third requirements, will necessarily have been met for the agreement to have qualified as a restrictive covenant in the first place. The result is that annexation occurs in this way *whenever the agreement exists as a restrictive covenant at all*. So whenever a restrictive covenant arises, its benefit is automatically annexed, and will pass likewise automatically, like that of an easement. Except, the courts have ruled,[51] such annexation does not occur

---

[44] See *Re Union of London and Smith's Bank's Conveyance, Miles v Easter* [1933] Ch 611, 628 (CA) and especially *J Sainsbury plc v Enfield London Borough Council* [1989] 1 WLR 590, 595–7 (Ch D). Even this extension is somewhat controversial: *Reid v Bickerstaff* [1909] 2 Ch 305, 329 (CA) and *Re Pinewood Estate, Farnborough* [1958] Ch 280, 286 (Ch D) seem to require express words. But according to the standard account, 'annexation' certainly cannot be found by reference purely to surrounding circumstances (*ibid*), except via 'statutory annexation', described below.

[45] 'You and your assigns' is also insufficient to annex: *Renals v Cowlishaw* (1878) 9 Ch D 125 (Ch D), affirmed (1879) 11 Ch D 866 (CA). The problem is that 'assigns' is ambiguous. It could mean 'persons to whom you transfer the land', in which case it is synonymous with 'successors in the land', a phrase which is sufficient to annex. But it could mean 'persons to whom you pass the right', which contemplates a separation between right and land, and so cannot annex.

[46] As in *Rogers v Hosegood* [1900] 2 Ch 388 (Ch D and CA).

[47] If the annexation is to land *A*, and you divide *A* into parts—say *A1* and *A2*—the question arises of whether the annexation survives the division. The annexing words can supply either answer (though if the answer is yes, the covenant, which must formerly have in fact benefited the whole, must now in fact benefit the newly created parts). If the words are ambiguous (eg simply 'to land *A*'), they are assumed to mean that annexation should survive the division: *Federated Homes Ltd v Mill Lodge Properties Ltd* [1980] 1 WLR 594, 606–7 (CA).

[48] [1980] 1 WLR 594 (CA).

[49] See especially G Newsom, 'Universal Annexation?' (1981) 97 *LQR* 32.

[50] 'A covenant relating to any land of the covenantee shall be deemed to be made with the covenantee and his successors in title and the persons deriving title under him or them ...'.

[51] *Crest Nicholson Residential (South) Ltd v McAllister* [2004] 1 WLR 2409 (CA).

unless the covenant document also identifies the dominant land;[52] or if the document shows an intention *against* annexing the rights.[53]

Assignment occurs when the rights are not annexed, but are passed with the dominant land by you to Kate. Given the wide scope of statutory annexation, it should hardly ever be relevant; it will apply only in the exceptions to statutory annexation, and in the absence also of express annexation. For assignment to be possible, the dominant land must be identifiable, but not necessarily from the terms of the covenant document: common sense inferences will suffice.[54]

A covenant right will remain enforceable on the basis of assignment only if it remains with the dominant land through the sequence of transfers of the land.[55] Say I covenant with you regarding the use of my land and so as to benefit you as owner of your land. Then I transfer my land to John. Assuming the covenant obligation is registered, you can enforce it against John, as it operates in rem. If you transfer your land to Kate, and simultaneously assign your covenant rights with it, Kate now has the right to John's obligation. But if you transfer your land to Kate and do not simultaneously assign your covenant rights with it (even if you assign them to her later), John is no longer liable to either you or Kate.[56]

The benefit of a covenant passes under a *building scheme* when the two pieces of land in question are contained within such a scheme, as described in § 10.2.2. Then, there is no need to show annexation or assignment: the benefit passes with the dominant land quite automatically. This is the closest the restrictive covenant rules come to their easement counterparts.

10.5.2 A Critique

The standard account thus presents this area of law as governed by a complex set of rules. It is prone to criticism on this account. But the complexity is the result of a failure properly to grasp the topic's key ideas.

[52] This ruling, which cannot be ascribed to the wording of s 78, aims to ensure that the person under the obligation can discover who is entitled to enforce it (eg so as to facilitate negotiations towards having it removed). But in this it fails, for it apparently tolerates a covenant such as 'for the benefit of the covenantee's nearby land': a formula which tells the covenantor and his successors rather little.

[53] s 78 appears not to allow for opting out of its effect in this way. The ruling seeks to meet the problem by reading a statement that a covenant is not to be annexed as one that it is not intended to benefit the covenantee as owner of his land at all. From the latter it would indeed follow, as explained in the text, that the covenant is not annexed by s 78. Unfortunately, however, the reasoning proves too much. It should also mean that the covenant's benefit cannot pass at all, even by assignment; and indeed that the agreement cannot even qualify as a restrictive covenant in the first place.

[54] *Newton Abbott Co-operative Society Ltd v Williamson & Treadgold Ltd* [1952] Ch 286, 297 (Ch D).

[55] *Chambers v Randall* [1923] 1 Ch 149 (Ch D); *Re Union of London and Smith's Bank Ltd's Conveyance, Miles v Easter* [1933] Ch 611, 629–34 (CA).

[56] If I have not transferred to John, however, Kate can enforce against me, for this is purely a matter of contract.

Essentially, the standard account depicts the benefit of a covenant as 'running' according to this set of rules, while its burden 'runs' under the circumstances described in §§ 10.2 and 10.4. But this is a fundamentally incorrect way of seeing the matter. The correct vision is as follows.

When I create a restrictive covenant in your favour, I attach its obligation to my land, whose use it controls. So if I transfer my land to John, the obligation will bind him, so long as it is registered.[57] All this is what we mean when we say that it is in rem.[58] We can if we wish put the point in a metaphor, using the figure of 'running'. But we should not say that the obligation runs: rather, it stays with the land, while I, John and so on run. Similarly with the covenant's benefit, or right. As explained in § 10.2.2, it is intrinsic to the make-up of a restrictive covenant that it benefits you—you have the right—in your capacity as owner of your land, rather than in your personal capacity. It follows that when you and the land part company, as when you transfer the land to Kate, it is the land with which the right should remain; Kate should acquire the right as part of the transfer. Like the obligation, then, the right does not run: it stays with the dominant land, and any running is done by you, Kate and so on. Hence the idea that restrictive covenants establish 'local law' between the pieces of land concerned: both obligations and rights are incurred simply by being there.

On this view, then, the trigger for covenant rights to pass should simply be the fact that the rights do and are intended to benefit you as owner of your land. This is in fact simply the second requirement that must be met for an agreement to take effect as a restrictive covenant at all.[59] It follows that whenever an agreement does take effect as a restrictive covenant (meaning that the second requirement, along with the first and the third, has been satisfied), the covenant right should automatically pass with the covenantee's land. Now we can grasp the essential difference between this view and the standard account. While this view treats the satisfaction of the second requirement as *sufficient* to make the right pass, the standard account treats it as only *necessary*, ruling (as explained in § 10.5.1) that the right will pass only if certain additional facts are shown.

The view for which we are arguing is in fact the same as that arrived at in *Federated Homes Ltd v Mill Lodge Properties Ltd*,[60] on the basis of section 78 of the Law of Property Act 1925. Though this is less commonly

---

[57] § 10.4.
[58] *Re Nisbet and Potts' Contract* [1905] 1 Ch 391 (Ch D), affirmed [1906] 1 Ch 386 (CA).
[59] § 10.2.2.
[60] [1980] 1 WLR 594 (CA). See at n 48 above. It is also the position favoured by the Law Commission for their proposed new 'Land Obligations': *Easements, Covenants and Profits à Prendre: A Consultation Paper* (Consultation Paper No 186, London, 2008) paras 8.66, 9.5–9.10.

understood, it was also taken, as a matter of basic principle, in *Rogers v Hosegood*,[61] the original leading case on the issue.

The judgments in the latter hold that, so long as the agreement both does and is intended to benefit you as owner of your land, the right it generates is 'annexed to' your land (and the obligation is likewise 'annexed to' my land).[62] Notice how this word is used: not (as in the standard account) to describe a step taken in order to *make* the right belong to your land, but to describe the situation where the right *does* belong to your land. Notice too how the judgments treat this approach's key question of whether, as well as in fact benefiting you as owner of your land, the agreement is intended to do so. The required intention can, according to the judgments,[63] be discovered either from the documents creating the covenant, or from the surrounding circumstances. On this view, then, 'express annexation' is simply annexation occurring when the evidence of the necessary intention happens to consist in the content of the covenant document. The judgments[64] present the existence of a building scheme as another (rather good) type of evidence for the same crucial intention, so it would be as logical to speak of 'building scheme annexation'. There is no ruling that the evidence cannot also take the form of other surrounding circumstances.[65] In principle, then, it should be possible to infer the necessary intention simply from the covenant's being in fact beneficial to you as owner of your land. All this is—as we should expect—identical with what we found in § 10.2.2, when looking at the same question (was the agreement intended to benefit you as owner of your land?) in its role as the second requirement for an agreement to take effect as a restrictive covenant at all.

This view thus integrates what the standard account calls 'express annexation' and the 'building scheme' rule into a single understanding of the circumstances in which a restrictive covenant right will pass with the covenantee's land: namely that it will do so whenever—as will necessarily be the case, if such a covenant right has arisen at all—the right does, and is found (for these or other reasons) to be intended to, benefit the covenantee as owner of his land. 'Statutory annexation' largely reproduces the effect of this view, but the reference to section 78 turns out to be unnecessary.

This view leaves assignment rather out in the cold, however. Assignment cannot be for cases where the conditions for annexation are not met, for on this view, the covenant would then not qualify as a restrictive covenant at all. An agreement could on the one hand qualify as a restrictive covenant, but on

---

[61] [1900] 2 Ch 388, 396–7 (Ch D), 404–8 (CA).
[62] *Ibid* 406–7.
[63] *Ibid* 396–7 (Ch D), 408 (CA).
[64] *Ibid*.
[65] The standard account treats the earlier decision in *Renals v Cowlishaw* (1878) 9 Ch D 125 (Ch D), affirmed (1879) 11 Ch D 866 (CA) as establishing such a rule. But *Rogers v Hosegood* [1900] 2 Ch 388, 407–8 (CA) treats that case merely as a decision on its facts, in which the

the other hand *not* have its rights automatically attach themselves to the covenantee's land and so pass only if assigned, only if the law positively allows opting-out from such attachment. Although introducing a complication, there is no essential reason why the law should not do so, if there is a demand for it.

10.6 A Comparison with Easements

Restrictive covenants have a basic similarity with easements (explored in Chapter 9),[66] in the sense that both are obligations in rem with 'appurtenant rights': that is, they can exist against me only if the rights to them benefit you not in your personal capacity but as owner of your land. Is there any reason why they should not be merged? To assess the possibility we need to take stock of their present differences. These are to be found principally on two[67] points.[68]

One relates to the obligation's content. Easements were developed in and for one application (the cross-exploitation of agricultural properties in the context of enclosure, and of town properties in the context of urbanisation), while covenants were developed in and for another (as a corrective to the discomforts of urbanisation). Each has however been applied more widely, to the extent possible without transgressing the rules reflecting the original applications, especially the requirement of dominant land. But in easements, there has been an attempt, albeit not a wholly thorough one, to limit the range of application, in the shape of the bias towards rights of a traditional, ordinary, agricultural, business nature.[69] There is no counterpart to this in

required intention could be discovered from neither the documentary words nor the surrounding circumstances.

[66] The link was made explicitly in *London & South Western Railway Co v Gomm* (1882) 20 Ch D 562, 583 (CA).

[67] At one time there might have been a third. Easement rights are regarded as belonging to the land which they benefit, and are transferred automatically with it; but on the standard account (criticised in § 10.5.2, however), this was not the case for restrictive covenants ... until *Federated Homes Ltd v Mill Lodge Properties Ltd* [1980] 1 WLR 594 (CA) made it so.

[68] The Law Commission, in *The Law of Positive and Restrictive Covenants* (Law Com No 127, London, 1984), advocated reform regarding covenants ostensibly calculated to bring them into line with easements, but paid virtually no attention to either of these differences. The report was also marred in other respects, notably its overstatement of the problems posed by the existing law (whatever the theoretical infelicities, covenants are almost always made by professional specialists, who are well able to skirt round these), and the rigidity and complexity of its proposed new approach. The report has not been taken forward.

[69] § 9.1.6.

the law of covenants, though in practice few novel applications seem to have been essayed for them.[70]

The reason why content matters is that obligations in rem are acceptable only if their usefulness outweighs the harm they necessarily do[71]; and their usefulness is a function of their content. The original applications of covenants and easements were evidently felt at the time to make them, on the whole, appropriate rights in rem: probably rightly: and that probably remains the balance of advantage today too. But novel applications require justification in the light of their own content, so the law on easements is right to be wary of them, and that on covenants wrong to give the appearance of insouciance on the point. If the two kinds of obligation were to be merged, then, it should not be on a basis which allows people to create appurtenant rights of whatever content they choose. This is especially important if, as argued in § 10.2.5, it should be possible to create covenants—and so, in the event of merger, easements too—involving positive obligations.

The other key difference between easements and covenants is in respect of the ways in which they can be created. It boils down to the issue whether it is right for the law to generate such obligations on the basis of utility (backed up by a weak element of consent), as it has traditionally done with easements but not with covenants. Where a right is not merely useful enough to merit acceptance as in rem, but exceptionally useful, there will be a case for allowing it to arise on that very basis. The law of easements reflects this point well in accepting non-intentional conferral in case of necessity, but misses it with its rule arising under section 62 of the Law of Property Act 1925[72] and its institution of prescription.[73] The law of covenants seems right not to contemplate non-intentional conferral, in that rights of the content to which it caters surely cannot be necessary. If the two kinds of obligation were to be merged, it should be on the basis that non-intentional conferral remains possible, but only where the right in question is in some sense necessary.[74]

---

[70] For those that have, see § 10.2.3.

[71] This is the *numerus clausus* principle: see § 1.2.2.

[72] § 9.2.5.

[73] §§ 6.3, 9.2.7.

[74] The Law Commission (*Easements, Covenants and Profits à Prendre: A Consultation Paper* (Consultation Paper No 186, London, 2008) pt 15) notices these two differences between easements and covenants (or 'Land Obligations', as it would call the largely identical replacement it envisages for the latter: *ibid* para 8.13)—even though its earlier treatment of the nature of easements (*ibid* pt 3) gave the impression that their content mattered little. Having noticed the two differences, however, it seems to favour preserving them in aspic, rather than considering their applicability to each type of right, and hence the possibility of merger, from first principles.

Leases

11.1 The Idea of a Lease

The next right in rem for consideration is a lease. The general idea of a lease is well known: I own some land, but allow you to have it for some period, usually in return for rent. The case that springs quickest to mind may be a domestic residential lease, under which you make the land your home, but there are also many other kinds of leases, such as commercial and agricultural.

In a moment we shall look at the detailed rules defining the concept of a lease. But first we shall deal with a puzzle about the concept's very nature: the relationship between leases and ownership.

11.1.1 Leases and Ownership

If you have an easement or a restrictive covenant against me, my obligation to you is relatively specific. I must refrain from using my land in some particular way (say, from building on it), or I must accept what would otherwise be a specified sort of trespass or nuisance by you (say, you crossing my land to reach your land). Although such obligations detract from the sum of the liberties I have in respect of my land, no one would say that they prevent me owning it, or that you own it instead.

If you have a lease of my land for some period, however, it might plausibly be said that you own the land, in my place, for that period (after which I resume ownership). This is because the rights and obligations involved in a lease are much more extensive than those involved in easements and covenants, making a lease something like the right to behave as the owner of the land in question for its duration. Having a lease of my land means that you can occupy it entirely, to a large extent excluding other people and even me, unless you choose to let us in. Subject to any restrictions in the lease's terms, you can also exploit the land economically, as for example by farming it, or running a shop on it, or sub-letting it to someone else, and keep the proceeds. You can also treat your lease as an asset in its own right, and transfer—'assign'—it to someone else. Conversely, the lease may place upon you the responsibility of maintaining the land.[1]

At the same time, we may still find ourselves saying that I, as your landlord, remain the owner of the land. I am of course owner-in-waiting, entitled to full rights again after your lease has finished, but the suggestion is that in some sense I remain owner during the lease. As we saw in § 1.3.3, 'ownership' is an elastic concept. But it really does not capture my position as a landlord, at any rate if your lease is of any significant duration. My rights for this period are very limited. I cannot go onto the land without your permission, except for special reasons allowed by the lease, such as to make emergency repairs. I may have the right to receive rent from you, but this is not always true, and even where it is, it does not seem to make me owner of the land. You may have to maintain the land, but since it is you who enjoys the land, this benefits me little during the lease, though it may help me get the land back in good order at the end. There is really only one sense in which I 'own' the land during the period of your lease. I can still sell it to John, albeit that John will normally be bound by your lease, as it is a right in rem.

Unlike lesser rights such as easements and restrictive covenants, therefore, leases create a true instance of fragmented ownership: you own the land for the period of the lease, and I own it thereafter, but during the lease no one has full ownership of it. We looked at the phenomenon of fragmented ownership in § 1.3.4. We saw that it is problematic, as impeding the sale of the land to someone wanting full ownership, and so damaging the land's marketability; and that as a result, the law has over the last century or so tended to suppress it, or create correctives to it. Leases have been excepted from this, however. They are much less damaging to the market: someone might well want to buy the landlord's interest during the lease, not only looking forward to the end of the lease but also for the sake of the rental income in the meantime. And the remaining damage seems to be outweighed by leases' usefulness. Allowing people to acquire most of an owner's rights in land for a limited period and for a proportionately limited investment—especially payable on a periodic basis—is valuable, particularly to businesses.

Perhaps because of difficulties of working with more ordinary words in a context of fragmented ownership, the law's terminology regarding leases is more than usually specialised. Your right, a lease, is also known as a 'demise' (though this word is old-fashioned), or especially as a 'term of years absolute',[2] often shortened to a 'term of years', or simply 'term'. You are a

---

[1] See further § 11.5.1.
[2] This is the expression used in the Law of Property Act 1925 s 1(1)(b).

tenant, or lessee, or 'termor'. As your landlord, I hold the land in 'fee simple absolute in possession', an expression which seems to cover my having mere title as well as it does beneficial ownership, but more specifically I have a 'reversion' (a word which emphasises my resumption of beneficial rights at the end of your term). I am a lessor, or 'reversioner'.

11.1.2 Enfranchisement and 'Right to Buy'

There is a further dimension to the insight that a lease is in some sense ownership. It underlies the right which some tenants have to 'enfranchisement': that is, to acquire the reversion of the land in question (or a new long lease over it), without the consent of the landlord and at a reduced price.

This right is the product of a number of pieces of legislation, aimed at a number of different contexts.[3] This has given the right a complex character, which will not be detailed here.[4]

Where the right is that of a tenant against a private sector landlord, the underlying idea is said to be that the tenant, rather than the landlord, deserves to own the reversion: either because he has made an up-front payment for the lease (a 'premium') as great as he would have had to pay for the freehold, or because he has spent money on maintaining the leased property (and sometimes even building it), on a scale giving him a moral entitlement to that property.[5] These arguments are not fully satisfactory, however, as they make sweeping, and arguably incorrect, financial assumptions.[6] If they were compelling, too, one would expect them to apply to all kinds of tenancies: yet the Acts cover only domestic, not commercial and agricultural, tenancies. In truth, at least part of the basis for the right seems to be an idea that certain tenants, simply because of their status as such, already 'own' the land in question, and this ownership entitles them to the reversion as well as the term. The power of this vision—and so the definition of the tenants in question—varies, obviously, with factors such as the length of time the tenants have had the property, but arguably also with context, so explaining the different treatment of domestic as opposed to commercial or agricultural tenants. Domestic tenants can be said to 'own' their leased

---

[3] Principally the Leasehold Reform Act 1967; the Housing Acts 1980 and 1985; the Landlord and Tenant Act 1987; the Leasehold Reform, Housing and Urban Development Act 1993; the Commonhold and Leasehold Reform Act 2002; and the Housing Act 2004.

[4] The various Acts take different approaches. The differences are only partly explicable by reference to the differences in context: to an extent they are the product of more general conceptual or political experimentation.

[5] Government White Paper, *Leasehold Reform in England and Wales* (Cmnd 2916, London, 1966).

[6] The argument that the tenant's expenditure on the property entitles him to own the property does not, moreover, explain why he should also have the right to acquire the underlying *land*. The arguments were put under little pressure during their examination by the European Court of Human Rights in *James v United Kingdom* (1986) 8 EHRR 123 (ECtHR).

property in an especially deep sense precisely because it is their home, with the qualitative enhancement of attachment that that entails.[7] This insight connects the enfranchisement right as it applies in the private sector with that operating in the public sector (the 'right to buy' one's council house[8]). The latter is not ascribed to a financial investment by the tenant, but is founded purely on a notion that the tenant has a political claim to full ownership. It is the very fact that his home is such a key aspect of his life, even his identity, that creates the imperative for him to have maximal dominion—full ownership—over it.

11.2 The Legal Definition of a Lease

11.2.1 'Exclusive Possession, Payment, Term'

In *Street v Mountford*,[9] the House of Lords, led by Lord Templeman, ruled that a right over another person's land counts as a lease (with some exceptions) if:

— it confers exclusive possession of the land;
— in return for a rent, and/or a lump sum payment (a 'premium'); and
— not indefinitely, but for a 'term'.

We shall examine these requirements in detail in a moment. The core ideas are simple, however. Exclusive possession is the right a tenant has to exclude other people, including the landlord, from the land. It is this requirement that is at the heart of the idea that the tenant owns the land in question. On the other hand, the requirements of payment[10] and especially of a term are what differentiate a lease from freehold ownership, showing that the land is not wholly the tenant's even during the lease, and that it will cease to be the tenant's at some point.

---

[7] The special attachment of a person to his home is recognised in the European Convention on Human Rights, Art 8 (right to respect for private and family life).
[8] Under (principally) the Housing Act 1985.
[9] [1985] AC 809 (HL).
[10] In fact, it is doubtful whether this requirement is essential: § 11.4.1. It is nonetheless an almost universal feature of leases.

According to *Street v Mountford*,[11] if your right to occupy my land does not meet these criteria and so does not amount to a lease, it will be a licence.[12] Licences are described fully in Chapter 15, but the key point is that a lease, involving especially excusive possession, makes you temporary *owner* of the land; whereas a licence, not involving exclusive possession, allows you to be on land which remains *mine*.

11.2.2 Leases and the Rent Acts

In turn, the distinction between a lease and a licence has traditionally reflected the boundaries of the Rent Acts.

'The Rent Acts' is the collective name for a series of pieces of legislation, which began in 1915, whose import is to restrict the level of rent that landlords can charge for, and the circumstances in which they can evict occupants from, residential accommodation.[13] The argument for the Acts is that, especially when something as important as residential accommodation is at stake, the law ought to restrain landlords from abusing the superior bargaining power they are thought to have: hence the regulation of the most crucial ways in which they might drive oppressive bargains. Even if one accepts the validity of this argument, however, there is also a counter-argument. There is nothing to make someone offer land for rental at all, and if the law regulates the value that landlords can extract from renting out their land to the point where they can do better by using it in some other way, they will do so: with the result that the supply of rental land will diminish, and would-be occupants will suffer simply by being unable to find accommodation at all. Hence the parallel provision of public sector rentals (especially 'council housing').

There have always been—must necessarily be—limits to the applicability of the Rent Acts regime. One such is the rule with which we are concerned: that, with some exceptions, the regime does not apply to the rental of a home under a licence rather than a lease. How is this rule to be accounted for?

One answer would say that it merely provides a device whereby the legislators could appear to be following the argument in favour of the Rent Acts, while in practice, mindful of the counter-argument, allowing the Acts' impact to be avoided. On this view, it should be possible for parties—and especially

---

[11] [1985] AC 809 (HL).

[12] This may not be quite correct. In theory, your right may alternatively be a 'tenancy at will': a right featuring exclusive possession, but terminable instantaneously by either party. The relationship between licences and tenancies at will is not well understood.

[13] Counterpart regimes have also existed for business and agricultural tenancies, though with differences of detail. In all these sectors, the law is nowadays much less protective of tenants than it once was. The current principal statute regarding residential accommodation is the Housing Act 1988.

landlords—to designate an arrangement which could be a lease, and so attract the Rent Acts, as a licence instead, and so opt out of the Acts.

This in fact was the position for a while. The arrangement in *Street v Mountford*[14] itself, for example, involved exclusive possession, rent and term, but described itself as a licence. The Court of Appeal, following the general understanding at the time, held that it was indeed a licence, and thus exempt from the Rent Acts.[15] When the House of Lords ruled that, having these features, the arrangement was *necessarily* a lease and thus attracted the Rent Acts, it gave the law a new direction. In drawing the line between leases and licences in this way, the decision inevitably accounted for the Acts' inapplicability to licences in a new way too, treating its newly established line between leases and licences as a principled boundary for the Acts. That is, it assumed that the rights it chose to define as leases deserve the application of the Acts; but that the rights it chose to define as licences do not.[16]

And this assumption is in fact difficult to accept. If anything, among those people who rent their homes, those with (what we now learn to be) leases, with their quality of temporary ownership, are the 'haves'; those with (what we now learn to be) licences, having no such quality, are the 'have nots'. Resort to a licence may well indicate that the occupant has an especially weak bargaining position. One would regard licensees, therefore, as if anything more in need of the kind of protection given by the Rent Acts than tenants. Significantly, current thinking favours applying the Rent Acts regime without distinction between leases and licences.[17]

The account given so far of the position produced by *Street v Mountford*[18] needs refinement, however. As we shall see, although the headline formula of 'exclusive possession, payment, term'—and so temporary ownership—broadly holds good, the precise concept of a lease developed in that and succeeding decisions has certain complexities. These complexities seem best explained not as necessary features of the concept, but as attempts by the judges to fine-tune the set of situations to which the Rent Acts apply.

---

[14] [1985] AC 809 (HL).

[15] (1984) 49 P & CR 324 (CA).

[16] The decision's reasoning states that the rules delineating leases and licences exist in their own right, uninfluenced by a desire to apply the Rent Acts or otherwise ([1985] AC 809, 819 (HL)). In reconfiguring these rules, however, it *necessarily* took a position on the correct scope of the Acts.

[17] Law Commission, *Renting Homes: The Final Report* (Law Com No 297, London, 2006) para 3.9.

[18] [1985] AC 809 (HL).

11.3 Exclusive Possession

11.3.1 The Idea of Exclusive Possession

Say you have a right to occupy a house which I own. You have 'exclusive possession' if your right entitles you to occupy the house on your own: that is, to exclude everyone else if you wish, aside from those able to enter regardless of permission, such as the police under certain circumstances. (This is not to say that you will be a hermit: simply that it is for you to say who shall join you.) If the right I confer on you is one which allows me to join you myself, or allows me to let others do so—even if I never take advantage of these possibilities—you do not have exclusive possession.

On this account, the question whether you have a lease turns on whether you have (the right of) exclusive possession. It does not matter whether you in fact occupy the house on your own, and so can be said to have 'exclusive occupation'. If you do have exclusive possession, you might nonetheless surround yourself with others; while if you do not have exclusive possession, you might in fact be left in peace. Lord Templeman in *Antoniades v Villiers*[19] suggests the contrary, however. He asserts that someone who in fact occupies exclusively (paying rent, for a term) is ipso facto a tenant, and thus necessarily acquires a tenant's rights ... including exclusive possession, regardless of any provisions in the agreement contradictory of this right. This view is normally regarded as incorrect.

11.3.2 'Conferring' Exclusive Possession

There is an ambiguity in the key idea of conferring exclusive possession on you.

Normally, I shall be the owner of the land in question. Then, if purport to confer exclusive possession on you, you will get it. That is because I myself (in my capacity as freehold owner) have such a right to give.

But sometimes I may purport to confer exclusive possession on you when I do not have it myself. This can occur in two kinds of case. One is where I am in the process of buying the land from John, its current owner, and I purport to set up a lease in your favour (ie confer exclusive possession on you) before the purchase is complete. At this point, I have no right at all in the land. The other is where I do have a right to the land, but it is a mere licence from the land's owner, John. As noted in § 11.2.1, a licence does not give me exclusive

---

[19] [1990] 1 AC 417, 461–2 (HL). See too *Aslan v Murphy* [1990] 1 WLR 766, 775 (CA).

possession of the land: yet I purport to give you a lease (ie confer exclusive possession on you) beneath me. Either way, I am purporting to give you exclusive possession when I do not have that right myself.

In such cases, since I do not have exclusive possession myself, and so cannot effectively confer it on you, you do not gain it and become a tenant in the normal sense. But in purporting to confer exclusive possession on you, I have *contracted* with you that that is what you shall be. So while you do not acquire exclusive possession itself, you do acquire a contractual right to it. Because a contractual right operates only in personam, however, you cannot enforce this contractual right against John himself or others whom he allows to enter (as, if you had become a tenant in the normal sense, you could enforce your exclusive possession against all comers). But you can enforce it against me: so obliging me not to intrude on you, and to compensate you if John or others do so. Your interest in this kind of case is therefore sometimes called a 'contractual lease'.[20] Contractual leases have some features in common with true leases,[21] but fundamentally they are quite different. The in personam character of their rights, especially the crucial right of exclusive possession, means that their effect falls far short of the ownership that is given by a true lease.

11.3.3 Two Complications

Subject to the side-issue covered in § 11.3.2, the idea of exclusive possession given so far depicts it as a right entitling you, for the duration of your lease, to exclude everyone else. This simple picture needs further development in two respects, however: as regards shared occupancy, and as regards the significance of a stipulation entitling the landlord to enter.

First, then, the case where the landlord gives a number of people the right to occupy the same property. Self-evidently, there can be only one right *exclusively* to possess a given piece of property. So if each occupant has an

---

[20] Alternatively, a 'non-estate lease'. In the first of our two cases, where I give you your lease in anticipation of acquiring the land myself, your right is usually called a 'tenancy by estoppel', but there seems to be no difference in the legal treatment. See generally *Bruton v London and Quadrant Housing Trust* [2000] 1 AC 406 (HL), where *X*, a licensee of land, purported to lease it to *Y*, with the consequences described in the text. (Much of the decision's reasoning is aimed at a distraction. The agreement between *X* and *Y* described the interest conferred on *Y* as itself only a 'licence'. If this description had held good, there would have been no contractual lease because *X* would not have been contracting that *Y* should be a tenant. But it did not hold good: the right that *X* purported to give *Y* was in substance a lease, and the word 'licence' was a mere misdescription, without effect. On misdescriptions, see further § 11.4.3.)

[21] For example, in *Bruton v London and Quadrant Housing Trust, ibid*, on the facts explained, the upshot was that *X* incurred in *Y*'s favour the obligations to repair the land imposed on landlords by the Landlord and Tenant Act 1985. In principle, it should be a matter of construction whether a given statutory rule about 'leases', certainly applicable to true leases, is applicable to contractual leases too. (The rules in the Land Registration Act 2002, for example, are obviously not. *Quaere* the rules imposing formality requirements.) But the decision does not explore this issue, merely assuming that the rule in question does have such an extended application.

individual right, the plurality of the rights means that they cannot be exclusive: none of the occupants has the right to exclude the others.[22] But a number of people can take a single right exclusively to possess the property, if they do so as 'joint tenants'[23] of the right.[24] This will be the case, however, only if they acquire their entitlement to the land together (not, say, at different moments,[25] or under separate agreements with the landlord[26]); and if their entitlement provides for them to have the land for the same period, and to share a single set of rights and obligations (as opposed, for example, to having separate liabilities to pay individual sums of rent).[27] So a couple renting a house will often share the right exclusively to possess it,[28] while a number of single people doing the same will often have a collection of individual rights to occupy it non-exclusively.[29]

The second complication, concerning the significance of access by the landlord, is more problematic. It is easy to see that a landlord who retains an unrestricted right to be in the property does not confer exclusive possession of it, while a landlord who retains no right to be in it does. But what of the

---

[22] Unless the landlord does indeed purport to grant each occupant an individual right exclusively to possess the same property, these rights therefore contradicting one another. Such a case is essentially the same as that where I purport to sell my car first to you, then to John. The solution is that the sale to you is effective, while that to John is not, because by the time I purport to make it I no longer have the car to sell. John is left with the right to sue me for breach of contract.

[23] The idea of joint tenancy is explained in detail in §§ 13.2.1–13.2.5. Two complications must be dealt with here. First, the word 'tenancy' here is not a reference to a lease: it is the old term for (in effect) ownership. So a statement that a number of people have a lease—or any other right—as joint tenants simply means that they share it. Second, the law recognises another form of co-ownership besides joint tenancy: tenancy in common. But tenants in common can only be beneficiaries under a trust, so persons sharing the legal title to a lease must do so as joint tenants.

[24] A joint tenancy is customarily said to require the presence of 'the four unities': see § 13.2.4. The following footnotes explain how the account in the text corresponds to three of these, but in essence both that account and its translation into the language of the unities simply detail the idea that joint tenants *share a single right*. The fourth unity is 'unity of possession', the gist of which is that the right must allow the persons in question to occupy a single piece, rather than separate pieces, of property. This unity is necessarily present in the context under discussion, which concerns the possibility that a number of persons may have exclusive possession *of the same piece of land*. (There is obviously no problem, for example, about a number of people separately having exclusive possession of the flats in a block.)

[25] 'Unity of time'.

[26] 'Unity of title'. This is not negated if a group of co-owners are given individual copies of the agreement: the crucial thing is that it is a single agreement between all of them and the landlord.

[27] 'Unity of interest'. Consistently with this, the members of the group can arrange between themselves who shall pay what, and the landlord may be happy to receive the rent in the shape of a number of separate payments from the individuals concerned. The key thing is that if the landlord wishes, he may call on all the members of the group to meet the entire liability.

[28] Though not always: the landlord may insist on renting to them as separate individuals, as in *Mikeover Ltd v Brady* [1989] 3 All ER 618 (CA), where in particular there were distinct liabilities to individual sums of rent. Nonetheless, a shared right to exclusive possession can be found if all such matters negating it can be dismissed as pretences: see § 11.3.5 below.

[29] As in *Stribling v Wickham* [1989] 2 EGLR 35 (CA); *AG Securities v Vaughan* [1990] 1 AC 417 (HL).

(very common) case where the landlord retains a limited right to enter? Landlords very often have obligations to maintain or repair the leased property, and a right of access in order to do so. Even where the obligations lie on the tenant, the landlord will often have the right to enter so as to check that the tenant is complying with them. Landlords sometimes also have an obligation to provide 'attendance or services' (eg cleaning), and a right to enter in order to do this.

According to one passage in *Street v Mountford*,[30] only the landlord's retention of an *unlimited* right to enter will negate the conferment of exclusive possession, ie produce a licence rather than a lease. The retention of a limited right 'only serves to emphasise the fact that the grantee is entitled to exclusive possession', and so has a lease: presumably on the ground that a landlord who has not conferred exclusive possession will necessarily have the right to enter at will, and so has no need to stipulate on the subject.

This view is unsatisfactory, however. It has a Catch 22 quality: surely the presence or otherwise of exclusive possession should be deduced from the arrangements that the parties have in fact made. And it is clear that the landlord's retention of even a limited right of entry will sometimes—though not always—negate exclusive possession, and so yield a licence. While access so as to inspect or repair does not negate exclusive possession, access for the purpose of cleaning does so, even if it is further limited as to the permitted time of day.[31] Unsurprisingly therefore, the question has been recognised as one of degree,[32] but given these distinctions, even this rather understates its difficulty: it clearly has a qualitative as well as a quantitative dimension.

Lord Templeman in *Street v Mountford*[33] proposes a touchstone by which to address it. He asserts that an occupant lacks exclusive possession only if he is the landlord's 'lodger'. One can understand the thought: if you rent premises from me, and I have access to them for cleaning purposes, the word 'lodger' may be appropriate to describe you; while if I have access only to inspect or repair, it is not. But as a tool for giving a comprehensive answer to our question (when does limited access by the landlord negate exclusive possession?), the 'lodger' idea is inadequate. It can be applied at all only in the context of residential accommodation: there is no such person as a commercial lodger.[34] And even in the residential context, while the concept

---

[30] [1985] AC 809, 818 (HL).
[31] In *Aslan v Murphy* [1990] 1 WLR 766 (CA), where the landlord had access only to clean and only between 10.30am and noon, it was assumed that exclusive possession was denied, yielding a licence. (A lease was, however, eventually found on the basis that this access provision was a pretence: see § 11.3.5.)
[32] *Aslan v Murphy, ibid* 770.
[33] [1985] AC 809, 817–18 (HL). See too *Aslan v Murphy, ibid* 770.
[34] *Booker Settled Estates Ltd v Ayers* [1987] 1 EGLR 50 (CA). In the commercial context, indeed, one can imagine a stipulation for the landlord to enter and clean which would not negate exclusive possession: the cleaning could be seen as a contract service packaged in with the tenancy. And if so there, why not also in the residential sphere?

of a lodger is intelligible, it cannot be sharply defined, so resorting to it merely replaces one unclear test with another. Ultimately, then, the law seems not to have solved the problem: the answer to the question whether limited access by a landlord negates exclusive possession seems to lie with the individual judge.

11.3.4 Exceptions

According to Lord Templeman in *Street v Mountford*,[35] there are some cases in which exclusive possession is present, but there is no lease.

At least some instances of this phenomenon are explicable on the basis that, even if there is exclusive possession, there is no payment or term. Freehold ownership is a plain example. Another seems to be the case where a prospective purchaser of land is allowed to occupy the land before the purchase is completed (or even before negotiations towards it begin).[36]

On proper examination of certain other instances, too, there turns out to be no exclusive possession after all. One such instance is the case of a 'service occupier', ie an employee given particular accommodation by his employer, because living there is essential or important for his duties: a school caretaker, perhaps. Here, the employee is regarded as occupying on behalf of the employer,[37] so he plainly does not have possession exclusive of the employer. Another is the case of a person given the accommodation as an 'act of friendship or generosity'. Here the point is that the parties do not intend to enter into obligations as between each other at all:[38] so again, exclusive possession (an obligation on the landowner not to enter his own land) cannot have been conferred.

In fact, it is unclear that there is any instance in which exclusive possession, payment and term are all present but the arrangement is not to be regarded as a lease. This is reassuring from the point of view of conceptual purity. But that in turn makes it all the more interesting that Lord Templeman should think of these cases as being, on the contrary, exceptions: cases in which the definition of a lease is satisfied but there is no lease. His taking this approach suggests that he in fact views a 'lease' as something not quite delineated by the technical definition after all.

---

[35] [1985] AC 809, 818–21 (HL).

[36] On this type of case, see *Ramnarace v Lutchman* [2001] 1 WLR 1651 (PC). It also seems questionable whether the prospective purchaser has a full right of exclusive possession: he may be able to exclude other people, but probably cannot exclude the seller.

[37] *Street v Mountford* [1985] AC 809, 818 (HL).

[38] *Ibid* 819–20. It is sometimes said that they do not intend 'to create legal relations', but that is inaccurate, as even a gratuitous licence involves legal relations.

11.3.5 Shams and Pretences

Say you and I agree that you will occupy a flat belonging to me, with me having the right to enter so as to provide you with attendance and services, or on the basis that you will share the flat with John, with whom I shall have a separate agreement. On the face of the matter, you do not have exclusive possession, so cannot have a lease.

But the law does not stop at the face of the matter. Instead, it asks whether any provisions of our agreement are 'shams', or 'pretences'. If they are, it disregards them, and considers whether our agreement *without them* gives you exclusive possession. So if the stipulation that I can enter the flat so as to provide you with attendance and services, or that you must share with John, is a sham or pretence, the law will disregard it. Without it, there is no reason to doubt that you have exclusive possession after all, so your right will be a lease. Equally, if your sharing with John is not a sham or pretence, but the separateness of my agreements with you both is, that separateness will be disregarded, giving you and John shared exclusive possession, and so a joint lease.

But what is a sham or pretence?

The original description of the concept, given by Lord Templeman in *Street v Mountford*,[39] reads: 'sham devices and artificial transactions whose only object is to disguise the grant of a tenancy and to exclude the Rent Acts'.[40] In applying this description in subsequent cases, the courts sometimes referred to earlier decisions that had used the term 'sham' in other contexts: principally *Snook v London and West Riding Investments Ltd*.[41] According to these earlier decisions, a provision is a sham if it fails to reflect the contract (if any) that the parties have in fact made.[42] This approach was taken, for example, by the Court of Appeal in *Antoniades v Villiers*.[43] A couple rented a flat. The rental document contained a provision allowing the landlord to introduce an additional occupant. As the flat had only one

---

[39] *Ibid* 825.

[40] In fact, the sham/pretence rule is not limited to provisions calculated to avoid the Rent Acts, but applies to provisions calculated to avoid other statutory regimes too. The Rent Acts regime is however the usual target of such provisions in arrangements which might be leases of land. For some exploration of the rule's overall scope, see B McFarlane and E Simpson, 'Tackling Avoidance' in J Getzler (ed), *Rationalizing Property, Equity and Trusts, Essays in Honour of Edward Burn* (London, 2003) ch 8.

[41] [1967] 2 QB 786, 802 (CA).

[42] According to some formulations, a provision is a sham only if we include it in our documentation *deliberately* so as not to reflect the contract we have in fact made. Other formulations omit this dimension, producing the picture given in the text. The latter approach (which merges the question of whether a provision is a 'sham' with the question of whether it is susceptible to rectification) seems correct in principle: for present purposes it should not matter whether the misleading provision was created deliberately or accidentally. But cf M Conaglen, 'Sham Trusts' [2008] *CLJ* 176.

[43] [1990] 1 AC 417 (CA). Likewise *Hadjiloucas v Crean* [1988] 1 WLR 1006, 1013–14 (CA).

bedroom, it would have been difficult[44] to do so. But the provision was not a sham in these terms, as it did indeed reflect the contract that the parties had made.[45] (It would only have been a sham in this sense if at the time of signing the document the landlord had, for example, said 'ignore that bit' and the couple had replied 'OK'.)

Findings of shams of this kind were rare, as a written document signed by the parties nearly always does reflect—because it defines—the contract in fact being made. When *Antoniades v Villiers*[46] went to the House of Lords, however, Lord Templeman moved to escape the narrowness of this approach and allow provisions to be discarded not merely when they failed to reflect the parties' contract but more widely. To this end, he dropped the word 'sham' in favour of 'pretence'.[47] The judgments go on to tell us that a provision counts as a 'pretence' if it was 'never seriously intended in fact';[48] if it does not reflect 'the substance and reality' of the transaction;[49] or if the parties do not regard it as a provision 'to which any effect would be given'.[50] The provision in question, allowing the landlord to introduce an additional occupant, was such a pretence. Even though it reflected the parties' contract, it was 'never seriously intended in fact', at odds with 'the substance and reality' of the transaction, and not destined to be put into effect. Similarly where, when I rent a house to you, our agreement provides that I will supply attendance and services, but I have no plan to do so.[51]

Consider the case where I rent a flat to you and John using two separate agreements, so that you and John have individual (and so necessarily non-exclusive) rights to occupy it. The agreements' separateness may be a pretence, as being at odds with 'the substance and reality' of the transaction: in which event it will be disregarded, leaving you and John sharing a

---

[44] Though not impossible. As well as a bedroom, there was a sofa-bed in the sitting-room, which was used for five or six weeks by a friend of the couple. But the resulting conditions seem to have been cramped and unsatisfactory.

[45] [1990] 1 AC 417, 444–7 (CA).

[46] [1990] 1 AC 417 (HL).

[47] *Ibid* 462.

[48] *Ibid* 469.

[49] *Ibid* 466; see also 467–8.

[50] *Ibid* 475; see also 462, 468, 476. Care is needed with this test, however. The question of whether effect *will be* given to the provision is not the same as the question of whether effect *has been*, or *is being*, given to it. The answer 'no' to the latter may *suggest* that the answer to the former is also 'no', making the provision a pretence, but explanations must be listened to. Say accommodation is rented to a group of people, with a provision allowing the landlord to choose replacements for those who leave. But in practice the landlord, out of reasonableness, kindness, politeness, does not insist upon the provision, instead allowing the remaining occupants to choose replacements for themselves. It should not be concluded that the provision was never intended to be exercised: *Stribling v Wickham* (1989) 21 HLR 381 (CA).

[51] *Aslan v Murphy* [1990] 1 WLR 766 (CA). But this decision blurs the distinction between 'sham' and 'pretence' approaches again, by stating the question to be whether the provision is part of the parties' 'true bargain'. 'True' is ambiguous between 'as recognised by the law of contract' (sham in the narrow sense) and 'substantial and real' (pretence).

single right of exclusive possession after all. The courts approach the matter via an inquiry into the nature of the relationship between you and John. If your relationship is close, as where you are a couple, your agreements will be seen as 'interdependent', and their separateness treated as a pretence[52]; whereas if you are no more than flatmates, your agreements are seen as 'independent', ie genuinely separate.[53] But this approach, requiring relationships to be allocated to one or the other of two categories in this way, is crude. Even if you and John are a couple, it is quite imaginable—even by yourselves—that you will split up. Say John leaves you: you may well feel it unnecessary to move out too, but instead stay in the flat and, being unable to afford the entire rent for it on your own, make the best of life with a new flatmate.[54] Equally, the fact that you and John are no more than flatmates does not mean that you are indifferent to each other's identity: on the contrary, you will each have a significant stake in the other's personality. In truth, just about all relationships have both interdependent and independent elements, in a subtle mix. It is impossible to characterise a given relationship one way or the other, and so make use of it to reveal pretences, without resorting to caricature. What emerges is that the 'substance and reality' of a transaction, on which the pretence doctrine depends, is a fragile—because ultimately impressionistic—concept.

There is a further, and more profound, difficulty with the 'substance and reality' idea, and so with the pretence doctrine.[55] It can be seen in the contrast between two sets of cases.

The first set is principally represented by *Gisborne v Burton*.[56] Here, a landlord agreed to rent land to a farmer. To avoid a statutory regime[57] that would have applied if he had leased the land directly to the farmer, the landlord leased it to his own wife, who then subleased it to the farmer. The court held that the inserted lease to the wife should be disregarded, inter alia as a pretence: it was at odds with the 'substance and reality' of

---

[52] As in *Antoniades v Villiers* [1990] 1 AC 417 (HL). See too the view taken, *ibid* 464 (and in *Street v Mountford* [1985] AC 809, 825 (HL)), of *Somma v Hazlehurst* [1978] 1 WLR 1014 (CA) and *Aldrington Garages Ltd v Fielder* (1978) 37 P & CR 461. But compare *Mikeover Ltd v Brady* [1989] 3 All ER 618, 625 (CA), where the facts may have been of this kind, but the court seems unwilling to engage with the issue.

[53] As in *AG Securities v Vaughan* [1990] 1 AC 417 (HL).

[54] In *Hadjiloucas v Crean* [1988] 1 WLR 1006 (CA), two ladies, who seem to have had a close relationship, rented accommodation under separate agreements. In *Antoniades v Villiers* [1990] 1 AC 417, 465 (HL) it is said that the ladies' relationship meant that the agreements were interdependent, ie their separateness was a pretence. But one of the two ladies had in fact left and been replaced.

[55] See further B McFarlane and E Simpson, 'Tackling Avoidance' in J Getzler (ed), *Rationalizing Property, Equity and Trusts, Essays in Honour of Edward Burn* (London, 2003) ch 8.

[56] [1989] QB 390 (CA).

[57] Under the Agricultural Holdings (Notice to Quit) Act 1977.

the transaction.[58] So the farmer was left in effect with a lease rather than a sublease after all. Rather similarly, in *Bankway Properties Ltd v Pensfold-Dunsford*,[59] a landlord leased accommodation to a tenant on a basis[60] which in principle gave the tenant security of tenure, but on terms whereby, after two years, the annual rent increased more than five-fold, to £25,000. The idea was not that the tenant should pay this sum: on the contrary, it was that he should not, so that his failure would put him into default, depriving him of his security of tenure and entitling the landlord to eject him. The court declared the rent increase provision invalid.[61]

For the second, contrasting, set of cases, consider *Hilton v Plustitle Ltd*[62] and *Kaye v Massbetter*.[63] In these, an individual wanted to rent accommodation. The landlord was willing to grant a lease, but not to the individual (in which case, the Rent Acts would have applied): only to a company (so that they did not). The individual therefore acquired a private company, specifically for the purpose; the landlord granted the company a lease; and the company allowed the individual to occupy the accommodation. Asking itself whether the insertion of the company was a pretence and should be disregarded, yielding in effect a lease from the landlord to the individual after all, the court held that it was not. The 'company let' was the 'substance and reality' of the transaction.

The contrast between these two sets of decisions lies in their operating two different understandings of the idea of 'substance and reality'. Those comprising the first set attend solely to the human story on the ground; while the assumption in the second set is that the parties' chosen legal vehicle is to be taken seriously—*is itself a kind of 'substance and reality'.*

The 'human story on the ground' approach is clearly the dominant one in the caselaw as a whole. Its correctness is assumed in the treatment of provisions allowing the landlord to introduce additional occupants, or requiring him to supply attendance and services, and of arrangements involving separate agreements. As regards all of these, it could be said that the parties had, irrespective of the distance from the human story on the ground, chosen the arrangement in question as the legal vehicle governing their relationship.

---

[58] One detail, which might be thought important as corroborating this conclusion, turns out to be deceptive. The terms of the lease to the wife seemed to require her to farm the land: which she obviously was not going to do, apparently making the lease to her a pretence for this reason too. But the terms went on to provide for subleasing, something which would obviously rule out farming by the tenant: so the farming provision could not mean what it appeared to—it must be taken to contemplate subleasing on terms requiring farming, which is what in fact occurred.

[59] [2001] 1 WLR 1369 (CA).

[60] An assured tenancy, under the Housing Act 1988.

[61] The reasoning did not quite follow the pretence analysis, but it seems possible to believe that applying that analysis in the same way as it was applied in *Gisborne v Burton* [1989] QB 390 (CA) would yield the same answer.

[62] [1989] 1 WLR 149 (CA).

[63] (1990) 62 P & CR 558 (CA). *Belvedere Court Management Ltd v Frogmore Developments Ltd* [1997] QB 858 (CA) is legally similar, though has a different factual make-up.

The courts' disregard of the latter reflection amounts to a rejection of it: to an affirmation that the 'substance and reality' to be attended to is of the 'human story on the ground' variety.

This position can be justified on the basis that, in the present context, those seeking to rent accommodation actually have little choice between the legal vehicles that might in principle be available: any such choices will in practice be made by the landlords: so the elimination of most of these vehicles is a measure properly calculated to restore renters' access to those vehicles it can be assumed they would wish to choose.[64] But the rejected view—that abstract legal concepts, and the choices that are available between them, can be just as significant (substantial, real) as more tangible phenomena in the shaping of people's lives—cannot simply be suppressed from the discourse. From time to time, especially where the parties do in fact seem to have bargained reasonably freely, it can be expected to bubble up (as it did in our second set of cases) ... leaving the pretence doctrine, shaped around the 'human story on the ground' understanding, enduringly somewhat unstable.

11.4 Other Aspects of the Legal Definition

As we saw in § 11.2.1, a lease is defined in *Street v Mountford*[65] as an arrangement whereby (with some exceptions) I grant you exclusive possession of my land, in return for payment, for a term. We looked at the requirement of exclusive possession in § 11.3. Now we shall look at the requirements of payment and a term, and also at the significance of the label ('lease' or 'licence') that the parties themselves give the right conferred. Finally, in § 11.4.4, we shall take what we have learnt about the various rules about the make-up of a lease, and the difficulties they exhibit; and attempt to understand the role they all play in the operation of the concept as a whole.

11.4.1 Payment

Leases are normally given in return for some kind of payment. Indeed, this is part of their *raison d'être*: they represent a way in which freehold owners can exploit their land, by turning its use into money, while those wishing to have

---

[64] Compare *Burdis v Livsey* [2003] QB 36 (CA), favouring the 'chosen vehicle' approach ... in a different context altogether, with the effect of *enhancing* consumer choice.
[65] [1985] AC 809 (HL).

access to land can do so on a more limited basis—and thus at a lower price—than by acquiring the freehold. In principle, however, there seems to be no reason why I should not give you a right exclusively to possess my land, for a term, and thereby grant you a lease, even without your paying for it.

The payment can be made as a lump sum, known in this context as a 'premium' or 'fine'. Leases for substantial periods are often acquired in this way. The price of a very long lease might well be little less than that of the freehold, even though, in contrast to a freehold, its value will necessarily diminish over time, eventually reaching zero. The other main form of payment is rent, ie a series of payments made at periodic intervals (weekly, monthly, quarterly, annual) over the life of the lease. The possibility of letting for a rent is especially valuable because it allows the temporary ownership of land to be sold to and bought by those unable or unwilling to pay up-front. (The possibility of buying freehold ownership with a mortgage serves the same purpose, however.)

In *Street v Mountford*,[66] although Lord Templeman states at one point that a lease requires either rent or a premium, he also says several times that there must be rent.[67] This was a curious position, given the entirely familiar possibility of a premium,[68] and the Court of Appeal subsequently refused to adopt it,[69] but Lord Templeman later reiterated it.[70]

11.4.2 Term

A lease must have a 'term': that is, it must be specified as having some particular duration.[71] So an arrangement expressed to last for a certain number of years (say 5, 7, 21, 99 ...)[72] can be a lease, while one expressed to last indefinitely cannot.

This rule is readily explained. It is simply a crystalline statement of the difference between two things that we may be trying to do, it being important to say which we have done. Either I mean to keep a reversion, in which case I

---

[66] *Ibid* 818.

[67] *Ibid* 816, 817, 818, 826, 827.

[68] And indeed the definition of a term of years absolute (lease) in the Law of Property Act 1925 s 205(1)(xxvii), which explicitly states rent to be inessential.

[69] *Ashburn Anstalt v Arnold* [1989] Ch 1, 9 (CA).

[70] *AG Securities v Vaughan* [1990] 1 AC 417, 454, 459, 462, 463 (HL); *Westminster City Council v Clarke* [1992] 2 AC 288, 299 (HL). But compare *Prudential Assurance Co Ltd v London Residuary Body* [1992] 2 AC 386, 390 (HL), where he defines a lease in terms which do not mention rent.

[71] It may of course terminate ahead of its nominal end, eg after breach of its terms (especially non-payment of rent) by the tenant, or by the agreement of landlord and tenant that it should do so.

[72] The rights under the lease will normally be active throughout the period specified, but this need not be the case: a timeshare arrangement, giving you the right exclusively to possess my land for say a particular fortnight each year, is a valid lease so long as its overall duration meets the rule under discussion (say, it lasts for 21 years).

necessarily do not grant you my land indeterminately: that is, I give you a lease. Or I do not mean to keep a reversion, in which case I necessarily do give you the land indefinitely: that is, I make you its freehold owner in my place.

There is a complication, however. Intermediate cases—cases where the arrangement is expressed neither to last for a definite time, nor to last indefinitely—are possible: for example, an arrangement expressed to last 'until you marry or die'. The rule is that, even if the arrangement's actual duration is not knowable from the outset, its *maximum* duration must be. So the arrangement just instanced would be invalid as a lease (its maximum duration cannot be known); but an arrangement 'to end after 21 years; or at such earlier time as you may marry or die' would be valid. This was decided by the House of Lords in *Prudential Assurance Co Ltd v London Residuary Body*.[73]

Our explanation for the headline rule does not account for this detail: even where we cannot know the arrangement's maximum duration from the outset, it is clearly different from an avowedly indeterminate arrangement, ie a freehold transfer. Indeed, the detail may well have no satisfactory basis.[74]

Before the ruling in *Prudential Assurance Co Ltd v London Residuary Body*,[75] other decisions had taken the contrary position, holding the only objectionable arrangement to be one of avowedly indefinite duration.[76] Even now, the law itself reworks an arrangement 'until you marry or die' as a valid lease for 90 years, finishing earlier in the event of your marriage or death.[77] This device keeps such cases within the ruling, but emphasises that the difference between the two formulations—one valid, the other not—may well be a narrow and practically unimportant one.

Moreover, the law has always accepted the validity of 'periodic tenancies': yearly, monthly or weekly tenancies. If I give you such a tenancy, you remain my tenant until one of us gives appropriate notice. Periodic tenancies were traditionally understood to operate as a single lease with neither a fixed nor a maximum duration, continuing until ended by notice.[78] On this account, they

---

[73] [1992] 2 AC 386 (HL): a purported lease of land until it was required for a road-widening scheme was therefore invalid. Likewise earlier authority, including *Lace v Chantler* [1944] KB 368 (CA), holding invalid a purported lease for the duration of the Second World War.

[74] For discussion, see S Bright, 'Uncertainty in Leases—Is it a Vice?' (1993) 13 *LS* 38.

[75] [1992] 2 AC 386 (HL).

[76] *Re Midland Railway Co's Agreement* [1971] Ch 725 (CA); *Ashburn Anstalt v Arnold* [1989] Ch 1 (CA). Both involved an arrangement expressed to last until the landlord needed the land for a specified purpose, very similar to that in issue in *Prudential Assurance Co Ltd v London Residuary Body* [1992] 2 AC 386 (HL).

[77] Law of Property Act 1925 s 149(6). Likewise, a purported lease for the duration of the Second World War was reworked as a lease for 10 years finishing on the earlier end of the war: Validation of War-time Leases Act 1944.

[78] *Gandy v Jubber* (1865) 5 B & S 15, 18 (Ex Ch); *Re Midland Railway Co's Agreement* [1971] Ch 725, 732 (CA). The latter decision overtly made this understanding of periodic tenancies the basis of its wider position that an arrangement even without a maximum period is valid, so long as it is not avowedly indefinite.

flatly contradict the theory that at least the maximum duration of an arrangement must be fixed, rather reinforcing the view that the only objection is to an avowedly indefinite arrangement. To square them with *Prudential Assurance Co Ltd v London Residuary Body*,[79] they are nowadays presented instead as comprising a series of individual leases, each for the period in question, put end to end.[80] But even if they can be analysed in this way, their use to create arrangements that in effect have no maximum duration, and the absence of any objection to this, suggests that there is no real fault to be found with such arrangements.[81]

11.4.3 Labels

In *Street v Mountford*,[82] the parties' agreement gave the occupant the right of exclusive possession, in return for a rent, and for a term, but asserted that the resulting arrangement should be a licence. If its nature had been fixed by this label, the arrangement would have fallen outside the Rent Acts, which applied only to (certain) leases. Reversing the decision of the Court of Appeal,[83] the House of Lords held that the arrangement's nature was not fixed by the parties' label. Rather, it followed from the presence or otherwise of the key indicators of a lease: exclusive possession, etc. These being present, the parties had created a lease, regardless of the label they had given it.

Lord Templeman explained the ruling by an analogy: 'The manufacture of a five-pronged implement for manual digging results in a fork even if the manufacturer, unfamiliar with the English language, insists that he intended to make and has made a spade.'[84] This, however, is bad reasoning (and not only because forks generally have four, not five, prongs).

Forks do indeed differ from spades in the matter of their having prongs rather than a blade, and in no other respect. The presence or absence of prongs is indeed determinative, therefore. But it cannot be assumed that the

---

[79] [1992] 2 AC 386 (HL).

[80] *Ibid* 394. See also *Hammersmith and Fulham London Borough Council v Monk* [1992] 1 AC 478, 492 (HL); *Barrett v Morgan* [2000] 2 AC 264, 272 (HL).

[81] Compare P Sparkes, 'Certainty of Leasehold Terms' (1993) 109 *LQR* 93, defending the requirement of maximum duration. Sparkes welcomes the requirement as allowing the courts to undo arrangements which the parties intended to last only a short time ('until the landlord is ready to redevelop the land', for example) but which have ossified, commonly with no provision for a rise in rent. (In *Prudential Assurance Co Ltd v London Residuary Body* [1992] 2 AC 386 (HL), the arrangement, pending a road-widening scheme, was made in 1930 at an annual rent of £30; by the date of the case, the market rent would probably have been about £10,000.) Even making the highly unlikely assumption that the law should rescue landlords from their incaution in this way, however, the rule in question goes too far: it renders such arrangements invalid from the very outset.

[82] [1985] AC 809 (HL).

[83] (1985) 49 P & CR 324 (CA).

[84] [1985] AC 809, 819 (HL).

presence or absence of exclusive possession etc is similarly determinative of the difference between leases and licences. This was the question that the court had to decide.

The court ruled in the affirmative. But the opposite answer was possible. The law might recognise a right featuring exclusive possession etc as having the potential to be either a lease or a licence, leaving the determinative factor to be something else—notably, whether the parties wish the right to be in rem (lease) or in personam (licence[85]).[86] On the latter view, the presence of exclusive possession etc equates with the presence of a handle and a usefulness for digging, features which forks and spades share; while the determinative contrast between prongs and a blade equates with the contrast between the parties' having characterised the right as in rem (lease) or as in personam (licence).

In fact, this latter view of the matter is in principle more likely than that given by the House of Lords. When parties, creating a right, give it features matching the requirements for some kind of right in rem (say, an easement), the law's standard position is that they still have a choice whether it shall be that right in rem, or whether it shall exist purely as a contractual provision between themselves.[87]

So in abstract terms, the position adopted by the House of Lords was not inevitable, or even probable. The decision to adopt it has a dual significance. First, it carries the illiberal implication that this kind of right (one involving exclusive possession etc) comes in only one version—in rem or in personam—as the law, not the parties, shall decide. (As if only one kind of digging implement—either the fork or the spade, as announced by the state—were allowed on the market.) And second, it announces the law's choice to be in rem. On the face of it, this is a surprising choice, as market considerations broadly run against rights operating in rem.[88] The explanation is, fairly obviously, not that for some exceptional reason we should want rights with exclusive possession etc always to be in rem, but an assumption by the House of Lords that, apart from the exceptional cases,[89] they should always be caught by the Rent Acts.[90]

---

[85] For licences as rights in personam, see § 15.1.1.

[86] Or, one might inquire, whether they wish it to attract the Rent Acts? But contracting out of the Rent Acts is assumed to be impermissible.

[87] As regards easements, this was recognised in *IDC Group Ltd v Clark* (1992) 65 P & CR 179 (CA): see § 9.1.5.

[88] § 1.2.2.

[89] See § 11.3.4.

[90] See further J Hill, 'Intention and the Creation of Proprietary Rights: Are Leases Different?' (1996) 16 *LS* 200.

11.4.4 An Interpretation

A right will deserve recognition as in rem only if its having that status will do enough good to outweigh the harm that it will also do, by impeding the market.[91] Whether this is the case will depend on the right's essential content. As explained in § 11.1.1, the essential content of a lease is temporary ownership. It is plainly appropriate to see *ownership* as a right in rem, because it connotes the ability to use land substantially as one wishes, with the boons of liberty and commercial advantage that this entails. And it is appropriate to treat *temporary* ownership as in rem too, as allowing most of the benefits of ownership to be sold and bought on a partial, rather than all-or-nothing, basis: so permitting fine-tuning of variables such as risk and cost, and in consequence further enhancing land's exploitability.

From this point of view, then, it is right to allow as much flexibility as possible over the configuration of leases: their duration, their cost, the other rights and obligations that can be built into them. It is essential, though, that the core idea of temporary ownership is maintained, so as to preserve the basis on which leases deserve to be rights in rem. It is correct, therefore, to insist on exclusive possession (ownership), and a term (making the ownership temporary). Which makes it seem as though the major authorities considered above—in particular, *Street v Mountford*[92] and *Prudential Assurance Co Ltd v London Residuary Body*[93]—merely state the obvious.

One cannot take such a simple view of these authorities, however. We have already seen how, as well as affirming the importance of these headline concepts, they and the rules developed in their wake also take a number of more detailed positions about the headline concepts' content and significance. Many of these positions, rather than simply explicating the idea of temporary ownership, give it a particular, stylised shape. *Street v Mountford*[94] is especially striking in this respect, and above all the ideas propounded by Lord Templeman there and subsequently.[95] Remember the equation of de facto exclusive occupation with the right of exclusive possession; the treatment of a landlord's rights of entry, making the word 'exclusive' not so determinative after all; the idea that exclusive possession is defined (negatively) by the concept of a 'lodger'; the view that certain situations, while involving exclusive possession, payment and term, are nevertheless not leases; the rule that aspects of the parties' arrangement can be discarded as being 'pretences', together with the unstable idea that a provision is a pretence if it does not represent the 'substance and reality' of the parties' arrangement, and the use of caricatured relationships in the

---

[91] See § 1.2.2.
[92] [1985] AC 809 (HL).
[93] [1992] 2 AC 386 (HL).
[94] [1985] AC 809 (HL).
[95] *AG Securities v Vaughan, Antoniades v Villiers* [1990] 1 AC 417 (HL).

construction of 'substance and reality'; the suggestion that rent is needed, whereas it is clearly inessential to the notion of temporary ownership; and the rule that the parties' own characterisation of the right as in personam rather than in rem can be disregarded as an incorrect 'label'. And *Prudential Assurance Co Ltd v London Residuary Body*[96] (the leading opinion again being given by Lord Templeman) contributes a strangely narrow understanding of 'term'.

These detailed positions are best understood as elements in a project to ensure that certain social situations are covered by the Rent Acts. The concept of a lease is relevant to this project only because it largely controls the Acts' applicability. If Lord Templeman thinks a particular situation ought (or ought not) to be covered by the Acts, he therefore has to announce that it is (or is not) a lease. Hence the relative inattention to the parties' legal positions; the emphasis instead on their positions on the ground; and the stereotyping of the kinds of people who are covered (eg those with 'interdependent' relationships), or not (eg 'lodgers', 'service occupiers'), by the 'definition'. The puzzling decision in *Prudential Assurance Co Ltd v London Residuary Body*,[97] while not concerned with the Rent Acts, has at least some resonance with this project: it reiterates the message that the law does not leave parties to organise their own version of temporary ownership, but insists on its own template.[98]

---

[96] [1992] 2 AC 386 (HL).

[97] *Ibid.*

[98] B McFarlane and E Simpson, 'Tackling Avoidance' in J Getzler (ed), *Rationalizing Property, Equity and Trusts, Essays in Honour of Edward Burn* (London, 2003) ch 8, discussing the pretence rule, suggest seeing it as an example of a statute about 'X' applying not to X as defined by the law, but to X as understood in some extra-legal way (as taxation statutes may sometimes do: *Macniven v Westmoreland Investments Ltd* [2003] 1 AC 311 (HL); cf now *Barclays Mercantile Business Finance Ltd v Mawson* [2005] 1 AC 684 (HL)). Specifically, the idea would be that the Rent Acts should be read as applying to leases in their social, rather than legal, understanding, the pretence doctrine being used to remove considerations of purely legal significance from the picture. In the end, however, the authors withdraw the suggestion, on the basis that *Street v Mountford* [1985] AC 809 (HL) gives 'lease' in the Rent Acts its legal meaning, ie exclusive possession, payment and term. But according to the argument in the text, the suggestion was right all along. While ostensibly applying the legal idea of a lease, the decision in fact constructs it by reference to the social situations which it was sought to bring under the Rent Acts.

11.5 Obligations in Leases

11.5.1 Kinds of Obligation

If an arrangement allowing you to occupy my land is to be a lease at all, I must have an obligation not to exercise what would otherwise be my own rights over the land, so that you can have it 'exclusively', as discussed earlier in this chapter. Normally, you will also have an obligation to pay me rent, unless you paid by way of an initial lump sum (and often even then). Most leases, however, impose on their landlord and/or tenant a number of additional obligations, usually called 'covenants'. Generally, though not always, these will relate to the treatment of the leased land itself. For example, you may be required to use the land for certain purposes, or not to use it for certain others,[99] possibly even to erect a building on it;[100] and one of us may be required to carry out maintenance and repairs as necessary.

We may make our covenants by express provisions in the lease, but they may also be implied. Implied covenants are mainly imposed by statute,[101] and operate principally to oblige landlords to keep domestic residential accommodation in good order, apparently on a basis of respect for basic human decency.[102] Such covenants tend to be interpreted fairly narrowly, however: in particular, a covenant requiring *repair* is not taken to demand *improvement*.[103] There are two pressures against greater

[99] The point of such obligations will often be to safeguard my commercial interests. Say I own a shopping mall. I lease out the individual units in it. In order to be able to extract the maximum profit, I may control the kind of goods that can be sold in each unit, so as to be able to promise each tenant freedom from competition within the mall, and/or the likelihood of passing trade generated by the presence in the mall of a magnet, such as a supermarket.

[100] An interesting type of obligation in that, at the end of your lease, the building (forming part of the land) will be mine. Of course, the price you have to pay for the lease should be smaller as a result.

[101] Principally the Landlord and Tenant Act 1985. Sometimes, however, an obligation is implied on ordinary contractual principles because it is necessary to the fulfilment of the parties' understanding. For example, a lease of 'a furnished dwelling-house' will impliedly require the landlord to ensure that the house is fit for habitation (*Smith v Marrable* (1843) 11 M & W 5 (Ex)): the house could hardy be let as a furnished (ie ready to use) dwelling-house otherwise. And a lease of a flat in a tower block will impliedly require the landlord to provide the stairs, lifts, rubbish chutes etc without which tower blocks cannot function (*Liverpool City Council v Irwin* [1977] AC 239 (HL)). In the context of 'occupation contracts', the Law Commission has recommended a higher baseline requirement: *Renting Homes: The Final Report* (Law Com No 297, London, 2006) pt 8.

[102] The protection for the 'home' given by the European Convention on Human Rights, Art 8 is relevant, but may not make a significant practical difference: see *Lee v Leeds City Council* [2002] 1 WLR 1488 (CA).

[103] *Wainwright v Leeds City Council* [1984] 1 EGLR 67 (CA).

intervention.[104] One is the idea that parties should be left to fix their own arrangements: if you want the option of leasing a derelict house from me, cheaply, and doing it up yourself, the law ought not to stop you; to insist that I do the work in advance, thus raising the rent, may not serve your interests. The other is the reflection that to require more, particularly by a wide interpretation of obligations in existing leases, will have the unfortunate result, in the case especially of public sector landlords, of distorting spending priorities.

11.5.2 Enforcement

If either of us breaches one of our obligations, remedies are available to the other.[105]

The set of available remedies includes some that are familiar from other parts of the law. In particular, I can sue you for unpaid rent; and I can sue you, and you can sue me, for damages for any loss resulting from breach of other obligations. We will generally be able to claim injunctions to prevent future breaches of obligations not to do something, and, under appropriate circumstances, specific performance of obligations to do something.[106] Less familiarly, self-help is also possible: if I fail in my responsibility to carry out repairs, under certain circumstances you can carry them out in my place and charge me for them; and if you are in arrears with your rent, I can sometimes have a court-authorised enforcement agent come onto the land, seize your belongings and sell them to recoup the debt.[107]

Under certain circumstances, a breach by one of us will also allow the other to terminate the lease. Where the breach is on the part of the landlord, the relevant rules are drawn from the law of contract, so the tenant will be able to withdraw if, but only if, the breach was a repudiatory one.[108] In

---

[104] See especially *Southwark London Borough Council v Mills* [2001] 1 AC 1 (HL); *Lee v Leeds City Council* [2002] 1 WLR 1488 (CA).

[105] Perceiving that ad hoc enforcement of individual obligations by domestic tenants against private landlords may not be fully viable or efficacious in practice, the Law Commission proposes the promotion of good standards via better regulation of landlords in this sector: *Housing: Encouraging Responsible Letting* (Law Com No 312, London, 2008).

[106] On the relatively restricted availability of specific performance, see *Co-operative Insurance Society Ltd v Argyll Stores (Holdings) Ltd* [1998] AC 1 (HL).

[107] Tribunals, Courts and Enforcement Act 2007, Part 3.

[108] *Hussein v Mehlman* [1992] 2 EGLR 87 (County Court). This decision, and others on which it rests (especially *National Carriers Ltd v Panalpina (Northern) Ltd* [1981] AC 675 (HL) and *Hammersmith and Fulham London Borough Council v Monk* [1992] 1 AC 478 (HL)), are often said to demonstrate the 'contractualisation' of leases. Care must be taken with this suggestion. These cases certainly rule that leases can end in ways derived from the law of contract, as opposed to the ways traditionally found in the law of leases. Another implication of 'contractualisation' might however be that the parties to a lease can structure it as they wish, ultimately perhaps not having to respect the law's differentiation between leases and other kinds of right at all. Although the courts have experimented with such a departure, their current position is against it (*Street v Mountford* [1985] AC 809 (HL), *Prudential Assurance Co Ltd v*

principle, one would expect the same rules to apply equally to a breach by the tenant, say a failure to pay rent. In the latter context, however, the law super-imposes a more specialised regime known as 'forfeiture', which is in some ways more, and in others less, favourable to the tenant.

For forfeiture to be a possibility, the terms of the lease must so provide, either in so many words or by labelling the obligation in question a 'condition'. If you breach such an obligation, I cannot terminate the lease without more, as I could a contract. First, I have to notify you of your position, and normally[109] must give you the chance to put your breach right—by paying your rent arrears, or compensating me for the damage done, and putting matters to rights for the future.[110] Then, even if you fail to put matters right, you may seek 'relief from forfeiture', ie an order by the court that I cannot forfeit after all.[111] If I am able to forfeit, I can do so either by obtaining a court order, or, except in the case of a residential lease,[112] by 're-entry', ie physically retaking the land.[113]

The landlord's ability to proceed by re-entry without a court order may, like other self-help remedies, be incompatible with Article 6 of the European Convention on Human Rights, requiring determination of civil rights and obligations by judicial proceedings.[114] The remaining details of the law on forfeiture are more complex than they need be,[115] but the essential idea is

---

London Residuary Body [1992] 2 AC 386 (HL): §§ 11.2–11.4), and many statutory rules relating to the content of leases are incapable of variation by the parties. See generally S Bridge, 'Leases—Contract, Property and Status' in L Tee (ed), *Land Law: Issues, Debates, Policy* (Cullompton, 2002) ch 4.

[109] I do not have to give you this chance if your breach is 'irremediable'. The test of this is not whether the fact of the breach can be undone: that is never the case. It is whether the damage can be put right in a practical sense: *Expert Clothing Service and Sales Ltd v Hillgate House Ltd* [1986] Ch 340 (CA). Using the leased land for 'immoral purposes' is a common instance of a breach found to be 'irremediable': it is said that such use gives the land a 'stigma' which discontinuance and compensation cannot remove (see eg *Rugby School (Governors) v Tannahill* [1935] 1 KB 87 (CA)). This view may be doubted, however. If the 'stigma' has a tangible impact (say by making the land harder to let in future), this surely can be remedied, by the payment of monetary compensation. If it does not, it is unclear how the landlord is damaged at all.

[110] There are separate regimes for rent (governed principally by the Common Law Procedure Act 1852 s 210, together with, for long residential leases, the Commonhold and Leasehold Reform Act 2002 ss 166–7) and for other obligations (the Law of Property Act 1925 s 146(1) and, for long residential leases, the Commonhold and Leasehold Reform Act 2002 s 168).

[111] Again, there are separate regimes for rent (see principally the Common Law Procedure Act 1852 s 212) and other obligations (principally the Law of Property Act 1925 s 146(2)). Other legislative regimes create yet further variations: see eg the Housing Act 1988 s 7 and Sch 2.

[112] Protection from Eviction Act 1977 s 3(1).

[113] In this case, you can apply for relief against forfeiture after my re-entry: *Billson v Residential Apartments Ltd* [1992] 1 AC 494 (HL).

[114] The Law Commission proposes abolition: *Termination of Tenancies for Tenant Default* (Law Com No 303, London, 2006) pt 7.

[115] The Law Commission has made proposals for streamlining: *Termination of Tenancies for Tenant Default* (Law Com No 303, London, 2006), and, in the particular case of 'occupation

clear. The law seeks to confine me to my legitimate interests, which it regards as being in the performance of your obligations under the lease in substance, even if not to the letter. If you deliver such a performance, a right to terminate the lease will give me advantages going beyond my legitimate interests. To take a plain instance, say you lease a house from me for 21 years for a lump sum; the terms oblige you not to make alterations without my consent; after a couple of years, you break this obligation in some minor way; an untrammelled right to forfeit would allow me on that account to evict you (retaining the lump sum while I re-let the property), or to induce you to pay me an additional amount (more than the mere cost of restoration) for fear that otherwise you will lose everything. To ensure that I cannot extract more than my legitimate interests in this way, forfeiture is not permitted in such a case. It is restricted to the case where you do not deliver a substantial performance, and my only way of enjoying my legitimate interests is to part company with you and move on.

The ideas in play here are also to be seen in the area of mortgages[116] and in further contexts involving the forfeiture of rights in land.[117] They have however been disavowed in other contexts, on the bases that forbidding a withdrawal from the transaction would amount to ordering its specific performance, the transaction being one not susceptible of specific performance;[118] and that it would involve an undesirable interference with the parties' own arrangements.[119] Allowing a tenant to retain a lease does not involve an order in the nature of specific performance against the landlord. It is however an interference with the parties' arrangements. Why should this be seen as unacceptable in other contexts, but accepted here? Perhaps because it is the shaping of the parties' arrangements in a free bargain that makes interference with them undesirable: but arrangements in leases are commonly not the product of a free bargain. Tenants are commonly less in control of lease transactions than landlords, and the 'legitimate interests' doctrine operates to give them the protection that they would take for themselves if they could. Moreover, in the context of leases, the desirability of respecting the parties' bargain is not the only, perhaps not even the most, fundamental value in

---

contracts', *Renting Homes: The Final Report* (Law Com No 297, London, 2006) pts 4 and 5. See further P Sparkes, 'Towards a Structure for the Law of Landlord and Tenant' in E Cooke (ed), *Modern Studies in Property Law, Volume 1* (Oxford, 2001) ch 13.

[116] § 12.2.2.

[117] *Shiloh Spinners Ltd v Harding* [1975] AC 691 (HL).

[118] So the courts will not prevent the withdrawal of a ship from a time charter for late payment of hire: *Scandinavian Trading Tanker Co AB v Flota Petrolea Ecuatoriana, The Scaptrade* [1983] 2 AC 694 (HL). But they may prevent forfeiture of a patent right: *BICC plc v Burndy Corp* [1985] Ch 232 (CA).

[119] So the possibility of relief was rejected in two cases involving heavily bargained agreements: *Scandinavian Trading Tanker Co, ibid*; *Sport International Bussum BV v Inter-Footwear Ltd* [1984] 1 WLR 776 (HL). But relief was granted despite this consideration in *BICC plc v Burndy Corp, ibid*.

play: respect has to be given to the human right to a home,[120] in domestic leases, and to a means of earning a livelihood, in many others: and the 'legitimate interests' doctrine serves this end.

11.6 The Acquisition of Leases

The rules regarding the creation of leases have been examined fully in § 4.5, and will be only briefly recapitulated here.

A new lease is given, and an existing lease transferred, normally by an intentional conferral. (Leases are occasionally given as relief for proprietary estoppel claims, and can also be acquired by adverse possession, as where you squat on land of which I am already a tenant.)

A lease for a fixed or periodic term of three years or less may usually be created orally.[121] Otherwise, the conferral requires a deed.[122] Once the term goes above seven years, and in certain other cases, its conferral is not effective unless it is also registered.[123] Remember, however, that if I purport to confer a lease on you but fail to use the necessary formality, the conferral may nevertheless have some effect. If our transaction is nevertheless in writing, it will give you an 'equitable lease': not dissimilar to the lease that was meant, but in certain ways not quite so robust.[124] Or if you begin paying me rent, you will probably be found to have a periodic tenancy. When we looked at this assembly of rules in § 4.5, we found that it can be understood up to a point, but is in some major ways unjustified. It is to be hoped that the rules introduced to provide for electronic registration will produce a more coherent treatment.

---

[120] As recognised in the European Convention on Human Rights, Art 8. According to *Kay v Lambeth London Borough Council; Leeds City Council v Price* [2006] 2 AC 465 (HL) and *Doherty v Birmingham City Council* [2008] 3 WLR 636 (HL), the level of protection required by the Article will generally be met by the existing rules controlling the termination of leases; a challenge to those rules for incompatibility with the Article remains a possibility, but should be handled in such a way as not to complicate routine cases.

[121] Law of Property Act 1925 s 54(2).

[122] *Ibid* s 52.

[123] Land Registration Act 2002 s 27(2)(b).

[124] § 5.2.

11.7 Alienating Reversions and Leases

If I lease my land to you, both you and I have rights somewhat in the nature of ownership over it—I because the freehold title remains mine, you because you have your lease—in the way explored in § 11.1.1. So in principle, both of us can alienate our rights to someone else.

We might of course wish to alienate only some limited aspect of our rights. For example, I might mortgage my reversion, or you might mortgage your term; or you might grant an easement or a licence over the land, necessarily for a period not longer than the remaining duration of your lease. Such cases pose no particular problems: they do not affect our remaining respectively landlord and tenant. We need to spend a moment, however, looking at the case where I alienate my whole interest as landlord, or you alienate the core of your interest as tenant—the right of exclusive possession itself.

Such an alienation can take two different forms: *assignment* (by the landlord or the tenant), and *sub-leasing* (by the tenant). The next two sections explore these, explaining how their effects are governed by an idea known as 'privity of estate'.

11.7.1 Assignment

An assignment is a complete transfer of the interest in question. So I might transfer my reversion to John. (I could do this simply by transferring the land itself. Your lease, as a right in rem, would bind John so long as the relevant rules of the Land Registration Act 2002 were satisfied,[125] leaving him with the reversion alone.) Or you might transfer your lease to Kate.

The effect of an assignment is captured in the idea of privity of estate. This connotes that the landlord-tenant relationship exists, ie the rights and obligations contained in the lease are enforceable, between anyone who holds the position of landlord or tenant under it at a given time: that is, between assignees as well as original parties. The reversion and the lease are regarded as actually *comprising* the respective sets of rights and obligations, so to assign one of them is necessarily to pass those rights and obligations to the assignee. The assignee thus automatically acquires all the rights and

---

[125] If the lease is one requiring registration in order to be effective at all (s 27(2)(b)), the same registration will make it bind a disponee. Otherwise, it will bind if it is registered (leases capable of oral creation cannot be registered: s 33(b); but all others can: s 34); or if it is overriding (legal leases are automatically overriding under Sch 3 para 1; an equitable lease can qualify as an overriding interest instead under Sch 3 para 2, if it is held by someone in actual and apparent occupation of the land in question).

obligations embedded in the interest assigned. So if I assign my reversion to John, John becomes your landlord in my place: henceforth, your liabilities are to him rather than me, and your rights are likewise against him rather than me. Conversely, if you assign your lease to Kate, Kate becomes my tenant in your place, and the liabilities and rights vis-à-vis me become Kate's rather than yours. And if both I and you have assigned, to John and Kate respectively, the landlord's and tenant's liabilities and rights now subsist between John and Kate.

Applying this idea requires us to say which rights and obligations are embedded in the interest assigned, ie affect the landlord and tenant in their capacities as such, as opposed to their personal capacities. The law has changed its approach to this task. Before the Landlord and Tenant (Covenants) Act 1995 came into effect in 1996, it asked whether the right or obligation was one 'touching and concerning', or 'having reference to',[126] the lease. If so, it was embedded, and thus passed on an assignment.[127] This remains the rule for leases made before 1996. It focuses on the correct issue, but uses concepts which, at the margin, are hard to pin down, generating uncertainty. The newer approach, applicable to leases made since 1996, instead treats all rights and obligations generated in the transaction creating the lease as embedded in the lease, unless they are expressed to be personal only.[128] The essential idea remains the same, but this technique of leaving the parties to opt out is a clearer way of getting at it: leases containing covenants over whose nature there might be doubt are likely to be professionally drafted, so the opting out rule will elicit the parties' own decision as to what is meant.

A final detail. When I lease to you, I almost certainly enter into a contract with you. So the obligations each of us has to the other are enforceable as a matter of contract ... and remain so even if we part with our reversion or term. Say you assign your lease to Kate, and Kate fails to perform an obligation which, as already explained, she thus now owes me as my tenant. I can enforce the obligation against Kate, but the fact of the contract between me and you means in principle that I can alternatively enforce it against you. And if for example Kate is insolvent, I might well wish to do so. Because this seems oppressive to you (you have probably moved on and naturally pay no attention to what ensues between Kate and me), the law protects you. If our lease was made before 1996, your exposure remains, but with certain limits and compensations.[129] If it was made more recently, your liability terminates

---

[126] For these concepts, see *Hua Chiao Commercial Bank Ltd v Chiaphua Industries Ltd* [1987] AC 99 (PC); *P & A Swift Investments v Combined English Stores Group Plc* [1989] AC 632 (HL).

[127] Law of Property Act 1925 ss 141, 142 (assignment of the reversion); *Spencer's Case* (1583) 5 Co Rep 16a (QB) (assignment of the term).

[128] Landlord and Tenant (Covenants) Act 1995 ss 2, 3; *BHP Petroleum Great Britain Ltd v Chesterfield Properties Ltd* [2002] Ch 194 (CA).

[129] Landlord and Tenant (Covenants) Act 1995 ss 17, 19.

upon your assignment,[130] though you can often be made to replace it with a new obligation creating a limited exposure after all.[131]

11.7.2 Sub-leasing

As explained in § 11.7.1, assignment is a complete transfer of the interest in question. So if you are my tenant, and you assign your lease to Kate, she becomes my tenant in your place. There is another way in which you, as my tenant, can alienate: by sub-leasing.

In this case, the alienation is not outright (that would be an assignment); it is for a period shorter than the remaining duration of your own lease. Say I give you a 10 year lease, and you immediately sub-lease to Liam for five years (or even for 10 years less one day). Unlike in an assignment, you keep your lease with me—you remain my tenant, I remain your landlord—but for those five years, you become Liam's landlord, and Liam becomes your tenant: and my sub-tenant. In such an arrangement, your lease is sometimes called a 'head lease'. There is no limit to the number of times the land may be sub-leased, so Liam (my sub-tenant) may himself sub-lease, for a period shorter than five years, to Meg, who is thus my sub-sub-tenant; and so on.

Combinations of assignment and sub-leasing are possible. So, say I lease to you. You sub-lease to Liam, and Liam sub-leases to Meg. I assign my reversion to John: he thus becomes overall landlord in my place. You assign your head lease to Kate: she thus becomes John's tenant, and Liam's landlord, in your place. (Or the chronology might be reversed: you might assign to Kate, then Kate might sub-lease to Liam.) Liam in turn sub-leases to Meg; either or both may also assign their interest.

In § 11.7.1, we saw how the effect of assignment is captured in the idea of privity of estate. The 'estate' is a given lease (such as mine to you), and the rights and obligations established in it operate between persons 'privy to' it: its original parties and their assignees. The effect of sub-leasing is likewise captured by privity of estate, but this time by its implicit connotation that the estate obtains, and its rights and obligations operate, *only* between the original parties and their assignees. That is, the landlord-tenant relationship exists, ie the lease's rights and obligations are enforceable, across only one level of letting at a time: so, between landlord (or his assign) and tenant (or his assign), and between tenant (or his assign) and sub-tenant (or his assign) ... *but not between landlord and sub-tenant*.

To revert to our example, then, there is a landlord-tenant relationship between me (or my assignee, John) and you (or your assignee, Kate) throughout. And when you sub-lease to Liam, there is a landlord-tenant

---

[130] *Ibid* s 5. By ss 6–8, there is a similar, though less thorough, rule terminating the contractual liability of landlords who assign.
[131] *Ibid* s 16.

relationship between you (or Kate) and Liam (and anyone to whom he may in turn assign). But there is no such relationship between me (or John) and Liam. And when Liam sub-leases to Meg, there is likewise no such a relationship between either me (or John) or you (or Kate) and Meg: only between Liam and Meg. So if I do not receive the rent which you and I agreed as a term of our lease, my only recourse is against you (or Kate): not against Liam or Meg.

11.7.3 Two Qualifications

But this account, focusing on privity of estate, does not give a true picture of the law as a whole. There exist two qualifications: two ways in which rights and obligations can after all be enforced across more than one level of letting at a time, say between landlord (eg me) and sub-tenant (eg Liam).[132]

First, by resort to forfeiture. If you are my tenant, and as a result of a breach of an obligation upon you I am able to forfeit your lease, everyone to whom you have given rights derived from that lease will lose those rights too. So if you have sub-leased to Liam, Liam's sub-lease will disappear, as will the sub-sub-lease that Liam later gives Meg.

At face value, indeed, this rule's effect goes beyond any idea of my 'enforcing' anything against Liam and Meg: I could be interested only in you, leaving Liam and Meg simply innocent victims of the logic of forfeiture. But the forfeiture regime permits the court, while allowing me to forfeit your lease, to protect anyone having a right derived from yours if it wishes.[133] The court will do so if it regards the person in question as not to blame for the situation precipitating the forfeiture. In practice, this allows me to put pressure on sub-tenants etc to respect the terms of the lease itself, even though they are not officially bound to me on them.

The second qualification consists in a special application of the rule whereby a restrictive (ie negative) covenant can, as a right in rem, bind anyone holding the land to which it applies.[134]

---

[132] In addition, certain other more general rules can sometimes be relevant. In particular, under the Contracts (Rights of Third Parties) Act 1999, if X, in a contract with Y, undertakes an obligation in favour of Z, Z (as well as Y) can enforce it against X. Say, then, in my lease with you I undertake responsibility for repairs ... then you sub-let to Liam. A lease will normally be a contract too, and the Act will therefore apply: so if my obligation is read as not merely for your benefit *but also for the benefit of anyone holding through or under you*, Liam (as well as you) will be able to enforce it against me. The key question, however, is whether my obligation should be read in that way. Arguably, a standard lease obligation is meant to be bounded by privity of estate, making such a reading inaccurate.

[133] Law of Property Act 1925 s 146(4). A sub-tenant protected in this way becomes tenant in the original tenant's place. Equally, if the fault leading to the forfeiture lies wholly with the sub-tenant, the court can allow the forfeiture to go ahead so far as it affects the sub-tenant, but relieve the tenant.

[134] That is, the rule in *Tulk v Moxhay* (1848) 2 Ph 774 (Ch).

Say that the property which I lease to you is my house A, and that in the lease there is a covenant prohibiting the use of house A for business purposes. As explained in Chapter 10, this covenant can operate in rem, so as to bind disponees of house A: but will do so only if it benefits another piece of land. So if I inserted it in the lease of house A so as to protect my neighbouring house B, the covenant will bind not only you (and your assignee, Kate), as a term of your lease: it will likewise bind Liam and Meg, for they are disponees of the servient land, and so caught by the covenant's in rem effect. This is an entirely routine application of the restrictive covenant rule, and involves no qualification to the idea of privity of estate: my right against Liam and Meg belongs to me not as landlord of house A, but as owner of house B. The rule's special application, which does qualify privity of estate, occurs when the land for whose benefit I insert the covenant in your lease of house A is not my neighbouring house B, but my reversionary (ie landlord's) interest in house A itself. The courts have decided that such an interest too qualifies as 'benefited land' for the purposes of this rule,[135] so the covenant will operate in rem in this instance as well: meaning that the covenant binds not only you (and Kate), but also Liam and Meg ... in my favour, *as landlord*.

This special application of the restrictive covenant rule involves a radical departure from the rule's original thrust. As we saw in § 10.2.3, the rule in its standard form makes obligations operate in rem if, *and because*, they protect the standard of amenity prevailing between neighbouring plots of (necessarily) physical land. By not conforming to that factual pattern, the special application therefore cannot rest on the same justification. It must have a basis of its own, on the lines that the distinction between assignee and sub-tenant (and sub-sub-tenant, etc) is unimportant: the protection of the landlord's reversionary interest requires that the lease's terms be effective against both. Contrary to the assumption made by the idea of privity of estate, that seems a very understandable position, resting on the idea that a tenant, on sub-leasing, should not be able to confer more (in the sense of an interest with fewer obligations to the landlord) than he himself has.

Because it is technically a special application of the restrictive covenant rule, this second qualification to privity of estate operates only on lease terms which impose a *negative* obligation on the tenant. Because (as we saw in § 10.2.4) the restrictive covenant rule does not extend to positive obligations, the qualification does not apply to terms creating a *positive* obligation, such as a covenant to pay rent or keep the house in good repair. The reach of the latter continues to be limited by privity of estate, ie to extend across only one level of letting at a time. This limitation seems inappropriate. The negativity requirement may or may not be justified as an aspect of the rule's standard

---

[135] *Hall v Ewin* (1887) 37 Ch D 74 (CA). The rule is preserved in the Landlord and Tenant (Covenants) Act 1995 s 3(5).

form.[136] But in the context of our special application, the requirement seems quite arbitrary. As we saw in the previous paragraph, the special application rests on the idea that a tenant should not be able to give away more than he himself has. And that idea makes as much sense for positive obligations as it does for negative ones. This lesson can best be absorbed, however, not by extending the restrictive covenant rule to positive as well as negative obligations, but by attacking the fundamental problem—privity of estate—itself.

---

[136] See § 10.2.5.

12

Mortgages

In common speech, the expression 'a mortgage' is often used to refer to a money advance, normally taken from a building society or bank so as to buy a house. In law, it has a slightly different meaning, though the two are connected. Put briefly, a mortgage is the right of resort that the building society or bank gains over the borrower's house, enabling it to repossess and sell the house so as to recoup itself if the advance is not repaid. As such, it is a right (held by the building society or bank) over (the householder's) land. It is also, as we shall discover, a right in rem. As such, it belongs in the series of rights in rem in land through which we are moving.

There are, naturally, a number of details to be looked at. On top of these, however, there are certain complications, arising from the roundabout way in which English law has evolved its current vision of a mortgage, and continuing to shape that vision. So we shall begin by sketching the essential idea of a mortgage of land. Then we shall turn briefly to the history, before examining the current rules in detail, noting the points at which the circuitous development of these rights has given them an odd configuration.

12.1 The Essential Idea of a Land Mortgage

12.1.1 Mortgages as Security Rights

Say you lend me some money. I incur a debt to you: that is, a legal obligation to repay you, which you can enforce, if necessary by suing me. Which is fine, except if I find myself under obligations to you and other creditors for a total amount that I cannot afford to repay, even if I go beyond my ready cash and draw on my assets as a whole—meaning, essentially, that I am bankrupt. You and my other creditors will not get all your money back. Instead, you will receive only your due proportion of my available assets.

But there is a way for you to improve your position. You can insist that my debt to you be 'secured' on my assets in general, or some particular item(s) within them: very possibly, my land. The effect of this is that, if I fail to repay the loan, you can resort to the asset comprising the security: take it away from me, sell it, and repay the debt from the proceeds. By securing my debt to you in this way, you separate yourself from my other creditors, whose rights are unsecured. The latter are sometimes called 'general creditors', and your security right gives you 'priority [over them] in [my] bankruptcy'. So long as the value of the asset comprising your security is at least as great as the sum I owe you, your ability to resort to this asset means that you will now recover this sum in full, while the general creditors continue to suffer a shortfall. Indeed, their position becomes worse, for the assets available to pay them no longer include the asset securing my debt to you, except to the extent that the latter's value exceeds that of the debt.

You might be unwilling to lend to me at all without the debt being secured in this way. Overall, however, I probably could find someone who is willing ... but only in return for a higher rate of interest. The risk of a loan going unpaid, ie of the lender losing all his money, is evidently greater where the loan is unsecured than where it is secured. An actuarial reckoning of this risk is one of the factors to which the lender will attend in deciding whether to make the loan, and more especially on what terms to do so: the greater the risk, the higher his return (the interest rate) will need to be so as to cover it. So secured loans, in presenting (*ceteris paribus*) a lower risk, will be at lower rates of interest.

Your security right over my asset is called a mortgage, or alternatively a charge.[1] I, the borrower, am the 'mortgagor', while you, the lender, are the 'mortgagee'. My paying off the debt I owe you, at which point you lose your security right, is called 'redeeming'. The asset over which you have your right is often itself called your 'security'.

---

[1] Strictly speaking, the two terms have different meanings. Both are security rights, but they arise in different ways. A 'charge' arises where I grant you a security right pure and simple. A 'mortgage' arises where I transfer my asset to you, on the basis that you will retransfer it to me (only) if I pay off my debt to you. § 12.1.4 explains the use English law has made of the two forms, and the current position. Where the distinction between them is not important, however, the words 'mortgage' and 'charge' are generally used as synonyms, the former being more common.

12.1.2 Mortgages as Rights in Rem

A mortgage is a right in rem. Unlike the other rights in rem discussed in this book, however, we should not in practice expect a mortgage to affect a transferee of the asset to which it relates. If I have mortgaged my land to you, then I transfer the land to John, I will normally use the purchase money I receive from John to redeem the mortgage, so that John acquires the land free of it. The more important manifestation of a mortgage's status as a right in rem is the very way it operates to give you security, and especially priority in my bankruptcy. It does so on the basis that, to the extent of your right to resort to the asset in question to repay the debt, the asset is yours. So if I become bankrupt, and my assets are taken and sold to pay off my debts, the security asset is excepted: to the extent of your right, it is not mine but yours. As explained in § 1.1.2, this—*'nemo dat quod non habet'*—is the basis on which rights are seen as in rem generally; effectiveness against disponees is another facet of it.

12.1.3 Mortgages of Land

So say I am negotiating to borrow a significant sum of money from you. You are willing in principle to lend it to me, but you are likely to require me to secure my obligation to repay it onto one or more of my assets. In practice, the asset on which we fix will commonly be some land that I own ... or will own by the time I incur the debt: my very object in seeking the loan might well be to assemble the money that I need in order to buy the land.

The latter scenario represents the enormously common case where I buy a house; cannot afford to pay for it in cash; so, usually after a small cash down payment, pay for the rest via a loan from a building society or bank. The picture we have of this situation may be that the lender now owns the house, until such time as I have paid all the instalments, when it becomes mine. In fact, however, the lender pays the loan money to me; I use it (together with my existing cash, whether savings or the net proceeds of selling my previous house) to buy the house, paying the seller the entire price for it up front, so that the house becomes quite literally mine; then I owe the lender the sum it has loaned me, and must repay it this sum, plus whatever interest falls due over the time it takes me.[2] The lender has its mortgage over the house, securing my payment of these liabilities, because it required me to grant it such a mortgage as a condition of giving me the loan. So at a single instant,

---

[2] There is room for a variation on the theme. An arrangement whereby I make direct repayments to the lender is called a 'repayment' mortgage. Sometimes, I will instead make payments to some other financial institution, which will invest them with a view to generating a lump sum with which I can, in due course, repay the lender in one go. An 'endowment' mortgage is an example of the latter kind of arrangement. Crucially, however, the responsibility of repaying the loan remains mine in either case: the difference is merely a choice on my part between different approaches to doing so.

the loan comes through; I use the money so raised to pay the seller for the house; the house becomes mine; and I give the lender its mortgage.[3] The reason why we do not normally notice all these complications is that they are handled on our behalf by the solicitors acting for me, the seller and the lender, largely as a matter of routine.

In enabling the instalment-purchase of houses in this way, mortgages are of huge importance in contemporary Britain: without them, the options would be to buy the ownership of the house for cash, which very few could afford, or to rent, and so never become owner oneself, which would leave many dissatisfied. But in its different way, the mortgaging of houses *after* purchase, so as to borrow money for spending on something else (often called 'equity release'), is also important. The 'something else' might be simple consumption: mortgages used in this way contributed to the consumer demand drive that featured prominently in the arrangement of the current British economy before the 2008 crash. Or it might be a project that empowers the borrower or those close to him in some more enduring way, such as enlarging his house or sending his children to university. Or it might be the establishment or expansion of his business, so creating employment and wealth more generally. As explained in § 12.1.1, even if loans for such purposes could be obtained without security, they would be more expensive, thus inhibiting the expenditure to which they might be devoted.

There is nothing in the abstract to say that my loan from you has to be secured on my land (nor even that a loan you give me to buy my house has to be secured on that house): in principle, any of my assets can be used. Land is commonly used partly because it is often by far the most valuable of my assets, and hence uniquely capable of securing a large loan. Partly too because it tends to retain its value well, especially over the long term, which is important for these purposes: you would be ill-advised to secure a 10 year loan for £1 million on my fleet of lorries, at the time worth that amount but obviously prone to depreciate over the 10 years to a small fraction of it, leaving the loan to that extent de facto unsecured. And partly because, thanks to the registration rules relating to land, I am unlikely to be able to conceal your rights in it so as to dispose of it, a move which could again otherwise leave your loan unsecured after all.

Because land is so commonly made the subject of security rights in this way, the rules on the subject can be expected to be especially detailed. And because land's other significances tend to be a particularly important—above all, the piece of land in question will often be my home—these rules can be expected to exhibit an unusual degree of complexity, the result of the balance that the law has to strike between the various relevant considerations. The

---

[3] And unless I am a first-time buyer, I simultaneously also transfer my old house to its buyer, receive his payment for it, pay off what remains of my mortgage on it, and put any remaining money into the payment I now make for my new house.

law fulfils these expectations. We shall look at the principal rules in §§ 12.3–12.7.[4]

12.1.4 The Current Legal Form of a Land Mortgage

Under the current law, a mortgage of registered land involves the borrower granting the lender a 'charge' over his land.[5] A charge is in principle a pure security right, as outlined thus far. But the law[6] views a charge over land as equivalent to a 3,000 year lease of the land from the borrower to the lender.

On the face of it, a security right and a lease are very different things. In particular, a lease entitles the lessee (the lender) to occupy the lessor's (borrower's) land, something not to be expected from a security right. It does not terminate when the debt is repaid. Nor, if the debt is not repaid, does it entitle the lessee to sell the freehold so as to recoup the amount outstanding, in the way that a security right demands. But by further rules, these inappropriate consequences of the lease are substantially removed, so as to produce an approximation to a pure security right after all.[7] Conceptually, however, the arrangement, with its introduction of a lease, remains grotesque. Moreover, the position today is only an *approximation* to a pure security right: there are points at which it still does not take quite the form one would expect of a pure security right. It derives from the history of the subject, prevailing—and showing these defects—today because the updating that has occurred has been insufficiently lucid. It will be necessary, therefore, to take a brief look at the history.[8]

---

[4] See further J Houghton and L Livesey, 'Mortgage Conditions: Old Law for a New Century?' in E Cooke (ed), *Modern Studies in Property Law, Volume 1* (Oxford, 2001) ch 10; M Oldham, 'Mortgages' in L Tee (ed), *Land Law: Issues, Debates, Policy* (Cullompton, 2002) ch 6. (These essays' references to the Consumer Credit Act 1974 are now out of date: the relevant provisions have been replaced by ss 140A–140D, introduced by the Consumer Credit Act 2006.)

[5] Land Registration Act 2002 s 23(1)(a).

[6] Law of Property Act 1925 s 87(1).

[7] As regards occupation, see § 12.6. As regards termination upon repayment, see the Law of Property Act 1925 s 85(1), to which s 87(1) refers. As regards sale of the freehold, see the Law of Property Act 1925 ss 88(1), 104(1), and § 12.5.

[8] See further A Simpson, *A History of the Land Law* (2nd edn, Oxford, 1986) 141–3, 242–7; G Watt, 'The Lie of the Land: Mortgage Law as Legal Fiction' in E Cooke (ed), *Modern Studies in Property Law, Volume 4* (Oxford, 2007) ch 4.

12.2 The History of Land Mortgages

12.2.1 The Historical Development of the Legal Form

In late medieval times, the borrower leased his land to the lender; or, a little later, transferred the freehold in it to him, with a provision for transfer back to the borrower when the debt was paid. If the debt was not paid, the lender could recoup himself from the interest so granted to him—the freehold version being better from this point of view than the lease. But at least as important, having the freehold or lease also allowed him to possess the land in the meantime. Such a general right to possess the land is out of place in a pure security interest,[9] but was vital at this time, when usury—lending money for profit—was prohibited. Having possession of the land, the lender was able to extract an income from it ... and this income took the place of interest on the loan.

Eventually, this latter consideration fell away, as the laws against usury were first changed so as to allow the taking of interest not exceeding a certain percentage, then dropped altogether, so that it became possible straightforwardly to stipulate for interest.[10] There was then no need for the lender to have a general right to possess the land: only a pure security right was in principle required. Inertia prevailed, however, and mortgages continued to be made principally by freehold transfer. But such a mortgage could in principle be made to emulate a pure security right almost exactly. If you lent me money, the terms of our arrangement could provide, for example, that you would allow me to remain in possession; that so long as I continued to be able to repay, I would not lose the land; and that if I did lose it, you would have to make over to me any difference between its value and the amount I still owed you. But one difference would necessarily remain: until I repaid, you were the owner of the land, rather than me. This was felt to be inappropriate, and was addressed in a change made in 1925, whereby I thenceforth gave you not my ownership, but a 3,000 year lease of my land.[11] So that I could continue to secure my debts on the freehold value of my land, however, further provisions had to be and were simultaneously introduced, enabling you—if I defaulted—to sell not merely this lease, but my freehold ownership after all.[12]

---

[9] The mortgagee's right to possess the land in today's law is examined in § 12.6.

[10] Maximum interest rates were applied in Tudor and Stuart legislation; final abolition came in the Usury Laws Repeal Act 1854.

[11] Law of Property Act 1925 s 85.

[12] *Ibid* ss 101, 104. *Mutatis mutandis*, all this applies similarly to the mortgage of a lease. Say I am not the freehold owner of some land, but a tenant of it under a reasonably long lease (a short

At some point, the possibility was recognised of a mortgage of land being made by pure security interest, leaving me as owner of the land but giving you, in the event of my default, the right to sell it so as to recoup yourself. The legislation of 1925 mentioned this form of interest—a charge—as an alternative to the mortgage by way of 3,000 year lease.[13] And in 2002, further legislation produced the current rule, whereby the charge is the only form of mortgage of registered land.[14] The 1925 legislation ruled, however, that despite the name 'charge', such mortgages should have the same effect as mortgages by 3,000 year lease,[15] and this remains the position. Given the ability of a mortgagee by long lease nonetheless to sell the freehold[16] (as the holder of a security interest over the freehold by definition can), this rule makes no practical difference.[17] But the law's overall approach—defining a charge over a freehold in terms of a lease, itself tweaked so as once more to emulate a charge—is bizarrely confused. It ought to be possible to create a mortgage of land by, and only by, granting a pure security interest, as outlined in § 12.1.1.[18]

12.2.2 Equity's Insistence that a Mortgage Give Only Security Rights

It was observed above that if I gave you a mortgage by way of freehold transfer, we could in principle structure the deal so as to emulate a pure security arrangement. Equally, though, we might not do so. In particular, our deal might provide for me to lose the land if I did not repay you in a certain way (by or on a particular date, at a particular place, in a particular currency, whatever), despite being able to repay in a more general sense. In fact, early

or periodic lease would hardly be of sufficient value to be useful as security). Before 1925, I could transfer the lease to you as security for my debt to you, on the basis that you would retransfer it when I paid. Under the Law of Property Act 1925 s 86, however, I cannot do this, but can grant you a sub-lease: not this time for 3,000 years, for that is likely to be longer than the term of my own lease, but for one day less than my own term.

[13] Law of Property Act 1925 s 85(1).
[14] Land Registration Act 2002 s 23(1)(a).
[15] Law of Property Act 1925 s 87(1); for registered land, the Land Registration Act 2002 s 51 in effect refers us back to s 87(1).
[16] Law of Property Act 1925 ss 88(1), 104(1).
[17] It might be thought to make a difference to the mortgagee's ability to possess—occupy—the land: a tenant normally can possess, without restriction, whereas we would expect the holder of a security right to be able to possess only to the extent demanded by the character of that right. On the best understanding, however, there is probably no such difference: the possession right of a mortgagee by way of lease is limited to what he requires as a mortgagee, ie to what he would have under a pure security right. But the issue is controversial: see § 12.6.3.
[18] The Law Commission has recommended that the law be reformed in this way: *Land Mortgages* (Law Com No 204, London, 1991), but no action has been taken. It is in fact already possible to create a pure security right over land, but this counts only as an equitable mortgage, as opposed to the common law mortgage being discussed in the text. Equitable mortgages have different rules, less advantageous to the lender, and are accordingly little used. The reform advocated would in effect be to merge the common law and equitable forms into a single, properly configured, pure security right.

mortgage arrangements were commonly formulated in this way, and were enforced at face value by lenders, with the assistance of the common law courts.

At some point, however, the position changed. Equity intervened, blocking the common law position and ruling that so long as I repaid in a practically sufficient way (and it was for equity to judge what this was), I could demand a retransfer of my land after all. The effect was, and was intended to be, that the parties could not bargain for a mortgage arrangement to give the lender more than a pure security right. Although it has other manifestations,[19] the idea was principally expressed as a demand that the mortgage be redeemable upon payment of the debt; that there be no 'clogs' or 'fetters' on the borrower's ability to redeem. This equitable right to redeem despite any contrary terms of the deal formed the principal element in what was called my 'equity of redemption'.[20]

It did not of course follow that I could simply withhold payment indefinitely, and still expect not to lose my land. My obligation to pay remained, and if I substantively failed to meet it, equity would retract its block, so that my land did indeed become yours. Such retraction of the block was called 'foreclosure'. The possibility of retraction was just as necessary—to ensure that mortgages did function as security rights—as the block itself, which ensured that they functioned as no more than that.

Modern mortgages achieve largely the same effect with less circumlocution. That is to say, not only the reality but also the appearance is closer to what one would expect of a pure security interest. The arrangement is unlikely to purport to allow you, if I do not repay exactly in some particular way, to take my land without further ado: modern mortgages do not normally stipulate for the legally impossible. And whatever the arrangement says on the subject, the law itself controls your ability to take my land through a detailed set of rules, allowing you to do so if, but only if, I default on my obligations *to a sufficient extent*. These rules are explained in § 12.5. But the essential idea of the original equitable intervention—that a mortgage may not be made irredeemable, or, more generally, confer more than a security right—continues to be understood[21] and invoked.[22] (That said, we shall see in § 12.7.4 that there is an argument,

---

[19] We shall notice three: the rules that a lender's sale powers may be used only so as to recoup the loan (§ 12.5.3); that a lender can possess the mortgaged land only where necessary for its role as security for the debt (§ 12.6.3); and that a lender cannot, in the mortgage agreement, stipulate for any other benefits (§ 12.7.1).

[20] The rule against irredeemability has another implication. If the land I mortgage to you is land that I lease, rather than own, the mortgage arrangement must allow me to redeem before the end of the lease. In *Fairclough v Swan Brewery Co Ltd* [1912] AC 565 (PC), the terms purported to disallow redemption until six weeks before the end of a 17 year lease; these terms were declared invalid. But cf *Knightsbridge Estates Trust Ltd v Byrne* [1939] Ch 441 (CA), where terms purporting to disallow redemption of a *freehold* for 40 years were upheld.

[21] *Knightsbridge Estates Trust Ltd v Byrne* [1939] Ch 441, 456–7 (CA).

[22] *Quennell v Maltby* [1979] 1 WLR 318, 322, 324 (CA): see § 12.6.3.

based on freedom of contract, to the contrary, and that the latter seems—probably rightly—to be in the ascendant.)

12.3 The Content of a Land Mortgage

Now we turn to look in more detail at the rules governing the operation of modern land mortgages. We shall see that in broad terms they provide appropriate fleshing out of mortgages' role as security rights, but that at certain points they remain redolent of the more tangential ways in which the law has approached the matter, and as a result appear dysfunctional.[23]

We shall focus in turn on a number of different rights enjoyed by a lender under a land mortgage: the underlying debt itself; the right to sell the mortgaged land, or alternatively foreclose the mortgage and take the land for oneself; the right to possess the mortgaged land; and the right to any additional benefits ('collateral advantages') stipulated for in the mortgage agreement.

12.4 The Debt

A mortgage gives the lender security for a debt that the borrower owes him. It thus presupposes such a debt. Once the debt is repaid, there is nothing to secure, so there can be no mortgage. Likewise if the debt is vitiated by duress, undue influence, or misrepresentation.

In English law, these traditional grounds for vitiating agreements operate in an 'all or nothing' way: if an obligation is affected by one of them, it is bad *in toto*, rather than rewritten into an acceptable form. Sometimes rewriting is possible, however. This is most prominently the case under the Unfair

---

[23] See further S Nield, 'Charges, Possession and Human Rights: A Reappraisal of s 87(1) Law of Property Act 1925' in E Cooke (ed), *Modern Studies in Property Law, Volume 3* (Oxford, 2005) ch 8. See also L Fox, *Conceptualising Home—Theories, Laws and Policies* (Oxford, 2007) and M Dixon, 'Mortgage Default and Mortgagee's Remedies' [2008] *Conv* 474, on the question whether the mortgage's identity as a security right should be balanced against other interests.

Contract Terms Act 1977 and the Unfair Terms in Consumer Contracts Regulations 1999. In the case of a debt in particular, it occurs also under the Consumer Credit Act 1974 sections 140A and 140B (aimed at 'unfair credit relationships')[24]; and[25] if the debt is vitiated by 'unconscionability', a concept explained in § 12.8.1. These latter rules allow an excessive interest rate to be changed to a proper one.[26] More generally, the Financial Services Authority's *Mortgages: Conduct of Business* rules[27] require financial institutions to undertake retail lending in a 'responsible' way, taking proper account of the customer's ability to repay, and treating him 'fairly': so, ensuring that interest rates are not excessive as compared with others available in the market.[28]

Other terms of a debt may be invalidated too, when they are objectionable in one of these ways. So, for example, if you lend me money on the basis that I cannot repay for a certain time—forcing me to continue paying you interest all the while—this prolongation may be set aside if it falls foul of one of the rules, say if the bargain in which I agree to it is an unconscionable one.[29]

12.5 Sale and Foreclosure

The most important element in a mortgage—the salient concrete manifestation of the security right it represents—is the fact that it allows the lender, if the borrower defaults sufficiently on the loan, to take the borrower's land and sell it so as to recoup the amount outstanding.

---

[24] These provisions were introduced into the 1974 Act by the Consumer Credit Act 2006. For their context and significance, see S Brown, 'The Consumer Credit Act 2006: Real Additional Mortgagor Protection?' [2007] *Conv* 316.

[25] Perhaps unexpectedly, for unconscionability seems to form part of a series with duress, undue influence and misrepresentation; and they, as noted, operate in an 'all or nothing' fashion.

[26] As in *Cityland and Property (Holdings) Ltd v Dabrah* [1968] Ch 166 (Ch D). The judge rejected the stipulated interest rate as being 'unreasonable', but *Multiservice Bookbinding Ltd v Marden* [1979] Ch 84 (Ch D) (reflecting *Knightsbridge Estates Trust Ltd v Byrne* [1939] Ch 441 (CA)) confirms that the correct test is not unreasonableness but unconscionability, as described in § 12.8.1. It is less clear, however, how the substitute rate is to be fixed.

[27] See http://fsahandbook.info/FSA/html/handbook/.

[28] Sections 11.3, 12.2.5. Section 12.2 further prohibits other kinds of charge (for early redemption, or for falling into arrears) from rising above the actual costs in question.

[29] In *Knightsbridge Estates Trust Ltd v Byrne* [1939] Ch 441 (CA) a 40 year debt term was attacked on this ground (among others), but was upheld because on the facts there was no unconscionability: the borrower was a business entity, adequately capable of looking after its own interests.

12.5.1 The Source of the Right to Sell

If I have granted you a mortgage over the freehold ownership of my house, and you now sell, say to John, you transfer the freehold ownership to John. As explained in § 12.2.1, before 1925 you generally had the very freehold ownership, with an obligation to restore it to me upon my repayment, so your ability to transfer it required no explanation. But since 1925 you will not have the very freehold ownership: nowadays, in the case of registered land, you will have a charge, though it will emulate a 3,000 year lease. Your ability nonetheless to transfer the freehold ownership rests on two foundations. First, the very nature of a charge, which is a security interest. By definition, this allows you to have resort to the charged asset if the debt in question is not paid. Second, the detail that the relevant rules put into 'have resort to'. They might, for example, have provided that the court shall take over the asset and sell it, returning the required sum to you. As it happens (but doubtless influenced by the pre-1925 history), in the present context they provide for you yourself to sell,[30] and give meaning to this by stipulating that, although you do not hold the freehold ownership, your sale nonetheless transfers it.[31]

12.5.2 The Availability of the Right to Sell

Say I borrow from you, and grant you a mortgage over my land to secure my debt. Normally our arrangement will require me to make monthly payments, either to you direct, or to a financial institution which will eventually put the sum generated by these payments towards discharging my debt. If I fail to make one of these monthly payments, I will be in default. But you cannot normally move to a sale immediately: the law delays you for a short period during which I can put matters right, and if I do so the possibility of sale disappears again. The rules[32] are complex and not easy to

---

[30] But not if you find yourself bound by the right of a beneficiary of a trust on which I, though purporting to own the land absolutely, in fact held it. Then, you will have to go via the court, under the Trusts of Land and Appointment of Trustees Act 1996 s 14. See §§ 14.2.2–14.2.5.

[31] Law of Property Act 1925 ss 88, 104. There are however possible complications, notably in the case where you purport to transfer to John despite having no right against me to do so (see § 12.5.2, on the availability of sale). Is the transfer nonetheless effective (leaving me to sue you for wrongfully but nonetheless effectively taking my land away)? There is an argument for saying 'no', so as to fully protect me, but there is also one for saying 'yes', so as to facilitate dealings in land. (Compare the parallel issue regarding the ability of trustees to transfer land free from the trust interests, when they act wrongly in purporting so to do: § 14.6.) In the case of registered land, the answer is offered by the Land Registration Act 2002 s 52. That section may have been intended to say simply 'yes', but its wording seems circular, apparently giving you the power to do ... what the law gives you the power to do. For (inconclusive) discussion, see G Ferris and G Battersby, 'The General Principles of Overreaching and the Modern Legislative Reforms 1996–2002' (2003) 119 *LQR* 94, 122–4.

[32] They are contained in the Law of Property Act 1925 ss 101 and 103.

understand.[33] But in broad terms you can sell if I have missed two months' interest payments ... or if (as is likely) the mortgage allows you to demand immediate repayment if I default at all, and you do so, giving me three months to comply, which I do not.

The rules thus give you the right to sell in the event of what may be called 'confirmed default' on my part. They are probably best regarded as concretised deductions from a more fundamental idea. As we saw in § 12.2.2, the law ensures that mortgage arrangements operate as security interests by disallowing lenders from using their rights so acquired otherwise than to deliver the payment of the relevant debt. The rules about the allowability of sale restrict the possibility of it to the cases where, in the eyes of the law, a lender really needs it so as recoup himself. But in allowing sale as soon as the borrower is in 'confirmed default', they are nevertheless not over-lenient. In practice, however, their rigour is mitigated in two ways.

First, building societies and banks tend not to proceed to a sale by any means so quickly, preferring instead to investigate the possibility of achieving repayment after all by rescheduling the debt over the remaining mortgage period (or sometimes longer).

And second, you will find it hard to *sell* unless you first gain *possession* of the land by evicting me[34]: and, as we shall see in § 12.6, your ability to obtain possession is normally narrower than your (theoretical) right to sell. If the mortgaged land is my home, confirmed default is not enough for you to take possession. You can do so only if I cannot show a likelihood of being able to pay off the debt even if, following normal bank and building society practice, it is rescheduled over the whole remaining mortgage period.[35] Like the rule concerning sale, this rule concerning possession is calculated to ensure that the lender's rights do not exceed what he needs to recoup the debt. But it evidently embodies a different—narrower—view regarding the scope of his need. There is no good reason for this discrepancy: the rules on the availability of sale and of possession as a prelude to sale should have the same profile. We shall return to this issue in § 12.6.4, arguing that the profile of the possession rule is the more appropriate.

[33] They were formulated with an eye on a bygone form of mortgage, where apparently I was to repay you the entire debt after only six months; as explained in § 12.2.2, this was unreal, given equity's insistence on permitting me to redeem so long as I am able to do so; but my failure to comply nonetheless counted as a default of sorts, upon which the provisions delaying sale are built. Modern mortgages try to give a clearer idea of what they mean, but this in turn produces a problematic relationship with the provisions.

[34] Otherwise, few will want to buy: under the circumstances, my lack of right to remain once the sale goes through will give a buyer little reassurance that I shall in fact leave when that time comes. The presence of the defaulting borrower is also likely to depress the price that can be got: few will eagerly bid, only to make him (and usually his family) homeless.

[35] Administration of Justice Act 1970 s 36; *Cheltenham & Gloucester Building Society v Norgan* [1996] 1 WLR 343 (CA).

12.5.3 The Lender's Duties Regarding Sale

When you sell my house to John, you will receive the price John agrees to pay you for it. You have first call on this money, to recoup what I owe you plus the expenses of the sale. If any money remains after this, you must pay it to me.[36] So, say I buy my house for £200,000, of which £180,000 is a loan from you secured on the house, and (given my failure to keep pace with your interest charges) I owe you £190,000 when I default; at which point you sell for £225,000, with expenses of £5,000. Of the £225,000, you will keep £190,000 + £5,000 = £195,000 for yourself, and must return the remaining £30,000 to me.[37]

But compare the following example. Say once more that my house cost me £200,000, of which £180,000 came by way of a secured loan from you, and that at the point you sell I owe you £190,000 ... but that your sale of my house fetches only £175,000, with expenses again of £5,000. The £175,000 is absorbed entirely by your call for £195,000; I not only get nothing but am left still owing you £20,000. This scenario, or the prospect of it, is called 'negative equity'.

I am thus crucially affected by differences—especially falls—between the value of the house when I grant your mortgage and the sum realised by your sale; the impact on you is likely to be much less. Sometimes a fall will be the result of a drop in the basic value of the house itself, as where it falls victim to subsidence or planning blight, or where house prices decline generally. But sometimes it will occur because, in selling, you fail to take the steps that I would have taken on my own account, so as to maximise the house's sale price. You might, for example, accept the first offer you receive, despite advice that you can realistically expect a better one; or you might neglect to market the house properly; or you might sell when the market is depressed, despite reason to believe that it will shortly pick up; or you might sell without making some obvious improvements that would more than repay their cost in a higher price. In such circumstances, I—as the principal sufferer—will be aggrieved. Do I have any legal recourse against you?

---

[36] Law of Property Act 1925 s 105, following plain security principles.

[37] Complications arise, however, where I have granted additional mortgages to other lenders: essentially, you must repay the sums I still owe them before returning any balance to me. Further complications arise where I purported to grant your mortgage over the full freehold ownership of the house, but in fact hold it on trust, say for myself and Kate equally. If you are bound by Kate's right, half of the £225,000 will be hers, leaving only £112,500 to meet your call for £195,000. You can sue me for the shortfall of £82,500, but probably not fruitfully. Whereas if you are not bound by Kate's right, the outcome is as explained in the text—you take your £195,000 and return £30,000 to me—and Kate must look to me (again, probably not fruitfully) for the £112,500 by which she is left down. For you and Kate, then, the question of whether you are bound by her right is an anxious one. For exploration of the way the law addresses it, see § 14.8.

The answer[38] has two elements. The first is that you, the lender, must always act in good faith. You will do so if you act genuinely so as to recoup the amount I owe you, no matter how much you harm me in the process; but not if you aim gratuitously to cause me loss.[39] The second element is that, *in your conduct of the actual sale but in no other respect*, you must take reasonable care to obtain a 'fair' or 'true market' or 'proper' (these seem to be synonymous) price.

In each of the examples just given, therefore, if you sell the house for less than its true value in bad faith, you must compensate me for the loss you thereby cause me. If you act in good faith but stupidly, however, you must compensate me where you inadvisably accept a poor first offer;[40] and where you neglect to market the house properly, say by failing to mention the existence of planning permission giving it development potential and thus a higher value;[41] but not where you make a damaging decision about the timing of any sale,[42] or about investing in improvements,[43] because these failures do not occur in the conduct of the actual sale.[44]

The law here is unstable, however. The courts in recent decisions have given a very confident account of it, but the confidence is misplaced.

The first element, requiring good faith, is unproblematic. Remember the law's demand (explained in § 12.2.2) that mortgage arrangements operate as security interests only, lenders being prohibited from using their rights under such arrangements otherwise than to recoup the debt. It follows that, even where sale is warranted so as to recoup the debt, a sale in fact carried out for some other end must be prohibited, and loss occasioned thereby must be made good.

The difficulty arises with the second element. It is hard to understand the distinction it requires between the actual sale and other aspects of the sale process, such as the timing of a sale and a decision not to improve the price by taking additional trouble. Indeed, it may not be possible firmly to say whether all given sets of facts count as occurring in the conduct of the actual sale or otherwise. Unsurprisingly, therefore, it is possible to find judicial

---

[38] As given in *Downsview Nominees Ltd v First City Corporation Ltd* [1993] AC 295, 312, 315 (PC); *Silven Properties Ltd v Royal Bank of Scotland plc* [2004] 1 WLR 997, [13]–[20] (CA).

[39] *Downsview Nominees Ltd, ibid.* So long as you do act with the proper motive, it does not matter that you have other motives too: *Meretz Investments NV v ACP Ltd* [2006] 3 All ER 1029, [314] (Ch D).

[40] *Palk v Mortgage Services Funding plc* [1993] Ch 330, 337–8.

[41] *Cuckmere Brick Co Ltd v Mutual Finance Ltd* [1971] Ch 949 (CA).

[42] *China and South Seas Bank Ltd v Tan Soon Gin* [1990] 1 AC 536 (PC).

[43] *Silven Properties Ltd v Royal Bank of Scotland plc* [2004] 1 WLR 997 (CA).

[44] See too section 13.6 of the Financial Services Authority's *Mortgages: Conduct of Business* rules: http://fsahandbook.info/FSA/html/handbook/. Like the cases, the section imposes a duty to obtain the best price that might reasonably be paid. A little differently from the cases, though, at least in emphasis, it requires that the sale should take place as quickly as possible—though recognising that there may be legitimate reasons why it should not.

assertions that care is *not* required as regards the actual sale[45]; and others, that care *is* required as regards other aspects. In *Palk v Mortgage Services Funding plc*[46] especially, the lender decided to postpone sale until the property market improved; the implication being that in the meantime, the debt would remain wholly unpaid, and would continue to generate interest liabilities for the borrower. The court viewed this plan as wrongful, for taking insufficient care of the interests of the borrower.[47] By way of remedy, the court pre-empted the wrong by itself ordering an immediate sale.[48]

It seems likely, then, that the rule should be the same for both contexts, ie as regards all a mortgagee's decisions about sale. But what form should that rule in principle take? Should it require good faith alone, or reasonable care too?

Certainly, no demand for reasonable care can be deduced from the basic idea of disallowing lenders from using their mortgage rights otherwise than for security.[49] But it does not follow that reasonable care should not be demanded for some other reason. In fact, in *Cuckmere Brick Co Ltd v Mutual Finance Ltd*,[50] where the demand's existence (for the conduct of an actual sale) was finally established, it was put in terms redolent of the tort of negligence: it is obvious that bad decisions regarding sale by the lender will injure the borrower, who bears the first impact of a failure to realise the property's potential value; so, following Lord Atkin's formula in *Donoghue v Stevenson*,[51] the borrower becomes the lender's 'neighbour', and the lender has to take reasonable care to avoid so injuring him. Now subsequent decisions have established that this formula is not to be applied literally; that situations can fall within its terms, but nonetheless not give rise to legal compensation rights. Nevertheless, it has clear moral force, so that if such rights are not to arise we want to know why. Why should there be an exception for bad decisions regarding sale by a mortgagee?

One might suggest: because the injury caused by such decisions will be economic, and many cases of economic injury are excepted from the application of Lord Atkin's formula. But while many such cases are excepted, some are not, so we need to decide which group the case under consideration

---

[45] See eg *Warner v Jacob* (1882) 20 Ch D 220, 224 (Ch D); *Kennedy v De Trafford* [1897] AC 180 (HL).

[46] [1993] Ch 330 (CA). See also *Standard Chartered Bank Ltd v Walker* [1982] 1 WLR 1410, 1415–16 (CA).

[47] This position is supported by the Financial Services Authority's *Mortgages: Conduct of Business* rules, http://fsahandbook.info/FSA/html/handbook/: section 13.6.1(1) envisages sales occurring as quickly as possible, unless there is a legitimate reason to the contrary.

[48] Under the Law of Property Act 1925 s 91(2). This decision is not contradicted, though its impact is complicated, by the position taken in *Cheltenham & Gloucester Building Society v Krausz* [1997] 1 WLR 1558 (CA), that if the sale would generate less than the entire sum owed, there is no jurisdiction to deny the lender *possession*: see n 66.

[49] *Downsview Nominees Ltd v First City Corporation Ltd* [1993] AC 295, 312 (PC).

[50] [1971] Ch 949, 966 (CA).

[51] [1932] AC 562, 580 (HL).

(where a mortgagor is injured by a mortgagee's bad decisions about sale) should belong to. The excepted cases seem (though the area is difficult) to involve, and turn upon, the presence of one of two significant characteristics. One characteristic is that the wrong in question is of a kind which might cause economic injury far and wide (whereas physical injury tends to be much more restricted in its occurrence): if there were liability for such a wrong, it would be disproportionate to the scale of the wrong, and/or not economically insurable.[52] The other is that, even if in the particular situation economic injury could befall only a limited class of victims, the wrongdoer's duty is discernibly to some of these only (whereas we have a duty to virtually all whom we might physically injure).[53] Our mortgage case displays neither of these characteristics. The class of potential victim is limited to mortgagors,[54] and there is no closer relationship with another type of victim to eclipse that between the mortgagor and mortgagee.

So one would have to explain the exception of our mortgage case on some third basis, possibly special to it. A candidate is a concern simply to minimise banks' exposure to risk, perhaps so as—by thus reducing their costs—to lower their interest rates, and thereby (at least under certain conditions) to boost the economy. There is evidence in other areas of land law for such a concern,[55] so it is no surprise to find a manifestation of it here too. But in no context can it be regarded as necessarily the dominant consideration, before which the rights of those injured must unquestionably be sacrificed. The present set of rules, whereby mortgagees are required to take care on the mortgagor's behalf in the conduct of the actual sale but not in their other decisions regarding sale, unsurprisingly reflects both views of the matter, but does so in the form of an unprincipled and therefore unsatisfactory compromise.

---

[52] This preoccupation can be seen in eg *Hedley Byrne & Co Ltd v Heller & Partners Ltd* [1964] AC 465, 483, 534, 536–7 (HL); *Spartan Steel and Alloys Ltd v Martin & Co Ltd* [1973] QB 27, 38–39 (CA).

[53] See *Murphy v Brentwood District Council* [1991] 1 AC 398 (HL); *Caparo Industries plc v Dickman* [1990] 2 AC 605 (HL) (though cf *White v Jones* [1995] 2 AC 207 (HL)). Constructing a special duty owed only to a subset of those potentially affected is also used as a way of allowing liability for economic loss without running into the first kind of difficulty: as in *Hedley Byrne & Co Ltd v Heller & Partners Ltd* [1964] AC 465 (HL) itself.

[54] It is true that a mortgagee's bad decisions regarding sale might impact on persons beyond the mortgagor: his dependants, say, or those for whom he held the property as trustee. Even where the bad decisions occur in the conduct of the actual sale, the law has declined to protect such further victims: *Parker-Tweedale v Dunbar Bank plc* [1991] Ch 12 (CA). The decision puts this rule on the basis that the mortgagor's duty arises not in negligence but in equity, and so is owed—like the duty to use his rights regarding sale in good faith—only to the mortgagor. But the same answer could be expected in negligence, on the second ground identified in the text.

[55] See especially § 14.8.2, offering a similar explanation for the way the law is profiled so that banks are not commonly affected by trust rights.

12.5.4 Foreclosure

As explained in § 12.1.1, saying that a creditor has a security right over an asset owned by a debtor means that the creditor can have resort to that asset so as to recoup the debt. Selling the asset is the main way of doing so, as this—turning the asset into money—enables fine-tuning of the outcome: as just noted, the creditor takes what is owed to him, but any surplus is returned to the debtor. The law does however maintain another way, known as 'foreclosure'.

If I secure my loan from you by a mortgage of my house, but default on my repayment obligations, and you foreclose, you simply become the owner of the house in my place. If the house is worth no more than I owe you, that is unproblematic, though of course you would do no better by sale. But in the more ordinary case where the house is worth more than I owe you, while sale would give you only what you are owed and the remainder to me, foreclosure gives you the remainder too; I lose what would otherwise be my share. This is of course attractive to you.

To understand the idea of foreclosure, remember what we saw in § 12.2.2. Long ago, a mortgage was effected by a freehold transfer with retransfer on payment of the debt, so that failure to pay precisely as stipulated meant losing the freehold; but equity blocked that outcome so long as the debtor was able to pay in a practical sense. Foreclosure is the lifting of this block when the court is persuaded that the debtor really cannot pay, leaving the freehold to be lost after all.

Foreclosure never was, however, properly conformable with the theory underlying this equitable intervention: that a mortgage arrangement shall give you no more than you need to obtain repayment of my debt. As well as meaning that you cannot keep my land if I am really able to pay, this ought to entail that, if I do indeed fail to pay, you can resort to my land (by a sale) only for the sum I owe you.[56]

Recognising foreclosure's unsatisfactoriness, the courts decided to allow it only with the rider that it can be 're-opened'—ie the lender ordered to return the property in question to the borrower—if at some later point the borrower unexpectedly manages to pay after all. And they made the borrower's right to re-open itself a right in rem, capable of binding someone to whom the lender went on to transfer the property. These measures, however, damaged the exploitability of foreclosed land. They therefore added further unsatisfactoriness, still without meeting the point explained in the previous paragraph, that

---

[56] Even if this objection is overlooked, foreclosure's place in the modern law is surprising for another, more technical, reason. Remember that nowadays, the mortgage arrangement gives you not the freehold in my land, but a lease over it: Law of Property Act 1925 ss 85, 87. So you would not naturally get to keep my freehold even if I did default. To preserve the possibility of foreclosure, the law has had to graft provision for it onto your rights as a lessee: *ibid* s 88(2).

[57] *Ibid* s 91(2).

foreclosure always was a mistake. More helpful is the modern rule that, if a lender seeks to foreclose, the court can order sale instead.[57] Except in the unlikely event of being confident that the sale price would equate to the outstanding debt, it would be amazing for the court to do otherwise. De facto, then, foreclosure is a dead letter. For the reasons explained, it deserves to be abolished altogether.

12.6 Possession

12.6.1 The Basic Rule

If you lend me money and secure my debt by taking a mortgage over my land, you will normally have no reason not to leave me in possession of the land. This is likely to alter, however, if I fail to repay you, and you wish—as your security right allows you—to resort to the land so as to recoup yourself. In particular, if you want to sell the land so as to pay off the outstanding debt, you will very probably want to take possession of it first, evicting me so as to have no problem about offering it for sale with vacant possession. In ordinary speech, such a proceeding is often referred to—not very accurately—as 'repossession'.[58]

But according to the standard account of the topic, your legal right to possession is much more extensive than this. The basic rule is that, simply as mortgagee of my land, you immediately gain the right to possess it (and exclude me), for any purpose you like.[59]

The basic rule has one qualification: a borrower can hold on to possession if he will imminently be repaying the whole outstanding debt.[60] But two or three months is the maximum time allowed under this qualification, and if the borrower proposes to repay by selling the land, the sale will need to be at an advanced stage before a court will view the proposal as sufficiently solid.

---

[58] For the practice, context and political significance of repossession (and thus, in a sense, of the phenomenon of acquisition via mortgage as a whole), see L Whitehouse, 'The Right to Possession: The Need for Substantive Reform' in P Jackson and D Wilde (eds), *The Reform of Property Law* (Aldershot, 1997) ch 9, and 'The Home-owner: Citizen or Consumer?' in S Bright and J Dewar (eds), *Land Law—Themes and Perspectives* (Oxford, 1998) ch 7.

[59] *Cholmondeley (Marquis) v Clinton (Lord)* (1817) 2 Mer 171, 359 (Ch); *Four-Maids Ltd v Dudley Marshall (Properties) Ltd* [1957] Ch 317, 320 (Ch D); *Birmingham Citizens Permanent Building Society v Caunt* [1962] Ch 883 (Ch D).

[60] *Birmingham Citizens Permanent Building Society v Caunt*, ibid 912; *Royal Trust Co of Canada v Markham* [1975] 1 WLR 1416, 1420 (CA).

So confined, the qualification is best regarded as an almost procedural matter, designed to prevent the pointless cost and upheaval of evicting the borrower and installing the lender only for a few weeks. Aside from this qualification, the thrust of the basic rule is that as soon as you have your mortgage over my house, you can decide that you would enjoy living in it, and evict me in order to do so.

It was originally natural that the lender should possess. As explained in § 12.2.1, in the late middle ages, when lending money for interest was prohibited as usury, the lender made a profit on the loan instead by taking the land and exploiting it, and took either a lease or the freehold in the land so as to make this possible. But when this functional need for possession fell away, mortgages nonetheless continued to be made by a freehold transfer of the land; later, a long lease of it; and today, a charge accompanied by the rights of such a lease. These forms, by their very nature, continue to entitle the lender to possess, and this seems to be the foundation of the basic rule that the lender has an essentially unqualified right to do so.

We should, however, expect this basic rule to be subject to the usual equitable intervention, designed to ensure that a mortgage arrangement gives the lender only a security right over the borrower's property, ie that his rights under the arrangement shall give him no more than he needs to obtain repayment of the borrower's debt. In these terms, there are only two reasons why a lender may need to possess the borrower's land. First, so as to maintain the land's value (eg by carrying out repairs on a house), so that it continues to secure the amount of the debt in question. (Say I borrow £200,000 from you, and grant you a mortgage over my house, which is then worth £250,000. If I neglect my house and its value falls to £150,000, it will no longer represent adequate security for my debt. So you should be able to come in and turn matters around.) And second, as a preliminary to extracting the value of the debt from it: that is, as a prelude to sale, in order to be able to sell with vacant possession.

In fact, the basic rule has two riders which partly—but only partly—align it with these principles. It has also been reformulated, wholly in accordance with these principles, by the Court of Appeal in *Quennell v Maltby*,[61] but many commentators refuse to accept the authority of this decision. The following two sections consider first the riders, then *Quennell v Maltby*.[62]

---

[61] [1979] 1 WLR 318 (CA).
[62] *Ibid.*

12.6.2 The Two Riders

The first rider is this. A modern lender can and will charge interest, so does not need possession in order to generate a return on his loan. If he nonetheless takes possession, he is not allowed to keep (he must 'account to the borrower for') the financial benefits of doing so. Instead, he must pay the borrower the profit he makes, or could make, from it (eg by renting the land out).[63] This rule does not, however, seek in any case actually to prohibit possession.

The second rider is established by the Administration of Justice Act 1970, section 36.[64] By this provision, the court should normally refuse possession if the borrower seems likely to be able to pay the debt over a period up to the planned term,[65] and the land's value is sufficient to secure the outstanding debt in the meantime.[66] (If the lender is denied possession under this rule, any further lapses by the borrower will probably result in immediate eviction.[67]) This rule is probably of little practical value to borrowers, for a lender will normally go to the trouble of seeking possession only if it has already become clear that the borrower's problems cannot be solved by rescheduling. But the rule is of some doctrinal importance: it seems to proceed on the theory that a lender can possess only if he needs to, in order to obtain repayment of his loan. It is prevented from giving full effect to that theory, however, by the statutory terms in which it is put.[68] It is confined to

---

[63] See *Robertson v Norris* (1859) 1 Giff 428 (Ch); *White v City of London Brewery Co* (1889) 42 Ch D 237 (CA). Nowadays, lenders normally take possession only as a prelude to sale, and keep it for such a short time that this liability is only theoretical.

[64] For discussion, see N Bamforth, 'Lord Macnaghten's Puzzle: The Mortgage of Real Property in English Law' [1996] *CLP* pt II 207, 231–43. An earlier judicial experiment on similar lines had ended in *Birmingham Citizens Permanent Building Society v Caunt* [1962] Ch 883 (Ch D), reaffirming the idea that a lender's right to possession is unqualified save in the respects already discussed.

[65] *Cheltenham & Gloucester Building Society v Norgan* [1996] 1 WLR 343 (CA); see also *Bristol & West Building Society v Ellis* (1997) 73 P & CR 158 (CA). The borrower's liabilities are not simply suspended for the planned term, in the hope that something may turn up. To refuse possession, the court must be satisfied that the *whole* debt is *likely to be paid* in this time. (Mortgage arrangements often stipulate that if the borrower defaults, the whole debt becomes repayable immediately, but the Administration of Justice Act 1973 s 8 instructs courts to disregard such stipulations in assessing the likelihood of repayment.)

[66] *Cheltenham & Gloucester Building Society v Krausz* [1997] 1 WLR 1558 (CA). So a lender is not denied possession where the borrower has a scheme (however sensible) to sell the mortgaged land and, from the proceeds, repay only part of the debt, leaving the remainder unsecured.

[67] *Cheltenham & Gloucester Building Society v Norgan* [1996] 1 WLR 343, 354 (CA).

[68] In addition to the features noted in the text, the rule's drafting has spawned a number of other problems, particularly regarding its applicability to different kinds of mortgages (see *Centrax Trustee Ltd v Ross* [1979] 2 All ER 952 (Ch D); *Habib Bank Ltd v Tailor* [1982] 1 WLR 1218 (CA); *Bank of Scotland v Grimes* [1985] QB 1179 (CA)), and to cases where the lender seeks possession otherwise than after default by the borrower (*Western Bank Ltd v Schindler* [1977] Ch 1 (CA)).

mortgages of a 'dwelling-house', ie a domestic residence.[69] And it applies only where the lender *sues* for possession, not where he enters in the borrower's absence, then prevents the borrower from returning; or sells, leaving the purchaser to take possession.[70] In terms of aligning the lender's right to possession with the principle that mortgage rights should be usable only to obtain payment of the debt, these are arbitrary limitations.

With these two riders, then, the law regarding the lender's ability to possess moves closer to the position we should expect, but not so far as to be in exact conformity with it.[71]

12.6.3 *Quennell v Maltby*

One judicial statement has been made, however, which would deliver such exact conformity. It consists in the decision of the Court of Appeal in *Quennell v Maltby*.[72] A lender wished to take possession of the mortgaged land for reasons unconnected with obtaining repayment of the debt. The court refused to allow her to do so, referring to the equitable principle and on that basis asserting that possession can be had only where it is sought for that purpose, and is reasonably calculated to deliver it.[73]

But this decision is rather isolated, and its rejection of the basic rule, and the latter's essentially unqualified right to possess, has been generally disparaged by commentators. This is odd: given the argument above, the

---

[69] Such a requirement is more intelligible as shaping a rule requiring the involvement in possession proceedings of certain other members of the borrower's family or former family, so that they can have the opportunity to escape eviction by taking the debt over: Family Law Act 1996 ss 30(3), 36(13), 55–56.

[70] *Ropaigealach v Barclays Bank plc* [2000] QB 263 (CA); *Horsham Properties Group Ltd v Clark* [2008] EWHC 2327 (Ch D).

[71] In addition to the two riders, in October 2008—in the context of the economic crisis then prevailing—the Civil Justice Council introduced a new Pre-Action Protocol, 'Pre-Action Protocol for Possession Claims based on Mortgage or Home Purchase Plan Arrears in Respect of Residential Property' (see http://www.justice.gov.uk/civil/procrules_fin/contents/protocols/prot_mha.htm). The Protocol declares that courts will normally expect lenders to have considered rescheduling before moving to repossess; but this was probably the position already. Complementing the Protocol, in December 2008 the Government announced a Homeowners Support Mortgage Scheme, whereby borrowers experiencing a significant and temporary loss of income as a result of the crisis could defer a proportion of the interest payments on their mortgage for up to two years, the deferred interests payments being guaranteed by the Government (see http://www.hm-treasury.gov.uk/press_132_08.htm).

[72] [1979] 1 WLR 318 (CA); followed, with further reference to the general equitable principle, in *Albany Home Loans Ltd v Massey* [1997] 2 All ER 609, 612–13 (CA).

[73] Lord Denning MR put it, at 322: 'A mortgagee will be restrained from getting possession except where it is sought bona fide and reasonably for the purpose of enforcing the security and then only subject to such conditions as the court thinks fit to impose.' The reference to conditions is a little speculative, but sound in principle as allowing the court to ensure that a mortgagee, having been granted a possession order, can use it only for the approved purpose. Templeman LJ put the same idea, at 324: 'The estate, rights and powers of a mortgagee ... are only vested in a mortgagee to protect his position as a mortgagee and to enable him to obtain repayment. Subject to this, the property belongs in equity to the mortgagor.'

decision seems undeniably correct, and the resilience of the basic rule is unexpected.[74] How are we to explain this resilience? Perhaps as tending, when lenders do seek properly to enforce their security rights, to remove obstacles from their path. It is not as if they will in practice commonly (ever?) want possession for any other reason: so maybe the idea is to regard that as sufficient reassurance, in the interests of allowing them to claim possession when they wish to do so without having to justify themselves in court.

If this is the explanation, however, it is not good enough. If the mortgage is of the borrower's home, Article 8 of the European Convention on Human Rights requires that home to be respected except to the extent necessary for the securing of certain other interests; and in all cases, Article 1 of the First Protocol to the Convention protects the peaceful enjoyment of a person's possessions except to the extent necessary for the securing of certain other interests. The lender's interest in recouping the loan undoubtedly qualifies as one of the other interests that these provisions recognise as capable of outweighing those protected. But for the lender to take possession of the mortgaged land for any other purpose—as the law permits, if one rejects *Quennell v Maltby*[75]—cannot be necessary for the securing of that interest, and so is unacceptable.[76]

12.6.4 Connecting Possession and Sale

To revert to an observation made in § 12.5.2: the law's rules about possession do not mesh with its rules about sale. This is problematic, given the intimate linkage between possession and sale, the former normally being of interest only as a prelude to the latter, and the two being combined in the idea of 'repossession'.

As explained in § 12.6.2, the provision in section 36 of the Administration of Justice Act 1970 partially tracks the idea that rights conferred by mortgage arrangements can be used only so as to recoup the debt. Even if the lender seeks possession with this motive, he can have it (where the land in question is a 'dwelling-house') only if the law regards it as necessary that he

---

[74] Even, it seems, within the industry. The Financial Services Authority's *Mortgages: Conduct of Business* rules require lenders to 'deal fairly with' customers in arrears, and treat it as an aspect of this that repossession should be used only as a last resort: see http://fsahandbook.info/FSA/html/handbook/, section 13.3.2.

[75] [1979] 1 WLR 318 (CA).

[76] In *Wood v UK* (1997) 24 EHHR CD 69 (ECommHR), the European Commission on Human Rights decided that taking possession did not infringe the Convention if it followed upon a failure to make repayments. Likewise, in *Horsham Properties Group Ltd v Clark* [2008] EWHC 2327 (Ch D), it was held that taking possession did not infringe the Convention if it was in aid of a legitimate right to sell. These decisions are, however, about the *unproblematic* use of possession.

should, and it does not take this view if the borrower seems likely to be able to repay over the mortgage period.

This construction of what is necessary for the recoupment of the debt is noticeably different from—narrower, more favourable to the borrower, than—the construction implicit in the rules indicating when the lender can *sell*. As explained in § 12.5.2, the latter treat sale as warranted as soon as the borrower is in 'confirmed default', regardless of the possibility of obtaining repayment after all, by rescheduling. The law thus declares that the lender can sell more often than he can claim possession in order to do so: an absurd position. The rules about sale and possession need to be aligned. And the alignment should be on the lines of the possession rule. This rule's construction of what is necessary for the recoupment of the debt is explicitly designed to reflect the view that banks and building societies take of their own needs.[77] Nothing wider can be justified.

In one context, the two constructions diverge in a different way. Where a borrower defaults on his repayments but there is negative equity, ie the house's value is below that of the outstanding debt, the borrower may want a quick sale (so as to reduce the amount of the debt on which interest liabilities would continue to accrue), while the lender may prefer to delay (in the hope that land values may rise, thus improving the chances of a sale eventually recouping the whole debt). On this sale issue alone, authority is in favour of the borrower, on the ground that the lender's approach shows insufficient care for the borrower's interest.[78] But given the negative equity, the present rules leave the lender entitled to possession,[79] effectively preventing the borrower from selling after all.[80] Evidently, again, embedded in these positions are two different constructions of what is 'necessary for the recoupment of the debt', one (that taken over possession) allowing the lender to transfer the effects of negative equity as far as possible to the borrower, the other (that taken over sale) requiring them to be shared. An argument could be made for both views, but the Financial Services Authority's *Mortgages: Conduct of Business* rules[81] favour the latter, requiring lenders to consider allowing the borrower to remain in possession and conduct his own sale. Once again, this position should therefore be adopted as regards both possession and sale.

---

[77] *Cheltenham & Gloucester Building Society v Norgan* [1996] 1 WLR 343, 353, 356–7 (CA), referring to the statement of the Council of Mortgage Lenders regarding the handling of borrowers who fall into arrears with their repayments.

[78] *Palk v Mortgage Services Funding plc* [1993] Ch 330 (CA): see at nn 46–48.

[79] *Cheltenham & Gloucester Building Society v Krausz* [1997] 1 WLR 1558 (CA): see n 66. For discussion, see M Dixon, 'Combating the Mortgagee's Right to Possession: New Hope for the Mortgagor in Chains?' (1998) 18 *LS* 279.

[80] Though it should not prevent the court from ordering sale, under the Law of Property Act 1925 s 91(2). This was the relief given in *Palk v Mortgage Services Funding plc* [1993] Ch 330 (CA).

[81] Section 13.3.2(1)(e): see http://fsahandbook.info/FSA/html/handbook/.

12.7 Collateral Advantages

In our review of the different rights comprising a land mortgage, we have so far looked at those rights that are automatically present: the lender's debt against the borrower, and his rights to sell or foreclose, and to possess. Now, finally, we look at the possibility that the parties may agree to give the lender other rights in addition. Such additional rights are known as 'collateral advantages'.

12.7.1 Collateral Advantages and their Evolving Treatment

Say I own a petrol station. To raise finance to modernise it, I make a deal with your oil company that you will lend me the money I need, my debt being secured by a mortgage over the land in question, in return for interest ... and additionally a stipulation—a 'solus tie'—that I buy all my petrol from you.[82] This solus tie would be a collateral advantage. The law of mortgages may disallow it.[83]

§ 12.2.2 explained how, if a mortgage arrangement purports to give the lender more than security—say, if it allows him to keep the mortgaged asset on a technicality, when the borrower is in substance able to pay—the additional rights will be unenforceable. From the late 17th to the turn of the 20th century, this position was taken with full rigour (give or take the aberrant rule about possession). A collateral advantage is an additional right: so it was struck down.[84]

But since the turn of the 20th century, collateral advantages have sometimes been upheld after all.[85] There has been no overt abandonment of

[82] Likewise if you, a brewery, lend me money to buy a pub, requiring me to buy all my beer from you (creating a 'tied house', as opposed to the 'free house' that it would be if I had no such obligation to a beer company); or if you, a bank, lend me money to buy my house, requiring me to buy other financial products, eg insurance, from you. Likewise too a converse arrangement, say where you, a cheese manufacturer, lend me money to buy a farm, requiring me to *sell* you all the milk I produce.

[83] As well as being disallowed under the law of mortgages as discussed here, some forms of collateral advantage—especially solus ties—may also run into problems with competition law.

[84] *Jennings v Ward* (1705) 2 Vern 520 (Rolls). Likewise certain decisions dating from a time when this straightforward approach had begun to be challenged: *Noakes & Co Ltd v Rice* [1902] AC 24 (HL); *Bradley v Carritt* [1903] AC 253 (HL).

[85] For early indications of the shift, see especially *Santley v Wilde* [1899] 2 Ch 474 (CA); Lord Lindley's dissent in *Bradley v Carritt* [1903] AC 253 (HL); and the expressions of dissatisfaction with the old position in *Samuel v Jarrah Timber and Wood Paving Corporation Ltd* [1904] AC 323 (HL). The shift was put beyond doubt in *Kreglinger v New Patagonia Meat and Cold Storage Co Ltd* [1914] AC 25 (HL).

the idea that a mortgage must give no more than security, but the courts have sometimes recognised collateral advantages as valid despite this seeming to have just that effect.[86] The (alleged) justifications for the shift cluster into essentially two approaches.

12.7.2 The First Approach

The first approach involves saying that the law of mortgages is applicable, but that, after all, the particular collateral advantage in question contravenes none of its principles.

The principle against which this approach measures collateral advantages is the principle (§ 12.2.2) requiring that the security must always be redeemable: ie that the lender's security interest (right to resort to the mortgaged asset) must come to an end when the borrower repays the debt.

It has accordingly been held that a collateral advantage is valid if it is expressed to end not later than the date when the loan is repaid.[87] Ending then, it cannot prevent redemption. It has also been held that a collateral advantage, even if expressed to extend beyond redemption, is valid if the security interest can nonetheless lift from the land. A distinction is necessary. Some collateral advantages do prevent the security interest from being lifted. Say, with your mortgage, I give you an option over my land (ie a right to demand that I sell the land to you on your demand). Continuing beyond redemption, such an option effectively extends your right of resort to my land: by exercising the option, you can still take the land, even though I have paid off the debt.[88] The option must therefore be invalid.[89] Other collateral advantages, however, do not prevent the lifting of the security interest from the land in this way. This is especially the case if, with your mortgage, I give you a solus tie. Your rights under this tie are not rights to resort to my land, ie to take it or sell it as your own. So even when the tie continues after my repayment of the loan, it does not

---

[86] For further discussion, see N Bamforth, 'Lord Macnaghten's Puzzle: The Mortgage of Real Property in English Law' [1996] *CLP* pt II 207, 213–31; G Watt, 'The Lie of the Land: Mortgage Law as Legal Fiction' in E Cooke (ed), *Modern Studies in Property Law, Volume 4* (Oxford, 2007) ch 4.

[87] *Biggs v Hoddinott* [1898] 2 Ch 307 (CA).

[88] Or at any rate, it does so if the price that the option requires you to pay for the land is below the market value. If it is the market value, the option certainly extends your right of resort to my land in the sense that you can insist on having it (even after repayment) despite my opposition. But in another sense, it falls short of doing so: resort despite repayment is objectionable because it gives you wealth to which you have no proper claim, and if you must pay the market value this is not the case.

[89] *Samuel v Jarrah Timber and Wood Paving Corporation Ltd* [1904] AC 323, 328–9 (HL); *Kreglinger v New Patagonia Meat and Cold Storage Co Ltd* [1914] AC 25, 50–51 (HL); *Lewis v Frank Love Ltd* [1961] 1 WLR 261 (Ch D).

prevent your right of resort from ending upon my repayment. The tie is therefore valid.[90]

In its own terms, this approach makes sense. But it has a weakness. The principle that it uses as its benchmark—the demand that the security must always be redeemable—while certainly not simply erroneous, is put too narrowly. When we discussed it in § 12.2.2, we depicted it in terms of a broader idea, that a mortgage must give only security rights. The existence of this broader idea is shown by the rule that a lender's sale powers cannot be used for other purposes than to recoup the debt,[91] and generates the argument that a lender's right to possession of the mortgaged land is similarly confined.[92] In the present context, it should entail that collateral advantages are unacceptable not merely when they impede redemption, but for the very fact that they—necessarily—mean the lender getting more from the mortgage than security alone. As noted in § 12.7.1, this was the view that was originally taken of them.

12.7.3 The Second Approach

The second approach to allowing collateral advantages involves saying that, in appropriate circumstances, the parties' deal for the collateral advantage does not form part of the mortgage transaction at all: so no matter what the law of mortgages has to say about collateral advantages within mortgage transactions, this particular collateral advantage is unaffected.

This approach is obviously sound in the abstract. If I grant you a solus tie over my petrol station (say, in return for certain pricing guarantees), then a decade later also borrow from you and secure my debt by a mortgage of my petrol station, the solus tie is plainly unconnected with the mortgage and will not be invalidated for inconsistency with the law of mortgages. What requires attention is the courts' use of this approach when the lack of connection between the collateral advantage and the mortgage is much less clear.

Some decisions indicate that a collateral advantage is unconnected with our mortgage, and so (in terms of mortgage law) good, if we establish it on a different day from the mortgage itself, however close the two days may be; or perhaps even if we establish both on the same day but in separate

---

[90] *Kreglinger v New Patagonia Meat and Cold Storage Co Ltd* [1914] AC 25 (HL). (So Lord Haldane LC's inquiries, at 39 and 41, as to whether the collateral advantage is 'outside and clear' of the mortgage, or 'outside the security ... independent of it', are aimed precisely at this question of whether the collateral advantage connects with the lender's right to resort to the borrower's asset.) For earlier statements of this approach, by Lord Lindley, see *Santley v Wilde* [1899] 2 Ch 474, 474–5 (CA); *Bradley v Carritt* [1903] AC 253, 276 (HL).

[91] § 12.5.3.

[92] § 12.6.3.

documents.[93] This deployment of the approach is wholly technical; it uses distinctions of no substantive merit.[94]

Other decisions assert that a transaction may place me under a debt to you, and give you a right of resort to my land for the recoupment of that debt, *and yet not be (or count for this purpose as) a mortgage* ... so that the mortgage rules do not apply, and a collateral advantage also conferred by the transaction will therefore be untroubled by those rules.[95] These decisions treat the classification of such a transaction, as a mortgage or not, as a matter for the parties' intentions. And they seem to regard the parties' intentions in this respect as indicated by the 'emphasis' of the transaction: if it centres on the loan, it will be a mortgage; while if it centres on the collateral advantage, it will not. (So on this approach, even an option in the lender's favour over the borrower's land will not necessarily be invalid.[96]) These decisions seem quite unstable. They in effect invite parties to opt into or out of the law of mortgages; and, in the idea of 'emphasis', use a highly subjective tool to discern the choice made.

12.7.4 The Key

The first approach thus accepts the applicability of mortgage principles, but takes too narrow a view of them. The second denies the applicability of mortgage principles, on unsatisfactory grounds. Both approaches are therefore unconvincing.

The root of the problem is the tension that exists between the proposition that a mortgage cannot give the lender more than a security right, and the idea of freedom of contract, whereby parties should be able to make whatever agreements they like. The judges themselves have noted this tension, and, unsurprisingly, have criticised the rule against collateral advantages for its inconsistency with freedom of contract.[97]

To address the problem, we need to regard freedom of contract as given (it is a very general idea, and rests on a liberal moral and political foundation which we find compelling). We need to regard it as likewise given that there should be, and are, exceptions to it (because its liberal foundation is either

---

[93] *Reeve v Lisle* [1902] AC 461 (HL); *Samuel v Jarrah Timber and Wood Paving Corporation Ltd* [1904] AC 323, 325 (HL).

[94] So in *Lewis v Frank Love Ltd* [1961] 1 WLR 261 (Ch D) an argument on these lines was rejected, and a collateral advantage held invalid despite separation in this way.

[95] *Kreglinger v New Patagonia Meat and Cold Storage Co Ltd* [1914] AC 25, 52–54 (HL); *Jones v Morgan* [2001] EWCA Civ 995, [55] (CA); *Warnborough Ltd v Garmite Ltd* [2003] EWCA Civ 1544, [69] (CA).

[96] *Warnborough Ltd v Garmite Ltd, ibid* [73].

[97] See especially *Samuel v Jarrah Timber and Wood Paving Corporation Ltd* [1904] AC 323, 325, 327 (HL); *Kreglinger v New Patagonia Meat and Cold Storage Co Ltd* [1914] AC 25, 46–47 (HL). The rule is disparaged also, on less precise grounds, in *Jones v Morgan* [2001] EWCA Civ 995, [86] (CA).

falsified or outgunned). We need to focus on the case for treating collateral advantages in mortgage transactions as one of these exceptions. Historically, two arguments for doing so have been advanced.

One lies in the old rules against usury, ie lending money in return for interest (later, excessive interest). A lender wanting to evade those rules might stipulate for a return in a different form—a collateral advantage—only for the courts, wishing to enforce the spirit of the rules, to declare this invalid.[98] This argument was certainly sustainable when the usury rules were in force, but their abolition by the Usury Laws Repeal Act 1854 has left it untenable since that time.

The other argument takes the line that if a borrower is vulnerable, a bargain for more than pure security will amount to an exploitation of that vulnerability, and so merits suppression as involving unconscionability on the part of the lender;[99] and continues that borrowers are so nearly always vulnerable that it is hardly worthwhile inquiring into the facts of the individual case: unconscionability can be presumed.[100] Freedom of contract should certainly yield in the face of the exploitation of vulnerability. But the argument's perception of borrowers as always vulnerable, so that lenders bargaining for more than security necessarily act unconscionably, is problematic. Perhaps when this position was originally taken, in the 17th century, it was backed by sound empirical observation, and/or a proportionate use of presumption in the prevailing forensic context. (An alternative hypothesis might be that, even then, it sprang from a prejudiced view of lenders.) Today, however, mortgage lenders operate in an environment that is both competitive and regulated,[101] and while most borrowers probably do remain at a disadvantage, factors such as the availability of independent advice limit its extent, and the possibilities for its exploitation. Where exploitation does occur, it can be dealt with ad hoc. This argument for generically suppressing collateral advantages is therefore untenable too.

There seems to be no other argument. It follows that the law should allow mortgage arrangements to contain stipulations for collateral advantages after all. The courts' decisions narrowing the scope of the rule against collateral advantages are steps towards this position, but, as we have seen, they leave the law unstable: stability will come only with the position's explicit adoption. It will, however, remain correct to argue that mortgages should

---

[98] The illegality of collateral advantages is explained in this way in *Kreglinger v New Patagonia Meat and Cold Storage Co Ltd* [1914] AC 25, 54–55, 58 (HL), citing *Chambers v Goldwin* (1802, 1803, 1804) 9 Ves Jun 254, 271 (Ch).

[99] For unconscionability, see § 12.8.1.

[100] This explanation for the illegality of collateral advantages is given in *Samuel v Jarrah Timber and Wood Paving Corporation Ltd* [1904] AC 323, 326 (HL), citing *Vernon v Bethell* (1761) 2 Eden 110, 113 (Ch).

[101] See especially the Financial Services Authority's *Mortgages: Conduct of Business* rules: http://fsahandbook.info/FSA/html/handbook/.

take the *form* of pure security rights, rather than of leases or whatever (§ 12.1.4). But the parties should be able to add *substantively* to them as they please. So if they wish (say) to give the lender, under certain circumstances, the right simply to take the mortgaged land, despite its value exceeding that of the outstanding debt; or the right to possess the land even when there is no need to do so in security terms; so—in principle[102]—be it.

12.8 The Creation of Mortgages

Mortgages are in practice always created by intentional conferral. In the case of registered land, such a conferral must (as we would expect: § 4.4) be effected by deed,[103] and completed by registration.[104]

It is however unnecessary for a mortgage to announce itself as such. If I grant you an interest in my land de facto as security for an obligation I owe you, the law recognises it as a mortgage. And if I give it features inconsistent with the law's idea of a mortgage, the law adjusts it so as to fit the perception of a mortgage as a security right. For example, there will be an insistence on redeemability. There will also be an insistence on the required legal form, as explained in § 12.1.4. So if I purport to secure my debt to you by transferring my freehold to you, as was possible in the past, the transaction will be translated (if the land is registered) into one creating a charge.[105]

---

[102] Arguably the parties' ability to agree on such things should be curtailed (in particular) where the land is a family home, as there is a paramount social interest in safeguarding homes.

[103] Law of Property Act 1925 s 52(1).

[104] Land Registration Act 2002 s 27(2)(f). This, however, goes only for legal mortgages, on which this chapter has focused. A mortgage may also be created in equity, either deliberately or as a fall-back from failure to use the formalities required for a legal mortgage (as explained in § 5.2.4). An equitable mortgage requires writing (Law of Property Act 1925 s 53(1)(a); Law of Property (Miscellaneous Provisions) Act 1989 s 2). Equitable mortgages do, however, also behave differently in certain respects, especially as regards the lender's right to sell.

[105] At one time, the law explicitly provided for such translation: Law of Property Act 1925 s 85(2), ruling that a mortgage purportedly by freehold transfer should take effect instead by a 3,000 year lease, that being the then prevailing form. There seems to be no corresponding provision translating a freehold transfer into the now prevailing form of a charge (Land Registration Act 2002 s 23(1)(a)), but it is assumed that the translation will occur nonetheless. There is a difficulty at a formal level, however. The register will necessarily show the freehold transfer, and not the charge. Presumably it will have to be altered so as to reflect the true substantive position.

12.8.1 Vitiation

The mortgage may of course be invalid for any of the usual reasons: if the transaction creating it occurred under duress, undue influence, misrepresentation ... or unconscionability.[106] Unconscionability requires special mention, as its profile for mortgages may differ from that for other kinds of contract. In the abstract, a stipulation is unconscionable if the promisee procured it 'in a morally reprehensible manner, that is to say, in a way which affects his conscience'.[107] As regards contracts generally, this is seen as occurring only where one party exploits some especial weakness from which the other suffers;[108] the straightforward exploitation of superior bargaining power is not enough.[109] In the mortgage context, however, it seems that the straightforward exploitation of superior bargaining power may be enough.[110] There is no warrant for this difference (perhaps it is a throwback to the idea that borrowers are conclusively presumed to be in desperate straits?), and the rules should be assimilated.

These vitiating factors may arise in their usual manner between the mortgagee and mortgagor. But they may also arise between a third person and the mortgagor, and affect the mortgage where the mortgagee has notice of them.[111] The context of mortgages is one of the principal areas in which this latter possibility is relevant. Say I own a house, and mortgage it to you, so as to secure a loan ... not, as in the usual case, from you to me, but from you to John, who is my husband. Commonly, John will have sought the loan in order to raise funds for his business. You will have demanded that his debt be secured on land. The land to which John has access is our house. But he and I own it in our joint names,[112] so John cannot mortgage it to you without

---

[106] *Knightsbridge Estates Trust Ltd v Byrne* [1939] Ch 441, 457 (CA); *Multiservice Bookbinding Ltd v Marden* [1979] Ch 84 (Ch D).

[107] *Multiservice Bookbinding, ibid* 110.

[108] *Fry v Lane* (1888) 40 Ch D 312 (Ch D); *Cresswell v Potter* [1978] 1 WLR 255n (Ch D); *Alec Lobb (Garages) Ltd v Total Oil (Great Britain) Ltd* [1983] 1 WLR 87, 94-5 (Ch D); *Boustany v Piggott* (1995) 69 P & CR 298, 303 (PC).

[109] *National Westminster Bank plc v Morgan* [1985] AC 686, 708 (HL) (denying the contrary view expressed in *Lloyds Bank Ltd v Bundy* [1975] QB 326, 336 (CA)).

[110] So, in the mortgage decision *Multiservice Bookbinding Ltd v Marden* [1979] Ch 84 (Ch D), the judge declares (at 110) that unconscionability is not limited to situations of especial weakness, and that 'the court can and should intervene where a bargain has been procured by unfair means'; before going on (at 111) to assess this in terms of the parties' relative bargaining strengths.

[111] *Barclays Bank plc v O'Brien* [1994] 1 AC 180 (HL); *Royal Bank of Scotland plc v Etridge (No 2)* [2002] 2 AC 773 (HL). For a fuller account, see eg M Chen-Wishart, *Contract Law* (2nd edn, Oxford, 2008) 361–6. For discussion, see M Thompson, 'Mortgages and Undue Influence' in E Cooke (ed), *Modern Studies in Property Law, Volume 2* (Oxford, 2003) ch 7.

[112] The same issues arise if the house is solely in my name, as in *Castle Phillips Finance v Piddington* [1995] 1 FLR 783 (CA). Alternatively, the house may be registered in John's name alone, but he holds it on trust for himself and me, so that he may be able to give you a mortgage taking precedence over my beneficial right only if he obtains my consent. The same issues again arise with regard to his doing so: *Scottish Equitable Life plc v Virdee* [1999] 1 FLR 863 (CA): see §§ 3.2.3–3.2.4, where the idea of 'notice' for these purposes is discussed more fully.

my participation. In securing my participation, he tells me lies about what is afoot. So there is misrepresentation between him and me, but this does not directly affect the validity of the mortgage as between me and you. It does so, however, if you have notice of it. This will be the case if you should realise the risk of John not behaving properly (generally from the nature of the deal and the relationship between John and me), but fail to insist that I obtain independent legal advice.

12.9 Mortgages' Effectiveness against Disponees

As explained in § 12.1.2, although a mortgage is a right in rem, we do not expect it in practice to bind a transferee of the land in question. Instead, we expect it to be redeemed using the purchase money, so that the transferee takes the land free from it. Its status as a right in rem is more significant as giving it priority in the borrower's bankruptcy. It does, however, also mean that the mortgage takes precedence over a disposition of the land short of a transfer.

Say, for example, I buy a house with a loan from you, mortgaging the house to you so as to secure my debt. Some time later, but before I have redeemed, I agree with John that he shall have a share in the house. I thenceforth hold the house on trust for John and myself.[113] But John's beneficial interest will be in the house *subject to the mortgage*. If you have occasion to repossess, John will not be able to prevent you doing so by pointing to his interest; and if you sell, John will have no claim against you to a share of the proceeds (though he will have a claim against me, to a share of the balance that you pay me after deducting what is due to you).[114]

As a right in rem, a mortgage is capable of binding a disponee in this way. For it actually to do so, the rules on this subject in the Land Registration Act 2002 must be observed. As explained in § 12.8, a mortgage has to be registered in order to exist at all.[115] This registration serves to make it bind,[116] but

---

[113] § 8.3.
[114] Contrast the situation where John's beneficial interest arises *before* I grant you the mortgage. In principle, John's interest then takes precedence over the mortgage. But the law maintains a number of rules which, in practice, produce the opposite effect. See § 14.8.
[115] Land Registration Act 2002 s 27(2)(f).
[116] *Ibid* s 29(2)(a)(i).

the requirement for it means that the mortgage cannot operate as an overriding interest.[117] This is as one would expect: mortgages are quintessentially rights created only in an organised way.

[117] Except that, if not completed by registration under the Land Registration Act 2002 s 27(2)(f), it can still take effect as an equitable mortgage (assuming that writing has been used: Law of Property (Miscellaneous Provisions) Act 1989 s 2), and as such could operate as an overriding interest ... though only in the unlikely event that you, the mortgagee, are in actual and apparent occupation of the land, so as to bring the case within the Land Registration Act 2002 Sch 3 para 2. This possibility will vanish with electronic registration: § 4.4.5.

Trust Rights 1

Our next right in rem is a beneficial interest under a trust. The topic is large and difficult, so our consideration of it will be divided between two chapters, this and Chapter 14.

13.1 The Basic Concepts

Trusts involve deep and complex ideas, many of which this book will not attempt to explore. But broadly speaking, a trust is 'a situation in which property is vested in someone (a trustee), who is under legally recognised obligations, at least some of which are of a proprietary kind [ie in rem], to handle it in a certain way, and to the exclusion of any personal interest. These obligations may arise either by conscious creation by the previous owner of the property (the settlor), or because some other legally significant circumstances are present.'[1] Commonly,[2] the trustee owes his obligations to another person, a 'beneficiary',[3] who thus has rights to their performance. These rights comprise the beneficiary's 'beneficial interest'. Commonly, too, the property vested in the trustee is a legal estate:[4] in the case of land, usually

---

[1] S Gardner, *An Introduction to the Law of Trusts* (2nd edn, Oxford, 2003) 2.

[2] Though not necessarily. Some trusts involve only obligations, not rights, which is why the description given focuses on obligations alone. See Gardner, *ibid* ch 14.

[3] Sometimes called by the old Law French name, '*cestui que trust*' (pronounced 'settee key trust').

[4] The alternative is that the property vested in the trustee, and held on trust for the beneficiaries, is itself an equitable interest. In broad terms, this makes no difference. But it could entail differences of detail regarding such things as formality, and, depending on their precise wording, the applicability of particular statutory provisions.

the freehold ownership, sometimes a lease, or some other legal interest such as a mortgage. Especially where it is the freehold ownership, the trustee is often therefore referred to as the 'legal owner', while the beneficiaries' rights under the trust are necessarily (because the trust concept was developed in the equity jurisdiction) equitable.

So, I might transfer a farm to you, on the basis that you will hold it on trust for John. This creates a trust, of which John is the beneficiary, you are the trustee, and I am the settlor. You are required to use the farm for John's benefit. Your doing so might take the form of renting it out to a tenant farmer and paying over the incoming rent to John (though it might take some other form instead). John has rights that you shall do so, which collectively add up to his beneficial interest. In this case, the trust arises because I create it. A trust arising in this way is called an 'express' trust.

Alternatively, I might own a house, but agree with you that we will share it equally. The upshot is that a trust arises against me in your favour, requiring me to treat the house as 50 per cent mine, 50 per cent yours.[5] I am the trustee, and, with our 50 per cent interests, you and I are the beneficiaries. This trust arises not because I (unilaterally) create it, but because our agreement amounts to a 'legally significant circumstance' leading the law to impose it. A trust arising on the basis of some 'legally significant circumstance' other than a settlor's wish in this way is usually, as in this example, a 'constructive' trust; sometimes, a 'resulting' trust.[6]

13.2 Where a Trust Has More than One Beneficiary

13.2.1 Concurrent and Consecutive Interests

Sometimes, a trust will have only one beneficiary: such as John, in the first example given above. Often, though, it will have two or more: such as you and me, in the second example. If it has two or more, their interests can either be concurrent (simultaneous) or successive (consecutive). In the second example above, you and I have concurrent interests: we are both entitled immediately and indefinitely, but alongside one another. An instance of

[5] See § 8.3.
[6] See S Gardner, *An Introduction to the Law of Trusts* (2nd edn, Oxford, 2003) 127–37 for the cases in which the trust is labelled 'resulting', and discussion of the (not universally accepted) view that such trusts arise, like constructive trusts, for reasons other than that a settlor intends them to.

consecutive interests would occur if, say, I transfer land to you on trust for John for his life, and thereafter for Kate.

There can be any number of successive interests, and any kind of event (so long as its occurrence will be sufficiently clear) can act as the boundary between one and another. A common arrangement is that already instanced, 'for John for his life, then for Kate', but I could make a trust 'for John until he dies, or is married, or reaches the age of 21, or becomes a student, or goes to live abroad, or is made bankrupt,' etc, 'then for Kate'; and I could limit Kate's interest in similar ways, providing that after her shall come Liam; and so on. The law's principal restriction on the creation of consecutive interests is a set of rules, collectively known as 'the rule against perpetuities', whereby (above all) I can stipulate for new beneficial interests to come into existence in this way only for a certain distance into the future. These rules are complicated, and a detailed treatment of them will not be attempted here.[7]

So far as concurrent interests are concerned, there can once again be any number, as where I make a trust of land 'for John, Kate, Liam, Meg,' and so on down the alphabet. But such interests can take two forms, and it must be decided which of these forms a given interest takes. Concurrent beneficiaries may either have a *shared single interest* in the particular piece of property, or a *set of separate interests* in it. (But not a set of interests in separate pieces of property, as say if I transferred house *A* to you on trust for John, and house *B* on trust for Kate. Then, John and Kate would not have beneficial rights in the same property at all.) Where concurrent beneficiaries have a shared single interest, they are called 'joint tenants'. Where they have separate interests, they are called 'tenants in common'.[8] Tenants in common are sometimes said to have 'undivided shares': this is another way of saying that they have separate interests ('shares'), but in the same property ('undivided').[9]

13.2.2 Joint Tenancies and Tenancies in Common

The principal difference between the two kinds of concurrent interest relates to the situation when one of the beneficiaries dies. Say I give you a house to hold on trust for John and Kate, then John dies. If John and Kate were *tenants in common*, John had a separate interest, which now devolves in the usual way, in accordance with his will or, if he has not left a will, under the intestacy rules. So say he leaves a will bequeathing all his property to Liam:

---

[7] The fullest account is R Maudsley, *The Modern Law of Perpetuities* (London, 1979). For a discussion of the rules' *raison d'être*, see Gardner, *ibid* 42–45, 49.

[8] The word 'tenant' in these expressions is not a synonym for 'lessee'. It is used in its etymological sense of 'holder'. (In the same way, someone who has the freehold to a piece of land is called, in technical language, a 'tenant in fee simple absolute in possession'.)

[9] On the two forms of concurrent interest, and their implications, see further L Tee, 'Co-ownership and Trusts' in L Tee (ed), *Land Law: Issues, Debates, Policy* (Cullompton, 2002) 132–48; R Smith, *Plural Ownership* (Oxford, 2005) pt II.

you now hold the house for Kate and Liam.[10] But if John and Kate were *joint tenants*, you now hold the house on trust for Kate alone. John and Kate previously shared a single interest, so upon John's death, Kate is simply left as sole owner of that interest. Liam does not inherit, because John did not have a separate interest upon which his will or the intestacy rules could operate. This expression of the nature of a joint tenancy is known as '(the right of) survivorship'.[11]

13.2.3 Should Joint Tenancy be Abolished?

It can be argued that joint tenancy is nowadays insupportable, and that it should therefore be abolished, leaving tenancy in common as the only possibility.[12]

The case against joint tenancy is that the difference between it and tenancy in common, namely survivorship, does harm, and no countervailing good. The harm occurs when a joint tenant dies unaware of his status as such, or of its implications. He probably assumes that his right will pass under an apparently relevant provision in his will (eg 'all my property to ...', or 'my share in the house to ...'), or under the intestate succession rules. But survivorship confounds his assumption, thus frustrating his wishes.

There is no such objection if our joint tenant is aware of his status as a joint tenant, and of its implications: he has the choice of becoming a tenant in common by severance (explained in § 13.2.6), and if he fails to do so he presumably wants survivorship to occur at his death. But the fact that it offers him the option of precipitating survivorship in this way, if he understands the position and wants this, is not an argument *in favour of* the joint tenancy. For he can achieve the same effect under a tenancy in common, by bequeathing his share to his fellow tenant(s) in common.

The following argument for the joint tenancy is sometimes made. Conceding the truth of the previous paragraph in general, it asserts that in certain circumstances, survivorship is beneficent as reflecting the way in which a deceased co-owner, dying intestate, would have wished to leave his right; or in which, regardless of his wishes, he ought to have left it. The 'certain circumstances' are, circularly, those where the co-owners' relationship is such that the one would or should have left his right to the other in this way ... above all, where the two were married, or civil partners, or had a similarly close but informal relationship.

---

[10] Who are likewise tenants in common: so if Kate dies, her interest will devolve in the same way, and so on.

[11] Sometimes the Latin is used: '*ius accrescendi*'.

[12] For further exploration, see M Thompson, 'Beneficial Joint Tenancies: A Case for Abolition?' [1987] *Conv* 29; A Pritchard, 'Beneficial Joint Tenancies: A Riposte' [1987] *Conv* 273; M Thompson, 'Beneficial Joint Tenancies: A Reply to Professor Pritchard' [1987] *Conv* 275.

This counter-argument fails, however, as once again survivorship is not the only way in which such work can be done; nor indeed is it the best way. The law has other rules specifically designed for these purposes,[13] and these will apply where a concurrent owner dies a tenant in common. Moreover, these rules operate in a subtler way than survivorship: they also benefit children of the relationship, and—above all—they operate on the basis of the relationship as it prevails at the time of death. By contrast, survivorship occurs on the strength of the joint tenancy that was established when the parties initially acquired their interests, regardless (unless there has been a severance) of supervening changes in their relationship making survivorship inappropriate. In an era when a relationship's closeness cannot be predicted to make it also enduring, this feature of the joint tenancy is especially damaging.

It may be concluded that joint tenancy, with its characteristic of survivorship, should be abolished, leaving tenancy in common as the only platform for concurrent beneficial rights.

13.2.4 The Four Unities

As the law stands, however, concurrent interests may exist under either a tenancy in common or a joint tenancy, and we need to be able to say which.

To capture the key idea that a joint tenancy is a shared single interest, it is commonly said that, if John and Kate are to be joint tenants, their concurrent rights must exhibit 'the four unities'. These are:

— *Possession*, meaning that their rights must be in the same piece of property (say, the house you hold on trust for them, rather than two separate houses, one apiece).
— *Time*, meaning that their rights must vest at the same time (this would not be satisfied, for example, if I transferred the house to you to hold on trust 'for John, and for Kate too if and when John marries her').
— *Title*, meaning that their rights must arise immediately from the same transaction (as where I establish them under the trust on which I give you the house; contrast the case where John later alienates his right to Liam, whereupon Kate and Liam are the beneficiaries but with rights which do not arise immediately from the same transaction).
— *Interest*, meaning that their rights must be of the same extent (eg both indefinite, or both for the duration of a certain lease) and size (ie, necessarily, equal; rather than say John's right being double Kate's).

---

[13] Intestates' Estates Act 1952; Inheritance (Provision for Family and Dependants) Act 1975. Of course, these rules may themselves be capable of improvement. In particular, in their current forms, they are not well adapted to informal relationships.

Unity of possession is indeed essential if John and Kate are to have a shared single interest, but only because it is essential if they are to have concurrent rights in the same property at all: that is, it necessarily characterises a tenancy in common as much as it does a joint tenancy. It is the other three unities that are supposedly crucial to the question whether concurrent rights are shares in a single interest, rather than a set of separate interests.

Plainly, John and Kate can have separate concurrent interests in the same property notwithstanding that these arise at different times, under different transactions, and are of different extents or sizes, and it follows that these unities are not required of tenancies in common. But equally plainly, they cannot share a single interest unless that interest was made at one time, under one transaction, and with a certain extent and size. In principle, however, the same need not be true of their *shares in* the single interest: in the abstract, there is no reason why these should not be of different relative sizes, or be acquired independently of one another. In particular, the idea of survivorship—that if John and Kate share a single interest, it becomes solely Kate's on John's death—makes as good sense regardless of the way in which their shares arose or of their relative sizes. Unsurprisingly, therefore, the idea that these three unities are essential to a joint tenancy has come under pressure.[14]

Moreover, the rights in question can exhibit the three unities (as well as unity of possession) and nevertheless amount to a tenancy in common rather than a joint tenancy. That is, they can arise at the same time, under the same transaction, and be identical in extent and size, and still be separate interests in the property, as opposed to shares in a single interest. So the unities do not, as might have been thought, actually *constitute* the single interest. They are (or perhaps are not quite, if the previous paragraph is right) necessary to the existence of such an interest, but not sufficient: those controlling the rights concerned must further intend them to exist in a combined state.[15] Where the unities are present, such an intention is presumed, but can be displaced by contrary evidence, showing either an intention at the outset that the rights should be separate, or a later intention that they should be separated ('severed'). These two possibilities are respectively considered in §§ 13.2.5 and 13.2.6.

---

[14] See especially R Smith, *Plural Ownership* (Oxford, 2005) 27–30 (querying indeed whether today's law requires unity of time at all), 44–46. On the other hand, it seems correct to say that joint tenants of a lease must have a single responsibility for the rent (as held in *Mikeover Ltd v Brady* [1989] 3 All ER 618 (CA); *AG Securities v Vaughan* [1990] 1 AC 417 (CA and HL)): the single responsibility is the counterpart of the single interest which, to be joint tenants, they must share.

[15] Or should one see the question, less metaphysically, as whether survivorship is intended? If so, is there the further implication that those with concurrent rights lacking the three unities can nonetheless opt into survivorship? This possibility would close the circle with the observation in the previous paragraph, that the three unities may not in fact be crucial to a joint tenancy anyway.

13.2.5 Separation at the Outset

So beneficial rights, exhibiting all four unities, will nonetheless be held in common rather than jointly if they are created with that intention. Such an intention can be discovered from the language in which the rights are created. If I create a trust 'for John and Kate', adding nothing, they will probably be found to be joint tenants. But if I add more or less anything—say, 'equally', or 'in equal shares'—the cases show that John and Kate will probably be found to be tenants in common.[16] Such additions are known as 'words of severance'.

The intention can alternatively be surmised from the surrounding circumstances. Say John and Kate have beneficial rights exhibiting all four unities in a house. If their relationship is of a business nature—for instance, they are dentists sharing surgery premises—it will be inferred that they do not intend to share a single interest (so that if John dies, Kate alone will take that interest, rather than John's share going to his estate: an inappropriate outcome in the circumstances).[17] Such an intention should also be found if John and Kate are friends who bought the house together because they wanted to 'get on the property ladder' and could not afford to do so separately. But not if they are a couple: then, survivorship is not contra-indicated.

The law's readiness to find especially words of severance suggests that it is not neutral on the question whether a joint tenancy or a tenancy in common has been created: that it has a preference for the latter answer. This is probably a reflection of the feeling, explored in § 13.2.3, that joint tenancies are an embarrassment, and that the law should cease to recognise them.

13.2.6 Subsequent Severance

An initial joint tenancy can be turned into a tenancy in common by subsequent severance.[18] Severance can occur in a number of ways:[19]

---

[16] See eg *Robertson v Fraser* (1871) LR 6 Ch App 696 (CA in Ch).

[17] *Malayan Credit Ltd v Jack Chia-MPH Ltd* [1986] AC 549 (PC).

[18] If there are only two joint tenants, say John and Kate, a severance necessarily leaves both as tenants in common. But say there are three—John, Kate, Liam—or more, and that John severs. John becomes tenant in common vis-à-vis Kate and Liam, so John's death will not benefit Kate and Liam by survivorship, nor will Kate's or Liam's death benefit John by survivorship. But (*ceteris paribus*) Kate and Liam remain joint tenants between themselves, so Kate's death will still benefit Liam by survivorship, and vice versa.

[19] Law of Property Act 1925 s 36(2); *Williams v Hensman* (1861) 1 J & H 546, 557–8 (Ch). In addition to those listed, perhaps also by the criminal killing of one joint tenant by another. Certainly, the killer does not take (unless relieved under the Forfeiture Act 1982), but this may alternatively be because survivorship does operate in the killer's favour, but the resulting gain is caught by a constructive trust for his victim's estate. See *Re K* [1985] Ch 85, 100 (Ch D).

— By written notice from one joint tenant to the other(s).[20]
— By agreement between the joint tenants concerned, or a 'course of dealing' (ie a set of pieces of behaviour) showing that they in fact regard the joint tenancy as having been severed.
— By 'an act operating on' one joint tenant's share,[21] such as where John, hitherto joint tenant with Kate, transfers[22] his right to Liam.

In § 13.2.5, we saw that in deciding whether concurrent rights exhibiting all four unities are initially established under a joint tenancy or a tenancy in common, the law shows a preference for the latter answer, ascribable to the unwelcome implications of the former. Unsurprisingly—all the more so given that changes in the parties' relationship may well make survivorship even less appropriate as time goes on—there are signs of the same tendency in the law's approach to discovering that a joint tenancy has subsequently been severed.

In particular, the courts are ready to find severance by written notice despite the piece of writing in question saying nothing about severance. A written document of any kind, passing from one joint tenant to another, will count as a notice of severance so long as the writer's desire to sever can be discovered by reflecting upon its content. Say land is currently held for John and Kate—perhaps brother and sister—as joint tenants. John, wishing to realise his share, applies to court[23] for an order that the land be sold and the proceeds divided between them. This application will necessarily be made in writing, and a copy of it served on Kate. Here is some writing passing from John to Kate ... and, although there is no mention of severance, it will count as a *notice of severance* because it plainly shows John as not wanting survivorship to continue to apply between himself and Kate.[24] In the same vein, an *agreement to sever* has been found despite those concerned making

---

[20] This method of severance was established by the Law of Property Act 1925 s 36(2). On a literal reading of s 36, it applies solely where the people concerned not only have concurrent beneficial rights as joint tenants, but also are trustees of the trust in question ('where a legal estate ... is vested in joint tenants beneficially ...'). This restriction is however unprincipled: severance affects only the relationship of the beneficial rights between themselves, not in any way the position of the trustees: so the identity of the trustees ought to be irrelevant.

[21] Severance by an act operating on one's own share is sometimes presented as logically inevitable: since Liam acquires his right from John, there is no unity of title between his right and Kate's, so they cannot be joint tenants. But in *allowing* a joint tenant to split his right out of a single interest in this way, the rule presupposes—like the other methods of severance—that the preservation of the single interest is optional, to be ended if those concerned so choose.

[22] Transfer of one's interest certainly counts as an act operating on it and thus severs. A mortgage of it probably does too. It is unclear whether the same is true of a lease of it.

[23] Under the Trusts of Land and Appointment of Trustees Act 1996 s 14: see §§ 14.2.2–14.2.5.

[24] *Re Draper's Conveyance* [1969] 1 Ch 486 (Ch D), approved in *Burgess v Rawnsley* [1975] Ch 429 (CA) and *Harris v Goddard* [1983] 1 WLR 1203 (CA). If the order that John seeks is made and carried out, the division of the money will end the unity of possession necessary for John and Kate to have concurrent rights in the same property at all: that is, they will at that point cease even to be tenants in common.

no reference to the issue, on the basis that they were negotiating to split the land in question between them.[25] And some judges have held that there is a severance by *course of dealing* if one joint tenant merely tells the other (orally is enough) of a desire on his part that is inconsistent with a continued joint tenancy:[26] a mere request to negotiate for a split would suffice.

But the cases also show a contrary tendency, sometimes taking a much narrower view of severance. The idea that unilateral oral notice amounts to a course of dealing has been disapproved:[27] a position that can certainly be supported on technical grounds,[28] but over which the judges concerned seem to shed no tears. Some decisions have declined to discern an agreement to sever, or even a shared treatment of the joint tenancy as severed, in unfinished negotiations towards a split.[29] And while there currently seems to be no doubt that a piece of writing need show only an implicit intention to sever, it has been held[30] that the intention must be for an immediate severance, a position for which there is no basis;[31] and that an intention to sever cannot be read into an application for a court order to reallocate a couple's property in the context of their divorce, a view which surely overlooks the significance of the applicant's desire for divorce itself. Finally, it might be thought that a generally distant relationship between joint tenants, either all along or evolving from something closer, should constitute a course of dealings showing that survivorship is not wanted; but the idea seems not even to have been argued, let alone judicially adopted.

How are these narrower treatments of severance to be explained? It is understandable that the judges should worry about joint tenancies being severed in nebulous circumstances. The effect of a severance, aborting survivorship, will generally not matter until one of the people concerned dies, possibly years or even decades later. If the law defines severance in such a way that it is hard to discern at such a distance, it will have created a recipe for undesirable litigation. From this point of view, it would be right to require that severance be by explicit writing alone (that is, if the law continues to maintain joint tenancies, and so have a place for severance, at all). But this argument seems not to account for the positions that the judges

---

[25] *Burgess v Rawnsley* [1975] Ch 429 (CA).

[26] *Re Draper's Conveyance* [1969] 1 Ch 486, 490–2 (Ch D); *Burgess v Rawnsley, ibid* 439–40, Lord Denning MR; perhaps also *Harris v Goddard* [1983] 1 WLR 1203, 1210–11 (CA), Lawton LJ.

[27] *Burgess v Rawnsley, ibid* 447, Sir John Pennycuick; *Harris v Goddard, ibid* 1211, Dillon LJ.

[28] If severance could occur by unilateral *oral* notice, there would be no need for the rule (Law of Property Act 1925 s 36(2)) specifically stating that it can occur by unilateral *written* notice.

[29] This view was taken in *Nielson-Jones v Fedden* [1975] Ch 222 (Ch D). That decision was criticised in *Burgess v Rawnsley* [1975] Ch 429 (CA), but the same view was again taken in *Gore and Snell v Carpenter* (1990) 60 P & CR 456 (Ch D).

[30] *Harris v Goddard* [1983] 1 WLR 1203, 1209 (CA).

[31] Severance by written notice is made possible by the Law of Property Act 1925 s 36(2), but the wording of this says nothing on the issue of immediacy.

have in fact taken against easy severance: though relatively narrow, they do not especially promote certainty.

Perhaps these positions are ascribable instead to a sense that, in an individual context, the survivor of two joint tenants positively ought to have the whole interest. Say John lives with Kate, who is separated but not divorced from her husband, in a house in which they have beneficial interests as joint tenants. Kate then dies intestate. A judge who finds severance will cause Kate's right to devolve to her estranged husband rather than to John. In these terms, even if the relationship between John and Kate had become troubled, it may remain more appropriate to treat the joint tenancy as remaining unsevered, so as to precipitate survivorship in John's favour. The same could be true even if John and Kate had parted, or indeed if Kate had recently found a new partner and made a will in the latter's favour: the basis of John's claim seems to lie less in the formal fact of his being Kate's partner than, substantively, in his having made his life with her over a significant and at any rate not too distant period. In their present forms, however, the intestacy and family provision regimes do not respond satisfactorily to this claim,[32] a deficiency which a judge can correct by refusing to find severance.

It is hard to say whether thinking of this kind was influential in the principal cases taking a narrow approach to severance,[33] as their facts are not fully enough reported. But they do seem to have involved a husband who, in the very throes of a divorce from his wife, dies, leaving his property elsewhere. So it is certainly possible that the court's perception of the wife's deserts, in terms of her role within the marriage, may have guided its treatment of the severance issue.[34] But such manipulation of the severance issue is ultimately an inappropriate tool for such work. It is available only where the parties were joint tenants in the first place, a point which is irrelevant to the true character of John's or the wife's claim; and where severance has not occurred beyond doubt (eg by an unequivocal written notice),[35] also an essentially irrelevant consideration.

---

[32] As Kate's unmarried partner, John will have no rights under the intestacy rules. He will have rights under the Inheritance (Provision for Family and Dependants) Act 1975 only if he still lived with Kate when she died, and then only to the extent of providing him with reasonable maintenance.

[33] *Nielson-Jones v Fedden* [1975] Ch 222 (Ch D); *Harris v Goddard* [1983] 1 WLR 1203 (CA); *Gore and Snell v Carpenter* (1990) 60 P & CR 456 (Ch D).

[34] Though the fact of the parties' marriage certainly creates a difficulty for this argument. The Inheritance (Provision for Family and Dependants) Act 1975 is more generous to bereaved spouses than to other kinds of family member or dependants, approaching quantum in a way similar to the regime applicable upon divorce (Matrimonial Causes Act 1973 s 24). So (except in *Nielson-Jones v Fedden* [1975] Ch 222 (Ch D), which predated the 1975 Act) the court could have used the 1975 Act to treat the wife as well as she would have been treated had the divorce gone through before her husband's death. In comparison, a tendentious refusal to recognise severance of the joint tenancy would have been a very blunt instrument.

[35] Perhaps aiming to neutralise this difficulty, Lord Denning MR in *Bedson v Bedson* [1965] 2 QB 666, 678 (CA) asserted that persons (or he may have meant specifically spouses) having concurrent beneficial interests in property as joint tenants may not sever their joint tenancy so

13.3 The Creation of Trust Rights in Land

13.3.1 Express and Constructive Trusts

As explained in the outline given in § 13.1, a trust can arise in two ways. First, because a settlor intends it to. The settlor may either transfer the property in question to the trustee on this basis, or keep it and declare himself trustee of it.[36] A trust arising in this way is an express trust. Second, because 'some other legally significant circumstances are present', in which case it is a constructive trust (or a resulting trust). The law operates a substantial number of sets of 'other legally significant circumstances'. Details of the rules concerning these can be found in books about trusts.[37] In most cases, the fact that the property in question is land rather than something else (eg money, stocks and shares) makes little or no difference, and so the rules merit no particular attention in a book about land law. This book will focus only on those rules to which it matters that the property is land, or whose exploration has occurred substantially in cases involving land.

One such type of constructive trust is that instanced in § 13.1, arising when I own some land, and you and I agree that you should have at least a share in it.[38] This type is discussed fully in § 8.3. Another type arises when I own some land and transfer it to you, stipulating that you should hold it on what would be an express trust, except that I fail to put this stipulation in writing, as I have to in order to create a valid express trust of land.[39] As explained in § 8.2, you hold the land on constructive trust instead.[40] A third type allegedly arises when I transfer property to you, you having promised to use it in a certain way (many of the relevant decisions involve land, though in fact the nature of the property seems inessential).[41] An obligation arises

---

long as one of them is in possession of the property in question. But, as Russell LJ observed *ibid,* at 690, there is no foundation for this position; and Russell LJ's view was accepted in *Re Draper's Conveyance* [1969] 1 Ch 486, 494 (Ch D) and *Harris v Goddard* [1983] 1 WLR 1203, 1208 (CA).

[36] It almost goes without saying that the finding of the required intention can be manipulated to serve other policy ends. See generally S Gardner, *An Introduction to the Law of Trusts* (2nd edn, Oxford, 2003) chs 2, 3.

[37] See Gardner, *ibid* chs 7, 8.

[38] *Gissing v Gissing* [1971] AC 889 (HL); *Lloyds Bank plc v Rosset* [1991] 1 AC 107 (HL); *Stack v Dowden* [2007] 2 AC 432 (HL); *Abbott v Abbott* [2008] 1 FLR 1451 (PC).

[39] Law of Property Act 1925 s 53(1)(b).

[40] *Rochefoucauld v Boustead* [1897] 1 Ch 196 (CA); *Bannister v Bannister* [1948] 2 All ER 133 (CA).

[41] *Binions v Evans* [1972] Ch 359 (CA); *Swiss Bank Corporation v Lloyds Bank Ltd* [1979] Ch 548 (Ch D); *Lyus v Prowsa Developments Ltd* [1982] 1 WLR 1044 (Ch D); *Ashburn Anstalt v Arnold* [1989] Ch 1 (CA).

against you: the authorities label it a constructive trust, though in truth it seems not to be a trust at all. This type too is explored in § 8.2.

13.3.2 A Complication regarding Tenancies in Common

Certain statutory provisions, read literally, appear to dictate that beneficial rights to be enjoyed by tenants in common can arise under an express trust,[42] but cannot arise under a constructive trust.

The ensuing gap would be substantial. In particular, consider the constructive trust that takes effect when I own some land, but you and I agree that you should have a share in it.[43] Unless your share is to be 100 per cent, so that I hold the land on a bare trust for you alone, you and I must emerge with concurrent beneficial rights. And we cannot be joint tenants (this is true even if we are each to have a 50 per cent share), as unity of title is absent: your share derives from the fact that the rule in play here imposes an obligation on me in your favour, while my share is my original entire ownership, minus what this obligation takes away from me.[44] If this rule is to generate beneficial rights at all, then, those holding them must do so as tenants in common. But the trust containing these rights is a constructive trust, and the statutory provisions referred to in the last paragraph say that a tenancy in common cannot arise under a constructive trust. It ought to follow that the rule under discussion cannot generate beneficial rights at all.

That is unthinkable, however. These trusts provide the law's principal way of allowing family members to acquire a greater share in their home than the title specifies, and if they are neither married to nor civil partners with the other party this will in turn be their principal means of sharing in the family's assets in the event of a breakdown. At the level of principle, moreover, there seems to be no reason why beneficial rights created via an express trust[45] can be held under a tenancy in common while those arising under a constructive trust cannot. Unsurprisingly, then, the courts have rejected this reading of the statutory provisions, and do allow beneficial rights created by constructive trusts to take effect under a tenancy in common after all.[46]

---

[42] Settled Land Act 1925 s 36(4) ... or under a statutory trust (§ 13.4) arising when I purport simply to transfer land to people as tenants in common, either *inter vivos* (Law of Property Act 1925 s 34(2)) or in my will (s 34(3)).

[43] § 8.3.

[44] The contrary is however asserted in *Hurst v Supperstone* [2005] EWHC 1309, [11] (Ch D).

[45] Or statutory trust: § 13.4.

[46] This position is implicit in, for example, *Bull v Bull* [1955] 1 QB 234 (CA); *Williams & Glyn's Bank Ltd v Boland* [1981] AC 487 (HL); *City of London Building Society v Flegg* [1988] AC 54, 74 (HL); *Abbey National Building Society v Cann* [1991] 1 AC 56 (HL). It is unclear how it is to be reconciled with the statutory wording.

13.3.3 Formalities for Express and Constructive Trusts

An express trust of land needs to be created in writing.[47] (If it involves a transfer from the settlor to the trustee of the interest to be held on trust, the formalities appropriate to the interest concerned must also be used. In the ordinary case, the settlor transfers the freehold ownership of the land to the trustee, and this requires a deed and registration.[48])

No formality is required in order for there to be a constructive or resulting trust.[49] Unlike an express trust, such trusts are not based on someone's intention to create them, and so can and commonly do arise without anybody intending them to. Any demand for formality would therefore not be complied with, and thus would normally prevent the trust from arising after all, frustrating the reasons why the law seeks its imposition.[50]

13.3.4 Trustees

If land is to be held on trust, so as to establish beneficial interests, there must be one or more trustees. The trustees are the people in whom the interest that is the subject-matter of the trust[51] is vested; as the outline given in § 13.1 explains, they then owe obligations to the beneficiaries, so generating the beneficiaries' rights. To complete our account of how trust rights are created, we need therefore to understand how people become trustees.

Say I wish to make an express trust for John of land that I have owned hitherto. I can transfer it to you as trustee for John. Usually, however, I will make the transfer to you *and at least one other trustee*, up to a maximum of four.[52] It is hard to find a direct authoritative statement on the point, but it appears that a trust of land ought to have a minimum of two trustees. As will be seen in § 14.6, two are required in order for the beneficial interests to be overreached from the land in the event of a disposition,[53] and the standard explanation is that this rule aims to reduce the risk of the proceeds being embezzled[54] ... implying that, if there is only a single trustee, it is his duty to seek the appointment of at least one colleague, at any rate before attempting to dispose of the land.

---

[47] Law of Property Act 1925 s 53(1)(b).
[48] *Ibid* s 52(1), Land Registration Act 2002 s 27: § 4.4.1.
[49] Law of Property Act 1925 s 53(2).
[50] See further § 6.1.2.
[51] Often, the very freehold ownership of the land, but it could be some other interest, such as a lease, or a mortgage, or indeed the trustee's own right as beneficiary of another trust.
[52] Trustee Act 1925 s 34.
[53] Law of Property Act 1925 s 27(2). But a single trustee will suffice if it is a 'trust corporation', eg the trustee department of a bank.
[54] *City of London Building Society v Flegg* [1988] AC 54, 74 (HL). This explanation is shaky, however. If a trust holds assets other than land all along, the danger of embezzlement seems at least as great, yet there is no rule against its being run by a single trustee.

There is an alternative way in which I can create an express trust: by 'declaring' it, ie retaining the land and making myself trustee of it. In this case, the need for at least two trustees will entail that I should seek the appointment of a second trustee alongside me. Likewise, if I own land and a constructive (or resulting) trust of it arises in John's favour, I again retain it, becoming trustee myself, and should find a second trustee. In this case especially, though, the likelihood is that I will not do so. I shall probably not realise that I hold the land on trust at all, let alone the need for such a trust to have at least two trustees. As we shall see in §§ 14.6 and 14.8.1, considerable problems follow when I, as a sole trustee, then purport to make a disposition of the land.

13.3.5 Multiple Trustees as 'Legal Joint Tenants'

When there are—as there should be—multiple trustees (ie two, three or four of them), they are said to hold the land as 'legal joint tenants'.

This statement makes use of the joint tenancy concept, discussed in §§ 13.2.1–13.2.6. There, the discussion was of the possible ways in which a trust's *beneficiaries* could have concurrent beneficial interests under it, these being as joint tenants or as tenants in common. When two or more people hold the legal title to the land as *trustees*, however, they cannot do so as tenants in common: legal estates cannot be co-owned under a tenancy in common, either from the outset or as a result of later severance.[55] Only the other alternative, a joint tenancy, is allowed.

Say, therefore, that a settlor transfers land to you and me on trust for John and Kate. No matter whether the settlor uses words of severance in the transfer (eg to you and me 'equally'), or whether the relationship between you and me is one that would ordinarily yield a tenancy in common (eg we are business partners): in taking the land as trustees, we necessarily do so as 'legal joint tenants'.

Because our positions as trustees cannot be held under a tenancy in common, they are incapable of severance and so of alienation—we cannot simply transfer them to others in our place. All either of us can do is die (or 'release', ie resign, our position), in which case survivorship takes effect in favour of the other. This indeed is the point of the rule. It ensures that the number of trustees of a given piece of land certainly does not rise, and tends to fall; and that the trustees probably remain a relatively close group. This in turn limits the number of obstacles potentially facing someone wishing to buy the land, which would otherwise reduce its marketability.[56] (The

---

[55] Law of Property Act 1925 ss 1(6), 34(1), 36(2).

[56] Even if the group is limited and close, however, the need for the trustees to number at least two introduces an obstacle which would be absent if the prospective buyer had to deal only with a single owner. But further rules are calculated to diminish this obstacle's size. Although in principle the trustees have to be unanimous in deciding to sell, their duty is to act in the

purchaser can normally disregard the beneficial rights under the trust, for these will be 'overreached', as explained in § 14.5.)

However: while this is the traditional account, it is not quite accurate. It is certainly correct to say that trustees cannot hold their positions as tenants in common, and that (therefore) these positions cannot be transferred, and that survivorship operates on death. But it is actually incorrect to say that trustees hold as joint tenants. If it were correct, the effect of death (or release) would be that a group of up to four trustees would, over time, dwindle to a single trustee: there would be no way of introducing new ones. The law could not allow that: as we have seen, trusts of land need at least two trustees. In fact, trustees of land can—unsurprisingly—be replaced (and, for that matter, removed), and additional ones appointed, in the same way as trustees of any other kind of property.[57] It is better, therefore, to regard those who hold property as trustees as doing so in a unique way: simply as co-trustees, under the rules explained in this section.

13.4 Statutory Trusts

13.4.1 The Nature of Statutory Trusts

As we have seen, concurrent beneficial interests in land can be created under an express trust, as where I transfer land to you on trust for John and Kate.

In the distant past, it used to be possible for me alternatively to transfer land directly to John and Kate as concurrent owners: that is, without creating a trust.[58] But nowadays, if I purport to do so, the law[59] interjects a trust, to like effect as if I had made an express trust: so if I try simply to transfer my house 'to John and Kate', without mention of a trust, the result

---

beneficiaries' (collective) best interests, so removing at least some of the reasons why unanimity might otherwise elude them; and where one or more vetoes a proposed disposition, the court can be asked (though of course it may not agree) to authorise it anyway (Trusts of Land and Appointment of Trustees Act 1996 s 14). In fact, a sale is effective and overreaches the beneficial interests even if the buyer deals with only two of the trustees (Law of Property Act 1925 s 27(2)), but if these two have gone against the wishes of their colleagues and have not obtained court approval they will generally be liable for breach of trust.

[57] The relevant rules are quite complex. See principally the Trustee Act 1925 Part III, together with the Trusts of Land and Appointment of Trustees Act 1996 Part II.

[58] § 1.3.4.

[59] Law of Property Act 1925 ss 34(2) and (3), 36(1).

will nonetheless be that the house is held on trust for them, their rights being as beneficiaries of this trust. Because the rule responsible for this is to be found in the Law of Property Act 1925, this trust is referred to as a 'statutory' trust.

If I establish an express trust, I will normally name its trustee(s). But if I thought I was making a simple transfer, I will not have done so. The law goes on to provide that the trustees of a purported transfer to concurrent owners will be the purported transferees themselves (or, if there are more than four of them, the first four named in the transfer).[60] My purported transfer 'to John and Kate', therefore, will take effect as a transfer to John and Kate as trustees, holding on trust for themselves as beneficiaries.[61]

13.4.2 The Rights in a Statutory Trust

Where I purport to transfer land to John and Kate and a statutory trust thus arises for John and Kate as its beneficiaries, their beneficial interests can exist under either a joint tenancy or a tenancy in common (and, if under a tenancy in common, in any proportions) in the usual way.

To decide their precise nature, we make use of the rules about the four unities and about initial separation, as explained in §§ 13.2.4–13.2.5. The task is assisted, however, by a Land Registry procedure. When land is transferred to multiple owners, the Registry, realising that the transferees must necessarily hold it on trust, requires that the trust's terms be expressly announced. So if land is transferred 'to John and Kate', its registration in their name will be accompanied by a statement telling us whether their beneficial interests are to be joint or in common, and if in common, in what proportions.

There is no question about the transferees' position as trustees, however. As explained in § 13.3.5, co-trusteeship can take only one form, traditionally (though not quite accurately) described as 'legal joint tenancy'. This rule's impact is especially noticeable in the case of a statutory trust. Say I purport to transfer land 'to John and Kate in equal shares'. Such a purported transfer has to take effect as a transfer to John and Kate on trust for themselves (§ 13.4.1). Containing words of severance, it is calculated to create a tenancy in common. It certainly does so in respect of John's and

---

[60] *Ibid* ss 34(2) (for purported transfers to tenants in common), 36(1) (for purported transfers to joint tenants). Children however cannot own legal estates in land (s 1(6)), so cannot become trustees in this way. So if I purport to transfer land to a group of people which includes children, the children will be disregarded in identifying the first four named, who will become the trustees.

[61] Parallel rules apply to two further cases where the law forbids a purported transfer of land from taking effect as expressed: where it is to a child (Law of Property Act 1925 ss 1(6), 4), or to transferees in succession (eg 'to John for life, then to Kate') (ss 1(1), 4). The approach to the location of trustees is necessarily different in such cases, however.

Kate's beneficial interests; but in their capacity as trustees, they necessarily hold as 'legal joint tenants'. So they can transfer their beneficial rights to others, whether during their lifetime or on death, as they please. But they cannot behave in this way with their positions as trustees. If, then, Kate sells her share in the house to Liam, Liam becomes beneficiary alongside John (as tenants in common), but (unless she also releases) Kate remains John's co-trustee.

13.4.3 The Point of Statutory Trusts

Why should the law read a purported transfer 'to John and Kate' as a transfer to John and Kate as trustees, on trust for John and Kate as beneficiaries, in this way? Anything that John and Kate might have wanted to do as outright transferees they can still do, in one or other of their two capacities (trustee and beneficiary): so why separate these?

The explanation is that interjecting a trust in this way preserves the land's future marketability, as explained in § 1.3.4: essentially, because a putative purchaser will need to deal only with the trustees, rather than with all those who would otherwise have been co-owners but who, under the statutory trust, are instead beneficiaries. While there can be any number of beneficiaries, and the number can grow over time through alienation (even an original joint tenancy can be severed and so treated in this way), we saw in §§ 13.3.4–13.3.5 how there can be no more than four trustees, and how trusteeships cannot be alienated.

The advantage is invisible so long as the trustees and beneficiaries remain the same people: John and Kate in our example. Here, the statutory trust seems a pointless complication. But the advantage becomes clearer if John and Kate (if necessary, sever and) alienate their beneficial interests, further fragmenting them in the process, so that by the time someone wishes to buy the land, the beneficiaries—if there were no statutory trust, the owners—have become a large and diffuse group. Likewise if the purported transfer is to more than four people concurrently from the outset.

Where trustees and beneficiaries are non-identical groups in this way, however, there is also a disadvantage. Although trustees must act in the interests of their beneficiaries, in practice this still leaves them considerable latitude. Those who are merely beneficiaries are correspondingly disempowered, as compared with people who are owners in their own right. This is the price of the statutory trust device. It is of course in principle no larger a problem than is intrinsic to an express or constructive trust (where the beneficiaries are necessarily no more than beneficiaries) anyway. And it is modulated by a further set of rules, discussed in §§ 14.2–14.3, which restrict the latitude enjoyed by trustees of land, giving (some) beneficiaries of such trusts of land an unusually large say in what should happen.

13.4.4 Statutory Trusts and Formalities

For formality purposes, a statutory trust counts as a constructive trust, and as such requires no formality.[62] My purported outright transfer to John and Kate takes effect (assuming of course that any formalities needed for the transfer itself have been used[63]), after which the statutory trust rule makes John and Kate trustees for themselves, regardless of my, or their, intentions.

13.5 A Worked Example

This chapter has looked at the main rules regarding the nature and creation of trust rights. These rules are complex. It may be helpful to illustrate their operation. The illustration will focus on a case involving the transfer of land to multiple transferees, as this scenario in particular can create confusion.

Say I am selling my house to John, Kate and Liam; let us imagine that they are three adult siblings who wish to live together. If I purport, literally, to transfer it 'to John, Kate and Liam', a statutory trust will arise, whereby John, Kate and Liam will hold the house on trust for themselves. More probably, John, Kate and Liam will have me transfer it to the three of them on an express trust for themselves. Either way, the upshot is that John, Kate and Liam become co-trustees ('legal joint tenants') of the house. The beneficiaries of the trust are themselves. On these facts—there being no words of severance or circumstances pointing to a tenancy in common—they hold their beneficial rights as joint tenants.

Some time later, John dies, leaving a will bequeathing all his property to Meg. What happens now depends on whether, before his death, the joint tenancy between John and Kate and Liam in respect of their beneficial interests had been severed, according to the rules explained in § 13.2.6, so that by the time of his death John was a tenant in common with Kate and Liam. If it had, John's rights as beneficiary of the trust will pass under his will to Meg. Otherwise, survivorship will occur, leaving Kate and Liam as the trust's sole beneficiaries.

But either way, the trustees are now Kate and Liam. Even if Meg inherits John's beneficial interest, she does not become a trustee in his place. The severance that led to her inheriting does not affect trusteeship; to put it

---

[62] § 13.3.3.
[63] Normally a deed (Law of Property Act 1925 s 52(1)), and registration (Land Registration Act 2002 s 27): § 4.4.1.

another way, there cannot be a legal tenancy in common, only a legal joint tenancy, to which survivorship applies. (Meg can, however, be appointed a trustee alongside Kate and Liam in John's place.)

In the end, then, the house is held on trust by Kate and Liam. If the joint tenancy between his beneficial right and the others had been severed before John's death, the trust's beneficiaries are Kate, Liam and Meg.[64] Otherwise, the beneficiaries are Kate and Liam alone.

---

[64] Although Meg certainly holds her interest as a tenant in common with Kate and Liam, as between themselves Kate and Liam may be either joint tenants or tenants in common. It depends on whether severance has occurred between them. If John's severance was unilateral, eg effected by written notice, there is no reason to doubt that Kate and Liam remain joint tenants; but if it was by agreement or course of dealings, the same agreement or course of dealings may (though it need not) show a severance between Kate and Liam too.

Trust Rights 2

In Chapter 13 we looked at the basic nature of the rights that exist under a trust of land, and at how they come into being. In this chapter, we go on to consider first the content of such rights, and then their impact on a disponee of the land.

14.1 The Possible Variety of Beneficial Rights

Beneficial interests can exist in a wide variety of sizes.

Sometimes they can be said to amount to ownership. Say you hold land on trust 'for John'. John is the only beneficiary; he is entitled indefinitely (so his interest continues to exist after his death, passing say under his will); and no other restrictions on his entitlement are mentioned. The land's legal title is vested in you as trustee, but in the nature of trusts, you must derive no benefit from this. So it is reasonable to regard John as in effect owning the land; reflecting the fact that trust rights are equitable, he is commonly described as having equitable ownership.[1] Or say you are trustee 'for John and Kate'. In this case, John and Kate once more have unrestricted and indefinite rights, such as we decided amounted to ownership in the first example. But here, they have concurrent interests, so the ownership entitlement is shared between them.[2] Or again, say you are trustee 'for John

---

[1] Assuming he is an adult and not suffering from mental incapacity, he can in fact require you to transfer the legal title to him, so as to make him owner of the full freehold estate, under the doctrine in *Saunders v Vautier* (1841) 1 Cr & Ph 240 (Ch). See S Gardner, *An Introduction to the Law of Trusts* (2nd edn, Oxford, 2003) 221–2.

[2] The doctrine in *Saunders v Vautier*, *ibid*, applies again, but requires John and Kate to agree on demanding the legal title.

for life, then for Kate'. Here, the overall ownership entitlement is again shared between John and Kate, but this time in a successive fashion, so that each has a distinct tranche. John's rights are for his life only, and Kate's, though indefinite, begin only with John's death. So neither John's nor Kate's interest amounts to ownership in the way that John's interest in the first example did.[3] But for the time that each prevails it confers quite a full set of rights, making it possible to regard John and Kate each as owner for a time, rather as lessees are. Of course, John's rights cannot allow him to damage what Kate gets after his death. In this respect, his position is again similar to that of a lessee, who must not damage the reversion.

Other examples can be given, however, featuring beneficial rights clearly *not* amounting to ownership. For instance, say you (more probably, you and a group of colleagues) are the trustee of a large benevolent scheme, and you hold your investments, including land (farms, shops, offices, blocks of flats), on terms requiring you to pay the income to the scheme's members, but in amounts decided by you. A trust of this kind is called a 'discretionary trust'. The members are beneficiaries of the trust, ie have rights to the performance of your obligations, but since each member will receive only what you decide, he cannot be described as owning the trust's land and other investments.[4]

14.2 Access to Particular Benefits 1: General Principles

14.2.1 The Ordinary Law of Trusts

The principal ways in which the beneficiaries of a trust of land may wish to enjoy their rights are by occupying the land, and by taking its financial value. In turn, there are a number of ways in which the beneficiaries could take the land's financial value. In principle, the land might for example be sold and the proceeds simply paid over to the beneficiaries, ending the trust; or sold and the proceeds reinvested in other assets so as to produce an income for the beneficiaries; or retained but rented out to tenants, again producing an income; or retained but mortgaged to secure a loan, itself used say to

---

[3] Nonetheless, John and Kate can once more combine to demand the legal title from you under the doctrine in *Saunders v Vautier, ibid.*

[4] In theory, the doctrine in *Saunders v Vautier, ibid,* applies here too, so that if all the members agree, they can demand the trust's assets. (The assets would have to be divided between them in such a way that they would also have to agree.) But when a trust has many beneficiaries, as here, this is unlikely to be feasible.

enhance the land's profitability (improving a farm, for instance) or to benefit one or more of the beneficiaries in some other way, perhaps by providing finance to set up or develop a business. But given this range of possibilities, how do we determine the way in which a beneficial right is in fact to be enjoyed?

In this section, we will review the general principles applicable to answering this question. These principles are, however, to some extent set aside in the situation where a beneficiary wishes to occupy the trust land. We shall look at the rules regarding that situation, and their relationship with these general principles, in § 14.3.

The dominant power to decide how a beneficial right is to be enjoyed lies with the beneficiaries, though they have this power only if they are all of full capacity and are unanimous about what they want. In this case, they can in the last resort remove their trustees, make themselves owners of the trust assets and so take their own decisions.[5] So if you hold land on trust for John alone, John can choose the way in which he wants to enjoy his interest. Likewise if your trust is for John for life, then Kate, or for John and Kate concurrently: John and Kate, if they agree, can choose how to enjoy their rights.

In English law, the beneficiaries' invocation of this rule prevails over even a settlor's explicit contrary instructions. But if the beneficiaries are not unanimous, or do not wish to go so far as to dismantle the trust, the next resort is to the settlor's stipulations. So if the terms of your trust indicate that the land must be used in a certain way, or cannot be used in some other way (or not without a certain person's consent), and the beneficiaries do not agree to dissolve the trust, you must abide by this.[6]

Where, however, the mode of enjoyment is not determined by the beneficiaries or the settlor in these ways, it becomes a matter for the trustees' discretion. But the ordinary law of trusts stipulates two requirements regarding the exercise of this discretion:[7]

— In making your choices under it, you, as trustee, must conduct yourself in your beneficiaries' interests.[8] Where there are two or more beneficiaries,

---

[5] This is the doctrine in *Saunders v Vautier*, *ibid*, again. If the known beneficiaries of full capacity all agree, but some of the beneficiaries are unable to agree because for example they are still children, the provisions of the Variation of Trusts Act 1958 may allow the court to agree on behalf of the latter. See S Gardner, *An Introduction to the Law of Trusts* (2nd edn, Oxford, 2003) 222–5.

[6] This is confirmed for trusts of land by the Trusts of Land and Appointment of Trustees Act 1996 s 8. There is an exception, however: the settlor cannot stipulate that the trustees must sell the land: s 4 gives trustees a power to delay sale indefinitely.

[7] On both requirements, see S Gardner, *An Introduction to the Law of Trusts* (2nd edn, Oxford, 2003) ch 9.

[8] *Cowan v Scargill* [1985] Ch 270 (Ch D); *Hayim v Citibank NA* [1987] AC 730 (PC).

this duty to serve the beneficiaries' interests requires you to be even-handed as between them.[9]

— You must act with the degree of prudence, care and skill that the law requires of trustees.[10]

These rules seem to apply equally to trusts of land,[11] together with an additional requirement to, 'so far as practicable', consult the adult beneficiaries with immediate interests, and follow the wishes of the majority by value, 'so far as consistent with the general interest of the trust'.[12] A settlor can however exclude this additional requirement,[13] and will often do so, in order to spare his trustees what could well be a headache; though the qualifications quoted must in any case deprive the requirement of much force, so the contrast with the ordinary law of trusts, which has no such requirement, is less marked than at first appears.

14.2.2 The Trusts of Land and Appointment of Trustees Act 1996, Section 14

The ordinary law of trusts continues to say that if you are not the only trustee, you and your colleagues will have to be unanimous in choosing what to do (a rule which in theory could produce paralysis, but in practice seems to pose few problems); but that, so long as you have complied with the rules in making it, your choice of what to do will stand: a judge will not normally substitute some other choice on the basis that, while yours is tenable, his is preferable.[14]

[9] *Raby v Ridehalgh* (1855) 7 De GM & G 104 (CA in Ch). In *Nestle v National Westminster Bank plc* [1993] 1 WLR 1260, 1279 (CA), the duty to be even-handed between beneficiaries was reformulated as a duty to be 'fair'. For consideration of this, see n 53.

[10] By *Re Whiteley* (1886) 33 Ch D 347, 355 (CA), 'the duty of a trustee is ... to take such care as an ordinary prudent man would take if he were minded to [act] for the benefit of other people for whom he felt morally bound to provide.' By the Trustee Act 2000 s 1(1), a trustee must exhibit 'such care and skill as is reasonable in the circumstances, having regard in particular—(a) to any special knowledge or experience that [the trustee] has or holds himself out as having, and (b) if he acts as trustee in the course of a business or profession, to any special knowledge or experience that it is reasonable to expect of a person acting in the course of that kind of business or profession'. These duties can however be excluded by the terms of an express trust: *Armitage v Nurse* [1998] Ch 241 (CA); Trustee Act 2000 Sch 1 para 7.

[11] The Trusts of Land and Appointment of Trustees Act 1996 s 6(1) confirms the trustees' discretion to choose the mode of enjoyment, by giving them the power to do anything with the trust land that an absolute owner might do. The text's two requirements regarding the exercise of the discretion are confirmed by s 6(5)–(8), requiring the trustees to 'have regard to the rights of the beneficiaries' and to act lawfully, including in compliance with the rules of equity; and by s 6(9), requiring them to act with the degree of care and skill demanded by the Trustee Act 2000 s 1(1). But there is an exception. In respect of a discretionary decision not to sell the land, trustees are exempted from the two requirements (they are not to be 'liable in any way': Trusts of Land and Appointment of Trustees Act 1996 s 4). This exemption apparently allows them, in this particular, to be self-interested, biased, careless and incompetent: an extraordinary rule.

[12] Trusts of Land and Appointment of Trustees Act 1996 s 11(1).

[13] s 11(2).

[14] *Tempest v Lord Camoys* (1882) 21 Ch D 571 (CA).

In these respects, however, the law is quite different where the trust is one of land. By the Trusts of Land and Appointment of Trustees Act 1996, section 14, it allows the court to take decisions regarding the management of the trust in lieu of the trustees.[15] So if trustees are divided over what to do, they can ask the court to adjudicate. And if a beneficiary, or any other person having a right in the trust land, does not like what the trustees are proposing to do or not do, he can ask the court to overrule them in favour of his preferred course.

14.2.3 The Justification for Section 14

Why does the law thus provide for judicial micromanagement of trusts where, but only where, they are trusts of land?

The ordinary rule, disavowing judicial micromanagement, is probably ascribable to a concern not to overload available judicial resources; and to a view of trusts as autonomous enclaves, into whose life judges should be slow to intrude.[16] These considerations are as relevant to trusts of land as to other kinds of trust, but in the case of trusts of land there is another, countervailing, pair of points which perhaps explain section 14.

First, groups of trustees are normally detached from the beneficiaries (that is usually one of the reasons for having a trust), and close-knit among themselves, so that irresolvable disagreements are rare. But the trustees of a trust of land are often the same people as the beneficiaries, most commonly a couple who have bought a house together.[17] If their personal relationship breaks down, they may well disagree over what should be done with the house, one perhaps wishing to continue living in it (maybe with their children), the other wishing to sell so as to be able to buy somewhere new.

Second, where a trust does not involve land, it is very probable that all concerned will regard its assets simply as investments. Where the trust holds land, however, occupation is quite likely to be an issue. In the former case, there may be differences of opinion over the choice of investments, but these will normally be less difficult than the arguments between rivals wishing to occupy, or between those wishing to occupy and those wishing to see the land used for financial gain.

On both counts, disagreements in trusts of land are likely to be more than usually heated—and someone's home will often be at stake, so that the dispute has an added social dimension. There is therefore a basis for a jurisdiction such as that established under section 14.

---

[15] It also allows the court to dispense trustees from a need to consult beneficiaries or to obtain consents.

[16] On the latter, see further S Gardner, *An Introduction to the Law of Trusts* (2nd edn, Oxford, 2003) 263–4.

[17] This generates a statutory trust of the land, as explained in § 13.4.

14.2.4 The Operation of Section 14: The Statutory Considerations

Section 14 does not, as one might have expected, leave the court to proceed simply as trustees should do, ie as described in § 14.2.1. To be sure, it seems not generally[18] to allow the court to order outcomes not available to the trustees.[19] For example, if the settlor has stipulated that the land shall not be sold before a certain date, section 14 does not allow the court to order otherwise. But the considerations to which the law requires attention in the *court's* exercise of the discretion are different from those to which the *trustees* are required, or indeed allowed, to attend. By section 15 of the 1996 Act, the court must ordinarily[20] take into account:[21]

— The intentions of the person(s) who created the trust (at the time they created it[22]).[23] This ought to refer only to the intentions of the settlor(s) of an *express* trust: constructive trusts are not 'created' by people (rather, they are made by the law, in reaction to what people have done), and the same is true of statutory trusts. But the general assumption is that, on the contrary, the intentions of those acquiring land as co-owners are indeed to be considered too. The intentions may be well documented, but are oftener inferred. A frequently encountered intention is that the land, a house, should provide a family home for a couple. Such an intention is rarely influential, however, as litigation under section 14 will not normally occur at all unless the couple are now estranged, so that the aim of providing them with a family home is no longer feasible. Another intention, which ought to be common, is often overlooked. Even where the land is also a home, it may be intended to provide the beneficiaries with a fund of wealth: most house purchasers will have at least some interest in this dimension of their acquisition, and for some it will be a major consideration. Where the couple are estranged, at least one of them may well want to unlock such wealth, in order to find new accommodation and move on with life.

— The purposes for which the trust's land is held (at the time of the litigation[24]).[25] It is the trustees who 'hold' the land, so the purposes must

---

[18] It does specifically allow the court to override an obligation not to act without consultation or consent: s 14(2)(a).

[19] See eg R Smith, *Plural Ownership* (Oxford, 2005) 156, referring to the Law Commission report which preceded the 1996 Act; but note the contradictory view, regarding occupation, discussed in § 14.3.3. Other jurisdictions exist to this effect, however: notably the Trustee Act 1925 s 57.

[20] It is quite different where sale of the trust land is sought by an insolvent beneficiary's trustee in bankruptcy (seeking to realise the beneficiary's assets so as to distribute the proceeds among his creditors). Then, the case is governed by the Insolvency Act 1986 s 335A. See § 14.2.6.

[21] See further R Smith, *Plural Ownership* (Oxford, 2005) ch 8.

[22] *White v White* [2004] 2 FLR 321, [23] (CA).

[23] Trusts of Land and Appointment of Trustees Act 1996 s 15(1)(a).

[24] *White v White* [2004] 2 FLR 321, [24] (CA).

[25] Trusts of Land and Appointment of Trustees Act 1996 s 15(1)(b).

presumably be theirs. (In most statutory trusts, of course, the trustees and the beneficiaries will be the same people.) A purpose that is not also an original intention might—though again, this is often overlooked—be the exploitation of a house, originally acquired purely as a family home, subsequently also for business, or as a fund of wealth. The fact that land is *used* in a particular way is neither necessary nor sufficient to show a *purpose* for which the land is held, however: the crucial thing is a sense, on the part of all the trustees, that the land *should* be used or usable in the particular way.[26] Finding such a sense will often be a matter of inference, however.

— The welfare of any children who occupy or might occupy the trust land[27]—most often, the children of the couple whose home the land is. Note 'welfare': it cannot be assumed, merely because there are children, that their *welfare* will be (significantly) affected by the relief being sought, eg the sale of the house:[28] children move house all the time, and usually without lasting bad effects, at any rate of a kind that weighs with adults. Something particular is needed, such as disruption of the child's education in the period immediately before public examinations ... though perhaps suffering not only the estrangement of his parents but also the loss of a familiar environment would, or should, count too.

— The interests of any beneficiary's secured creditors:[29] notably, of a bank which has loaned the beneficiary money, taking a mortgage over his interest in the land. So long as the mortgage payments are being made and the security remains adequate, the creditor will not normally have an interest in any particular outcome, but if payments are in arrears, it may be asking for a sale.[30]

— The circumstances and wishes of the majority (by value) of adult beneficiaries with immediate rights.[31] Note the inattention to future

---

[26] *White v White* [2004] 2 FLR 321, [24] (CA).

[27] Trusts of Land and Appointment of Trustees Act 1996 s 15(1)(c).

[28] *First National Bank plc v Achampong* [2004] 1 FCR 18, [2003] EWCA Civ 487, [65] (CA).

[29] Trusts of Land and Appointment of Trustees Act 1996 s 15(1)(d).

[30] A creditor will need to seek a sale of the land under s 14 in this way, moreover, only where the mortgage security does not comprise the entire beneficial entitlement to the land. Say John and Kate hold a house on trust for themselves and their parents, and mortgage it to a bank. Because in this case the loan money will be paid to two trustees, *all* the beneficial interests will be overreached (§ 14.5.1). That is to say, the bank will be unconcerned with them, so if it later seeks to repossess and sell the house to recoup the debt, it can do so without needing to enter into arguments under s 14 with beneficiaries who oppose sale. But say John alone is the trustee. Here, the beneficial interests will *not* be overreached, and so may bind the bank. (They will do so if the beneficiary was in actual and apparent occupation at the time the mortgage was created, and did not consent to it. If they do not bind the bank, the bank will be unconcerned by them, just as if they had been overreached.) Beneficial interests thus binding upon the bank will rank at the same level as the mortgage; so in order to sell (if the beneficiaries oppose this), the bank will need to obtain an order under s 14. See further § 14.8.1.

[31] Trusts of Land and Appointment of Trustees Act 1996 s 15(3).

beneficiaries, like Kate in the case of a trust for John for his life, thereafter for Kate.

These five considerations are however non-exhaustive. So the court could, for example, view a house as a fund of wealth, available (via an order for sale) to help an estranged couple move on, even if this was neither the intention with which the couple acquired the house nor a purpose to which they subsequently put it.

14.2.5 The Operation of Section 14: The Aim of the Jurisdiction

When, in operating section 14, reference is made to a consideration, it is not enough to say that the consideration is indeed a live issue in the individual circumstances: thought must be given to its weight. For example, the mere presence of children is irrelevant. A threat to their welfare is relevant, but inconclusive. To arrive at an outcome, a value must be put on the threat, and be entered into a calculus alongside the values put on all other relevant considerations.[32] But how are comparable values to be assigned to such incommensurables? It can only be, by assessing their message for the common meta-consideration that is the *aim* of the jurisdiction. (Just as apples and oranges may be compared in terms of—inter alia—their money value; or volume, or mass, or density; or water or vitamin or sugar or acid content; depending on what we are interested in.)

The statutory scheme, however, does not identify this common meta-consideration or aim.

According to the ordinary principles of the law of trusts, as noted in § 14.2.1, the aim ought to be even-handedly to maximise the trust's benefit to its beneficiaries. The statutory scheme does not work in this way, however. The direction to attend to the circumstances and wishes of adult beneficiaries with immediate rights,[33] no mention being made of others, reads as an invitation not to be even-handed; and the intention of the trust's creator(s)[34] (save as embedded in the specification of the beneficial interests), its purpose,[35] and the welfare of children[36] seem at best tangential to this consideration. Nor does the key lie in viewing the aim as even-handedly to maximise the trust's benefit to its beneficiaries, *but not necessarily in financial*

---

[32] *Mortgage Corporation v Shaire* [2001] Ch 743 (Ch D). *White v White* [2004] 2 FLR 321 (CA) involved a couple who had separated. The woman wanted the house to be sold, so as to realise her share of the capital tied up in it, while the man wished to retain the house for occupation by himself and the children. Sale was ordered despite the consequence of requiring the man to find a cheaper and smaller house for himself and the children, perhaps obliging them to share a bedroom.

[33] Trusts of Land and Appointment of Trustees Act 1996 s 15(3).

[34] s 15(1)(a).

[35] s 15(1)(b).

[36] s 15(1)(c).

terms (albeit that even-handedness cannot easily be judged otherwise than in financial terms). The same evidence defeats this possibility too.

Indeed, for the most part, the statutory considerations invite the court to step outside the thinking required or allowed by the ordinary law of trusts, and this seems to be the whole reason for the Act's mention of them. They can, however, plausibly be read as calculated to deliver a form of[37] family welfare among the beneficiaries and their dependants.[38] Hence the preference for immediate beneficiaries over remoter ones; the attention to non-beneficiary children, alone among those persons not recognised by the ordinary law of trusts itself; and the tendency (noted in § 14.2.4) to think of intentions and purposes predominantly in domestic terms.

If family welfare is the aim, the law is not wholly unprincipled, since (as we have seen) a trust is needed for land to be concurrently owned, and doubtless land is concurrently owned most commonly when it is a family home. But there is nonetheless a substantial mismatch. If family welfare is the aim, the trust seems irrelevant. (The welfare needs are the same, whether the home is concurrently owned or not.[39]) At the same time, if the aim of the jurisdiction is family welfare, it has nothing to say about the many cases in which there is a trust of land, but the land held on trust is *not* a family home.

Moreover, if family welfare is the aim, the reference to the interests of secured creditors does not belong: the vindication of such interests, normally by selling the land, is likely to be categorically inimical to family welfare, at least in an immediate perspective.[40] Such interests can be included in the calculus only if the jurisdiction's focus is one, necessarily at a higher level of abstraction, to which both they and the family welfare considerations are germane. In *Mortgage Corporation v Shaire*,[41] it was correctly held that the Act requires the interests of secured creditors to be weighed against all other

---

[37] 'A form of', because family welfare is not itself a single idea: it can be viewed in a number of ways. Since the considerations in the Trusts of Land and Appointment of Trustees Act 1996 s 15 are relatively unspecific in content and in any event non-exhaustive, we cannot say just what view is taken for this Act. It may or may not coincide with that adopted by or under the Matrimonial Causes Act 1973 s 24, dealing with the treatment of property on the dissolution of a marriage or civil partnership; or the Children Act 1989 Sch 1, dealing with the orders that can be made for (*inter alia*) the reallocation of land in the interests of a child. The latter Acts certainly have a wider reach, not requiring a trust as their starting point and allowing the court to adjust property interests, but that does not necessarily indicate a difference in aim. It is, however, not easy to discover the 1973 Act's precise aim, either: both the statute itself and the cases under it lack precision.

[38] See further J Dewar, 'Land, Law, and the Family Home' in S Bright and J Dewar (eds), *Land Law—Themes and Perspectives* (Oxford, 1998) ch 13.

[39] So, where both the Trusts of Land and Appointment of Trustees Act 1996 and the Matrimonial Causes Act 1973 apply, the latter takes precedence: *Tee v Tee* [1999] 2 FLR 613 (CA). The same is presumably true of the Children Act 1989.

[40] In the longer term, eroding the value of such security interests would tend to reduce the availability or raise the cost of the credit on which families rely in order to acquire a home, and in some cases other benefits too.

[41] [2001] Ch 743 (Ch D).

relevant considerations, thus positing the existence of such a focus, but no guidance was given as to its nature. In the individual case, no such guidance was necessary: sale was refused on the basis that the beneficiary opposing it bought out the secured interest, so that both she and the creditor should have been happy ... it is hard to see why the case came to court. Guidance is however needed for the more usual sort of litigated case where the beneficiary cannot afford such a solution and a choice has to be made. But the guidance has never been given; it is simply observable that secured creditors are normally awarded sale.[42]

14.2.6 The Special Case of Insolvency

The law deals separately with the case where one of the beneficiaries has become insolvent, and the court is asked by the bankruptcy authorities to order sale of the trust land so as to pay his creditors. Because the need to weigh the creditors' interests against other relevant considerations is the very crux of this case, we might expect greater transparency about how the weighing is to be done. But again, it is not to be found.

For the first year after the bankruptcy, the court has a task—and a problem—similar to that discussed above: it is required to take account of the claims both of the creditors and, if the land in question is their home, of the bankrupt's spouse or civil partner and children,[43] but the law does not declare the basis on which these are to be compared. (Bizarrely from the viewpoint of the ordinary law of trusts, the provision makes no reference at all to the interests of other beneficiaries under the trust. Aside from the creditors' interests, its sole preoccupation is with the welfare of the bankrupt's family.) Thereafter, the court must order sale 'unless the circumstances of the case are exceptional'.[44] Even then, there is a choice. The court

---

[42] See eg *Bank of Ireland Home Mortgages Ltd v Bell* [2001] 2 FLR 809 (CA). For further work on how to evaluate the various ideas in play, see L Fox, *Conceptualising Home—Theories, Laws and Policies* (Oxford, 2007).

[43] Insolvency Act 1986 s 335A(2).

[44] s 335A(3). The courts treat 'exceptional' as meaning 'unusual'. Exceptional circumstances were found, and sale refused, in *Claughton v Charalamabous* [1999] 1 FLR 740 (Ch D), where the bankrupt's spouse was severely disabled and the house had been adapted accordingly (see too *Judd v Brown* [1998] 2 FLR 360 (Ch D); *Re Rave* [1998] 2 FLR 718 (Ch D)). But the hardship to the bankrupt's family routinely associated with insolvency is (therefore) not 'exceptional', and not considered: *Re Citro* [1991] Ch 142 (CA). Section 335A(3) may infringe the European Convention on Human Rights, Art 8, which requires respect for family life and homes except as proportionately required for, *inter alia*, the protection of the rights of others (here, the creditors' rights to the money owed them). The 'usualness' of the circumstances seems irrelevant to this. According to *Barca v Mears* [2004] EWHC 2170, [38]–[42] (Ch D), the need to ensure proportionality also demands a more ad hoc examination of the rival (relevant) considerations in individual cases; but *Nicholls v Lan* [2006] EWHC 1255 (Ch D) doubts this, aligning itself with the position taken, in a different context, in *Kay v Lambeth London Borough Council; Leeds City Council v Price* [2006] 2 AC 465 (HL) and *Doherty v Birmingham City Council* [2008] 3 WLR 636 (HL). See further T Allen, 'The Human Rights Act (UK) and Property Law' in J McLean (ed), *Property and the Constitution* (Oxford, 1999) ch 7, 161–4.

should still order sale unless the 'exceptional' circumstances are compelling enough to demand otherwise, reviving the same conundrum.[45]

14.3 Access to Particular Benefits 2: the Right to Occupy Trust Land

14.3.1 The Rules

Say you hold land on trust for John and Kate. Under certain circumstances, John and/or Kate will have a right to occupy it. This right is established by sections 12 and 13 of the Trusts of Land and Appointment of Trustees Act 1996.[46]

Under these provisions:

— A beneficiary of a trust of land is 'entitled' to occupy that land if this is one of 'the purposes of the trust', or 'the land is held by the trustees so as to be' available for occupation by him, so long as it is in fact available and suitable.[47]
— Where this formula gives two or more beneficiaries simultaneous rights to occupy the same piece of land, but they cannot realistically do so, the trustees must choose which of the beneficiaries shall occupy,[48] and can make the chosen beneficiary compensate those not chosen.[49]
— A beneficiary already occupying the trust land cannot be removed except by a court order.

These provisions evidently cut back the discretion that, as we saw in § 14.2.1, the trustees otherwise have to decide the form in which the beneficiaries shall enjoy their interests. That said, the 'entitlement' to occupy is less solid than at first appears. The concepts in which the provisions' requirements are expressed ('purposes', 'held ... so as to be', 'available', 'suitable')

---

[45] See further L Fox, *Conceptualising Home—Theories, Laws and Policies* (Oxford, 2007).
[46] See further R Smith, *Plural Ownership* (Oxford, 2005) ch 7, and other contributions reviewed there; S Pascoe, 'Right to Occupy under a Trust of Land: Muddled Legislative Logic' [2006] *Conv* 54.
[47] s 12.
[48] s 13(1).
[49] s 13(6). This provision was applied in *Stack v Dowden* [2007] 2 AC 432, [93]–[94] (HL). The approach taken is, however, questionable; cf the dissenting analysis of Lord Neuberger, *ibid* [148]–[157].

lack conceptual clarity, and the facts at which they are aimed will often be disputable. So in practice, a significant degree of discretion creeps back in after all.

14.3.2 An Objection

There is a major objection to these provisions. Contrary to the law's ordinary thinking, as explained in § 14.2.1, they require outcomes that are not even-handed among the beneficiaries.

Where their requirements are (held to be) satisfied, the provisions allow one beneficiary to occupy the trust land despite the loss this may cause other beneficiaries, relative to the land being treated as an investment. Say you hold the land on trust for John and Kate concurrently. If you rent the land out, the resulting income will go to John and Kate in their due shares. But if John occupies, and if as a result Kate gets nothing, they will not have been treated even-handedly.

At first sight, there seems to be an answer to this complaint, in the rule that the beneficiary who is chosen to occupy can be made to pay compensation to his fellow beneficiaries.[50] The compensation that John will thus pay Kate will restore even-handedness after all. But the compensation rules are organised in such a way that even-handedness may not in fact always be secured.

The first problem is that the rules give no guidance as to how this compensation's quantum should be fixed. Say the house is modest in itself, so that its rental value is unremarkable, but it is strategically placed, so that it has a high sale (and hence reinvestment) value. Kate will not be treated even-handedly—on the contrary, she will subsidise John—if you choose John to occupy and require him to pay Kate no more than the rental value.

Moreover, the rules do not provide for John to compensate Kate at all unless Kate too is entitled to occupy the house under the Act's scheme, but you have chosen John to occupy over her.[51] Yet Kate is nonetheless a beneficiary, and the absence of compensation will mean that she is not treated even-handedly. Say John and Kate have successive interests, as in a trust 'for John for life, then for Kate'. John has the right to occupy during his lifetime, so you must allow him to do so, but Kate does not,[52] so John cannot be made to compensate her.

All should be well if the trust property is the freehold ownership of the house, as, even though in the meantime you retain it for John's occupation, it will meet Kate's essential need for an investment asset that at least maintains

---

[50] s 13(6).

[51] Strictly speaking, s 13(3) allows you to impose any reasonable condition on John, which could in the abstract include a duty to compensate Kate; but s 13(6), making particular mention of requirements to compensate other beneficiaries *entitled to occupy*, seems to limit this.

[52] Her interest is not 'in possession', as required for an entitlement to occupy under s 12(1).

its real value over John's life. Not so, however, if the trust property is for example a 99 year lease of the house, for this will diminish in value over John's life. To safeguard Kate's interest in succeeding to capital whose real worth is at least as great as when the trust begins, your natural course would be to sell the lease, and invest the proceeds so as to secure their real capital value for Kate and also to pay an income to John. If the house is to be retained for John's use, John should have to pay such sums as will produce an equivalent result for Kate. But given Kate's lack of an entitlement to occupy, the Act does not provide for you to require him to do so.

Equally, say John and Kate have concurrent interests, but the house you hold for them is a multi-storey house, which is suitable for occupation by John ... but not by Kate, who is disabled and needs a bungalow. Under the Act, the fact that the house is unsuitable for Kate means that she is not entitled to occupy it, which in turn means that, although you must allow John to occupy it, there is no provision for requiring him to pay compensation to Kate. She is therefore not treated even-handedly.

So, in its provisions giving beneficiaries a right to occupy trust land, the 1996 Act derogates from the ordinary law's requirement that trust assets be managed in a manner that is even-handed as between beneficiaries. Is there a principled basis for this derogation? Presumably, the right to occupy can be ascribed to a concern to vindicate people's rights to their home. That is a proper project for the law. But so is the even-handed treatment of beneficiaries: a departure from this principle is in effect a confiscation of one beneficiary's rights for the benefit of another. If the two principles conflict, the law can legitimately treat the former as capable of taking precedence over the latter, but to treat it as automatically doing so, as the 1996 Act does, is objectionable because it is disproportionate.[53]

There may be a partial answer to this objection. Remember that the problem arises from the combination, in the 1996 Act, of a right allowing one beneficiary (John) to occupy, to the financial disadvantage of another (Kate), without sufficient provision for redressing that disadvantage. Outside the Act, however, there exists a wider mechanism, known as 'accounting', which may be usable to redress the disadvantage in at least some cases. Accounting was commonly used before 1996, in cases where two beneficiaries had once lived together in the same house, but one had moved out as it was

---

[53] In *Nestle v National Westminster Bank plc* [1993] 1 WLR 1260, 1279 (CA), the duty to treat beneficiaries even-handedly was reformulated as a duty to be 'fair', and was said to allow trustees to favour one beneficiary over another so as to redress an imbalance between the two beneficiaries' other wealth. Even if it were uncontroversial in itself (which it is not), this position would not justify the approach of the Trusts of Land and Appointment of Trustees Act 1996. The 'fairness' rule requires the trustees to consider the relative claims of the individual beneficiaries involved, whereas the Act discriminates against classes of beneficiary defined without reference to their deserts.

no longer realistic for them to cohabit,[54] to require the other to pay 'rent' for having the house to himself. Some of its territory—the case where both parties have a right to occupy under the 1996 Act and the trustees choose one of them over the other—has now been taken over by the Act's own compensation provision.[55] But accounting remains available in all other cases where parties have concurrent interests in land but cannot realistically be expected to occupy it together.[56] It would, then, avail Kate in the case where she and John have concurrent interests, but due to her disability she has no statutory right to occupy, and so no statutory claim to compensation. It would not, however, avail her in the case we took first, where her interest is successive to John's. In this case, she could not expect to occupy at all during John's life: so neither the statutory provision, nor accounting, can help her. Our objection to the approach taken by the 1996 Act thus remains.

14.3.3 Intervention by the Court

In the event of dissatisfaction with the trustees' decisions under sections 12 and 13, the court can be asked to substitute decisions of its own, under the jurisdiction conferred by section 14 of the 1996 Act, discussed in §§ 14.2.2–14.2.5. So the court can overrule the trustees' judgments about whether the conditions under which a right of occupation arises are satisfied, and about which of two entitled beneficiaries shall occupy.

But, as we have seen,[57] section 14 appears to address the exercise by the court of discretions *possessed by the trustees*, not to give the court additional discretions. So it appears not to allow the court to override a right to occupy—to say that, despite the requirements of section 12 being satisfied, no beneficiary is to occupy the land.[58] The commentators however appear to

---

[54] As where their relationship had broken down: *Dennis v McDonald* [1982] Fam 63 (Fam D and CA); *Bernard v Josephs* [1982] Ch 391 (CA).

[55] In this case, the old accounting mechanism has been superseded by the statutory provision: *Stack v Dowden* [2007] 2 AC 432, [94], [150] (HL).

[56] *Byford v Butler* [2003] EWHC 1267 (Ch D); *French v Barcham* [2008] EWHC 1505 (Ch D). This position is problematic, however. It assumes that the non-resident co-owner has, as such, a right to occupy the land (*French v Barcham* at [34]); the 'rent' he can recover is compensation for his exclusion from the benefits of that right. Before 1996, it was thought that all co-owners had such a right. Under the 1996 Act, however, a co-owner has a right to occupy the land only if he is covered by s 12 (ie if his occupation is one of the purposes of the trust, or the land is held by the trustees so as to be available for occupation by him, and it is in fact so available and suitable). If a co-owner is—like Kate—not within s 12, yet can still have accounting, it must be on the basis that the non-statutory right to occupy continues to exist. The restrictions of s 12 (purpose, availability, suitability) would then be left nugatory: an unlikely reading of the Act.

[57] At nn 18–19 above.

[58] Such a possibility might seem to be contemplated by s 13(7), providing that, if a beneficiary currently occupies the trust land, the trustees can evict him *if the court so approves*. But s 13(7) makes it clear that the eviction (if the court approves it) occurs under the trustees' s 13(1) power to choose which of two beneficiaries, each entitled to occupy, may do so. Section 13(7) does not, therefore, allow the court—any more than the trustees—to exclude both, in order to sell.

think, on the contrary, that the court *can* order sale in such cases.[59] The issue seems not to have been explicitly litigated so far. In certain cases, notably *Mortgage Corporation v Shaire*,[60] it logically should have been, but was not: although the court seems to have assumed, with the commentators, that it can order sale despite an occupation right.

Although apparently excluded by its wording, this view certainly makes the best sense of section 14. Most section 14 disputes will be over the question whether the land should be sold, and the party opposing sale will very often have a right to occupy. So unless section 14 allows the court to override that right, the practical scope of section 14 is small.

This view is also the more desirable stance for the law in terms of substantive justice, as allowing the court to address the concerns expressed in § 14.3.2 regarding the absolute right of occupation.[61] Even-handedness may well require the land to be sold. So may considerations of family welfare: as where a house is held for a couple; their relationship having broken down, they need to find separate accommodation; to this end, at least one of them needs to take their entitlement in the form of money; and this cannot be delivered without selling the existing house. The court should therefore be able to order sale despite a beneficiary having a right to occupy, and insisting on it. Better still, of course, the occupation right should itself be abolished, so that trustees too can allow occupation only where it is right to do so.[62]

---

[59] See eg R Smith, *Plural Ownership* (Oxford, 2005) 157.

[60] [2001] Ch 743 (Ch D).

[61] Provisions regarding occupation and allowing the various considerations to be weighed against each other in this way are to be found in the Family Law Act 1996. Commentators assume that even where the land in question is the subject of a trust, thus attracting the Trusts of Land and Appointment of Trustees Act 1996, it is the Family Law Act that takes precedence. This may matter even if the former allows the court to order sale despite a right to occupy, as the considerations to be taken into account differ a little between the two Acts. But it certainly matters if this is not the case, for then the right to occupy, if absolute under the Trusts of Land and Appointment of Trustees Act, turns out not to be absolute after all. The Acts themselves, however, say nothing about their interrelationship.

[62] It can be argued that s 12 already has this shape. Say you hold a house for John and Kate, and that at first sight, the s 12 requirements are satisfied, giving John a right to occupy, even though your duty to treat your beneficiaries even-handedly, or the court's family welfare responsibilities under s 14, would otherwise indicate selling the house. The argument is that the factors indicating sale make the house 'unavailable' for occupation, with the result that the s 12 requirements are not satisfied after all, and that John has no right to occupy. The problem with the argument, however, is that it leaves the 'right' to occupy surprisingly narrow. On this reading, the right would arise and make a difference only where, although Kate does not agree that John should occupy, her reasons are subjective, rather than justified complaints in terms of even-handedness or family welfare.

14.4 Trust Rights' Effectiveness against Disponees

At least some of the obligations and rights arising under every trust are in rem, and thus capable of binding disponees of the land or other property to which they relate.[63] So if you hold land on trust for John, then you transfer the land to Liam, Liam may in principle be bound by John's interest. As compared to the question whether a disponee is bound by any other kind of right in rem, however, the question whether Liam is in fact bound by John's trust right is an unusually complex one.

There are two principal issues, though each of them has a number of detailed aspects.

One of these issues is that to which we are by now accustomed: the message of the rules, mainly to be found in the Land Registration Act 2002, stating the circumstances in which a right that is capable of binding Liam will actually do so. This issue will be covered in § 14.7.

Before that, however, we need to explore the other issue: the possibility that John's right, while in principle a right in rem capable of binding Liam as a right affecting the land which Liam acquires, may become detached from the land ('overreached') as part of your transfer to Liam. If this occurs, John's right ceases to be capable of binding Liam after all, so we do not need to continue to the issue of whether Liam is in fact bound: he simply cannot be. We look at this issue next, therefore, in §§ 14.5–14.6.

Finally, in § 14.8 we shall come to a worked example, covering the various aspects of both issues, and offering a perspective on the topic as a whole.

14.5 Overreaching 1: the Key Ideas

The present group of sections looks at the idea of trust rights being overreached by a disposition, explaining what happens when they are, and

---

[63] The view that only some trust obligations and rights are in rem, while others are in personam, while likely from first principles, is not well established: it is more usually said that *all* such obligations and rights are in rem. (See further S Gardner, *An Introduction to the Law of Trusts* (2nd edn, Oxford, 2003) 247–50; R Nolan, 'Equitable Property' (2006) 122 *LQR* 232.) The issue will not be explored further in this book, for it is unnecessary to our concern, which is with those obligations and rights that are in rem.

giving an evaluation. When the disposition involves an impropriety, however, the rights may not be overreached after all (and so may endure to bind the disponee). We shall look at this complication in § 14.6.

14.5.1 The Idea of Overreaching

When trustees dispose—properly—of a piece of property that they hold on trust, the beneficial rights, which would otherwise remain with the property, instead detach themselves from it, so that the disponee cannot be affected by them. Then the rights re-attach themselves, once more as rights in rem, to the replacement property (usually money) that the trustees receive from the disponee: it becomes the trust property instead.

This phenomenon is called 'overreaching'.[64] Overreaching is thus a device by which rights in rem are made, temporarily (ie in favour of a disponee under a proper disposition), to behave as though they were rights only in personam. On the strength of their susceptibility to overreaching, beneficial rights in land are sometimes said to lie behind a 'curtain', so that a disponee of the trust land cannot be affected by them.[65]

14.5.2 The Value of Overreaching

Trustees of land have a power to dispose of the land.[66] This enables them to deal with it in various ways that are potentially advantageous to their beneficiaries: to exchange it for other land, or turn it into cash, or rent it out, or secure loans against it. But the power to dispose would be valueless without overreaching.

By definition (as explained in § 13.1), trustees can have no beneficial interest in the trust property themselves: their obligations to the beneficiaries must be so exhaustive as to deny them any such interest. So if they sought to dispose of the property with these obligations (in other words, the beneficiaries' rights) still attached, so that the disponee became bound by them, the disponee could acquire nothing of value to him: he would become a mere trustee in turn. No one would want to take (buy, rent, accept a security right over) property from trustees in such circumstances. Coupling the power to dispose with overreaching transforms the picture, enabling a disposition of trust property to confer its full value on the disponee, and so opening up the possibility that someone might indeed want to take the property after all.

---

[64] See too § 1.3.4.

[65] In the case of trusts of land, overreaching is provided for by the Law of Property Act 1925 s 2.

[66] As an aspect of their power to do anything that an ordinary owner can do, conferred by the Trusts of Land and Appointment of Trustees Act 1996 s 6(1). As explained in § 14.2, however, this power can be withdrawn or subjected to conditions by the settlor (s 8), and overridden by a court order (s 14), as well as by the agreement of the beneficiaries.

This matters not only for the story of an individual trust. By making it feasible for trustees to sell trust property, the combination of a power to dispose and overreaching also exposes trust property to the market, so benefiting the economy. Remember an inherent disadvantage of rights in rem: that they damage the economy by making the property to which they apply less exploitable, and therefore less valuable.[67] The ability to overreach beneficial interests on a disposition of trust property enables their in rem effect to be temporarily cancelled, undoing its capacity for damage.

The law's interjection of a statutory trust whenever I purport simply to transfer land to two or more people, as explained in § 13.4, springs from the same considerations. Without such a trust, the ownership of the land in question would be shared between the transferees, rather than held by trustees. This in turn would make the land less readily marketable, as someone wishing to buy it outright (and buying a lesser interest would not often be worthwhile) would need to deal with all the sharers: a relatively time-consuming and expensive task at best, and perhaps a fruitless one (an awkward individual could block the whole transaction, or at best hold it to ransom). The difficulty is exacerbated by the possibility of the sharers' interests being alienated to new owners. The interjection of a trust means that the title to the land is instead held by the trustees, and that the sharers' fragmentary interests take effect as beneficial rights. Adding a power for the trustees to dispose of the land and overreach the sharers' beneficial rights, the law allows the would-be disponee to acquire the land outright without dealing with the sharers—only with the trustees—after all.

14.5.3 The Settlor's and Beneficiaries' Perspective

For their part, a trust's settlor (if any) and beneficiaries will welcome a power to dispose and overreach if they see the—or a—point of the trust as being to provide money benefits. Say a farm is held on trust, and rented out so as to produce an income which the trustees then pay over to the beneficiary. The farm is essentially an investment, and it could be as valuable to the beneficiary to receive the profits from another piece of land, or indeed some other form of asset. A power to dispose and overreach enables the trustees to trade between assets so as to maximise the return to the beneficiary. *Mutatis mutandis*, a similar account can be given if the aim is to provide a residence for the beneficiary. It may benefit the beneficiary for the trust to be able to switch from one property to another, so as to gain a nicer home, or to take a new job in a different part of the country, or in response to a change in the make-up of his family.

---

[67] § 1.2.2.

But not all settlors and beneficiaries will want their trust's land to be tradable in this way. To take an extreme case, say a family's ancestral estate is held on trust for the members of the family. They may see the particular land in question as important in its own right and to be retained, rather than as to be held only until something different is needed or wanted. Or take the more mundane case of an ordinary home held on trust because it is co-owned by a couple. While the couple will value the ability to dispose and overreach in principle, under particular circumstances at least one of them may prefer to be able to insist on the house being retained: above all, where they separate and, while one wants a sale so as to liquidate his share, the other wants to continue living in the same house.

At one time—before the late 19th century—the law did not insist on disposal and overreaching where these were unwelcome to the settlor and beneficiaries, and indeed did little to provide for them even where they were wanted. During this period, land was put in trust principally to secure its retention within a family in a dynastic fashion, something once seen as valuable. But eventually there emerged a political movement, with several bases, seeking to make land more exposed to the market.[68] To this end, the law (especially the Settled Land Act 1882) went to the other extreme, making rather rigorous provision for disposal and overreaching even where the settlor and beneficiaries did not want it. In effect, the law chose to conceive the dynastic trusts on which these new rules operated as about wealth rather than specifically land, and imposed this choice on settlors and beneficiaries.

Today, however, the law's position is different again. It has swung away from an insistence on disposal and overreaching. This is unsurprising, given how commonly ordinary homes will nowadays be held on trust. As we have seen, in today's law, land owned by more than one person must be held on trust[69] ... and a very common case of this is where a couple co-own their home.

Under the current rules, then, there is full provision for disposal and overreaching where the beneficiaries do want it, but a preference to the contrary will be given respect, though it will sometimes be outweighed. The default rule remains that trustees have a power to dispose of the trust land and to overreach the beneficial interests.[70] But settlors can exclude this power,[71] or (normally a wiser course) allow it to stand but stipulate that it cannot be exercised without the consent of one or more identified

---

[68] See H Perkin, 'Land Reform and Class Conflict in Victorian Britain' in J Butt and I Clarke (eds), *The Victorians and Social Protest* (Newton Abbott, 1973) 177; F Thompson, 'Land and Politics in England in the Nineteenth Century' (1965) *Transactions of the Royal Historical Society* 5th series, vol 15, 23.

[69] §§ 1.3.4, 13.4.

[70] Trusts of Land and Appointment of Trustees Act 1996 s 6(1); Law of Property Act 1925 s 2(1).

[71] Trusts of Land and Appointment of Trustees Act 1996 s 8(1).

individuals.[72] For their part, unless they are unanimous,[73] beneficiaries are unable to say that the land shall never be disposed of, or to veto a particular impending disposition; but they may be able to block it by asserting an occupation right inconsistent with the proposed disposition, or by persuading the court to order against it. We reviewed the latter possibilities in §§ 14.2–14.3. The overall effect is that, while overreaching itself is not compromised, the underlying power to dispose is heavily qualified, presumably on the basis that the market advantages of a wider power are often outweighed by other considerations.

14.5.4 Why does Overreaching Apply Only to Trust Interests?

Why does overreaching apply only to trust interests, and not to other kinds of right in rem? Say you own land that is subject to a lease or an easement in favour of John. When you transfer the land to Liam, why should not John's lease or easement, instead of binding Liam, likewise be converted into a right against the money Liam pays you?

One might answer, 'Because a right to occupy a specific piece of land, or to cross it, can exist only in respect of that specific piece of land. It cannot sensibly be turned into a right in money.' That is not right, however. Rendition into money is possible: it happens whenever a lease or easement exists over land which is compulsorily purchased, and is itself bought out in the process. The key is rather the degree of usefulness that the law perceives in the particular type of right, relative to the damage that its attachment to the land will do to the market.

In not applying overreaching to non-trust rights—leases, easements, etc—the law seems to have been persuaded of their net usefulness. This is no surprise. Each chapter has explored the reasons why such rights are allowed in rem status at all, despite the ensuing market damage: these are also the reasons why the rights are not to be overreached. The same cannot necessarily be said for trusts, however. In their case, the question depends on the use to which they are in fact put. This explains the variable extent to which the law has in fact subjected them to overreaching. When they were used to service dynasties and this was thought to be all-important, overreaching was not emphasised. When the priority became the exposure of land to the market, it was. With their contemporary role of allowing the co-ownership of family homes, the balance has changed again, and, as we have seen, overreaching has once more been de-emphasised.

---

[72] *Ibid.* If a required consent is withheld, however, the court has a discretion to supply it instead: s 14(2)(a).

[73] In which case they can invoke the rule in *Saunders v Vautier* (1841) 1 Cr & Ph 240 (Ch), enabling them to take control of the land and do what they like with it: see at nn 1–5 above.

14.6 Overreaching 2: the Effect of Impropriety

At the start of § 14.5.1, it was explained that overreaching occurs when trustees 'properly' dispose of land that they hold on trust. The word 'properly' requires some attention, to see when a disposition counts as improper, and what happens if trustees make (or purport to make) such an improper disposition.

14.6.1 'Impropriety'

A number of duties bind trustees as they make a disposition of trust land. For example, if the terms of a trust require the trustees to obtain a certain person's consent before making the disposition in question, the trustees have a duty to do so.[74] The trustees must act only in the interests of the beneficiaries:[75] so they will act wrongfully if, for example, they mortgage the land to secure a loan which they plan to spend on themselves. Trustees of land are often required to consult their beneficiaries before making a disposition of it.[76] And in making the disposition, they must exercise appropriate care and skill (say, in negotiating the price).[77] The most celebrated among these duties is, however, that of ensuring that any money produced by the disposition—eg the price for which the land is sold—is paid to at least two trustees.[78] This duty is known as the 'two-trustee rule', and exists to lessen the chances of the purchase money being embezzled.

If the trustees act contrary to such duties, they will certainly be in breach of trust, entitling their beneficiaries to sue them for an injunction to prevent the behaviour in question, or for financial relief against its consequences. There may also be implications for the disponee. Our focus is on the latter issue. It needs to be considered in terms of two contrasting scenarios: where the duty in question is noted on the register by means of a 'restriction' (§ 14.6.3), and where it is not (§§ 14.6.4–14.6.5).[79]

---

[74] Trusts of Land and Appointment of Trustees Act 1996 s 8(2).

[75] *Cowan v Scargill* [1985] Ch D 270 (Ch); *Hayim v Citibank NA* [1987] AC 730 (PC), applied to trusts of land by the Trusts of Land and Appointment of Trustees Act 1996 s 6(5) and (6).

[76] *Ibid* s 11. 'Often', because this section lists a number of exceptions.

[77] *Ibid* s 6(9).

[78] Law of Property Act 1925 s 27.

[79] The rules discussed are those for registered land. The position of unregistered land is not dissimilar in overall effect, but different techniques are used to achieve this. See principally the Trusts of Land and Appointment of Trustees Act 1996 s 16.

14.6.2 Restrictions

A 'restriction' is an entry on the register recording the duty.[80] The law allows such an entry to be made precisely so as to help ensure that the duty is obeyed. But it seems that not all duties relevant to dispositions of trust land can be recorded by a restriction. A restriction can be entered only if, in the nature of the duty, obedience can be easily verified by the Registry staff.[81]

This will be so, and a restriction can therefore be entered, in the case of the duty to pay two trustees, and a duty to obtain someone's consent before making a disposition. It will be plain whether or not these duties have been obeyed. But it is otherwise in the case of the duty to act solely in the beneficiaries' interests, or to exercise due care and skill. It is impossible for the Registry staff to verify whether these duties have been obeyed: even if the staff can discover all the relevant facts, deciding whether these amount to obedience involves applying the relevant rule, and that requires the exercise of judgment, which is vested solely in a court with appropriate jurisdiction.

So in terms of our two scenarios, the first (where the duty is noted by a restriction on the register) will involve duties which are of the former kind and which have been registered. The second scenario (where the duty is not noted by a restriction on the register) will involve duties which are of the former kind and so could have been registered, but have not been; together with duties of the latter kind, which simply cannot be registered.

14.6.3 The First Scenario: Where there is a Restriction

If a restriction has been entered and the duty to which it refers is obeyed, the disposition of course goes through, and the trust rights are overreached, as explained in § 14.5.1. But if a restriction has been entered but (the Registry staff conclude) the duty to which it refers is *not* obeyed, the disposition is generally blocked.[82] There will then be no question of overreaching: the land will remain with the trustees, and beneficial rights will continue to bind it in their hands.

Say you and I are trustees of a piece of land for John, and are in the course of transferring it to Liam. If the register contains a restriction noting that a disponee of this piece of land must pay two trustees, and Liam pays us both, the transfer will be successful: Liam will acquire the land, and John's interest will be overreached. But if there is such a restriction but Liam pays only one of us, Liam will not acquire the land at all, and John's interest will

---

[80] Land Registration Act 2002 s 42.

[81] *Ibid* s 43 forbids the entering of restrictions unless checking on compliance 'would ... be straightforward, and ... not place an unreasonable burden on [Registry staff].

[82] *Ibid* s 41. Specifically, the disposition cannot be registered. But (s 27) in the case of freehold transfers, leases for more than seven years and ordinary mortgages, registration is required for the disposition to take effect at all.

continue to bind it in our hands. Likewise if there is a restriction noting that John's consent is required before we can make the transfer. If John does consent, the transfer will be successful and will overreach John's interest; but otherwise, the transfer will simply fail, and there will be no question of overreaching.

14.6.4 The Second Scenario: Where there is No Restriction

The second scenario is that where the duty has not been recorded by a restriction, no matter whether or not it could have been.

If the duty is obeyed, the lack of a restriction is irrelevant: the disposition goes through and the beneficial interests are overreached. It is where the duty is not obeyed that the complications start. The relevant law was changed in 2002. But the new rules appear not simply to replace the old ones, so we need to look at both.

Before 2002, when an improperly made disposition of trust land was not prevented by a restriction, the disposition took effect; but sometimes without overreaching the beneficial rights. Say you and I held land on trust for John, and had a duty not to dispose of it without John's consent, but this duty was not registered. Say then that, without obtaining John's consent, we purported to transfer the land to Liam. The transfer to Liam succeeded, but John's right was not overreached (and so could go on to bind Liam). The icon of this set of rules was the decision of the House of Lords in *Williams & Glyn's Bank Ltd v Boland*,[83] where overreaching was blocked by a breach of the two-trustee rule (and the unoverreached right went on to bind the disponee). But while we know that improprieties of these two kinds—failure to obtain consent, and breach of the two-trustee rule—blocked overreaching, we are less sure about others, such as failure by the trustees to act solely in the beneficiaries' interests, or to exercise due care and skill, in making the disposition. It is possible that in these cases, the impropriety had no impact on the disposition at all: that the disposition not only took effect, but also overreached the beneficial interests, notwithstanding the impropriety.[84]

The change that occurred in 2002 was the arrival of section 26 of the Land Registration Act 2002. By this section (but with a possible exception mentioned in a moment), the previous law's blocks on overreaching are

---

[83] [1981] AC 487 (HL). For a challenge to the decision's correctness, however, see N Jackson, 'Overreaching in Registered Land Law' (2006) 69 *MLR* 214 (and 'Overreaching and Unauthorised Dispositions of Registered Land' [2007] *Conv* 120). For more on the relationship between the two-trustee rule and overreaching, see *City of London Building Society v Flegg* [1988] AC 54 (HL).

[84] In theory, the effect of such other improprieties could be gathered from the wording of the relevant provisions of the Trusts of Land and Appointment of Trustees Act 1996, but in practice the wording gave no clear indication. For an effort to quarry answers nonetheless, see G Ferris and G Battersby, 'The General Principles of Overreaching and the Modern Legislative Reforms 1996–2002' (2003) 119 *LQR* 94, 95–108; but the arguments used there often seem strained.

lifted. The section achieves this by ruling that a duty unprotected by a restriction is to be treated, vis-à-vis a disponee,[85] as if it never existed.

So: (there being no restriction) the disposition continues to take effect, as before, but now the beneficial interests are always overreached, despite the impropriety. In other words, a breach of a duty regarding the disposition of trust land *cannot* result in the disposition taking effect but without the beneficial interests being overreached, so that the disponee is bound by them. If the duty is protected by a restriction, its breach means that the disposition will fail altogether. If the duty is not protected by a restriction, then, notwithstanding the breach, section 26 ensures that the disposition takes effect and that the beneficial interests are overreached after all.

Except, perhaps, where the impropriety is of one particular (but very important) kind: a breach of the two-trustee rule. The relationship between section 26 and this rule has not yet received attention from the courts, but has been much discussed by commentators.[86] There is a consensus among the latter that the section does not apply to such a breach. If this is right, the pre-2002 position—that such a breach blocks overreaching—continues to prevail: the law continues to be as it was stated by the pre-2002 decision in *Williams & Glyn's Bank Ltd v Boland*,[87] which itself involved a breach of the two-trustee rule. That is, (there being no restriction) the disposition takes effect, but the beneficial rights are not overreached: they remain with the land as rights in rem capable of binding the disponee.

14.6.5 Does, and Should, Section 26 Apply where there is a Breach of the Two-trustee Rule?

The wording of section 26 gives little or no support to the view that it does not apply to breaches of the two-trustee rule.[88] Beyond that, however, *ought*

---

[85] The duty continues to apply between the trustee(s) and the beneficiaries, so disobeying it continues to operate as a breach of trust by the trustee(s), who can be sued for this by the beneficiaries. Moreover, if the transaction shows dishonesty on the part of the disponee, he becomes accessory to the wrong, committed by the trustee(s), of breaking the rules regarding the disposal of the trust property, and can be sued alongside the trustee(s) for this: see S Gardner, *An Introduction to the Law of Trusts* (2nd edn, Oxford, 2003) 273–8. It is additionally possible that a disponee who acquires the land with an 'unconscionable' awareness or lack of awareness of the beneficial interests will also be liable to the beneficiaries for the loss arising from the interests' failure to affect him as rights in rem. But the nature of this liability is controversial. The preferable understanding (*ibid* 281–2) is that it reacts to losses arising from breaches of trust on the part of those who, receiving trust property from trustees, are bound by the beneficial interests as rights in rem. Disponees protected by s 26 are precisely not so bound, for on the section's assumption that the duty in question never existed, the disposition takes effect and the beneficial interests are overreached.

[86] The fullest account is G Ferris, 'Making Sense of Section 26 of the Land Registration Act 2002' in E Cooke (ed), *Modern Studies in Property Law, Volume 2* (Oxford, 2003) ch 6.

[87] [1981] AC 487 (HL).

[88] See G Ferris and G Battersby, 'The General Principles of Overreaching and the Modern Legislative Reforms 1996–2002' (2003) 119 *LQR* 94, 120–2; R Smith, *Plural Ownership* (Oxford,

305 OVERREACHING 2: THE EFFECT OF IMPROPRIETY

such breaches to remain—as the consensus has it—outside section 26, so that, in this case (alone), the beneficial interests can survive the impropriety and be capable of binding the disponee? Arguably so. The argument runs as follows.

As we saw in § 14.6.4, under the pre-2002 law (as exemplified by *Williams & Glyn's Bank Ltd v Boland*[89]), a disponee could be affected by an impropriety, by taking the land but with the beneficial interests still attached. This was objectionable in that, the duty in question not being recorded by a restriction, the disponee might not have been able to anticipate the problem and avert this damaging outcome. The issue of the two-trustee rule apart, section 26 means that this can no longer occur. Either the duty in question will be recorded by a restriction, in which case a breach of it will block the disposition itself, but the disponee will have every opportunity to anticipate the problem and avert this outcome by noticing the restriction and complying with it to ensure that there is no breach. Or there will be no restriction, in which case a breach will not affect the disponee at all: the disposition will take effect and the beneficial interests will be overreached.

It might be asked, 'Why do we need section 26 to ensure that a disponee can anticipate difficulty over an impropriety? Under the pre-2002 rule, even if the impropriety meant the beneficial interest not being overreached, the interest did not actually bind the disponee unless the beneficiary was in actual and apparent[90] occupation of the land,[91] and surely this alerted the disponee to the potential problem?'

For most improprieties, however, this was not the case. Certainly, the disponee could discover the beneficiary's *occupation*, and so his interest, in the manner described. But this did not normally alert the disponee to the risk of an *impropriety*, and so to the risk of that interest actually *binding* him, rather than being harmlessly overreached. (Some duties apply only to some trusts: such as a duty to obtain a consent. Other duties apply to all trusts, but the disponee would not know whether the trustees were in breach: such as the

2005) 192–8. Perhaps the best argument is as follows. Under s 26, a disponee is unaffected by any (unregistered) 'limitation' upon the disponor, ie the trustee. The word 'limitation' is apt to refer to duties of the trustee, such as a duty to obtain a certain consent. But it is not apt to refer to the two-trustee rule, which operates as a demand upon the disponee rather than as a duty of the trustee. This argument seems unsuccessful, however, for two reasons. First, because the two-trustee rule probably does involve a duty of the trustee (if you are a single trustee, you may not try to make a disposition without securing the appointment of a colleague). Second, even if that is wrong, because the word 'limitation' is capable of referring not only to duties of the trustee, but also to rules otherwise controlling the effect of a trustee's disposition ... notably the two-trustee rule.

[89] [1981] AC 487 (HL).

[90] In fact, the pre-2002 rule required only actual occupation, but its counterpart today requires the occupation also to be apparent (Land Registration Act 2002 Sch 3 para 2). The question is whether this was the only adjustment needed, leaving s 26 unnecessary.

[91] Thereby allowing the unoverreached interest to bind the disponee as an overriding interest: see further § 14.7.

duties to act solely in the beneficiaries' interests, and to exercise due care and skill.) Section 26 was needed, therefore, so as to protect the disponee against surprise, in the manner described.

Breaches of the two-trustee rule are different, however. Unlike other duties, not only does this rule apply to nearly[92] every disposition of trust land, but a breach of it will also be obvious to the disponee. So in this instance, the disponee, aware of the beneficial interest itself, can also anticipate the risk of being bound by it, and act to avert this risk. The additional protection of section 26 is unnecessary.

Indeed, not only is it unnecessary: it would be positively inappropriate. If the disponee can (despite the absence of a restriction) anticipate the impropriety in this way, it is right to expect him to play his part in averting it, for the sake of the beneficiary, whom the duty exists to protect. Applying section 26 in such circumstances would relieve him of that responsibility.

In this way, then, the consensus view—that the section does not apply to breaches of the two-trustee rule, and that the pre-2002 decision in *Williams & Glyn's Bank Ltd v Boland*[93] remains, on its (two-trustee rule) facts, good law—can be supported.

14.7 Binding Disponees

As a result of the rules about restrictions and section 26, then, if a disposition of trust land takes effect at all, the beneficial rights will at least normally be overreached and so be incapable of affecting the disponee. But the position may be different where the disponee pays the purchase money to only one trustee. If there was no restriction requiring payment to two trustees, the disposition will take effect. And if breaches of the two-trustee rule lie outside the scope of section 26 (as the commentators think, but it is far from certain), overreaching will be blocked. So in this case (alone), the beneficial rights will remain attached to the land and capable, as rights in rem, of binding the disponee.

Whether, in such a case, the beneficial rights actually do bind the disponee depends on the usual rules regarding the operation of rights in rem. Two issues require attention. First (§ 14.7.1), how do the relevant rules in the Land Registration Act 2002 apply to such rights? Then (§ 14.7.2), how does the consent

---

[92] It does not apply if the disposition does not produce purchase money, as for example where the land is exchanged for other land: *State Bank of India v Sood* [1997] Ch 276 (CA).
[93] [1981] AC 487 (HL).

principle described in Chapter 3 (that if the holder of a right consents to its not binding the disponee, it will not do so) apply to these rights?

14.7.1 Unoverreached Beneficial Rights as Overriding Interests

There is no question of the beneficial rights binding through registration. They cannot be registered by notice.[94] This is because, if a right is protected by a notice, it necessarily binds a disponee. In the case of a trust right, the preferred outcome[95] is that the right is overreached, so that the disponee is not bound. If those involved with the trust are able to register it, therefore, they must do so by a restriction,[96] the effect of which is—as explained in § 14.6.3—to ensure that, if a disposition of the trust land occurs at all, the rights under the trust will be overreached. But if the rights are overreached, there will, by definition, be no question of them binding the disponee. So in thinking about whether unoverreached beneficial rights will bind a disponee, we are necessarily concerned with the case where there is no registration. The remaining question, then, is whether the rights operate as overriding interests.

This question is answered by reference to Schedule 3 of the Land Registration Act 2002. The schedule makes no specific mention of beneficial rights, but they can qualify under paragraph 2, which gives overriding effect to a right in rem if (with some exceptions) its owner is in actual and apparent occupation of the land in question at the time of the disposition. If the beneficiary is in actual and apparent occupation of the trust land when the trustees dispose of it, his unoverreached right will therefore generally operate as an overriding interest to bind the disponee.

This is appropriate. A breach of the two-trustee rule is most likely to occur when the trust in question has only one trustee. This is in turn likely to be where the trust is a constructive (or resulting) one: as for example where you are the registered owner of a house, and agree with John that he should have a share in it, which creates a constructive trust under the doctrine explored in § 8.3. Beneficial rights under constructive (or resulting) trusts clearly arise in a disorganised way. As a result, it is neither reasonable to expect nor sensible to require their registration (in this case, via a restriction). As explained in §§ 2.2.2–2.2.3, therefore, it is right that they should be able to operate instead as overriding interests, at any rate where actual and apparent occupation makes them discoverable.

In a case of this kind, too, it is extremely common for John to live in the house. The possibility of a disponee being bound by John's right, on account of a breach of the two-trustee rule together with John's being in actual and apparent occupation, is therefore a routine one.

[94] Land Registration Act 2002 s 33(a).
[95] § 14.5.2.
[96] Land Registration Act 2002 s 42.

14.7.2 The Consent Principle

One final issue. Say you hold land on trust for John, then transfer it (on your own, and therefore in breach of the two-trustee rule) to Liam. Assuming that section 26 of the Land Registration Act 2002 does not apply and that the transfer therefore takes effect without John's beneficial right being overreached (§§ 14.6.4–14.6.5), and that John is in actual and apparent occupation of the land (§ 14.7.1), John's right will bind Liam as an overriding interest ... unless John has consented to its not doing so.

The rule that an interest that would otherwise bind a disponee can be 'postponed' by consent in this way[97] is explained in detail in Chapter 3.

Although in principle this rule can apply to any kind of right in rem, it is especially associated with trust rights. It will normally be possible to find an *implied* consent only where you (the disponor) and John (the owner of the right) are closely connected, in such a way that Liam (the disponee) will understandably read the disposition as a shared project between you and John.[98] This will be the case almost exclusively where the land is your and John's shared home, and, given this, the right in question (John's right in the land, whose postponement to Liam's right John assents to) will most commonly be a beneficial interest. In fact, a putative disponee will commonly seek the safety of an *express* consent, by proceeding with the transaction only when all occupants of the land in question have signed a form postponing their rights (if any) to his. Again, it is only where the disponor (you) and the owner of the right (John) are closely connected in this way that such a signature is likely to be forthcoming: someone whose interests were not aligned with the disponor's would have no reason to supply it.

14.8 A Worked Example, and an Appraisal

14.8.1 A Worked Example

§§ 14.5–14.7 show that beneficial rights under trusts thus affect disponees of the land in question according to more complex rules than other rights in

---

[97] *Bristol and West Building Society v Henning* [1985] 1 WLR 778 (CA); *Paddington Building Society v Mendelsohn* (1985) 50 P & CR 244 (CA).
[98] § 3.2.1.

rem in land. It may be helpful to work through an illustration covering the issue as a whole, together with its possible consequences.

In our discussions so far, the disposition has tended to be instanced as a transfer of the trust land. But for the present example, let us make it instead a mortgage of the land, by the trustee. The rules are essentially the same, but it is in mortgage cases that their difficulties appear in the most practically acute form.

So: say you are registered as the owner of a house, and you mortgage it to a bank. In due course, however, you fail to keep up the payments, and the bank wishes to repossess the house and sell it. At this point John intervenes, saying that you held the house on trust for yourself and him in equal shares, by virtue of a common intention to that effect.[99] The register contained no restriction reflecting such an interest, however. Our task is to assess John's intervention, and determine its impact on you and, especially, the bank. To perform this task, we need to ask and answer seven separate questions.

— *Question 1: did John indeed have a beneficial interest in the house?* So long as John can substantiate his assertion of a common intention, the answer should be yes. Remember (§ 8.3) that the requisite 'common intention' may be genuine (express or implied), or imputed—ie invented—by the court, on the basis of your and John's 'whole course of conduct in relation to [the property]'.

— *Question 2: did John acquire his beneficial interest before the bank took its mortgage?* If he did not, the bank cannot be affected by his interest.[100] Sometimes this rule is easy to apply. Say you acquired the house with money the bank lent you, so that the mortgage arose at the moment the house became yours ... but it was five years later that you met John and his interest came into being: the mortgage obviously predates John's interest. Conversely, say you acquired the house on the basis of your agreement with John, so that his interest in the house arose at the moment the house became yours ... and you mortgaged it to the bank, maybe to raise funds for your business, only five years later: John's interest obviously predates the mortgage. The hard case is the very common one where you acquired the house *both* with money the bank lent you, *and* on the basis of your agreement with John: so that, seemingly, the mortgage and John's interest arose simultaneously, at the moment the house became yours. In this situation, the law—for no sufficient reason[101]—treats the mortgage as having arisen first, with the result

---

[99] § 8.3.

[100] *Abbey National Building Society v Cann* [1991] 1 AC 56 (HL).

[101] *Abbey National Building Society v Cann, ibid*, offers two justifications. First, John's interest did not predate the bank's; so the bank's must have predated John's. Wrong: it is correct to say that John's interest did not predate the bank's because they arose simultaneously, so the bank's interest did not predate John's either. Second, even if the bank's interest did not in fact arise

that it cannot be affected by John's interest. It can be affected by John's interest only in the case of a post-acquisition mortgage. In many cases, the possibility of John's right binding the bank will therefore proceed no further.

— *Question 3: was John's interest overreached by the mortgage disposition?* On the given facts, you being the only trustee, there has been a breach of the two-trustee rule. Since there was no restriction requiring compliance with the rule, the mortgage nonetheless takes effect.[102] But assuming that breaches of the two-trustee rule are not within the scope of section 26 of the Land Registration Act 2002,[103] John's interest was not overreached by the mortgage, and so remained attached to the land, capable of binding the bank.[104]

If these three questions are answered in John's favour, John had, at the time you mortgaged the house, a right in rem in it, capable of binding the bank. Questions 4 and 5 tell us whether it actually did bind the bank.

— *Question 4: did John's unoverreached right qualify as an overriding interest?* This question[105] has to be addressed by reference to the terms of Schedule 3 paragraph 2 of the Land Registration Act 2002. The answer depends principally on whether, at the time you granted the mortgage, John was in actual and apparent occupation of the house. Given that (as explained in answer to question 2) the mortgage will need to have been a post-acquisition mortgage, there is a good chance that he was, but of course everything will depend on the particular facts.[106]

If John's right does qualify as an overriding interest in this way, the bank is bound by it[107] ... unless the answer to question 5 dictates otherwise.

---

first, it *deserves* to be treated as though it did, because you could not have bought the house without the bank's help. Again, wrong: it may be true that you needed the bank's help, but if so you probably needed John's help (eg his contribution to repaying the mortgage) too.

[102] § 14.6.4.

[103] §§ 146.4–14.6.5. If this is wrong, and breaches of the two-trustee rule *are* within the scope of s 26, we must instead pretend in the bank's favour that two trustees were not required, leaving no reason why the bank should be affected by John's interest. In this event, John's claim against the bank can proceed no further. (Just as if John's argument against overreaching was any other kind of impropriety in the mortgage, such as your having taken the loan for yourself alone: s 26 certainly applies then.) John could however proceed against you, to recover his share of the mortgage money.

[104] As in *Williams & Glyn's Bank Ltd v Boland* [1981] AC 487 (HL).

[105] § 14.7.1.

[106] For the meaning of 'actual occupation', see § 2.1.2.

[107] As the bank was bound by Mrs Boland's right, operating as an overriding interest on the basis of her actual occupation, in *Williams & Glyn's Bank Ltd v Boland* [1981] AC 487 (HL).

— *Question 5: can the bank say that John consented to the mortgage?* If so, he loses[108] the ability to assert his right against the bank.[109] The meaning of 'consent' in this context is discussed fully in §§ 3.2–3.3, but, in brief, it is wide. John will probably be found to have consented so long as he was aware that you were creating a mortgage and did not oppose you, or even so long as he consented in this way to an earlier mortgage, which this one (perhaps quite unknown to him) replaced.[110] However, if John appeared to consent, but his consent was vitiated by the manner in which you obtained it, the bank may not be able to rely on it: §§ 3.2.3–3.2.4.

If questions 4 and 5 are answered in John's favour, his right actually does affect the bank. That is to say, the mortgage binds your interest in the house, but not John's. It remains to be seen where this leaves John in practice.

— *Question 6: if you default on the mortgage repayments, and the bank (naturally enough) wishes the house to be sold so as to recoup its loan, can John prevent this?* The answer lies in the court's discretion, under section 14 of the Trusts of Land and Appointment of Trustees Act 1996.[111] In brief, if you have been bankrupt for a year or more, the house will almost certainly have to be sold;[112] otherwise, it will probably have to be sold,[113] unless John is able to take the mortgage over himself.[114] So while John's beneficial right does (if the previous five questions have been answered in his favour) bind the bank, it is unlikely that he can on this account simply ignore the mortgage. He may well have to leave the house, and be content with a substitute entitlement.

— *Question 7: if the house is sold, what rights does John have?* If the bank succeeds in its request for a sale, the proceeds of that sale will be divided in the same proportions as the beneficial interests: if you and John had equal rights, 50:50. Your share will go to the bank so as to pay off your debt and any sale expenses (you will receive any surplus, of course), and John's share will go to him. Contrast the position if John's right had *not* bound the bank, so that the bank could repossess the house and sell it without regard to John. Then, the bank would have been entitled to retain as much of the proceeds as it needed to pay off the loan, before paying any surplus to you. John would still have been entitled to half the sale price, but his

---

[108] As in *Bristol and West Building Society v Henning* [1985] 1 WLR 778 (CA); *Paddington Building Society v Mendelsohn* (1985) 50 P & CR 244 (CA). In *Williams & Glyn's Bank Ltd v Boland, ibid,* the bank did not argue that Mrs Boland had consented to the mortgage: presumably because there was no evidence that she even knew about it at the time her husband was granting it.

[109] § 14.7.2.

[110] *Equity and Law Home Loans v Prestidge* [1992] 1 WLR 137 (CA).

[111] §§ 14.2.2–14.2.6, 14.3.3.

[112] Insolvency Act 1986 s 335A; *Re Citro* [1991] Ch 142 (CA).

[113] *Bank of Ireland Home Mortgages Ltd v Bell* [2001] 2 FLR 809 (CA).

[114] *Mortgage Corporation v Shaire* [2001] Ch 743 (Ch D).

claim for it would have been only against you, his trustee. In theory, then, John is entitled to half the sale price of the house either way. But in practice, his chances of actually getting his hands on this money are far greater if he has a right against the bank (because it is a bank) than if he does not, and has to resort to claiming from you (who by definition—since the bank wants a sale—are over your head in debt).

The ability to claim money from the bank rather than from you is the real-time advantage John can hope to gain from asserting that he has a beneficial right in the house, binding on the bank. From the bank's point of view, of course, the difference between the two outcomes is even greater: if it is bound by John's right it can take only half the proceeds of sale, while otherwise it can keep all the proceeds up to the value of your debt.

The difference both to you and to the bank is most acute if, as is likely, the bank, taking you to have full rights in the house, loaned you a sum greater than the value of the 50 per cent share you actually had. Say, for example, the house was worth £200,000; the bank loaned you £180,000; £160,000 is outstanding; and the house is now sold, for £240,000 (net of expenses). If the bank is *not* bound by John's interest, it takes its £160,000 first, then pays the remaining £80,000 of the sale money to you, leaving John with the unpromising prospect of claiming his half share of the sale money—£120,000—from you. But if the bank *is* bound by John's interest, the £240,000 will go £120,000 to John and £120,000 to the bank: the bank will not recover the whole outstanding debt, there will be no surplus to come to you, but John will receive his full entitlement.

14.8.2 An Appraisal

The law embedded in § 14.8.1's seven questions (especially the first five of them) gives John a rather slim chance of being able to look to the bank, rather than you, in this way. This is probably no accident. Not merely overreaching,[115] but the whole set of rules regulating the impact of trust rights on disponees of land can be seen as calculated to ensure that trust rights remain 'behind the curtain', ie that a disponee is not normally affected, and need not normally fear being affected, by such rights.[116]

---

[115] § 14.5.

[116] Discussing the leading authority on Question 2, *Abbey National Building Society v Cann* [1991] 1 AC 56 (HL), R Smith, 'Mortgagees and Trust Beneficiaries' (1990) 106 *LQR* 545, 548 observes that it 'comes perilously close to a simple assertion that a mortgagee wins because he is a mortgagee'. See further M Dixon, 'Equitable Co-Ownership: Proprietary Rights in Name Only?' in E Cooke (ed), *Modern Studies in Property Law, Volume 4* (Oxford, 2007) ch 2; L Fox, *Conceptualising Home—Theories, Laws and Policies* (Oxford, 2007).

This is an intelligible position for the law to adopt, for it enhances land's commerciability, and so lubricates the economy; and if we focus especially on the question whether beneficial rights should bind mortgagee banks,[117] it reduces the bank's risk, and so facilitates a lower interest rate, and fuels the economy in that way. The position is by no means unavoidable, however: one could see banks as having social responsibilities in respect of the damage that can occur (to persons such as beneficiaries) in transactions involving them, because of their position as 'gate-keepers' of such transactions.[118] Moreover, even the position in fact adopted by the law does not quite imply a disregard for the protection of beneficiaries, even where their desire to stay with the land leaves them unhappy with overreaching: rather, it involves seeing their protection as the responsibility normally of their trustees alone, and not of outsiders taking a disposition of the land.

This position would, however, be more simply expressed by a rule that (at least in the case of land) trust rights operate in personam only. As the law stands, there is considerable conceptual overkill. It treats such rights as in principle in rem, but then cuts back the significance of this to almost zero, by the multifarious and tortuous rules described in this chapter. So we find rules to the effect that the right in rem may be overreached ... but that overreaching will in principle be blocked by certain, but not all clearly identified, improprieties in the disposition ... but that in fact the block is lifted by pretending that the impropriety was not an impropriety, though it is unclear whether in every case ... and so on.

If trust rights are viewed as essentially in personam, the implication is that, after a disposition, a beneficiary will need to be content to enjoy his right in a money form.[119] To be sure, this may conflict with his actual preference, which may well involve enjoying—and continuing to enjoy—his right against the physical trust land itself, usually by occupying it. The vision treating trust rights as essentially in personam has no quarrel with this as a preference, but regards it as a matter solely between the beneficiary and his trustees, to be addressed *prior to* a proposed disposition. Although (as we saw in §§ 14.2–14.3) they are configured in an unsatisfactory way, the provisions of the Trusts of Land and Appointment of Trustees Act 1996—giving a right to occupy, and allowing trustees' proposals for the operation of the trust to be challenged in court—are in principle calculated

[117] On this, see further C Sawyer, 'A World Safe for Mortgagees?—Registering a Scintilla of Doubt' in E Cooke (ed), *Modern Studies in Property Law, Volume 1* (Oxford, 2001) ch 12.

[118] Some of the rhetoric in *Barclays Bank plc v O'Brien* [1994] 1 AC 180 (HL) views banks in this way, though the detail of that decision and especially of its successor, *Royal Bank of Scotland plc v Etridge (No 2)* [2002] 2 AC 773 (HL), is aimed more at allowing banks to discharge these responsibilities with minimum effort.

[119] This is obvious where the disposition is a sale or a lease; where it is a mortgage, he may be able to occupy so long as the mortgage is being repaid, but in the event of default he will have to go. The key point is whether his presence is compatible with the rights conferred on the disponee.

to allow this.[120] On this view, the beneficiary's preference should not be capable of impinging on a disponee at all, let alone doing so via issues that essentially have no relevance to that preference, such as whether the money arising upon a disposition was paid to two trustees rather than one.

[120] For another possible approach, see Law Commission, *Overreaching: Beneficiaries in Occupation* (Law Com No 188, London, 1989), proposing that adult beneficiaries in actual occupation of trust land should have a veto (removable at the discretion of the court) on proposed dispositions of that land.

15

Licences

15.1 What is a Licence?

15.1.1 Licences as Residual Consensual Rights in Personam to Be on Another's Land

Given the liberal suppositions of English land law, you gain a right to be on my land only if I consent to you doing so, or if the law contains a specific rule requiring it in particular circumstances. That is, you can acquire such a right without my consent only in a finite number of specified ways, and then only in a form that the way in question allows.[1] But if I consent to your having a right to be on my land, I can in principle give that right any form I like.

Of the infinite variety of rights over my land that I can therefore create by consent, however, only some are allowed to operate in rem. This is because of the *numerus clausus* principle: the phenomenon explained in § 1.2.2 whereby, because a right in rem is damaging to the market in land, the law allows it to arise only where some stronger argument indicates that it should. This argument will be a function of the right's nature, as reflected in its definition. (An easement, for example, is a right in rem because a right with the characteristics required for an easement deserves to operate in rem, despite the harm that this does.[2]) Of the infinite variety of possible consensual rights over land, the residue thus operates in personam only.

---

[1] Rights of this non-consensual kind include, for example, your right to enter my land under certain circumstances so as to search it; a right arising from my responsibilities towards you as a member of my family, under the Family Law Act 1996 Part IV; or your 'right to roam' over my land, under the Countryside and Rights of Way Act 2000. The qualification of my ownership by such rights can (normally) be justified, of course; and can be seen either as an intrinsic limitation on the idea of ownership, or as the net outcome of the competition between the arguments for allowing me to exclude you and those to the contrary. See § 1.3.3; and further K Gray and S Gray, 'Private Property and Public Propriety' in J McLean, *Property and the Constitution* (Oxford, 1999) ch 2.

[2] § 9.1.6.

And within this residue of consensual rights in personam over land, certain ones are referred to as 'licences'. The term is normally applied only to rights of this kind that allow you to *be on* my land. Say, by contrast, I agree to use my land on your behalf in some other way: perhaps to grow flowers there, for you to sell in your shop. Your right regarding my land is of the residual kind: ie consensual, and, as it does not match the specification of any right in rem, in personam only. But as it does not involve your actually being on my land, it is not called a licence. While not referred to as licences, however, rights of this latter kind (which have no generic name of their own) seem to give rise to essentially the same issues, and to attract essentially the same rules, as licences.

It is possible to give instances of licences by contrasting them with rights in rem (arising by my consent, and allowing you to be on my land) to which they bear some, but necessarily not a full, resemblance. For example, if we have an agreement entitling you to occupy my house, but for one reason or another your right is not exclusive, you do not have a lease[3] ... but you do have a licence. Or if you rent a cottage on my large country estate, and I give you, but only you, a right to ride your horse around the estate, you do not have an easement[4] ... but you do have a licence.

At the same time, we can notice certain very common kinds of right that are in fact licences. If you come and visit me at my house, for example, the reason you are not a trespasser is because you have a licence (a right, arising from my consent) to be on my land. Likewise if you go into a shop, or a restaurant, or a theatre or cinema or museum or gym or sportsground ... Likewise too if you are a guest in my hotel, or a lodger in my house. (In none of these cases do you have the exclusive possession of my land needed for your right to be a lease; nor does your right accommodate other land owned by you, so as to be a potential easement.)

In all these examples, you are known to the law as a 'licensee'; I am a 'licensor'.

15.1.2 Kinds of Licence

It is usual to discern three different kinds of licence: bare licences, contractual licences and licences coupled with an interest (or with a grant). We shall examine each kind in turn. As we do so, we shall discover certain departures from the position we have just worked out, that a licence over another's land is necessarily a right in personam. These departures will need careful consideration.

---

[3] § 11.2.1.
[4] § 9.1.3

15.2 Bare Licences

15.2.1 The Nature of a Bare Licence

If I give you a bare licence to be on my land, I merely give you permission to do so. The permission can of course be explicit (as where I make you a formal invitation to visit me), or tacit (as with the permission I extend to all comers—or at any rate all bona fide comers—to walk up my garden path so as to ring at my front door). But it is no more than a voluntary permission. It is in this respect that bare licences differ from especially contractual licences. If I give you a contractual licence to be on my land, I still give you permission to do so ... but it is not simply a voluntary permission: I am obliged to give you it because I have entered into a contract to that effect. For example, say I have sold you a ticket to visit my stately home: we have a contract obliging me to allow you to do so. A bare licence is one that lacks this obligatory element.

15.2.2 Duration

The fact that you have a licence—my permission to be on my land—means that you are not a trespasser when you are there. (Another way of speaking of your licence is to say that you have the defence of *volenti non fit iniuria* to the tort of trespass that you would otherwise commit against me.[5])

If I state a limit to my permission, therefore, you become a trespasser if you stay on my land past that limit. So if I say that you can remain only until midnight, you do not (unless I extend the licence) have permission to remain beyond midnight. If you are still on my land a moment after midnight, you are trespassing: it is your responsibility to ensure that you do whatever it takes to get yourself away before the clock strikes twelve.[6]

But my saying, even solemnly promising, that you can remain until midnight does not mean that you can certainly stay even that long. Promises made without consideration are not binding: so I can change my mind and revoke my permission. Similarly if my permission is open-ended: whether or not you have the impression that this means you can stay permanently, I can revoke it.

---

[5] *Winter Garden Theatre (London) Ltd v Millennium Productions Ltd* [1948] AC 173, 188 (HL).

[6] I may also limit your licence in other ways, express or implied. Say I permit you to come into my house: if you in fact enter with the object of stealing from me, you will be a trespasser because you are acting outside the terms on which I surely gave that permission: *R v Jones and Smith* [1976] 1 WLR 672 (CA).

I cannot however simply announce, 'your licence is now over' and instantly make you a trespasser. After my announcement, you certainly have enough time to take yourself and where relevant your belongings off my land before you commit trespass. This rule is surely intrinsic to the idea of trespass, confining your liability to the case where your presence on my land can properly be ascribed to your agency at all.

But the relevant law is surprisingly confused,[7] and contains some support for two further propositions. The first is that I must express my announcement so that it takes effect only after a reasonable delay (eg 'your licence will be over in 24 hours' time'). This may simply be another way of couching your basic right to enough time to leave, making it inoffensive unless misunderstood, and cumulated with that basic right: there seems no reason why you should have both. The second proposition assumes that the first does indeed represent the law, then goes on to assert that its requirement of 'a reasonable delay' means enough time not merely to leave, but also to make alternative arrangements. This seems dubious: it is hard to see why your future needs are my concern, rather than something for you to consider before setting so much store by a mere gratuitous permission.[8]

15.2.3 Effect on Disponees

The authorities on bare licences are fully aligned with the idea that licences operate in personam only.[9] Given the ease with which such licences can be revoked, the question will rarely require attention, let alone litigation ... unless it is true that you can claim enough time to make other arrangements, for this could be considerable.

[7] See J Hill, 'The Termination of Bare Licences' [2001] *CLJ* 89. The principal authorities are *Canadian Pacific Railway Co v R* [1931] AC 414 (PC); *Winter Garden Theatre (London) Ltd v Millennium Productions Ltd* [1948] AC 173 (HL); *Governing Body of Henrietta Barnett School v Hampstead Garden Suburb Institute* (1995) 93 LGR 470 (Ch D). Each contains unreconciled traces of all the ideas referred to in the text.

[8] Unless, by coming or staying on my land rather than making other arrangements, you have acted in detrimental reliance on an assurance from me that *you can stay*. Then you have an estoppel right, which may entitle you to remain on my land in this way. But care is needed in deciding whether I have indeed assured you that you can stay: it may not be right to read a bare revocable permission in that way.

[9] The point is made in a passage from an antique case in another context (*Thomas v Sorrell* (1673) Vaugh 330, 351 (Ex Ch)), adopted for the present context in *Winter Garden Theatre (London) Ltd v Millennium Productions Ltd* [1948] AC 173, 188 (HL).

15.3 Contractual Licences

15.3.1 The Nature of a Contractual Licence

As said in § 15.2.1, if I give you a contractual licence to be on my land, I give you permission to do so ... but this time I am obliged to give you this permission, because I have entered into a contract to that effect.

The obligation to let you be on my land may be an express term of the contract (as where I sell you a ticket to visit my stately home), or an implied term, implied normally so as to give business efficacy to the more explicit aim of the contract (as where you visit my restaurant; our contract focuses on your meal, but impliedly obliges me to allow you to sit at a table to eat it).[10] The contract may give you a right alone (in neither of the foregoing examples do you have to enter or remain on my land, if you change your mind), or it may give you a right enabling you to perform an obligation which the contract simultaneously imposes on you (as where you are my employee; our contract obliges you to work on my farm; so it necessarily also obliges me to let you be on my farm for that purpose).[11]

15.3.2 Duration

As with a bare licence, it is your responsibility to keep within the confines of your licence. So if you book a room in my hotel for one week, but then refuse to leave and stay for another, during this second week you will be a trespasser. Also as with a bare licence, if I have given you an open-ended permission, I can terminate it; in which event, I must certainly allow you enough time to remove yourself and your belongings, and perhaps also give you reasonable notice beforehand, and/or enough time to make other

---

[10] In *Tanner v Tanner* [1975] 1 WLR 1346 (CA), the very contract seems to have been invented, so as to allow the court to give protection in the name of a contractual licence. On very similar facts, no contract—and so no contractual licence—was found in *Horrocks v Forray* [1976] 1 WLR 230 (CA). In these cases, a woman had a close relationship with a man, and was in some degree materially dependent on him. He provided her with a home, but later sought to evict her. She could probably be said to have relied on an understanding between them that he would house her, giving her an estoppel claim (Ch 7). Even if the estoppel requirements are not truly present, moreover, the courts will often invent them so as to enforce what are perceived as the defendant's family responsibilities: § 7.4.5.

[11] The contract may be between me and you, or between me and someone else for your benefit—as where you attend my theatre, but your father buys your ticket. In such a case you will normally be able to enforce your father's contract against me, under the Contracts (Rights of Third Parties) Act 1999.

arrangements.[12] But in the case of a contractual licence, this default rule may be overlain by more specific arrangements (usually more generous to you) required by the express or implied terms of the contract: in particular, the contract may state your licence to be terminable on, say, a month's notice.

The most important difference between bare and contractual licences arises, however, where I purport to end your licence prematurely, ie inconsistently with my promise. Say I promise that you can stay for a year. If my promise is gratuitous, I can legitimately revoke it any time, and you must leave (though I must give you at least a reasonable time in which to do so). But if my promise is in a contract, I cannot legitimately revoke it.[13] You can insist on staying;[14] and if I use force to eject you—even no more force than I can lawfully use against someone who really is a trespasser—I therefore commit an assault on you, as you are not a trespasser.[15]

Given the contractual quality of the licence, an account of this rule needs to begin with the ordinary law of contract. In these terms, my purported revocation counts as a repudiation. Two possibilities follow. One is that you accept my repudiation (ie accept that the licence is over, and take yourself away), and, if you suffer loss, claim this from me as damages for breach of contract. The other is that you affirm the contract, so that we are both obliged to continue performing it (ie I must let you stay on my land for the remainder of the year after all). But you do not have a free choice between the two possibilities. The former is always available, but you can opt for the latter only in two situations. First, if you can claim specific performance—an equitable order for the performance of the contract—against me. This is only exceptionally the case. And second, without specific performance, only if you can keep the contract going by your own activities alone, and the law allows you to do so. This is not always the case. In particular, it is not if, to continue, you need my co-operation; and you are seen as needing my co-operation if keeping the contract going will involve your using my property.[16] Affirming

---

[12] *Winter Garden Theatre (London) Ltd v Millennium Productions Ltd* [1948] AC 173 (HL). Such a possibility of revocation tends to be found even if the contract seems to allow you to stay forever: *Staffordshire Area Health Authority v South Staffordshire Waterworks Co* [1978] 1 WLR 1307 (CA) (in a different context). In theory, it follows that a contract apparently permitting you to stay for some *fixed* time could likewise be read as allowing earlier termination on notice. But in general such a reading would be surprising.

[13] Unless my revocation is an acceptance by *me* of an earlier repudiatory breach on *your* part: eg if you have abused your licence by harassing me. *Thompson v Park* [1944] KB 408 (CA), where the licensor's termination was held to render the licensee a trespasser, is commonly explained in this way.

[14] *Winter Garden Theatre (London) Ltd v Millennium Productions Ltd* [1948] AC 173 (HL); *Hounslow London Borough Council v Twickenham Garden Developments Ltd* [1971] Ch 233 (Ch D).

[15] *Hurst v Picture Theatres Ltd* [1915] 1 KB 1 (CA); approved, *Winter Garden Theatre (London) Ltd, ibid* 191, 193–4, 202–3; accepted as the law, *Hounslow London Borough Council v Twickenham Garden Developments Ltd, ibid* 254–5.

[16] *Hounslow London Borough Council v Twickenham Garden Developments Ltd, ibid* 252–4, discussing *White & Carter (Councils) Ltd v McGregor* [1962] AC 413 (HL).

your contractual licence and continuing to enjoy it will plainly involve your using my land. Affirming and continuing to enjoy your licence will not, therefore, be possible unless you can claim specific performance of our contract against me.

This, then, is the position we should expect under the ordinary law of contract. The cases about the revocability of contractual licences are broadly consonant with it; but, as we shall see, they also display certain unexpected features.

The story begins with *Wood v Leadbitter*.[17] This early decision held that my repudiation of the contract simply terminates the licence. It was taken purely with reference to the common law, ie without considering the possibility of specific performance, which is a purely equitable remedy. Given that limitation, it reached the outcome that the account above leads us to expect.[18]

But it was glossed, and in effect reversed, by subsequent cases, which adverted additionally to equity's position on the matter (giving this priority, for equity takes precedence over the common law[19]). This makes a difference because (these cases held) the licensee can demand specific performance[20] of the contract, obliging the licensor to let him stay on the land if he is currently there,[21] or to let him enter if he is not.[22] And further, because (they also held)

---

[17] (1845) 13 M & W 838 (Ex). This decision did, however, disapprove some even earlier authority to the contrary, especially *Tayler v Waters* (1817) 7 Taunt 374 (CP). The basis of the latter is unclear. *Wood v Leadbitter* deals with the case by treating it (not very convincingly) as concerned with a different type of licence altogether, a 'licence coupled with an interest'. See further § 15.4.

[18] The decision does not however explicitly base itself on that account. Its reasoning is not easy to follow, but appears to boil down to an assertion that, at common law, you have the right to be on my land against my will only when you have a right in rem to that effect, and a contractual licence is not such a right. (There is much reference to the need for a deed, but the point of this seems to be that a deed is often needed to create a right in rem.) On reflection, however, perhaps this does connect with the account given in the text: the only other way in which you might have a right to be on my land against my will is by virtue of our contract, and, as the account explains, this in fact delivers no such right in these circumstances.

[19] § 1.5.

[20] The discussion in *Winter Garden Theatre (London) Ltd v Millennium Productions Ltd* [1946] 1 All ER 678, 685 (CA) speaks not of specific performance of my promise to let you be on my land, but of an injunction enforcing my promise not to revoke my permission for you to be on my land. The latter is an odd way of approaching the matter (treating the permission—licence—as one entity, and the required promise not to revoke it as another: an analysis which the judgment, at 680, rejects), and one which fails to acknowledge that to enforce the licence is, by whatever name it is called, in effect to grant specific performance of the contract. The language of specific performance is used in *Hounslow London Borough Council v Twickenham Garden Developments Ltd* [1971] Ch 233, 254–5 (Ch D); see also *Hurst v Picture Theatres Ltd* [1915] 1 KB 1, 9, 14, 15 (CA).

[21] *Winter Garden Theatre (London) Ltd v Millennium Productions Ltd* [1946] 1 All ER 678, 685 (CA); approved, [1948] AC 173, 202–3 (HL); accepted as the law, *Hounslow London Borough Council v Twickenham Garden Developments Ltd, ibid* 247, 254–5 (Ch D).

[22] As in *Verrall v Great Yarmouth Borough Council* [1981] QB 202 (CA). In that case, there was an additional reason for granting specific performance: to protect the licensee's right of free speech (he had hired the licensor's conference centre for a political event which the licensor no longer wished to see happen). But the logic of the surrounding law suggests that specific performance should be granted even without such a special factor.

even if the licensee has no opportunity to obtain specific performance, the *availability* of specific performance means that he can again treat the licence as still operative. So if the licensor, having unsuccessfully asked the licensee to leave, goes on to evict the licensee by force in the same way as he would a trespasser, the licensee is seen as entitled to be on the land, meaning that the force is an assault.[23] These propositions represent the prevailing law.

The theme of this treatment—its focus on specific performance as making all the difference—is fundamentally correct. As explained above, in a context like this, it is only by claiming specific performance that a licensee can affirm the contract, and so keep the licence in being. But the treatment has two surprising features.

First, it seems to suppose that a licensee, faced with a licensor's repudiation, can always claim specific performance. But this remedy is usually seen as obtainable only where damages for breach of contract would not be adequate. Why should that always be the case where a licence is involved? Say you hire space to keep your (quite ordinary) goods in my (quite ordinary) warehouse for a year, and after six months I ask you to remove them. Surely your interests are adequately covered by my liability to pay you your removal expenses, plus any amount by which equivalent replacement accommodation costs you more. The notion that specific performance is always available in licence cases seems rather to be aimed at teeing up the further proposition that a licensee can treat the licence as still operative, even without obtaining an order of specific performance.

The second surprise is that further proposition: the idea that, even if specific performance is available, a licensee need not actually obtain it, but can simply proceed on the basis that the licence remains operative. This idea depends on the doctrine 'equity looks upon as done that which ought to be done', as applied to the specific performance of the licence contract. That is, because specific performance would (let us assume) be given if it were sought, we pretend that it has been given and complied with: and therefore that the licensor's permission still stands, making the licensee not a trespasser. But this doctrine's pedigree is as a rule about contracts to confer interests, operating in the fashion described in § 5.2.1. To apply it to a contract to permit what would otherwise be a trespass is clearly to take it outside this pedigree.[24] Viewed substantively, however, the resulting rule perhaps represents an effort to discourage licensors from, at all events, using force to evict their licensees. That is intelligible, resonating with a more

---

[23] *Hurst v Picture Theatres Ltd* [1915] 1 KB 1 (CA); approved, *Winter Garden Theatre (London) Ltd v Millennium Productions Ltd* [1948] AC 173, 191, 193–4, 202–3 (HL); accepted as the law, *Hounslow London Borough Council v Twickenham Garden Developments Ltd* [1971] Ch 233, 254–5 (Ch D).

[24] And so was declared impossible in Phillimore LJ's dissenting judgment in *Hurst v Picture Theatres Ltd* [1915] 1 KB 1, 18–19 (CA).

general perception that self-help is an undesirable way for a landowner to deal even with an undoubted trespasser.[25]

If this suggestion is right, it would be possible to disentangle the law by adopting a general rule against the forcible eviction by landowners even of trespassers, and leaving the subsistence of contractual licences in the face of a licensor's repudiation to the ordinary law of contract: meaning that the licensee can always have damages for breach of contract, and specific performance in appropriate cases. But a general rule against forcible eviction of trespassers seems politically unachievable, so the law is likely to remain in its present analytically unsatisfactory state.

15.3.3 Are Contractual Licences Rights in Personam or in Rem?

In § 15.1.1, we saw that licences comprise those consensual rights to be on land that are not rights in rem, and as such must be in personam. The prevailing view regarding contractual licences is that they are indeed in personam.

The cases have not all told the same story, however. To be sure, in *King v David Allen & Sons Billposting Ltd*[26] and *Clore v Theatrical Properties Ltd*,[27] the House of Lords and Court of Appeal respectively treated contractual licences as rights in personam. But in *Errington v Errington*,[28] the Court of Appeal (or some of its members) subsequently treated such licences as rights in rem. The House of Lords in *National Provincial Bank Ltd v Ainsworth*[29] discouraged this development when it once again drew attention to the earlier decisions, though without quite disapproving the development as a matter of substance;[30] it did not pursue the issue further, however, as it was not relevant to the case in hand. Certain later decisions of the lower courts[31] nevertheless continued to treat such licences as in rem, though the explanations given for this position, and especially for its ability to co-exist with *King v David Allen & Sons Billposting Ltd*[32] and *Clore v Theatrical Properties Ltd*,[33] lacked clarity.[34] Eventually, the Court of Appeal in *Ashburn Anstalt v*

---

[25] *McPhail v Persons (Names Unknown)* [1973] Ch 447, 456 (CA).

[26] [1916] 2 AC 54 (HL).

[27] [1936] 3 All ER 483 (CA).

[28] [1952] 1 KB 290 (CA).

[29] [1965] AC 1175 (HL).

[30] *Ibid* 1239–40, 1254.

[31] *Binions v Evans* [1972] Ch 359 (CA) (the judgment of Lord Denning MR); *DHN Food Distributors Ltd v Tower Hamlets London Borough Council* [1976] 1 WLR 852 (CA); *Re Sharpe (a bankrupt)* [1980] 1 WLR 219 (Ch D); *Midland Bank Ltd v Farmpride Hatcheries Ltd* (1980) 260 EG 493 (CA).

[32] [1916] 2 AC 54 (HL).

[33] [1936] 3 All ER 483 (CA).

[34] The key statement is that by Lord Denning MR in *Binions v Evans* [1972] Ch 359 (CA). He appears to reach the conclusion that the licence operates in rem on two grounds. First (at 367), on the facts there the licence was for the duration of the licensee's life, and older authority

Arnold[35] declared the in rem view unsupportable, and since then contractual licences have been accepted as operating in personam only.[36] (The court did however draw attention to the rule—examined in § 8.2—whereby a disponee who promises to honour the licence will be obliged to do so, under a 'constructive trust'.)

As a matter of principle, however, is there anything to be said in favour of the experiment with in rem status?

A number of arguments seem possible, but most of them are unconvincing. First, it has been said that contractual licences deserve in rem status—and have been given it—(only) when they are identical in substance to a recognised right in rem, which is absent only because of a want of formality.[37] The supposed identification with another kind of right in rem is often dubious, however, and the want of formality certainly cannot be dismissed as unimportant. It is easier to say, secondly, that where a contractual licence is present, there is (almost always) a proprietary estoppel claim too,[38] which may yield the same (expectation) response;[39] and that since an estoppel claim operates in rem,[40] it is therefore only sensible that the

---

treated licences for life as rights in rem. This is correct, but: (i) the older authority proceeded on the basis that a 'licence for life' in fact amounted to a beneficial interest for life under a trust, which is a right in rem (§ 14.4); (ii) Lord Denning MR had already (at 366) rejected that analysis (for insufficient reasons, though in the end correctly: *Dent v Dent* [1996] 1 WLR 683 (Ch D)); (iii) in any case, such reasoning did not apply to licences other than for life. Second (at 368), because if the land is transferred to someone who promises to honour the licence, the latter is bound by a 'constructive trust' to do so (§ 8.2) ... such a promise can be implied ... and, according to Lord Denning MR (at 369), apparently always is implied. But (i) it is fanciful to think that the required promise is always given; (ii) when it is given, the transferee is necessarily bound by it—not, as with a right in rem, only if the relevant detailed rules are satisfied (ie the right is registered or qualifies as an overriding interest); (iii) the 'constructive trust' obligation can arise only upon the transfer, whereas a right in rem operates as such from its very creation, which can make a difference to its behaviour even before any transfer occurs (as in *DHN Food Distributors Ltd v Tower Hamlets London Borough Council* [1976] 1 WLR 852 (CA) and *Re Sharpe (a bankrupt)* [1980] 1 WLR 219 (Ch D)).

35 [1989] Ch 1 (CA).

36 It is sometimes suggested that, in registered land, contractual licences have become in rem as a result of the Land Registration Act 2002 s 116(b), declaring 'a mere equity' to be a right in rem. 'A mere equity', however, is a very different kind of right from a contractual licence. If I transfer land to you under a contract vitiated by misrepresentation, undue influence, etc, the law allows me to rescind the contract and so regain my land. My (as yet unexercised) right to do so is a 'mere equity', which s 116(b) declares to be a full right in rem, making it capable of binding John, to whom you have transferred the land in the meantime.

37 S Moriarty, 'Licences and Land Law: Legal Principles and Public Policies' (1984) 100 *LQR* 376.

38 For proprietary estoppel, see ch 7. The offer, acceptance and consideration needed for the contract are *a fortiori* to the claimant's belief and reliance, ascribable to the defendant, needed for estoppel (unless the consideration remains wholly executory). Estoppel is wider, however: belief and reliance, ascribable to the defendant, may exist without amounting to offer, acceptance and consideration.

39 Though it may not. For estoppel relief, see § 7.3.

40 This is now established (for registered land) by the Land Registration Act 2002 s 116(a), but was probably the law all along. See § 7.5.2.

contractual licence should too—otherwise the outcome in this respect depends on the choice between two equally correct labels. This argument, however, overlooks the fact that proprietary estoppel is a (disorganised) method of generating rights. Where the right is itself in rem, it makes sense for the estoppel claim to be likewise in rem; but where the right is itself in personam (as a contractual licence is), the estoppel claim ought to be in personam too.[41] Thirdly, it might be said that the law's vindication of contractual licences always (as we saw in § 15.3.2) by specific performance demonstrates a view that it is important to protect such licences in specie, rather than see them dissolve into a right to damages against the original licensor: and after a disposition, protecting them in specie requires that they be capable of binding the disponee, ie operate in rem. There is merit in this argument,[42] but it starts from a weak premise, for as we saw in § 15.3.2, specific performance's role in the protection of contractual licences is essentially technical, aimed at securing them against premature termination by the licensor.

These arguments, moreover, fail to engage with the central question, ie whether contractual licences—seen simply as themselves—ought to be rights in rem rather than in personam.

As we saw in § 15.1.1, in principle 'licences' comprise all consensual rights allowing you to be on my land, but not amounting to established rights in rem. By definition, then, they are in personam. This does not mean, however, that they necessarily *should be* in personam. The class of rights deserving to operate in rem is not static.[43] As social conditions change, the arguments for allowing a given kind of right to operate in rem will fluctuate in strength. As a result, the balance between these arguments and the harm done to the market can alter too. Sometimes the balance regarding an existing right in rem will change to the point where it ought to be reclassified as in

---

[41] § 7.5.2.

[42] More merit than is recognised in *National Provincial Bank Ltd v Ainsworth* [1965] AC 1175, 1253–4 (HL). It is certainly true that the availability of specific performance to enforce a contract does not automatically entail its operation in rem, but, as explained in the text, the information it ought to give us about the right is also relevant to the question of whether it should be in rem.

[43] Note that the text says, 'the class of rights *deserving to* operate in rem is not static'. Arguably, the class of rights (over land) actually *allowed to* operate in rem is indeed static, or at any rate not to be added to, for the Law of Property Act 1925 s 4(1) appears to rule that only those rights recognised as in rem in 1925 can have that status. Such a rule can be defended if, although reclassifying a particular right in personam as a right in rem would in itself promote the greater good, the process of reclassification would create so much upset (to the market) that it would at least cancel this out. This is, however, unlikely to be true of all such reclassifications, as a matter of principle; the law ought therefore to retain the flexibility to make them, taking the ensuing upset into account in effecting the required calculus. Section 4(1) has accordingly been largely ignored by commentators, and even more markedly by the courts: even when arguing against a new right in rem (as in *Ashburn Anstalt v Arnold* [1989] Ch 1 (CA)), the judges tend to speak ad hoc, avoiding reference to the absolutism of s 4(1).

personam;[44] sometimes the movement will be the other way, so that a right hitherto in personam should be reclassified as in rem.

It is, however, highly unlikely to be the case that all rights in personam regarding land—or even those to be on land—ought simultaneously to become rights in rem in this way. Rather, some such rights, defined by their content, may merit reclassification, while the remainder do not. The selective nature of the phenomenon should not be obscured by the fact that, while in personam, all such rights are called 'licences'. Those deserving to become in rem need to be identified, by reference to their characteristics, and, for clarity's sake, given an appropriate name. That name will then join the series 'lease, easement, etc', representing the class of rights which, on account of their nature, it is right to except from the normal in personam rule, and make operate in rem. Those not deserving to be in rem will remain 'licences': that is to say, rights in personam. In short, the identity between licences and rights in personam does not entail that a given kind of right, currently classified as a licence, alias in personam, is properly so classified.

So, when some judges said that 'contractual licences' were, or ought to be, rights in rem, they probably meant that *a particular set* of licences—not simply all those covered by a contract, but those also possessing particular substantive characteristics—merited identification and recognition as a new right in rem in this way. Those substantive characteristics were never sharply identified, but the licences at issue in the cases favouring in rem status mostly fit a certain pattern. They are nearly all domestic residential licences.[45] The cases disfavouring in rem status,[46] on the other hand, involve commercial licences.

The idea that domestic residential contractual licences should be in rem is certainly defensible. It aligns with the treatment of respect for people's homes as a fundamental human right.[47] In large measure, the law has already absorbed this argument. More recently than the decisions depicting such licences as in rem, and before the confirmation that they are only in personam, *Street v Mountford*[48] declared (as we saw in § 11.4.3) that 'licences' conferring exclusive possession of land must be seen instead as leases. Many

---

[44] The law's current treatment of trust rights, supposedly in rem but in reality closer to in personam (§ 14.8.2), may be seen as reflecting such an adjustment.

[45] This is true of *Errington v Errington* [1952] 1 KB 290 (CA), *Binions v Evans* [1972] Ch 359 (CA), *Re Sharpe (a bankrupt)* [1980] 1 WLR 219 (Ch D) and *Midland Bank Ltd v Farmpride Hatcheries Ltd* (1980) 260 EG 493 (CA). It is not true of *DHN Food Distributors Ltd v Tower Hamlets London Borough Council* [1976] 1 WLR 852 (CA). There, the licence was over a commercial warehouse. A local authority compulsorily purchased the warehouse in order to redevelop the site for housing, destroying the licensee's business. Under the relevant rules, the licensee could demand compensation for this if, but only if, its right was in rem. The court's decision in its favour can be understood as aimed at this specific outcome.

[46] *King v David Allen & Sons Billposting Ltd* [1916] 2 AC 54 (HL), *Clore v Theatrical Properties Ltd* [1936] 3 All ER 483 (CA) and *Ashburn Anstalt v Arnold* [1989] Ch 1 (CA).

[47] European Convention on Human Rights Art 8.

[48] [1985] AC 809 (HL).

domestic residential 'licences' are caught by this ruling, and translated by it (as leases) into rights in rem. It would be wrong, however, to think that the case for regarding domestic residential contractual licences as in rem has thereby been completely addressed. Those arrangements not conferring exclusive possession are left as licences: including the situations where the landlord has access to the premises in question so as to provide services (the cases of lodgers, then, and of elderly people living in residential care), and where two or more people occupy the premises but do not share a single right to do so (as is true of many flatmates). While these situations fall outside the law's definition of a lease, the premises concerned may easily (as in these examples) be the occupant's home. And this returns us to the argument that, even if it is a contractual licence rather than a lease, the occupant's right to it merits in rem status.

15.4 Licences Coupled with an Interest

15.4.1 Characteristics

Say I sell you the right to shoot—and keep—game from my wood. My wood is in the middle of my estate, so in order to enjoy this right you additionally need the right to be on my land. The right to do so may be given expressly with the shooting right, but otherwise it will be given impliedly, so as to ensure that you can take advantage of the shooting right.

A right of this kind is commonly called a 'licence coupled with an interest', or (meaning the same thing) a 'licence coupled with a grant'. This denotes that it is a licence (ie a permission on my part allowing you to be on my land), but a licence with legal characteristics different from bare and contractual licences.

Unlike a bare licence, though like a contractual licence, I cannot terminate it prematurely—that is, while you are still entitled to enjoy your 'interest'. If your shooting right is for 12 months, therefore, the licence coupled with it will be for 12 months too. So I may not treat you as a trespasser during that time.

And, it is said, unlike a bare or contractual licence, a licence coupled with an interest operates in rem.[49] So if, during the 12 months, I transfer the land

---

[49] The only authority for this, however, seems to be *Webb v Paternoster* (1619) Poph 151 (KB), which cannot be definitively seen as concerning a licence coupled with an interest at all: see n 58.

containing the wood to John, your right to access the wood (as well as your right to take the game[50]) will be capable of binding John.

15.4.2 What Counts as a Licence Coupled with an Interest?

Your right to be on my land counts as a licence coupled with an interest if you have an 'interest', to enjoy which you need to be on my land. But what counts as the required 'interest'?

Two sorts of right are firmly recognised as 'interests' for this purpose. One is a right in rem in my land. Your right to take my game is a right of this kind: it is a profit à prendre, a kind of right entitling you to take something from my land, which until that moment counted as part of my land. The right to take my game—or my fish—counts because the law regards the animals or birds or fish, before you take them, as part of my land. Other instances are the right to excavate my gravel or coal or stone, or to cut my meadow-grass or my trees.[51] Another kind of right in rem in my land, with which a licence might be coupled in this way, is presumably a lease, as where I lease you a barn situated in my field: the access right you need in order to reach it can be regarded as a licence coupled with the 'interest' which it represents.

The other firmly recognised type of 'interest' is a right in rem in chattels (ie property other than land) situated on my land. In such cases, the right in question is usually ownership. So if I sell you some logs that are in my yard, leaving you to come and fetch them, you necessarily have the right to be on my land so as to do so: and this right counts as a licence coupled with an interest, the 'interest' being the ownership of the logs given to you by the sale.[52]

There is some authority for a third type of 'interest', consisting in a right of any other kind, to enjoy which you need to be on my land: as where you buy a ticket to watch the film being shown in my cinema, to do which you need to enter and remain in the cinema.[53] The prevailing view, however, is that there is no such third kind of 'interest': only the two described above.[54]

---

[50] This is a profit à prendre, a recognised type of right in rem.

[51] *James Jones & Sons Ltd v Earl of Tankerville* [1909] 2 Ch 440 (Ch D). *Frogley v Earl of Lovelace* (1859) John 333 (Ch) also involved an interest of this kind, and is commonly regarded as likewise exhibiting a licence coupled with it.

[52] The authority for this is said to be *Wood v Manley* (1839) 11 Ad & El 34 (QB), holding a buyer of hay entitled to collect it from the seller's land despite the seller's refusal to allow this. Once something growing in or on the land is harvested—for example, once a tree or a field of hay is cut—it ceases to count as land, so a right to it is not a profit à prendre.

[53] *Hurst v Picture Theatres Ltd* [1915] 1 KB 1, 7 (CA). This decision also treated your right on these facts as a contractual licence, and reached the same conclusion—that I cannot prematurely terminate it—on that basis: see at n 23.

[54] *Hounslow London Borough Council v Twickenham Garden Developments Ltd* [1971] Ch 233, 243–5 (Ch D). There, a construction firm contracted to build on the council's land. This was held to give the firm the access it needed to do so as a contractual licence, but not as a licence coupled with an interest: ie its right to perform the contract did not count as an 'interest'.

This seems correct. As already noted, a licence coupled with an interest is thought to operate in rem, ie to be capable of binding a disponee of the land in question. It can hardly do so unless the interest in question, which the licence exists to support, is itself in rem. The alleged third type of 'interest' is by definition (by virtue of the contrast between it and the other two types) a right only in personam: usually a contractual right, which is prevented from affecting a disponee of the land in question by the doctrine of privity. So for a licence associated with it to operate in rem would be absurd.

15.4.3 Does this Concept Exist?

An argument can be made that there is little reason, and no need, to think that the law maintains the concept of a licence coupled with an interest at all.

As a matter of authority, the concept has no great support. A key decision exemplifying it is said to be *Wood v Manley*.[55] There, a buyer of some cut hay was to collect it from the seller's land, and the court held that the seller could not revoke the buyer's licence to do so. This licence could have been seen simply as a contractual licence (an implied term of the contract selling the hay, obliging the seller to let the buyer enter and collect it). Then, the case would have decided that contractual licences are irrevocable. A few years later, however, the contrary was held in *Wood v Leadbitter*,[56] as we saw in § 15.3.2. In the course of doing so, it distinguished *Wood v Manley*, treating the latter as dealing not with contractual licences but with 'licences coupled with an interest'. But the reasoning in *Wood v Manley* makes no reference to this concept, whether by name or by unmistakable allusion,[57] and it is arguable that *Wood v Leadbitter* identified it solely for this purpose.[58] Its genuineness has subsequently been assumed, but in a set of authority which is neither large nor powerful.[59]

---

[55] (1839) 11 Ad & El 34 (QB).

[56] (1845) 13 M & W 838 (Ex).

[57] The reasoning raises the possibility that the licence was irrevocable simply because of the sale contract (ie a contractual licence), though apparently without conviction; but firmly asserts the licence's irrevocability on the ground that the buyer acted upon it: ie on the faith of the seller's promise to allow collection of the hay, the buyer contracted to buy it and indeed paid for it. This idea of a 'licence acted upon' has had a sporadic and not always comprehensible existence in the law. It may be best regarded as subsumed in the doctrine of proprietary estoppel (ch 7).

[58] The judgment seems to ascribe the concept to two earlier decisions, *Webb v Paternoster* (1619) Poph 151 (KB) and *Thomas v Sorrell* (1673) Vaugh 330 (Ex Ch), but neither refers to it by name, or describes it in terms leaving it clearly distinct from other possible analyses. Likewise other old decisions sometimes referred to as exemplifying it, both before and after *Wood v Leadbitter* (1845) 13 M & W 838 (Ex): eg *Doe d Hanley v Wood* (1819) 2 B & Ald 724 (KB), *Muskett v Hill* (1839) 5 Bing NC 694 (CP), and *Frogley v Earl of Lovelace* (1859) John 333 (Ch).

[59] See principally *James Jones & Sons Ltd v Earl of Tankerville* [1909] 2 Ch 440 (Ch D) and *Hurst v Picture Theatres Ltd* [1915] 1 KB 1, 7 (CA): considered at nn 51 and 53 above.

Do we need the concept of a licence coupled with an interest? Consider how the cases in question would be handled without it.

So far as revocability goes, the absence of the concept would make little difference. Usually, I will give you your interest—the right to catch my game, or the ownership of my crop of hay—via a contract. If I do, you will have an access right in the form of an implied contractual licence. And in the modern law (as it has developed since *Wood v Leadbitter*[60]), a contractual licence is irrevocable, just as a licence coupled with an interest is. At the same time, if the interest I give you (via a contract or otherwise) is itself a right in my land—a profit or a lease—your access right can take the form of an easement.[61] And easements too are irrevocable. The remaining case is where I give you a chattel interest without using a contract. In this case, your access right can only be a bare licence. So here there would be a difference: unlike a licence coupled with an interest, a bare licence is revocable. But, as explained in § 15.2.2, I cannot revoke even a bare licence without giving you at least enough time to take yourself and your belongings off my land. So where you have a bare licence so as to access your chattel that is on my land, I must still allow you to collect the chattel.

The absence of licences coupled with an interest would make a greater difference to the question whether your access right would affect a disponee of my land. Where your interest is a right in my land, again, you can claim an easement. An easement is a right in rem, so there is no difference there. But in other cases, claiming a contractual or bare licence, you have only a right in personam. So if I sell or give you some logs stacked in my yard, on the basis that you are to collect them, and before you do so I transfer my land to John, your having only a contractual or bare licence would mean you could no longer enter and take them: whereas if we re-introduce the concept of a licence coupled with an interest, it seems that you may be able to do so.

In the end, then, the question whether or not to acknowledge the concept of a licence coupled with an interest largely resolves into the question whether access rights associated with chattel interests should, against the background of the *numerus clausus* principle, be accepted as rights in rem. It is very arguable that they should not. Even though you cannot demand entry to John's land to collect your logs, they remain yours, and if you are prevented from retrieving them, you can still sue me and/or John for their value. That is probably protection enough.

---

[60] (1845) 13 M & W 838 (Ex).

[61] As explained in § 9.1.2, an easement requires a dominant tenement. A lease counts as a dominant tenement, as does a profit (*Hanbury v Jenkins* [1901] 2 Ch 401, 422–3 (Ch D)). A chattel right, of course, does not. The easement would be impliedly granted as part of the grant of the interest, on the principles described in § 9.2.2.

15.5 Creation of Licences, and their Operation against Disponees

As things stand, no formalities are required to establish a bare or a contractual licence. The formality rules relevant to dealings with land focus solely on the conferral of a right in rem in the land, or a contract to confer such a right.[62] And as we have seen, bare and contractual licences are not rights in rem.

Similarly, bare and contractual licences have no engagement with the Land Registration Act 2002. As explained in Chapter 2, the rules in this Act detail the precise circumstances in which a right in rem, ie capable of binding a disponee, will actually do so. They have nothing to say about a right which is simply *not* capable of binding a disponee. So a bare or contractual licence cannot be registered.[63] And even if the licensee is in actual and apparent occupation of the land in question at the time of the disposition, his licence will not affect the disponee as an overriding interest.[64]

If there is such a concept as a licence coupled with an interest, however, it seems to be (as we saw in § 15.4.1) a right in rem. As such, the formality rules should apply, meaning that writing must certainly be used,[65] and in certain circumstances arguably a deed.[66] In some cases, the same requirements will apply also to the conferral of the interest with which the licence is associated, and the valid conferral of the interest will therefore automatically entail the valid creation of the licence, on the basis that the latter is implied into the former. This is true in particular where the interest in question is a profit. (To validly grant you your profit, I will have to use a deed[67]; and the same deed will suffice to confer the licence coupled with the profit.) But where the interest is in a chattel such as the logs in our illustration, no formalities will normally be required for its conferral, or used in practice. So the apparent

---

[62] Law of Property Act 1925 ss 52, 53; Law of Property (Miscellaneous Provisions) Act 1989 s 2.

[63] Land Registration Act 2002 s 32(1), allowing registration by notice only of 'an interest affecting' the land in question: this being code for a right in rem relating to it.

[64] To qualify as an overriding interest under the Land Registration Act 2002 Sch 3 para 2, a right must be an 'interest': again, code for a right in rem.

[65] Law of Property Act 1925 s 53(1)(a); Law of Property (Miscellaneous Provisions) Act 1989 s 2.

[66] If the licence is indefinite or for a term of years, it appears to count as a legal estate (Law of Property Act 1925 s 1(2)(a), (4)), and as such must be conferred by deed (s 52). It also requires registration under the Land Registration Act 2002 s 27(2)(d) ... unless it is implied, as such licences commonly are.

[67] Law of Property Act 1925 s 52: profits are analogous to easements, whose formality requirements are discussed in § 9.2.8.

need for formality so as to establish the associated licence becomes more of a problem, and one which has not been addressed by the courts.

As rights in rem, licences coupled with an interest should qualify for registration, and for operation as overriding interests. In practice, they will not normally be registered, so the latter possibility is the important one. Since a licence coupled with an interest is by its nature merely an access right, however, the licensee will not normally occupy the land concerned, so such a right will not normally qualify as an overriding interest on that particular basis ... and the only other basis on which it might do so is that it can be regarded also (as explained in § 15.4.3) as an easement, implied into a grant of a profit or lease over the land in question.[68]

The confused and probably unsatisfactory picture regarding licences coupled with an interest is a further reason to suspect that the concept does not actually exist.

---

[68] Such an easement can operate as an overriding interest under the Land Registration Act 2002 Sch 3 para 3: see § 9.3.

Index